University Casebook Series

August, 1988

ACCOUNTING AND THE LAW, Fourth Edition (1978), with Problems Pamphlet (Successor to Dohr, Phillips, Thompson & Warren)

George C. Thompson, Professor, Columbia University Graduate School of Business.

Robert Whitman, Professor of Law, University of Connecticut.

Ellis L. Phillips, Jr., Member of the New York Bar.

William C. Warren, Professor of Law Emeritus, Columbia University.

ACCOUNTING FOR LAWYERS, MATERIALS ON (1980)

David R. Herwitz, Professor of Law, Harvard University.

ADMINISTRATIVE LAW, Eighth Edition (1987), with 1983 Problems Supplement (Supplement edited in association with Paul R. Verkuil, Dean and Professor of Law, Tulane University)

Walter Gellhorn, University Professor Emeritus, Columbia University.

Clark Byse, Professor of Law, Harvard University.

Peter L. Strauss, Professor of Law, Columbia University.

Todd D. Rakoff, Professor of Law, Harvard University.

Roy A. Schotland, Professor of Law, Georgetown University.

ADMIRALTY, Third Edition (1987), with Statute and Rule Supplement

Jo Desha Lucas, Professor of Law, University of Chicago.

ADVOCACY, see also Lawyering Process

AGENCY, see also Enterprise Organization

AGENCY—PARTNERSHIPS, Fourth Edition (1987)

Abridgement from Conard, Knauss & Siegel's Enterprise Organization, Third Edition.

AGENCY AND PARTNERSHIPS (1987)

Melvin A. Eisenberg, Professor of Law, University of California, Berkeley.

ANTITRUST: FREE ENTERPRISE AND ECONOMIC ORGANIZATION, Sixth Edition (1983), with 1983 Problems in Antitrust Supplement and 1988 Case Supplement

Louis B. Schwartz, Professor of Law, University of Pennsylvania.

John J. Flynn, Professor of Law, University of Utah.

Harry First, Professor of Law, New York University.

BANKRUPTCY (1985)

Robert L. Jordan, Professor of Law, University of California, Los Angeles.

William D. Warren, Professor of Law, University of California, Los Angeles.

BANKRUPTCY AND DEBTOR–CREDITOR LAW, Second Edition (1988)

Theodore Eisenberg, Professor of Law, Cornell University.

BUSINESS ORGANIZATION, see also Enterprise Organization

BUSINESS PLANNING, Temporary Second Edition (1984)

David R. Herwitz, Professor of Law, Harvard University.

BUSINESS TORTS (1972)

Milton Handler, Professor of Law Emeritus, Columbia University.

CHILDREN IN THE LEGAL SYSTEM (1983) with 1988 Supplement

Walter Wadlington, Professor of Law, University of Virginia.
Charles H. Whitebread, Professor of Law, University of Southern California.
Samuel Davis, Professor of Law, University of Georgia.

CIVIL PROCEDURE, see Procedure

CIVIL RIGHTS ACTIONS (1988)

Peter W. Low, Professor of Law, University of Virginia.
John C. Jeffries, Jr., Professor of Law, University of Virginia.

CLINIC, see also Lawyering Process

COMMERCIAL AND DEBTOR–CREDITOR LAW: SELECTED STATUTES, 1988 EDITION

COMMERCIAL LAW, Second Edition (1987)

Robert L. Jordan, Professor of Law, University of California, Los Angeles.
William D. Warren, Professor of Law, University of California, Los Angeles.

COMMERCIAL LAW, Fourth Edition (1985)

E. Allan Farnsworth, Professor of Law, Columbia University.
John Honnold, Professor of Law, University of Pennsylvania.

COMMERCIAL PAPER, Third Edition (1984)

E. Allan Farnsworth, Professor of Law, Columbia University.

COMMERCIAL PAPER, Second Edition (1987) (Reprinted from COMMERCIAL LAW, Second Edition (1987))

Robert L. Jordan, Professor of Law, University of California, Los Angeles.
William D. Warren, Professor of Law, University of California, Los Angeles.

COMMERCIAL PAPER AND BANK DEPOSITS AND COLLECTIONS (1967), with Statutory Supplement

William D. Hawkland, Professor of Law, University of Illinois.

COMMERCIAL TRANSACTIONS—Principles and Policies (1982)

Alan Schwartz, Professor of Law, University of Southern California.
Robert E. Scott, Professor of Law, University of Virginia.

COMPARATIVE LAW, Fifth Edition (1988)

Rudolf B. Schlesinger, Professor of Law, Hastings College of Law.
Hans W. Baade, Professor of Law, University of Texas.
Peter E. Herzog, Professor of Law, Syracuse University.
Mirjan P. Damaska, Professor of Law, Yale Law School.

COMPETITIVE PROCESS, LEGAL REGULATION OF THE, Third Edition (1986), with 1987 Selected Statutes Supplement

Edmund W. Kitch, Professor of Law, University of Virginia.
Harvey S. Perlman, Dean of the Law School, University of Nebraska.

CRIMINAL LAW, Second Edition (1986)

Peter W. Low, Professor of Law, University of Virginia.
John C. Jeffries, Jr., Professor of Law, University of Virginia.
Richard C. Bonnie, Professor of Law, University of Virginia.

CRIMINAL LAW, Fourth Edition (1986)

Lloyd L. Weinreb, Professor of Law, Harvard University.

CRIMINAL LAW AND PROCEDURE, Sixth Edition (1984)

Rollin M. Perkins, Professor of Law Emeritus, University of California, Hastings College of the Law.
Ronald N. Boyce, Professor of Law, University of Utah.

CRIMINAL PROCEDURE, Third Edition (1987), with 1988 Supplement

James B. Haddad, Professor of Law, Northwestern University.
James B. Zagel, Chief, Criminal Justice Division, Office of Attorney General of Illinois.
Gary L. Starkman, Assistant U. S. Attorney, Northern District of Illinois.
William J. Bauer, Chief Judge of the U.S. Court of Appeals, Seventh Circuit.

CRIMINAL PROCESS, Fourth Edition (1987), with 1988 Supplement

Lloyd L. Weinreb, Professor of Law, Harvard University.

DAMAGES, Second Edition (1952)

Charles T. McCormick, late Professor of Law, University of Texas.
William F. Fritz, late Professor of Law, University of Texas.

DECEDENTS' ESTATES AND TRUSTS, Seventh Edition (1988)

John Ritchie, Late Professor of Law, University of Virginia.
Neill H. Alford, Jr., Professor of Law, University of Virginia.
Richard W. Effland, Professor of Law, Arizona State University.

DOMESTIC RELATIONS, see also Family Law

DOMESTIC RELATIONS, Successor Edition (1984) with 1988 Supplement

Walter Wadlington, Professor of Law, University of Virginia.

EMPLOYMENT DISCRIMINATION, Second Edition (1987), with 1988 Supplement

Joel W. Friedman, Professor of Law, Tulane University.
George M. Strickler, Professor of Law, Tulane University.

EMPLOYMENT LAW (1987), with 1987 Statutory Supplement and 1988 Case Supplement

Mark A. Rothstein, Professor of Law, University of Houston.
Andria S. Knapp, Adjunct Professor of Law, University of California, Hastings College of Law.
Lance M. Liebman, Professor of Law, Harvard University.

ENERGY LAW (1983) with 1986 Case Supplement

Donald N. Zillman, Professor of Law, University of Utah.
Laurence Lattman, Dean of Mines and Engineering, University of Utah.

ENTERPRISE ORGANIZATION, Fourth Edition (1987), with 1987 Corporation and Partnership Statutes, Rules and Forms Supplement

Alfred F. Conard, Professor of Law, University of Michigan.
Robert L. Knauss, Dean of the Law School, University of Houston.
Stanley Siegel, Professor of Law, University of California, Los Angeles.

UNIVERSITY CASEBOOK SERIES—Continued

ENVIRONMENTAL POLICY LAW 1985 Edition, with 1985 Problems Supplement (Supplement in association with Ronald H. Rosenberg, Professor of Law, College of William and Mary)

Thomas J. Schoenbaum, Professor of Law, University of Georgia.

EQUITY, see also Remedies

EQUITY, RESTITUTION AND DAMAGES, Second Edition (1974)

Robert Childres, late Professor of Law, Northwestern University.
William F. Johnson, Jr., Professor of Law, New York University.

ESTATE PLANNING, Second Edition (1982), with 1985 Case, Text and Documentary Supplement

David Westfall, Professor of Law, Harvard University.

ETHICS, see Legal Profession, Professional Responsibility, and Social Responsibilities

ETHICS AND PROFESSIONAL RESPONSIBILITY (1981) (Reprinted from THE LAWYERING PROCESS)

Gary Bellow, Professor of Law, Harvard University.
Bea Moulton, Legal Services Corporation.

EVIDENCE, Sixth Edition (1988 Reprint)

John Kaplan, Professor of Law, Stanford University.
Jon R. Waltz, Professor of Law, Northwestern University.

EVIDENCE, Eighth Edition (1988), with Rules, Statute and Case Supplement (1988)

Jack B. Weinstein, Chief Judge, United States District Court.
John H. Mansfield, Professor of Law, Harvard University.
Norman Abrams, Professor of Law, University of California, Los Angeles.
Margaret Berger, Professor of Law, Brooklyn Law School.

FAMILY LAW, see also Domestic Relations

FAMILY LAW Second Edition (1985), with 1988 Supplement

Judith C. Areen, Professor of Law, Georgetown University.

FAMILY LAW AND CHILDREN IN THE LEGAL SYSTEM, STATUTORY MATERIALS (1981)

Walter Wadlington, Professor of Law, University of Virginia.

FEDERAL COURTS, Eighth Edition (1988)

Charles T. McCormick, late Professor of Law, University of Texas.
James H. Chadbourn, late Professor of Law, Harvard University.
Charles Alan Wright, Professor of Law, University of Texas, Austin.

FEDERAL COURTS AND THE FEDERAL SYSTEM, Hart and Wechsler's Third Edition (1988)

Paul M. Bator, Professor of Law, University of Chicago.
Daniel J. Meltzer, Professor of Law, Harvard University.
Paul J. Mishkin, Professor of Law, University of California, Berkeley.
David L. Shapiro, Professor of Law, Harvard University.

FEDERAL COURTS AND THE LAW OF FEDERAL–STATE RELATIONS (1987), with 1988 Supplement

Peter W. Low, Professor of Law, University of Virginia.
John C. Jeffries, Jr., Professor of Law, University of Virginia.

UNIVERSITY CASEBOOK SERIES—Continued

FEDERAL PUBLIC LAND AND RESOURCES LAW, Second Edition (1987), with 1984 Statutory Supplement

George C. Coggins, Professor of Law, University of Kansas.
Charles F. Wilkinson, Professor of Law, University of Oregon.

FEDERAL RULES OF CIVIL PROCEDURE and Selected Other Procedural Provisions, 1988 Edition

FEDERAL TAXATION, see Taxation

FOOD AND DRUG LAW (1980), with Statutory Supplement

Richard A. Merrill, Dean of the School of Law, University of Virginia.
Peter Barton Hutt, Esq.

FUTURE INTERESTS (1958)

Philip Mechem, late Professor of Law Emeritus, University of Pennsylvania.

FUTURE INTERESTS (1970)

Howard R. Williams, Professor of Law, Stanford University.

FUTURE INTERESTS AND ESTATE PLANNING (1961), with 1962 Supplement

W. Barton Leach, late Professor of Law, Harvard University.
James K. Logan, formerly Dean of the Law School, University of Kansas.

GOVERNMENT CONTRACTS, FEDERAL, Successor Edition (1985)

John W. Whelan, Professor of Law, Hastings College of the Law.

GOVERNMENT REGULATION: FREE ENTERPRISE AND ECONOMIC ORGANIZATION, Sixth Edition (1985)

Louis B. Schwartz, Professor of Law, Hastings College of the Law.
John J. Flynn, Professor of Law, University of Utah.
Harry First, Professor of Law, New York University.

HEALTH CARE LAW AND POLICY (1988)

Clark C. Havighurst, Professor of Law, Duke University.

HINCKLEY JOHN W., TRIAL OF: A Case Study of the Insanity Defense (1986)

Peter W. Low, Professor of Law, University of Virginia.
John C. Jeffries, Jr., Professor of Law, University of Virginia.
Richard C. Bonnie, Professor of Law, University of Virginia.

INJUNCTIONS, Second Edition (1984)

Owen M. Fiss, Professor of Law, Yale University.
Doug Rendleman, Professor of Law, College of William and Mary.

INSTITUTIONAL INVESTORS, (1978)

David L. Ratner, Professor of Law, Cornell University.

INSURANCE, Second Edition (1985)

William F. Young, Professor of Law, Columbia University.
Eric M. Holmes, Professor of Law, University of Georgia.

INTERNATIONAL LAW, see also Transnational Legal Problems, Transnational Business Problems, and United Nations Law

INTERNATIONAL LAW IN CONTEMPORARY PERSPECTIVE (1981), with Essay Supplement

Myres S. McDougal, Professor of Law, Yale University.
W. Michael Reisman, Professor of Law, Yale University.

INTERNATIONAL LEGAL SYSTEM, Third Edition (1988), with Documentary Supplement

Joseph Modeste Sweeney, Professor of Law, University of California, Hastings.
Covey T. Oliver, Professor of Law, University of Pennsylvania.
Noyes E. Leech, Professor of Law Emeritus, University of Pennsylvania.

INTRODUCTION TO LAW, see also Legal Method, On Law in Courts, and Dynamics of American Law

INTRODUCTION TO THE STUDY OF LAW (1970)

E. Wayne Thode, late Professor of Law, University of Utah.
Leon Lebowitz, Professor of Law, University of Texas.
Lester J. Mazor, Professor of Law, University of Utah.

JUDICIAL CODE and Rules of Procedure in the Federal Courts, Students' Edition 1988 Revision

Daniel J. Meltzer, Professor of Law, Harvard University.

David L. Shapiro, Professor of Law, Harvard University.

JURISPRUDENCE (Temporary Edition Hardbound) (1949)

Lon L. Fuller, late Professor of Law, Harvard University.

JUVENILE, see also Children

JUVENILE JUSTICE PROCESS, Third Edition (1985)

Frank W. Miller, Professor of Law, Washington University.
Robert O. Dawson, Professor of Law, University of Texas.
George E. Dix, Professor of Law, University of Texas.
Raymond I. Parnas, Professor of Law, University of California, Davis.

LABOR LAW, Tenth Edition (1986), with 1986 Statutory Supplement

Archibald Cox, Professor of Law, Harvard University.
Derek C. Bok, President, Harvard University.
Robert A. Gorman, Professor of Law, University of Pennsylvania.

LABOR LAW, Second Edition (1982), with Statutory Supplement

Clyde W. Summers, Professor of Law, University of Pennsylvania.
Harry H. Wellington, Dean of the Law School, Yale University.
Alan Hyde, Professor of Law, Rutgers University.

LAND FINANCING, Third Edition (1985)

The late Norman Penney, Professor of Law, Cornell University.
Richard F. Broude, Member of the California Bar.
Roger Cunningham, Professor of Law, University of Michigan.

LAW AND MEDICINE (1980)

Walter Wadlington, Professor of Law and Professor of Legal Medicine, University of Virginia.
Jon R. Waltz, Professor of Law, Northwestern University.
Roger B. Dworkin, Professor of Law, Indiana University, and Professor of Biomedical History, University of Washington.

LAW, LANGUAGE AND ETHICS (1972)

William R. Bishin, Professor of Law, University of Southern California.
Christopher D. Stone, Professor of Law, University of Southern California.

LAW, SCIENCE AND MEDICINE (1984), with 1987 Supplement

Judith C. Areen, Professor of Law, Georgetown University.
Patricia A. King, Professor of Law, Georgetown University.
Steven P. Goldberg, Professor of Law, Georgetown University.
Alexander M. Capron, Professor of Law, University of Southern California.

LAWYERING PROCESS (1978), with Civil Problem Supplement and Criminal Problem Supplement

Gary Bellow, Professor of Law, Harvard University.
Bea Moulton, Professor of Law, Arizona State University.

LEGAL METHOD (1980)

Harry W. Jones, Professor of Law Emeritus, Columbia University.
John M. Kernochan, Professor of Law, Columbia University.
Arthur W. Murphy, Professor of Law, Columbia University.

LEGAL METHODS (1969)

Robert N. Covington, Professor of Law, Vanderbilt University.
E. Blythe Stason, late Professor of Law, Vanderbilt University.
John W. Wade, Professor of Law, Vanderbilt University.
Elliott E. Cheatham, late Professor of Law, Vanderbilt University.
Theodore A. Smedley, Professor of Law, Vanderbilt University.

LEGAL PROFESSION, THE, Responsibility and Regulation, Second Edition (1988)

Geoffrey C. Hazard, Jr., Professor of Law, Yale University.
Deborah L. Rhode, Professor of Law, Stanford University.

LEGISLATION, Fourth Edition (1982) (by Fordham)

Horace E. Read, late Vice President, Dalhousie University.
John W. MacDonald, Professor of Law Emeritus, Cornell Law School.
Jefferson B. Fordham, Professor of Law, University of Utah.
William J. Pierce, Professor of Law, University of Michigan.

LEGISLATIVE AND ADMINISTRATIVE PROCESSES, Second Edition (1981)

Hans A. Linde, Judge, Supreme Court of Oregon.
George Bunn, Professor of Law, University of Wisconsin.
Fredericka Paff, Professor of Law, University of Wisconsin.
W. Lawrence Church, Professor of Law, University of Wisconsin.

LOCAL GOVERNMENT LAW, Second Revised Edition (1986)

Jefferson B. Fordham, Professor of Law, University of Utah.

MASS MEDIA LAW, Third Edition (1987)

Marc A. Franklin, Professor of Law, Stanford University.

MENTAL HEALTH PROCESS, Second Edition (1976), with 1981 Supplement

Frank W. Miller, Professor of Law, Washington University.
Robert O. Dawson, Professor of Law, University of Texas.
George E. Dix, Professor of Law, University of Texas.
Raymond I. Parnas, Professor of Law, University of California, Davis.

MUNICIPAL CORPORATIONS, see Local Government Law

NEGOTIABLE INSTRUMENTS, see Commercial Paper

NEGOTIATION (1981) (Reprinted from THE LAWYERING PROCESS)

Gary Bellow, Professor of Law, Harvard Law School.
Bea Moulton, Legal Services Corporation.

NEW YORK PRACTICE, Fourth Edition (1978)

Herbert Peterfreund, Professor of Law, New York University.
Joseph M. McLaughlin, Dean of the Law School, Fordham University.

OIL AND GAS, Fifth Edition (1987)

Howard R. Williams, Professor of Law, Stanford University.
Richard C. Maxwell, Professor of Law, University of California, Los Angeles.
Charles J. Meyers, Dean of the Law School, Stanford University.
Stephen F. Williams, Judge of the United States Court of Appeals.

ON LAW IN COURTS (1965)

Paul J. Mishkin, Professor of Law, University of California, Berkeley.
Clarence Morris, Professor of Law Emeritus, University of Pennsylvania.

PATENTS AND ANTITRUST (Pamphlet) (1983)

Milton Handler, Professor of Law Emeritus, Columbia University.
Harlan M. Blake, Professor of Law, Columbia University.
Robert Pitofsky, Professor of Law, Georgetown University.
Harvey J. Goldschmid, Professor of Law, Columbia University.

PLEADING AND PROCEDURE, see Procedure, Civil

POLICE FUNCTION, Fourth Edition (1986), with 1987 Case Supplement

Reprint of Chapters 1–10 of Miller, Dawson, Dix and Parnas's CRIMINAL JUSTICE ADMINISTRATION, Third Edition.

PREPARING AND PRESENTING THE CASE (1981) (Reprinted from THE LAW-YERING PROCESS)

Gary Bellow, Professor of Law, Harvard Law School.
Bea Moulton, Legal Services Corporation.

PROCEDURE (1988), with Procedure Supplement (1988)

Robert M. Cover, Late Professor of Law, Yale Law School.
Owen M. Fiss, professor of Law, Yale Law School.
Judith Resnik, Professor of Law, University of Southern California Law Center.

PROCEDURE—CIVIL PROCEDURE, Second Edition (1974), with 1979 Supplement

The late James H. Chadbourn, Professor of Law, Harvard University.
A. Leo Levin, Professor of Law, University of Pennsylvania.
Philip Shuchman, Professor of Law, Cornell University.

PROCEDURE—CIVIL PROCEDURE, Fifth Edition (1984), with 1988 Supplement

Richard H. Field, late Professor of Law, Harvard University.
Benjamin Kaplan, Professor of Law Emeritus, Harvard University.
Kevin M. Clermont, Professor of Law, Cornell University.

PROCEDURE—CIVIL PROCEDURE, Fourth Edition (1985), with 1988 Supplement

Maurice Rosenberg, Professor of Law, Columbia University.
Hans Smit, Professor of Law, Columbia University.
Harold L. Korn, Professor of Law, Columbia University.

PROCEDURE—PLEADING AND PROCEDURE: State and Federal, Fifth Edition (1983), with 1988 Supplement

David W. Louisell, late Professor of Law, University of California, Berkeley.
Geoffrey C. Hazard, Jr., Professor of Law, Yale University.
Colin C. Tait, Professor of Law, University of Connecticut.

PROCEDURE—FEDERAL RULES OF CIVIL PROCEDURE, 1988 Edition

PRODUCTS LIABILITY (1980)

Marshall S. Shapo, Professor of Law, Northwestern University.

PRODUCTS LIABILITY AND SAFETY (1980), with 1985 Case and Documentary Supplement

W. Page Keeton, Professor of Law, University of Texas.
David G. Owen, Professor of Law, University of South Carolina.
John E. Montgomery, Professor of Law, University of South Carolina.

PROFESSIONAL RESPONSIBILITY, Fourth Edition (1987), with 1988 Selected National Standards Supplement

Thomas D. Morgan, Dean of the Law School, Emory University.
Ronald D. Rotunda, Professor of Law, University of Illinois.

PROPERTY, Fifth Edition (1984)

John E. Cribbet, Professor of Law, University of Illinois.
Corwin W. Johnson, Professor of Law, University of Texas.

PROPERTY—PERSONAL (1953)

S. Kenneth Skolfield, late Professor of Law Emeritus, Boston University.

PROPERTY—PERSONAL, Third Edition (1954)

Everett Fraser, late Dean of the Law School Emeritus, University of Minnesota.
Third Edition by Charles W. Taintor, late Professor of Law, University of Pittsburgh.

PROPERTY—INTRODUCTION, TO REAL PROPERTY, Third Edition (1954)

Everett Fraser, late Dean of the Law School Emeritus, University of Minnesota.

PROPERTY—REAL AND PERSONAL, Combined Edition (1954)

Everett Fraser, late Dean of the Law School Emeritus, University of Minnesota.
Third Edition of Personal Property by Charles W. Taintor, late Professor of Law, University of Pittsburgh.

PROPERTY—FUNDAMENTALS OF MODERN REAL PROPERTY, Second Edition (1982), with 1985 Supplement

Edward H. Rabin, Professor of Law, University of California, Davis.

PROPERTY—PROBLEMS IN REAL PROPERTY (Pamphlet) (1969)

Edward H. Rabin, Professor of Law, University of California, Davis.

PROPERTY, REAL (1984), with 1988 Supplement

Paul Goldstein, Professor of Law, Stanford University.

PROSECUTION AND ADJUDICATION, Third Edition (1986), with 1988 Case Supplement

Reprint of Chapters 11–26 of Miller, Dawson, Dix and Parnas's CRIMINAL JUSTICE ADMINISTRATION, Third Edition.

PSYCHIATRY AND LAW, see Mental Health, see also Hinckley, Trial of

PUBLIC REGULATION OF DANGEROUS PRODUCTS (paperback) (1980)

Marshall S. Shapo, Professor of Law, Northwestern University.

PUBLIC UTILITY LAW, see Free Enterprise, also Regulated Industries

REAL ESTATE PLANNING, Second Edition (1980), with 1980 Problems, Statutes and New Materials Supplement

Norton L. Steuben, Professor of Law, University of Colorado.

REAL ESTATE TRANSACTIONS, 1988 Edition, with Statute, Form and Problem Supplement (1988)

Paul Goldstein, Professor of Law, Stanford University.

RECEIVERSHIP AND CORPORATE REORGANIZATION, see Creditors' Rights

REGULATED INDUSTRIES, Second Edition, (1976)

William K. Jones, Professor of Law, Columbia University.

REMEDIES, Second Edition (1987)

Edward D. Re, Chief Judge, U. S. Court of International Trade.

RESTITUTION, Second Edition (1966)

John W. Wade, Professor of Law, Vanderbilt University.

SALES, Second Edition (1986)

Marion W. Benfield, Jr., Professor of Law, University of Illinois.
William D. Hawkland, Chancellor, Louisiana State Law Center.

SALES AND SALES FINANCING, Fifth Edition (1984)

John Honnold, Professor of Law, University of Pennsylvania.

SALES LAW AND THE CONTRACTING PROCESS (1982)

Reprint of Chapters 1–10 of Schwartz and Scott's Commercial Transactions.

SECURED TRANSACTIONS IN PERSONAL PROPERTY, Second Edition (1987) (Reprinted from COMMERCIAL LAW, Second Edition (1987))

Robert L. Jordan, Professor of Law, University of California, Los Angeles.
William D. Warren, Professor of Law, University of California, Los Angeles.

SECURITIES REGULATION, Sixth Edition (1987), with 1988 Selected Statutes, Rules and Forms Supplement and 1988 Cases and Releases Supplement

Richard W. Jennings, Professor of Law, University of California, Berkeley.
Harold Marsh, Jr., Member of California Bar.

SECURITIES REGULATION, Second Edition (1988), with Statute, Rule and Form Supplement (1988)

Larry D. Soderquist, Professor of Law, Vanderbilt University.

SECURITY INTERESTS IN PERSONAL PROPERTY, Second Edition (1987)

Douglas G. Baird, Professor of Law, University of Chicago.
Thomas H. Jackson, Professor of Law, Stanford University.

SECURITY INTERESTS IN PERSONAL PROPERTY (1985) (Reprinted from Sales and Sales Financing, Fifth Edition)

John Honnold, Professor of Law, University of Pennsylvania.

SENTENCING AND THE CORRECTIONAL PROCESS, Second Edition (1976)

Frank W. Miller, Professor of Law, Washington University.
Robert O. Dawson, Professor of Law, University of Texas.
George E. Dix, Professor of Law, University of Texas.
Raymond I. Parnas, Professor of Law, University of California, Davis.

SOCIAL RESPONSIBILITIES OF LAWYERS, Case Studies (1988)

Philip B. Heymann, Professor of Law, Harvard University.
Lance M. Liebman, Professor of Law, Harvard University.

SOCIAL SCIENCE IN LAW, Cases and Materials (1985)

John Monahan, Professor of Law, University of Virginia.
Laurens Walker, Professor of Law, University of Virginia.

TAX, POLICY ANALYSIS OF THE FEDERAL INCOME (1976)

William A. Klein, Professor of Law, University of California, Los Angeles.

TAXATION, FEDERAL INCOME, Second Edition (1988)

Michael J. Graetz, Professor of Law, Yale University.

TAXATION, FEDERAL INCOME, Sixth Edition (1987)

James J. Freeland, Professor of Law, University of Florida.
Stephen A. Lind, Professor of Law, University of Florida and University of California, Hastings.
Richard B. Stephens, Professor of Law Emeritus, University of Florida.

TAXATION, FEDERAL INCOME, Successor Edition (1986), with 1988 Legislative Supplement

Stanley S. Surrey, late Professor of Law, Harvard University.
Paul R. McDaniel, Professor of Law, Boston College.
Hugh J. Ault, Professor of Law, Boston College.
Stanley A. Koppelman, Professor of Law, Boston University.

TAXATION, FEDERAL INCOME, VOLUME II, Taxation of Partnerships and Corporations, Second Edition (1980), with 1988 Legislative Supplement

Stanley S. Surrey, late Professor of Law, Harvard University.
William C. Warren, Professor of Law Emeritus, Columbia University.
Paul R. McDaniel, Professor of Law, Boston College.
Hugh J. Ault, Professor of Law, Boston College.

TAXATION, FEDERAL WEALTH TRANSFER, Successor Edition (1987)

Stanley S. Surrey, late Professor of Law, Harvard University.
Paul R. McDaniel, Professor of Law, Boston College.
Harry L. Gutman, Professor of Law, University of Pennsylvania.

TAXATION, FUNDAMENTALS OF CORPORATE, Second Edition (1987)

Stephen A. Lind, Professor of Law, University of Florida and University of California, Hastings.
Stephen Schwarz, Professor of Law, University of California, Hastings.
Daniel J. Lathrope, Professor of Law, University of California, Hastings.
Joshua Rosenberg, Professor of Law, University of San Francisco.

TAXATION, FUNDAMENTALS OF PARTNERSHIP, Second Edition (1988)

Stephen A. Lind, Professor of Law, University of Florida and University of California, Hastings.
Stephen Schwarz, Professor of Law, University of California, Hastings.
Daniel J. Lathrope, Professor of Law, University of California, Hastings.
Joshua Rosenberg, Professor of Law, University of San Francisco.

TAXATION, PROBLEMS IN THE FEDERAL INCOME TAXATION OF PARTNER-SHIPS AND CORPORATIONS, Second Edition (1986)

Norton L. Steuben, Professor of Law, University of Colorado.
William J. Turnier, Professor of Law, University of North Carolina.

TAXATION, PROBLEMS IN THE FUNDAMENTALS OF FEDERAL INCOME, Second Edition (1985)

Norton L. Steuben, Professor of Law, University of Colorado.
William J. Turnier, Professor of Law, University of North Carolina.

TAXES AND FINANCE—STATE AND LOCAL (1974)

Oliver Oldman, Professor of Law, Harvard University.
Ferdinand P. Schoettle, Professor of Law, University of Minnesota.

TORT LAW AND ALTERNATIVES, Fourth Edition (1987)

Marc A. Franklin, Professor of Law, Stanford University.
Robert L. Rabin, Professor of Law, Stanford University.

TORTS, Eighth Edition (1988)

William L. Prosser, late Professor of Law, University of California, Hastings.
John W. Wade, Professor of Law, Vanderbilt University.
Victor E. Schwartz, Adjunct Professor of Law, Georgetown University.

TORTS, Third Edition (1976)

Harry Shulman, late Dean of the Law School, Yale University.
Fleming James, Jr., Professor of Law Emeritus, Yale University.
Oscar S. Gray, Professor of Law, University of Maryland.

TRADE REGULATION, Second Edition (1983), with 1987 Supplement

Milton Handler, Professor of Law Emeritus, Columbia University.
Harlan M. Blake, Professor of Law, Columbia University.
Robert Pitofsky, Professor of Law, Georgetown University.
Harvey J. Goldschmid, Professor of Law, Columbia University.

TRADE REGULATION, see Antitrust

TRANSNATIONAL BUSINESS PROBLEMS (1986)

Detlev F. Vagts, Professor of Law, Harvard University.

TRANSNATIONAL LEGAL PROBLEMS, Third Edition (1986) with Documentary Supplement

Henry J. Steiner, Professor of Law, Harvard University.
Detlev F. Vagts, Professor of Law, Harvard University.

TRIAL, see also Evidence, Making the Record, Lawyering Process and Preparing and Presenting the Case

TRIAL ADVOCACY (1968)

A. Leo Levin, Professor of Law, University of Pennsylvania.
Harold Cramer, of the Pennsylvania Bar.
Maurice Rosenberg, Professor of Law, Columbia University, Consultant.

TRUSTS, Fifth Edition (1978)

George G. Bogert, late Professor of Law Emeritus, University of Chicago.
Dallin H. Oaks, President, Brigham Young University.

TRUSTS AND SUCCESSION (Palmer's), Fourth Edition (1983)

Richard V. Wellman, Professor of Law, University of Georgia.
Lawrence W. Waggoner, Professor of Law, University of Michigan.
Olin L. Browder, Jr., Professor of Law, University of Michigan.

UNIVERSITY CASEBOOK SERIES—Continued

UNFAIR COMPETITION, see Competitive Process and Business Torts

UNITED NATIONS LAW, Second Edition (1967), with Documentary Supplement (1968)

Louis B. Sohn, Professor of Law, Harvard University.

WATER RESOURCE MANAGEMENT, Third Edition (1988)

Charles J. Meyers, Esq., Denver, Colorado, formerly Dean, Stanford University Law School.
A. Dan Tarlock, Professor of Law, II Chicago-Kent College of Law.
James N. Corbridge, Jr., Chancellor, University of Colorado at Boulder, and Professor of Law, University of Colorado School of Law.
David H. Getches, Professor of Law, University of Colorado School of Law.

WILLS AND ADMINISTRATION, Fifth Edition (1961)

Philip Mechem, late Professor of Law, University of Pennsylvania.
Thomas E. Atkinson, late Professor of Law, New York University.

WORLD LAW, see United Nations Law

University Casebook Series

THE SOCIAL RESPONSIBILITIES OF LAWYERS: CASE STUDIES

By

PHILIP B. HEYMANN
Professor of Law
Harvard University

LANCE LIEBMAN
Professor of Law
Harvard University

Westbury, New York
THE FOUNDATION PRESS, INC.
1988

Library of Congress Cataloging-in-Publication Data

Heymann, Philip B.

   The social responsibilities of lawyers : case studies / by Philip
Heymann, Lance Liebman.

     p.   cm. — (University casebook series)

   ISBN 0-88277-645-2

   1. Legal ethics—United States. 2. Attorney and client—United
States. I. Liebman, Lance. II. Title. III. Series.

KF306.H44 1988

174'.3'0973—dc19   88–16505

                                                  CIP

H. & L. Soc.Resp.Lawyers UCB

For Jim Vorenberg, a good lawyer who encouraged us to study the social responsibilities of lawyers.

*

PREFACE

Since de Tocqueville, foreigners have marvelled at the importance of lawyers in American society. Today, more than 600,000 lawyers work in a wide variety of settings, giving advice to individuals, businesses, and government agencies, and operating the vast state and federal justice systems. One estimate of the "gross national product" for the legal profession in 1980 was $30 billion, or about one and one-half percent of total GNP.

But what do lawyers do, and how is the profession structured? On the whole, American law schools have not studied that subject. Law schools study "the law": rules, doctrines, policies. Law students read appellate cases: opinions issued by judges to explain decisions. But most lawyers never appear in an appellate court; and most citizens make contact with the legal system in circumstances far less refined than those studied in law schools.

The case studies included in this book are the product of an effort to broaden the available materials for studying the American legal system. These are not cases in the traditional law school sense: appellate decisions. Rather, they are cases as the term is used in business schools and schools of public policy: stories reporting events, institutions, choices, and outcomes. These stories show lawyers working in a wide variety of professional roles: representing large businesses and poor individuals; working in government and for private interests; doing criminal defense work and lobbying in Washington. These cases offer more flavor and context about the work done by lawyers than is available in most of the literature.

The case studies focus on the role society wants lawyers to play and the rules society wants them to follow. Should a lawyer fight energetically for a client, even if the result may be harm to a child or continuation of fraud? Should the organized bar oppose no-fault auto insurance because the tort system provides a good living for many lawyers? What should a government lawyer do when a newly elected president wants the Department of Justice to switch sides on a case already pending in the Supreme Court? These cases offer depth and context for tackling questions of lawyer ethics. Students can see the lawyer's choices in a credible context.

But the stories also demand attention to larger questions about lawyers in the United States. The most important ethical issues facing the system of justice are not the dilemmas that confront individual lawyers from time to time. Rather, they are the issues that affect the entire bar and the entire system of justice. Are legal services satisfactorily allocated? Is it fair that many important claims cannot be pressed because individuals cannot afford lawyers? How should we run such programs as Workers' Compensation so that the society gives injured employees a fair response to their claims without spending too much money on lawyers and judges? The stories in this book also address questions of that sort.

Lawyers are important to the United States. They provide services that assist individuals and institutions to comply with rules, to find imaginative solutions to problems, and simply to get along in a diverse and changing society. The United States gives lawyers so much power, fun, and money because the society needs their work. Therefore lawyers and non-lawyers must consider whether the legal system should be organized differently and whether the rules and norms governing lawyer conduct should be changed. Is the legal profession socially responsible today? How could it contribute more in the future? That discussion can only take place in the context of an accurate picture of the diversity of the profession and the reality of its contributions.

The conventional model for understanding the lawyer's role imagines an individual lawyer, a client making choices and decisions, and a neutral judge who will—if necessary—decide between two adequately represented parties. But the world is not like that, and probably never was. You are unlikely to have *a* lawyer, just as you rarely now have *a* doctor. Instead, you need specialists on different sorts of law, and you can only hope someone will coordinate the entire effort from your point of view. But "the client" is also often a myth. When a lawyer represents a business, is the client the management, the shareholders, the workers, or some combination of these? How can a lawyer get clear guidance when the client is the migrant farmworkers of California or a grandmother ambivalent about whether she wants to have custody of a nine-year old? And independent judicial decision is often barred by cost, delay, or inadequate representation for important interests. The case studies in the book seek to stimulate discussion of these questions.

This book had enthusiastic encouragement from Dean James Vorenberg, who initiated Harvard Law School's Program on the Legal Profession. The Program was made possible by support from the Alfred P. Sloan Foundation. Research on the case studies was done and initial drafts were written by an excellent team of student research assistants. They were Randy Bellows (Notes of a Public Defender), Ken Bresler (Lawyering for Fun and Profit), Maxwell Chibunda (When to Give Up a Law Suit), James Cramer (M. & A.: The Conoco Takeover), David Crane (No-Fault, No Fee), Kevin Darken (ShelterAd Inc.), Sula Fiszman (Law Offices of Lewin & Associates), Stephen Hitchner (California Rural Legal Assistance), Diane Hoffman (Food For Thought and When to Give Up a Law Suit), Leila Kern (Rita's Case), Darlene Reid-Dodick (Asbestos Litigation and OPM Leasing), Bill Rubenstein (Rita's Case and California Rural Legal Assistance), and Eric A. Stern (The Case of the Segregated Schools). We are grateful to faculty colleagues at Harvard and elsewhere who helped with supervision as the case studies were written and who gave us comments after teaching versions of the cases. Penny Pitman Merliss and Rose Zoltek provided administrative and intellectual leadership to the project. There would be no book had not Darlene Reid-Dodick edited and rewritten the cases over two years, encouraging us to complete our part of the work. Enice Matera, Joanne Burkert, and Tom Potter tolerated repeated revisions.

PHILIP B. HEYMANN
LANCE LIEBMAN

May 1988

*

TABLE OF CONTENTS

*

THE SOCIAL RESPONSIBILITIES OF LAWYERS: CASE STUDIES

*

I. Lawyer and Client

Rita's Case: Legal Services and Family Law *

Introduction

In April of 1982, Keith Maynard, director of Philadelphia Legal Aid (PLA), sat down to consider whether he would encourage one of his young attorneys, Joan Kiladis, to pursue a child custody case for which she had done an intake the previous day. There would be no problem with PLA handling such a suit—the client appeared to meet the income requirements of the organization and the lawyers at PLA routinely handled child custody cases.

But the issue for Maynard was whether he wanted Kiladis, a young lawyer in her third year out of law school, on this suit. She had devoted most of her time for the past year to a child custody case and although that legal battle had ended—Kiladis's client having gained custody of her eleven year old grandchild—Kiladis's involvement with the client, Gladys, and her granddaughter, Rita, had really just started. Kiladis still saw the family regularly: she took Rita to the zoo or to the museum or on other day trips, she often helped Gladys by driving her to and from her therapy appointments or to the grocery store or to Rita's school, and from time to time she dropped by their apartment with food for the family or gifts for Rita.

Maynard, although proud of Kiladis's work on Rita's case, had two concerns: first, he was worried that another custody case would again occupy Kiladis's time with extra-legal affairs. He could not afford to have one of his lawyers spend as much effort on such a routine matter; nor, Maynard thought, could Kiladis afford to spend so much emotional energy on her lawsuits. Second, he was concerned that Kiladis's intense involvement in Rita's case was not proper for a lawyer. Maynard had been taught that a lawyer must be a detached advocate for—not intimately involved with—her clients' interests. He was worried that Kiladis might be departing from limitations on the lawyer's proper role with her participation in her clients' lives.

For her part, Kiladis wanted nothing more than the opportunity to handle another custody case. Rita's case was the highlight of her time at PLA; rather than shuffling forms and preparing memos, she had had an opportunity to get involved with a family and had had what she considered a positive impact on their lives. She relished the personal dimension of the case. But she also knew that Maynard would be reluctant to let her delve immediately into a new custody suit; so she wrote him a note asking him to consider the work she had done on

---

* This case is fiction, adapted from several actual disputes in cities other than Philadelphia.

Rita's case and asking for an opportunity to discuss this new case with him.

Before he called Kiladis in to discuss the new case with her, Maynard did as Kiladis asked—he pulled out the file to reconsider Rita's case and to think again about Kiladis's involvement in that case.

Rita's Background

Rita was born in Bellevue Hospital in New York City in December 1971. Her mother, Carllota, had entered the hospital in labor, just four hours after taking a shot of heroin. Rita's father, who had been living with Carllota for a number of years and who had fathered her two other children, was not present, nor was his name entered on Rita's birth certificate. Carllota abandoned Rita in the hospital, where the infant remained for three months, being treated for both heroin addiction and syphilis. Rita's maternal grandmother, Gladys, obtained legal guardianship and took Rita home in March 1972.

When Maynard later discussed Rita's case, he could not recall how Gladys had been named guardian; grandparents had no special status in guardianship cases and certain factors in Gladys's home life argued against her being named guardian. Maynard guessed that some social worker had filed the necessary papers and pushed the guardianship through.

Rita lived with her grandmother for the next two and one-half years. First they resided in New York City; then, with the New York court's approval, they moved to West Philadelphia where they lived in a house next door to a low-income public housing project. Although many members of the family—aunts, uncles, cousins—also lived with Gladys at various times during this period, two others were relatively permanent members of the household, both in New York and in Philadelphia. One was Manuel, Rita's first cousin. Three years older than Rita, Manuel had also been born out-of-wedlock, to Rita's aunt, Maria, and had been raised by Gladys from birth. Maria, like her sister Carllota, was addicted to heroin. The second semi-permanent member of the household was Juan. Born in 1950, Juan had been brought up by Gladys since he was 15. In 1977, when he was 27 and Gladys was about 51, Juan became Gladys's third husband, thus becoming Rita's step-grandfather.

In August 1974, Gladys turned to the Department of Public Welfare in Philadelphia (DPW) for help with Rita. The child, although only two and one-half years old, was very difficult to handle; according to Gladys, she had become manipulative, aggressive, and unmanageable. Gladys was scheduled for gall bladder surgery and needed help caring for Rita. The Department suggested that Gladys place Rita in the Catholic Home for Children where the child could be evaluated and receive appropriate therapy, if needed. The Home requested that St. Christopher's Hospital evaluate and provide therapy for Rita while she resided at the Home.

Maynard later remembered that Gladys's feelings toward Rita seemed to indicate ambivalence: "Gladys loved Rita, but also couldn't control her, was somewhat older and not feeling well. There was this, 'I want her away, I want her back.' " Perhaps this ambivalence explains why, when she had recuperated from her gall bladder operation, Gladys did not bring Rita back from the Catholic Home for Children. Maynard remembered, "Once Gladys got home, and a period of time passed as she recovered from major surgery, she found she had a situation that was not so bad. So Gladys left things alone. It is similar, I think, to what some parents in other class settings who are ambivalent about their children do; they put their children in boarding school."

From August 1974 until June 1976 Rita seemed to thrive at the Catholic Home. She visited her family frequently on weekends, and her grandmother was often at the Home during the week as well. But Gladys could not adapt to the "boarding school" regime; she was not comfortable with the rules. "I think the Home found Gladys to be a pain in the ass," added Maynard. She could not do anything on time. She came to visit Rita during the week; she baked birthday cakes for other children's birthdays. She often brought Rita back late after a weekend home visit. Sometimes after such visits Rita's face and clothes were dirty and her hair uncombed, which shocked Home personnel.

Although Gladys viewed the Catholic Home as a temporary residential facility where children could receive help and then return to their families, the DPW often used the Home as a clearinghouse for children needing foster care. Because of Gladys's erratic behavior, the home decided that Rita would be better off in foster care. This decision was reinforced by Gladys's failure to state clearly that she wanted Rita back. Accordingly, in June 1976, the Home decided to place Rita with a foster family in a lower-middle-class Philadelphia suburb. Gladys continued to visit Rita and take her home on weekends during the seven months that Rita lived there.

Relations between Gladys and Rita's foster family quickly became strained. The foster parents complained to the Home that Gladys was not sticking to the visitation schedule, and Gladys complained to DPW that Rita's foster parents were abusing Rita. Maynard commented:

> I believe that Gladys intentionally undermined this placement.
> She was extremely threatened that she had failed as a mother

again and that she was going to lose Rita permanently. Gladys did not have the ability to say directly to the Home, "I want my child back." So, I think she made it very difficult for the foster family. When she talked to Rita about it, Rita picked up signals about what Gladys wanted to hear. So Rita started saying things about what was being done to her. There's no way of knowing whether they were true or not.

Nonetheless, Gladys complained to the DPW social worker about the alleged abuse and corroborated her tale with a description of bruises on Rita's buttocks, back, and sides; the social worker had Rita returned to Gladys within three days. By this time, February 1977, Juan and Gladys had married.

At first, everything seemed fine when Rita returned to Gladys. But soon Gladys became depressed. She could not handle Rita at all, and something seemed to be wrong with the child—she was aggressive and difficult, biting other children and throwing temper tantrums. Gladys turned to her social worker therapist, Elizabeth Reilly, who had Rita evaluated at the Learning Disabilities Center where Reilly worked. Reilly doubted Gladys's ability to care for Rita given her own physical problems and Rita's antics. Reilly was finally able to convince Gladys to place Rita back at the Catholic Home for Children. She also began a process of convincing Gladys to put Rita up for adoption.

During the following 18 months, Rita again settled into the routine at the Home. Although there were still many home visits, Gladys was again having difficulty maintaining the visiting schedule. She often did not arrive when she had promised to, and she frequently left early. Occasionally, Rita's mother, who had herself moved to Philadelphia, visited Rita at the Home. Home personnel noted that Rita often returned from visits to Gladys appearing distressed.

Within a year of Rita's return to the Home, when Rita was six years old, plans were again made to move her to a foster family. Maynard remarked:

> The planning came from the judgment of the people at the Home that Rita really ought to be permanently placed somewhere, and that grandma should remain grandma. There should be visits, but Rita should slowly be weaned away from her grandmother. This was a judgment that was concurred in by Elizabeth Reilly, Gladys's therapist. And there was something in writing—some document from the Home that indicated consent by Gladys to an adoption. Interestingly enough, when we got discovery, that document was missing; but I had seen it.

The plans to move Rita into a foster placement were greatly accelerated when a young, inexperienced psychology student, after six play-therapy sessions with Rita, concluded that Rita had been sexually abused. Looking back on Rita's case, Kiladis commented:

> The student was being supervised by someone whose "thing" was sexual abuse. What wasn't so clear to us and took us a while to find out was that half of the children in the Home had been placed there as a result of being sexually abused. This student felt that Rita was acting out various sexual behaviors. What was somewhat unfair about it was that apparently this went on all the time. Kids often playacted, partly as a way of working through some of what they've been through, and obviously it rubbed off on some of the other kids. But this student really freaked out about what was going on.

Although it was possible that Rita had been exposed to some sexual behavior, it was not clear exactly what had occurred or where. The Home suspected Juan, Rita's step-grandfather, and filed with DPW a form CY47 report of possible abuse. The Home also decided to place Rita out of Gladys's reach. Although the Home stated that it was cutting off visitation because of the sexual abuse issue, Gladys's failure to cooperate with the first foster care placement was also a major concern of the Home's. "All of the social workers' notes were loaded with things like that, that Gladys was and had continuously been difficult." Rita was then moved to a foster placement with the Biancos, a middle-class family in Jenkintown, a well-to-do suburb of Philadelphia about 20 miles from Gladys's home in West Philadelphia. Gladys was not given Rita's address or her phone number.

The Home promised Rita's new foster parents in Jenkintown that the child was theirs to adopt. Kiladis later reflected that this promise might have been part of "a deliberate cover-up" of Rita's exposure to either sexual abuse or sexual activity at the Home itself. At first Gladys reacted passively to Rita's placement in a foster home, as she had when Rita was placed in Germantown the first time. But when the new DPW worker on the case, who had met Gladys only once before, bluntly told her that Rita was being placed a second time— adding "I'm not going to let you see her"—and furthermore made accusations about sexual abuse of Rita by Juan, Gladys's attitude suddenly altered. Maynard recalled: "Gladys went to her therapist Reilly and Reilly's staff and drove them crazy, screaming at them, 'You've got to help me!' and they in turn called us." Maynard added:

> I got a call from Reilly saying that we had to help this woman. There had been accusations of sexual abuse and her child had been taken away. Reilly didn't say anything to me about the fact that she had been moving Gladys toward adoption, that

she herself felt that that might be both in Gladys's and Rita's best interests. I learned of these things only after the case came to us.

Maynard, after some investigation, took Gladys as a client. In a complicated series of moves he was able to negotiate a visitation schedule for Gladys while Rita was being evaluated by a group of specialists at St. Christopher's who dealt with sexually abused children. After several weeks, however, the "games began again." As Kiladis later put it: Gladys and the Biancos competed for Rita like divorcing parents. Gladys was never on time when she brought Rita back and never returned her to the Biancos in the same clothes in which she had left. The Biancos often dressed Rita inappropriately—for example, dressing her in a party dress when they knew that Gladys was taking Rita on a picnic. The Biancos would then complain when Rita's dress became soiled. Each family criticized the other's way of life. The Biancos were not Hispanic, and Jenkintown had essentially no Hispanic population. Rita, who had been bilingual, could no longer speak much Spanish. In fact the Biancos severely reprimanded her for any tendencies to use Spanish. At school in Jenkintown she was exposed to racial slurs and made to feel inferior for being Spanish. Rita claimed that the Biancos told her that if she returned to West Philadelphia she would become "scum like the rest of them," but that their home offered a fine suburban lifestyle.

Legal Strategy

Taking the Case

Maynard remembered how he analyzed the case after getting the call from Reilly:

Invariably I begin investigating these sorts of cases as if the facts are there to be assembled for decision at some future date. But in my gut I know that the decision will not be the same once the investigation is completed. Memories, perceptions, and positions will all have been affected—influenced by the investigation itself. What might look very bad for a client before a lawyer gets into a case can look very different after the lawyer's influence is felt. On the other hand, what are the choices? This is not an extreme case where I suspected that the child was being abused by my client. I did suspect, and this turned out to be true, that Rita's mother was involved much more than Gladys was telling us. Rita had Carllota's phone number and often spoke with her, and Carllota was often at Gladys's house. In addition, Rita went over to her mother's house more often than any of us realized, and the exposures over there that would be bad for a child were enormous. But this wasn't enough to alter what I did in the case. I simply chose the right of Gladys to make the decision about her grandchild over the right of other people to make it. I did not decide that I was the lawyer to decide what was best for Rita. Within certain limits, I really did and do allow my role as an advocate in the situation to take its course.

By the time Kiladis entered the case, then, Maynard had gotten to know Gladys well: he did not believe that there was sexual abuse in Gladys's home, and he believed that losing Rita permanently would be a terrible blow for Gladys. If, during the course of the prolonged legal maneuverings, Gladys's anger and anxiety would dissipate and she committed herself to adopting Rita, Maynard would be amenable.

Kiladis's approach to representing Gladys was somewhat different. Kiladis had let Maynard know, when she first became involved with the case, that she had to speak with Rita before she could make a commitment to represent Gladys. If DPW were correct in its evaluation of the situation and if Rita had developed a strong positive bond with the Biancos, then Kiladis felt she would not have "the emotional energy for the case." But if Rita reported that life with the Biancos was very different from the way both the Home and DPW described it, then "it would be very important to help her." Kiladis recalled:

> Ultimately it put me in a bit of a bind. It wasn't clear whose attorney I was; what I was advocating for and so on. Knowing Rita's needs as well as Gladys's and eventually even Carllota's created a lot of tension for me. Their needs were different, and it was not clear how to bargain them out; whether to try to get the maximum good for everyone or just for our client, Gladys.

Aside from the question of what might or might not be in Rita's best interests, Maynard had first been confronted with the problem of Gladys's best interests. Gladys wanted Maynard to move immediately to get Rita back for her. Here Maynard had two concerns: first, that he might lose if he went to court at a time when suspicions of sexual abuse were being raised; and second, that a court battle would take its toll on Gladys herself. Gladys was not emotionally able to withstand the upheaval of a prolonged court procedure. Early in the case Maynard had come to realize that it would be extremely painful for her to be evaluated as a parent by an outsider.

Although he intended to be Gladys's advocate and to try to intervene with DPW, Maynard's legal instincts told him he could best manage the case by drawing things out for a while despite Gladys's desire that he act immediately. Maynard therefore decided that it did not make sense to force the issue to a hearing right away:

> One, I couldn't win. Two, I thought this would be bad for Gladys. And three, the expert who had been doing therapy all of this time could not make a good witness for Gladys. So I went back to Gladys and I said: "I don't think that I can win it now. I don't think I can even get you visitation now, although if you tell me that I have to, I will try. I also don't think that Elizabeth Reilly will be as good a witness for you as she needs to be. I have got to do a lot of work with her, and you should start talking to her as well. . . ."

Initial Legal Maneuvers

From March through May, Maynard asked for visits at critical times: a confirmation ceremony in the family, illness of a close relative, a whole range of similar events. Each time, the visits were refused, yet there was constant negotiation with DPW about visits.

On May 10, 1979, more than two months after Gladys had come to him, Maynard drafted a letter for her. Essentially the letter was a statement by Gladys that she wished to terminate DPW's custody of Rita and a demand that Rita be returned to her. Maynard knew that this would precipitate action on the part of the Department, and it did. Since the time Gladys had voluntarily placed Rita with DPW, the Department had had custody of the child. Now, on May 25, 1979, the Department moved to formalize its custody by filing a motion in the appropriate Philadelphia court. Judge Warren granted temporary custody to the DPW, pending further proceedings.

But by then Maynard had begun the process he described as "obtaining information from, and trying to neutralize" the professionals involved in the case, and he was ready to proceed in court. On June 8, 1979, Maynard filed two motions: one for visitation and one for the payment of expert assistance for a psychological evaluation of Rita concerning the alleged sexual abuse. When he went into court on June 11, Maynard did not press the first motion:

> What I said to them was that Gladys should be allowed to visit. I asked them why they felt that she shouldn't. They told me that it was too dangerous, that Gladys, or someone in her household, was going to sexually abuse the child. Then I brought up the notion of having an independent expert decide that issue. I used the two motions to get them to concede to the motion for expert assistance.

In fact, the court never acted on the visitation motion. Maynard continued to pursue that goal through negotiation. On the other hand,

Judge Warren allowed the motion for payment of expert assistance because DPW did not oppose it. All parties agreed that expert assistance was a good idea; that Gladys really could not afford it; and, moreover, that it should be provided by the team of specialists at St. Christopher's. Maynard's choice of that team was a deliberate one:

> Before I went on the motion, I went to St. Christopher's. I had two meetings with the people there. They had never seen Gladys, but I had two meetings with them. I had a long talk with them about what I saw was going on and about how important it was that they look into it. I also went to see the fellow who runs the clinic, knowing that at that time St. Christopher's was involved in an internal struggle over whether to support DPW's approach to child custody issues, an approach which many saw as extreme intervention.

Maynard felt that many of the specialists on the team at St. Christopher's had attitudes that were ideal for his client. They were internally involved in a fight about whether they should be supportive of DPW's approach to removing children from their homes; they were sympathetic to poor people; they did not respect social workers (who generally stood at the bottom of the hierarchy of mental health professionals); and they believed that the social workers' decisions were often ill-advised and unsympathetic to poor people. Maynard recalled, "I knew they would bend over backwards to be non-interventionist in a case with PLA; I knew they would take the general position that these kids belong at home." In this particular case, where a child was being taken from an Hispanic environment and being removed to a distant suburb where she was not being allowed to see her relatives, Maynard thought the team would surely begin with an attitude sympathetic to Gladys. By the time Maynard had met with them twice, he knew that he had a "fairly receptive audience."

Maynard told Judge Warren that he had been to see the people at St. Christopher's. He indicated that they would be willing to accept the appointment from the court. Maynard was relieved that neither David Slade—a lawyer the court had appointed to represent Rita—nor the DPW counsel objected to the choice of St. Christopher's as evaluator. Had he been on the other side, Maynard noted, he would have demanded a different appointment, recognizing that the attorney who got to the expert first established a relationship that was likely to set up the case to some extent in his favor. But, in Maynard's words, "They were so relieved to give up this fight on visitation for a period of time that they went along with the appointment of St. Christopher's as an evaluator."

It was not until August 1980 that Rita's court-appointed lawyer, Slade, voiced concern about the evaluation being done by St. Christopher's. At that time he moved for an additional psychological evaluation and payment of costs. Although this evaluation was also to be conducted by St. Christopher's, Slade specified that the report evaluate Gladys's household as a potential home for Rita rather than limiting itself to the question of whether or not abuse had occurred there. Although Maynard knew that Slade might have realized that the St. Christopher's team was going over to Gladys's side, Maynard went along with the motion for a new evaluation because "I knew we had St. Christopher's; once you've got them that far, you've got them."

Lull

The evaluation process was very drawn out. But that also, Maynard thought, worked in Gladys's favor in the long run. In the interim, the PLA attorneys had succeeded in building up Gladys's visitation with Rita, bit by bit; they also were able to speak with all of the actors in the case—a therapist in Jenkintown to whom the Biancos had taken Rita, a nun at the Home, the DPW social workers, and Gladys's therapist, Reilly. Every interview had a dual purpose: it was an opportunity to get information and an opportunity to "neutralize" the speaker to ensure passive acquiescence in (if not active support for) a result favoring Gladys. Maynard commented that "all of those contacts were negotiations as well as interviews. The whole strategy was to bring the professionals around so that they saw Rita's placement as something that ought to change."

A great deal had changed under the influence of PLA. A schedule of day visits had been established. The St. Christopher's team was evaluating the situation, and though Gladys was cooperating fully with them, Betty Bianco was not. Because Betty refused to bring Rita to Philadelphia to go to St. Christopher's, Joan Kiladis was driving out to Jenkintown to pick up Rita and bring her downtown. Gladys was still in therapy with Elizabeth Reilly, whom Maynard felt was now moving toward siding with Gladys.

The team at St. Christopher's was aware that Rita was feeling tension because of the racism in the Jenkintown school she was attending. By March 1980, a talk between Gladys's attorneys and the staff at St. Christopher's indicated that the St. Christopher's evaluators were coming to three conclusions, summarized in a memo in the PLA file:

> (1) While the St. Christopher's team cannot state categorically that there has been no sexual abuse, nothing in Rita's language or behavior indicates any basis for the CY47. If she was abused, she is no longer cognizant of the fact. The team believes that the filing of the CY47 was ill-advised; that a lot of the behavior cited is characteristic of institutional living.

(2) Rita wants to go home to her grandmother, cannot understand why she is moved from place to place, and is apprehensive that her therapists will be taken away from her. (3)
Because of the above, the team would recommend that Rita be
returned to Gladys's home and continue in therapy at St.
Christopher's.

Yet St. Christopher's was unwilling officially to exonerate Juan of
sexual abuse; nor would the evaluators address the possibility that Rita
was being beaten by the Biancos. Rita had written a letter to her
therapist at St. Christopher's, saying that she was being beaten and
generally mistreated by the Biancos and that she wanted to go home to
her grandmother and "pappy," her name for Juan. Although Kiladis
had not actually handed Rita the pencil and paper to write it, she felt
somewhat implicated in the letter-writing process because she frequently urged Rita to be frank with the people she saw at St. Christopher's,
reassuring her that what she told her therapist there would not get
back to the Biancos.

Kiladis had also told Rita to be frank with David Slade, but as it
had turned out, Rita never got to talk with Slade. Although he was the
child's attorney, and according to Maynard had left "no legal stone
unturned," Slade never went out to see the child or asked to have her
brought to his office. Maynard recalled, "We did not sit down with
Slade and say, 'you should see the kid.' If we had, I think that he
would have gone. But we didn't do that." Kiladis said that both Rita
and Gladys had called Slade's office on numerous occasions and left
messages on his answering machine, but their calls were never returned. Maynard added:

> Slade lived in another world. He lived in the downtown world
> of big firms. Those attorneys don't go to Jenkintown, and they
> don't go out to people's houses. The last thing he was going to
> do was to go to Gladys's house in West Philadelphia. I think
> that that is part of the class structure of the bar, and I think
> it's a shame. Those attorneys miss the chance for the type of
> practice that a doctor who is a general practitioner has. I have
> a life as full of people as of law, law as a human service. It's
> not for everybody, but it's for more people than you'd think if
> they'd give it a chance.

It was also not clear to Maynard what Slade was advocating. At
first, Maynard said, Slade had gone along with DPW, but later he
opposed them as well and asked for continuances. He seemed to feel
that Rita had already lost her identification as an Hispanic, and that
therefore ethnicity was no longer at issue. "Slade was not even present
at the final two hearings in the case," Maynard noted.

Further, the PLA attorneys were able to turn to Rita's advantage Kiladis's friendship with two of the women at DPW who were involved with the case. Memos in the PLA file indicate that Kiladis had long telephone conversations with Susan Goldman, the supervisory social worker. Goldman had often called Kiladis at her home to discuss Rita's case. They also discussed the form CY47 report of possible abuse that the Home had filed with DPW more than two years earlier but that had never been substantiated or officially pursued. Goldman felt that the psychology student who had made the first report of sexual abuse had been under considerable pressure—pressure to find instances of such abuse for her supervisor's book. Goldman and Kiladis discussed the question of why the Home had chosen to move Rita into foster placement at a time when many of the professionals involved were warning against any change. Kiladis told Goldman of her own belief that Juan was a stabilizing influence on the family and that his youth counted in the family's favor if any concerns about Gladys's failing health might arise. Kiladis reassured Goldman that DPW need not rely upon its own judgment that Gladys and Juan were "okay as parents," since St. Christopher's was certainly very competent and would be making a favorable report.

Similarily, Kiladis was continually in contact with Grace Myers, the counsel for DPW. Before Myers became the attorney of record on the case, Kiladis had met her at the Philadelphia courthouse. Kiladis explained:

> I had several long conversations with Grace. I knew her from law school. When I talked with her at the courthouse, I knew that some of what I was saying would get back to the Department. I told her that we had a lot of cases with the Department in which we concurred with the moves that the Department was making, but that we had a few where we felt that the Department's behavior was off-the-wall. The Department occasionally overreacted, and Rita's case was an example of that; they were much more upset than was warranted.

Kiladis knew that her relationship with Myers "cut a lot of red tape." Kiladis did not tell Myers that she thought Gladys would fall apart if she had to take care of Rita without the necessary support services from DPW. Instead she told her that there were support mechanisms in place, that Gladys was doing well with them, that Gladys was being very cooperative, and that when the department told Gladys to do something differently with Rita she did so. Myers, according to Kiladis, "knew that I believed in what I was saying, that Rita wanted to go to Gladys, that Gladys wanted her, and that there were support mechanisms at work that I had no objection to."

Final Legal Matters

On January 29, 1981, Kiladis filed a petition for Gladys and Juan to adopt Rita. By then Kiladis herself had been with the case for six months and knew all of the professionals involved, as well as the "principals"—Rita, Gladys, Betty Bianco, Carllota, and Juan. Since Juan spoke very little English, Kiladis's acquaintance with him was limited. She had participated in a conference at St. Christopher's and knew that the hospital team's second report, which would come out on February 1, 1981, would contain a recommendation that Rita be returned to Gladys after a period of gradually increased visitation. The adoption petition, although filed, was not immediately acted upon.

DPW agreed to St. Christopher's recommendations, and Rita returned to live with Gladys, Juan, and Manuel in March 1981. She was, however, still under the legal custody of DPW. Rita and Gladys attended therapy sessions each week at St. Christopher's. Juan refused to go from the beginning. Kiladis believed that his resistance arose from a combination of his residual distress about having been accused of sexually abusing Rita and the traditional "macho" notion that men do not talk about their feelings. For whatever reasons, Juan said that if he had to attend therapy sessions he would move out. And shortly thereafter he did so, moving in with a woman his own age.

Gladys, Rita, and Manuel—Rita's cousin—were now living together at Gladys's home in West Philadelphia. Gladys was in therapy with Elizabeth Reilly, and Rita and Gladys continued to go to therapists at St. Christopher's. DPW remained involved. Finally, in January of 1982, Kiladis convinced Susan Goldman that it was time for DPW to release Rita from its custody by moving to dismiss the original DPW motions for custody and to dispense with Carllota's consent to Rita's adoption. A hearing was set for February 2. Because Rita was ill that day, she and Gladys did not attend. Kiladis was there, along with Grace Myers for DPW; David Slade was not present. Since there was no opposition to the dismissal of the two motions filed by DPW, the judge was willing to dismiss them. But, he asked, who would then be Rita's guardian? Myers mentioned that Gladys was legally Rita's guardian because of the New York court order. Kiladis, not convinced of the validity of that order in Pennsylvania, told the judge that she had filed an adoption petition for Gladys and Juan. Myers voiced some concern about allowing Rita to be adopted by Gladys and Juan. Both women were concerned about the possibility that if adopted, Rita might become the object of a custody dispute between Gladys and Juan in the event that their separation ended in divorce. Judge Warren ordered a continuance.

In April Rita's Case appeared before Judge Warren again. Rita and Gladys were present with Kiladis, and DPW was represented by Grace Myers and Susan Goldman. David Slade again did not appear. The judge allowed DPW to dismiss its two motions, entered into the record an agreement between Gladys and DPW for after-care services, and allowed the petition for Gladys and Juan to adopt Rita, even though Juan was not present and the judge knew that Juan and Gladys were living separately. Rita ran up to the bench and hugged the judge.

Conclusion

After he finished reviewing Rita's case, Maynard concluded that it was Kiladis's involvement that had won the case for Gladys. Kiladis not only spent many hours talking with Susan Goldman and Grace Myers; she also spent a great deal of time with Gladys and Rita. While Rita lived in Jenkintown, Kiladis drove her to and from St. Christopher's and to and from Gladys's for visits. She met Carllota and recognized the extensive contact that Rita still had with her mother. Kiladis in many ways became an advisor and counselor to Gladys, talking with her about the best school placement for Manuel and, eventually, Rita, as well as answering Gladys's questions about various presents for Rita while the child was still living with the Biancos. Maynard recalled Kiladis had told him, "I had to set limits or I would have been making up grocery lists for her."

But Maynard was still not convinced Kiladis had successfully set those limits:

> She came as a new student and gradually became more experienced. As she began to grow and I had more confidence in her, I gave her more and more of the case. She developed an excellent relationship with Gladys. I was anxious for that to happen because I needed to separate myself from it psychologically. But what I also saw develop was the classic problem of overcommitment. It seemed to me that Joan took every little piece of anything that was there and blew it up. At the same time she was driving Rita around town and making Gladys's domestic arrangements. She made the case because of the amount of energy and effort that she put into it.

Before Kiladis went in to speak with Maynard, she thought about the many things she knew about Rita's case that Maynard did not know. She thought of Carllota's continuing involvement with Gladys and Rita and the potential dangers in Rita's exposure to a drug-dominated environment. Moreover, there was the fact that Gladys received a full monthly allowance from the federal AFDC (Aid to Families with Dependent Children) program, even though (unbe-

knownst to the government) Gladys and Juan owned the building that
Gladys and the children were living in and had not reported the rent
they were receiving from the two apartments in the building; and the
couple also owned a building in Puerto Rico which, since it was not
occupied by either of them, would disqualify Gladys for welfare as well.
Additionally, Kiladis knew that Gladys was working on one job under a
false Social Security number. Where did Kiladis's duty to her client
begin and end?

Characters

Joan Kiladis—Lawyer at PLA

Gladys—Client, Rita's grandmother

Rita—Subject of case

Keith Maynard—Lawyer at PLA; Kiladis's supervisor

DPW—Department of Public Welfare

Carllota—Rita's mother; Gladys's daughter

Manuel—Rita's first cousin; Carllota's sister's son

Maria—Rita's aunt; Gladys's daughter; Carllota's sister; Manuel's
    mother

Juan—Gladys's third husband; Rita's step-grandfather

Catholic Home for Children—Rita's residence 9/74–6/76, 6/77–12/78

Germantown foster family—Rita's home 6/76–2/77

Elizabeth Reilly—Gladys's counselor, social worker

Biancos—Jenkintown foster family, Rita's home 1/79–3/81

David Slade—Rita's court-appointed lawyer

Susan Goldman—DPW supervisor of social workers

Grace Meyer—DPW legal counsel

Appendix A. Rita's Places of Residence

12/71–3/72	NYC hospital at which she had been abandoned
3/72–8/74	Gladys's homes in New York and Philadelphia, where Gladys moved with permission of New York court
8/74–6/76	Catholic Home for Children, as suggested by DPW
6/76–2/77	Germantown foster family, as suggested by Home
2/77–6/77	Gladys and Juan's home, as suggested by DPW
6/77–12/78	Catholic Home for Children, as suggested by DPW
1/79–3/81	Bianco family, Jenkintown foster parents, as suggested by Home

3/81–present   Gladys's home, as suggested by Gladys and arranged by
                PLA

Discussion Questions

1. What must Keith Maynard or Joan Kiladis decide before they can
represent Gladys in her attempt to obtain custody of Rita? Kiladis wants
Maynard to assure her that obtaining custody for Gladys is in Rita's best
interest; but when Maynard agreed to represent Gladys, he had no way of
knowing what was the best outcome for the child.

In part, the moral problem is a familiar one for any lawyer. A client seeks
representation. The position to be taken is defensible, but not necessarily
correct. The conventional justification of the lawyer's role is that competing
positions will be represented and the judicial process will decide.

But how can Kiladis and Maynard rely on that justification? If they
commit their organization's resources to Gladys, her position will be zealously
pressed. It is unlikely that competing positions will be represented with equal
skill and aggressiveness. Maynard and Kiladis can be virtually certain that *all*
legitimate interests will not be vigorously represented.

Does this mean that Maynard and Kiladis should decline to represent
Gladys if their initial guess is that she should not be Rita's custodian? The
California Business and Professional Code provides in § 6068(h) that it is a
lawyer's duty "never to reject, for any consideration personal to himself, the
cause of the defenseless or the oppressed." Would this provision require
Maynard or Kiladis to represent Gladys? Or is Rita more defenseless than
Gladys? In any event, is the California provision in conflict with DR 5–101(A)
of the ABA's Code of Professional Responsibility, which tells a lawyer not to
accept a representation (except with the client's consent after full disclosure) if
his or her professional judgment "may be affected by his own . . . personal
interest"? Is Kiladis's concern for Rita's well-being a "personal interest"?

Can Maynard simply say that Gladys walked in the door, meets the office's
income test, and therefore will be his client, even if the outcome she seeks
(custody) is harmful to Rita and contrary to the public interest? Doesn't every
lawyer make decisions as to whom she will represent before committing her
talents to a client's purposes? Every lawyer chooses to do certain work, in a
particular institutional context, rather than other work. Every lawyer allo-
cates limited time among various clients. Every lawyer chooses the approach
to take to particular matters. Do Maynard and Kiladis face additional responsibilities? If so, is it because they know that they must turn away many
clients; that the public pays the bills; that a child's life is at stake? If
Maynard and Kiladis should consider the social desirability of particular
results, what guidance do they have in reaching their conclusions?

2. Does the manner of representation change when opposing interests are
poorly represented? Maynard and Kiladis *know* that if they fight hard for
Gladys to get custody, there is a very good chance that will be the outcome,
whether or not it is the outcome they would favor if they were in the role of
neutral fact-gatherer or decision-maker. Does that give them special responsi-

bilities they would not have if they were confident all positions would be equally well represented? Is there a position between the "hired gun" on the one hand and, on the other hand, the lawyer as one who shares moral responsibility for the client's ends and means? What is that in-between position?

Should the fact that Maynard and Kiladis do not face determined and able opposition limit them in pressing for certain results? Note that the first thing Maynard does for (or to) Gladys is to tell her it is too soon to sue for custody. One reason for this is that, on the existing record, he is not sure she would win. But perhaps he is also delaying until he himself becomes more confident about what the result should be. Yet if Maynard and Kiladis will not work aggressively for what Gladys says are her goals, should they not tell her that there are limits to their advocacy for her; and are they not failing to provide what the Model Code of Professional Responsibility calls "zealous" representation? Does Gladys know, when she retains Maynard, that he will be approaching her cause through the filter of his own evaluation of a desirable result? Should he tell her? Would the legal system work well if every lawyer held Kiladis's view: that she will only pursue client goals with which she agrees?

On the other hand, given the imbalance of representation, are you troubled by the role of Maynard and Kiladis in creating the facts—the story—on the basis of which the official decision will eventually be made? In our system, a judge rules on a case created and presented by others. Perhaps that is satisfactory when advocates are competing to establish versions of the facts. Here, as it turned out, the Biancos did not obtain a lawyer—the cost would be great, and perhaps they were diffident about "fighting over" a child for whom they cared deeply. The Catholic Home would not go to the expense of hiring a lawyer. The court appointed a lawyer for Rita, but he did not do his job. The welfare department saw no reason to invest the time of its lawyers in this case. Carllota, Rita's mother, might have wanted to participate, but Philadelphia Legal Aid was the most likely place for her to obtain representation, and they were already working for Gladys.

Thus Maynard and Kiladis had no competition as they helped Gladys revise the story that she initially brought to them so as to make it more acceptable to the legal system. What if the story as told to them by Gladys had such extensive holes or contradictions or implausibilities that it would have raised serious questions about Gladys's character? Is hiding that evidence of untruthfulness a proper role, perhaps even a responsibility, of Gladys's lawyers? Should Maynard ask Gladys for proof? Must he either "buy" the story and agree to represent its teller, or decline representation?

To these familiar choices of lawyers, the case adds additional dimensions because of the very close involvement of the lawyers with the daily lives of Gladys and Rita and the energetic efforts by Maynard and Kiladis to control the elaborate decision making process. Kiladis inevitably changed the facts when she became close to Rita. In conversations, Kiladis supported certain recollections and interpretations of Rita's past and discouraged others. And the fact that Rita could lean on Kiladis made Rita and Gladys appear more stable to the judge. Is it a problem that the role of Rita's friend is played by a lawyer attempting to win a case? Is it not very likely that after Kiladis obtains a result by showing the court a Rita befriended by Kiladis, Kiladis will move on to other things, and Gladys, not Kiladis, will now be in charge of Rita? Does this mean that Kiladis's double role has the result of changing the facts? Does that make it wrong?

Similarly, Maynard and Kiladis use their relationship with helping professionals—the hospital personnel who evaluate Rita—to obtain opinions useful to the result they seek. They know a great deal about Gladys that does not become part of the official decision. They manage to downplay inquiry into the validity of the New York custody determination. They steer away from possible competing claims by Rita's mother. These actions are both effective advocacy and manipulations of the official processes. Did Maynard and Kiladis behave properly in seeking so successfully to control the decision making process? Have they made themselves rather than the judge the final decision-maker? Is your answer to that question different from the answer you would give if the positions opposed to Gladys's attempt to obtain custody were as well represented as Gladys's position?

As to each evaluation of an action taken by Maynard and Kiladis, are you influenced by the fact that a child's welfare is at stake? Should the ethical responsibilities for a lawyer dealing with custody of a young person differ from the obligations of a lawyer merely fighting over (what may be a large amount of) money?

Note that the discussion of special responsibilities for a lawyer who has no (or weak) opposition is relevant in many situations other than that of legal aid lawyers representing a poor grandmother. Many times, lawyers for business can invest greater resources in a case than their opponents—consumers, workers, or even a government agency. In that situation, do those lawyers have special responsibilities? (The situation for government lawyers varies widely. Sometimes those lawyers have nearly unlimited resources compared to those of their opponents; other times, government lawyers with limited resources face vast battalions of well-financed business counsel.)

3. Did the adversary process "work" in Rita's Case?

What needs to happen for society to make a satisfactory decision on a matter such as the proper placement of Rita? What information is needed? Who is the proper decision-maker?

In this instance, the court system offered a procedure—a judge and a courtroom. The judicial system waited, as it usually does, for represented parties to proceed. Not surprisingly, the only position that had an effective advocate prevailed. If that is to be our system, is it not essential to make sure all important positions are represented? Is there any way to do that?

The alternative to using the adversary system is a "neutral" decision-maker ferreting out the facts and the law. The judge in this case was neutral, but he did not play an active role in structuring the decision. He waited, and then ruled on what was brought to him. A second neutral, in a sense, was the lawyer appointed to represent Rita. He was free to decide what was best for her and then to argue for that result. Why was he so ineffective here? Could the process be made satisfactory by appointing a better lawyer for the child who is the subject of the proceeding? How would that lawyer find out what was best for Rita? Would that lawyer just be substituting his or her own values, preferences, and biases for those of the majority who enacted the statutes on custody, guardianship, and adoption? (Note that the statute uses general language such as "best interests of the child" as the legal standard. Could the legislature give more specific guidance than it has done here?)

The state agency was a neutral party. We would not need an adversary proceeding or a judicial decision if we trusted trained government professionals. In other countries social service experts would play the dominant role on a matter such as Rita's Case. Is that feasible in the U.S.? What are the impediments here? For all our doubts about unchecked bureaucratic power, does this story give you confidence that court review can be a major improvement on bureaucratic decision? Certainly Rita's Case shows an example of the worst of all worlds: no vigorous competing advocacy, yet no effective neutral espousing and implementing a clear public policy.

Epilogue

As this book was going to print, Rita had turned 17 years old. She was still living with her grandmother, Gladys, although Gladys's husband Juan had moved out of the house and divorced Gladys. Juan was remarried to a woman close to his own age. Although Rita was living with her grandmother, she was still very much in the court system. As a result of truancy and delinquency at school, she had been in juvenile court defending charges brought by the school system and by the Department of Public Welfare. These charges stemmed from her actions in school where she had been "acting out," and was neither a good nor a popular student. Kiladis was no longer in communications with Rita or her grandmother, although she had recently run into them in the halls of the Philadelphia Probate Court.

II. Lawyer Roles

A. Lawyers for a Political Movement

California Rural Legal Assistance *

Gary Bellow

Bellow's Background

Gary Bellow grew up in Brooklyn, attended Yale as an undergraduate, and received his LL.B. from Harvard Law School in 1960. He spent the next year at Northwestern University studying criminal law and then went to work for the public defender agency in Washington, D.C., where he quickly rose to the position of deputy director. In 1964, he was named Young Lawyer of the Year by the District of Columbia Bar Association.

Early in 1964, a member of Washington's United Planning Organization (UPO) approached Bellow and asked him to draft the proposal for UPO's Neighborhood Legal Services Project (NLSP). The Ford Foundation funded Bellow's proposal for NLSP in November 1964, and he was asked to join the Board of the new organization. In April 1965, Bellow left the public defender agency to join UPO as its administrative director. Several months later he was promoted to deputy executive director. In both positions, he shared the responsibility for general oversight of the legal services project, but he was not directly involved in its operations. He continued to serve on NLSP's board of directors, and in the fall of 1965 he was invited to join the National Advisory Council to the newly created United States Office of Economic Opportunity (OEO) Legal Services Program as one of its charter members.

At UPO Bellow was responsible for training community organizers, coordinating organizational efforts, and building political strategies around issues of welfare, housing, and community planning. His work led him directly into such activities as organizing tenant groups and conducting rent strikes. This experience convinced Bellow that UPO was not using effectively the full potential of legal services as an organizing tool. The NLSP seemed to be misdirecting its energies. Bellow agreed fully with the criticism of the legal services program voiced by Kenneth Pye, chairman of NLSP's board:

> NLSP gradually became service oriented without any decision by its board to proceed in that direction. . . . During its

---

* This case is based on interviews with some participants in the relevant events. Some names have been changed.

first year it failed to realize the objectives of an experimental program which would re-examine systematically the legal rules and procedures affecting the poor, which would investigate new areas and utilize new methods in the representation of the poor, which would coordinate effectively legal and social services for a joint approach to the problems of the poor. It did not develop into a program in which attorneys, relieved of heavy caseloads, could concentrate on a limited number of cases of significance to the community, could develop drafts of new rules, regulations and statutes, and could provide leadership in the formation and representation of neighborhood organizations. . . . The staff attorneys performed their tasks with an attitude of dedication and provided aggressive representation for individual clients. But many demonstrated an approach of cautious conservatism towards the subjects of group representation, participation in attempts to organize groups, and relationships with social workers and UPO organizers. . . . An atmosphere did not develop in which the neighborhoods could look to staff attorneys for leadership in community affairs. NLSP attorneys were outsiders who came to the neighborhoods to represent those needing legal services and who left when the task was done.

Bellow shared Pye's view that NLSP had become at best a first-rate legal aid society of the traditional type. He was convinced of the need for a new approach to legal services.

Approaches to Legal Services

Bellow described the original concept behind legal services as the "service model." Here the idea is to increase the availability of legal services to poor persons so that they will be adequately represented within the political and economic system. Neighborhood legal offices will help individual clients with problems stemming from such things as landlord-tenant relations, wage garnishments, welfare, consumer credit, and family relations. This model assumes that the social order is fundamentally sound, with the legal services program serving as a means of ensuring that the proper authorities hear poor people's grievances. This has been the attitude traditionally adopted by the American Bar Association and other bar groups. The service model generally leads to extremely heavy caseloads, since legal services offices try to help every client who comes to them. Unfortunately, lawyers who are overwhelmed by heavy caseloads may fail to see areas where the model's basic assumption is faulty—where the law itself must be reformed before the poor can obtain equal justice.

This realization led many proponents of legal services to endorse the "law reform model," which emphasizes rule change and the representation of groups of poor people. Based on the example of *Brown v. Board of Education,* 347 U.S. 483 (1954), the objective of legal services under the law reform model is to establish broad legal principles and to change administrative rules in a way that relieves the plight of poor people. The basic instrument for this purpose is the test case, which is brought to attack unfair practices of government agencies or private companies and to establish new rights for the poor. Under the law reform model, service to individual clients is provided only as a means for winning the confidence of the poor community and for learning about the problems poor persons face.

In 1964 and 1965, most lawyers in the legal services community espoused some combination of service to individual clients and law reform with increasing emphasis on the latter. Gary Bellow, however, believed that both these models of legal services were inadequate. He approached the problem from a different perspective.

> I had been a criminal defense lawyer and then had gone to UPO, where for a year and one-half we did street organizing. . . . I saw legal services as an arm of community organization, that is, the lawyer was to function as part of a political effort, at times as a lawyer, at times as an organizer, an educator, teacher, and PR man.

He was particularly sensitive to what he saw as the shortcomings of the law reform model of legal services:

> The worst thing a lawyer can do—from my perspective—is to take an issue that could be won by political organization and win it in the courts. And that is what legal services agencies did all over the country. They took the most flagrant injustices—the ones that had the potential to build the largest coalitions—and they took them into the courts, where, of course, they won. But there was nothing lasting beyond that. . . .
>
> The basic theory of test case litigation is that a court case can be framed and directed toward the elimination of a particular wrong, like maldistribution of income, and can be a vehicle for the elimination of injustice. For test case lawyers, the problem is merely finding the particular rule or doctrine which embodies or causes the injustice and challenging it. This approach is a dead end for a number of reasons. First, it misconstrues the problem. The problem of unjust laws is almost invariably a problem of distribution of political and economic power; the rules merely reflect a series of choices

made in response to these distributions. If a major goal of the unorganized poor is to redistribute power, it is debatable whether judicial process is a very effective means toward that end. This is particularly true of problems arising out of disparities of wealth and income. There is generally not much doctrinal judicial basis for dealing adequately with such problems, and lawyers find themselves developing cases whose outcomes are peripheral to the basic issues that these problems raise.

Secondly, rule change, without a political base to support it, just doesn't produce any substantial result because rules are not self-executing: they require an enforcement mechanism. California has the best laws governing working conditions of farm laborers in the United States. Under California law, workers are guaranteed toilets in the fields; clear, cool drinking water, covered with wiremesh to keep flies away; regular rest periods; and a number of other "protections." But when you drive into the San Joaquin Valley, the drinking water is neither cool, nor clean, nor covered. If it's provided at all, the containers will be rusty and decrepit. It doesn't matter that there's a law on the books. There's absolutely no enforcement mechanism. Enforcement decisions are dominated by a political structure which has no interest in prosecuting, disciplining, or regulating the state's agriculture interests. It's nonsense to devote all available lawyer resources to changing rules.

According to Bellow's analysis, the problem is:

the creation of a mechanism that can create a substantial and lasting change in behavior, governmental and private. This is inevitably a political as well as a legal problem. We can try to generate pressures on the parties involved by bringing public attention to the problem, or try to develop sanctions for non-compliance with existing laws, or attempt to develop institutional mechanisms to keep the problem visible. Sometimes a legal decision can produce conforming behavior. But what happens when we go away—when the pressure abates? Legal victories can be so easily circumvented. If one avenue is blocked, five other alternatives remain open.

To his question "What happens when we go away?" Bellow's answer was that the legal service lawyers must leave behind poor people who have organized to keep the pressure on the governmental authorities. In other words, he believed that legal services should be based on the model of "lawyer-organizers" who provide legal services to help organize poor communities. In cases where no organizational efforts are under way, this might mean that lawyers would themselves function as the organizers.

Bellow was explicit in describing how he thought lawyer-organizers should operate. Even though they might use test cases and other tools of the law reformers, their aims and methods would be very different:

> If litigation is directed toward the different goal of organizing, the potentials and methods in pursuing a law suit significantly change. In such a context, law suits can consciously be brought for the public discussion they generate, and for the express purpose of influencing middle class and lower class perspectives on the problems they illuminate. They can be vehicles for setting in motion other political processes and for building coalitions and alliances. For example, a suit against a public agency may be far more important for the discovery of the agency's practices and records which it affords than for the legal rule or court order it generates. An effective political challenge to the agency may be impossible without the type of detailed documentation that only systematic discovery techniques can provide. It is on this base that coalitions and publicity can be built, and that groups can be organized to limit previously invisible authority.

> This, of course, suggests a different orientation for the attorney interested in political change. He will spend a great deal more time in political organizing, in working on cases and priorities that reflect the group demands of his clients and in developing cases in a way which reinforces their political integration and cohesion. Let me give you an example: Assume an attorney is seeking an injunction and he must make a decision as to the type of preliminary relief he will ask of the court. What criteria should govern that decision? An attorney focusing on political organizing might well delineate the narrowest rather than the broadest ground in seeking preliminary relief. For example, in a landlord-tenant dispute he might seek a restraining order preventing the landlord from using force or self-help. This is, of course, a clear legal right in California, and the likelihood of obtaining such an order would be high. Why would it be sought? Twenty tenants would go in with the attorney to court asking that they not be thrown out by the landlord before he goes to court and they'd walk out with a paper in their hands restricting the landlord's power. More than the protection, they'd have won a victory. They can go back to the forty other tenants who didn't go to court and say "We won our first fight. Now we'll try a harder fight."

Financing The CRLA

Frustrated by his inability to redirect NLSP and tired of Washington, Bellow decided early in 1966 to look for a new position where he would be closer to the actual delivery of legal services and could better try out his ideas. He hoped to demonstrate the utility of the lawyer-organizer model to OEO and the legal services community:

> I thought legal services was on the wrong track with its separation from community organization and its tendency to slip into law reform without recognizing the political dimensions of that approach, so I began looking for a place where the lawyer could function as an organizer.

Thinking that his approach would be particularly helpful to poor people in a rural area, Bellow investigated legal services programs in Florida and Arizona. Finally, Earl Johnson, Deputy Director of OEO's Office of Legal Services, told him about an ambitious program that was about to start in California. The prime mover behind the California program was Jim Lorenz, a 26–year–old associate at a major Los Angeles law firm. Lorenz had gone to Phillips Andover Academy, graduated Phi Beta Kappa from Harvard College, and earned his LL.B. at Harvard Law School, where he had won first place in the Ames moot court competition. He was being assisted in planning the new program by two students from the Yale Divinity School, Tom Jensen and Barry Clark, who had been organizing farm workers in the San Joaquin Valley.

Johnson showed Bellow the funding proposal for California Rural Legal Assistance (CRLA), which Lorenz had prepared. Bellow was immediately excited about the idea because it involved a good deal of community organizing. While the CRLA lawyers could do some of this organizing, they also would be dependent on establishing a good relationship with Cesar Chavez and his union, which was already organizing the farm workers. Bellow was also excited by Lorenz's proposal itself. It began with a quote from a Woody Guthrie song that the farm worker "comes with the dust and is gone with the wind." The proposal proceeded to describe the farm workers' situation in the following terms:

> Few will debate the desperate plight of these farm workers. Their average individual hourly farm wage is $1.35 as compared with the statewide average factory wage of $3.05 an hour. Those who work at least 25 days a year in agricultural employment still are employed an average of only 134 days. It is not surprising, then, that the farm worker's average annual income from both agricultural and non-agricultural employment is approximately $1,378, which is less than half the

$3,000 level at which poverty supposedly begins in this coun-
try. His median income is only $674.00. More than 84 per-
cent of all farm workers in California—approximately 252,000
persons—earn less than $3,000 a year.

When measuring the farm worker's impotence, it should
be noted that he is exempt from the protections of the National
Labor Relations Act, which guarantees other workers the right
to bargain collectively; the Federal Fair Labor Standards Act,
which sets the basic minimum wage and maximum hours for
industries engaged in interstate commerce; and the Federal
Unemployment Tax Act, which subsidizes 60 percent of the
state unemployment insurance programs. On the state level,
he is not covered by unemployment insurance, by a minimum
wage, or by a maximum hours provision. His wife and children will receive a minimum hourly wage of $1.30 if they
undertake farm work but this rate does not apply to employers
hiring less than five women and children, does not extend to 20
percent of the piece work which is performed for any employer,
and is not accompanied by maximum hour or overtime provisions. If the farm worker is a Mexican American, an Oriental,
or a Negro, as most farm workers are, he is sometimes discriminated against. In the words of the Senate Subcommittee on
Migratory Labor, the farm worker's plight is "shocking"; he is
the "always excluded American," according to the Director of
the Office of Economic Opportunity, and as he himself says,
"We're always goin' some place but we never git no place."

After painting this depressing picture, the proposal continued: "So
far as the rural poor are concerned, the familiar saying that we are a
society of laws, not of men, is, at best, a half truth. Laws are passed,
interpreted, and enforced by men: legal rights depend upon political,
economic, and legal representation. Yet this is what the rural poor,
particularly the farm workers, have consistently lacked." Because of
this lack of representation, the proposal maintained:

it is not surprising that the laws which are intended to protect
the rural poor frequently go unenforced. Section 923 of the
California Labor Code guarantees to the individual worker full
freedom of association and the right to organize and engage in
concerted activities; but in practice, organizational picketing
by farm workers, which is essential to any successful organizational campaign, is often enjoined. Under present California
case law, trial courts possess broad discretion to enjoin picketing, even where the acts enjoined are non-violent, so long as
the court determines as a matter of fact "that future picketing,

even though conducted peacefully, would probably, if not necessarily, be regarded as sinister in purpose."

The State of California has extensive housing codes governing the operation and upkeep of labor camp housing, but the President's Committee on Migratory Labor has estimated that only a quarter to a third of the labor camps comply with these laws.

Working conditions in the field are also regulated: employers are required to provide their workers with drinking water, toilets and hand washing facilities and periodic rest periods. Yet it has been observed that less than 20 percent of the employers in the state comply with these requirements.

The State Labor and Education Codes contain extensive regulations governing the employment, working conditions, and hours of minors, but inspectors from the Department of Labor find children working illegally on 60 percent of the farms they inspect.

Employers are required to furnish their workers an itemized written statement showing income earned and deductions made; but the nebulous and changing working relationship between farm workers and employers and the common practice of paying workers on a piece-rate basis means that accurate records are rarely kept or made available to employees. As a result the benefits of the Social Security Act and the Old Age, Survivors and Disability Insurance Program are frequently not received by workers, even though they are legally entitled to such benefits.

Criminal prosecutions are permitted under the Labor Code, but they are rare. In 1957, for example, only one California farm employer was prosecuted for violating the State Labor Laws.

Many violations of the law go unreported because farm workers are fearful of retaliation, or because they are unaware of their rights: while many of the rural poor speak Spanish, the statutes contained in the State Labor Code and the regulations published by the State administrative agencies are written in English. When complaints are made to the Labor Commissioner and other state agencies, many are determined to be unfounded or unsubstantiated, because the complainants have no clear idea of their legal rights and what they must prove to enforce these rights. Complaints which are filed may not be successfully prosecuted because necessary witnesses, who migrate to other areas of the State, cannot be found. Sometimes, even the complainant disappears.

It is little wonder, then, that the California State Senate Fact Finding Committee on Labor and Welfare concluded in 1961 that the manpower for compliance work is still far short of that necessary to accomplish a minimal adequate job. This fact is recognized by Federal and State administrators of the program, growers, and organized labor.

Lorenz argued that a legal services program could make a significant contribution to bettering the condition of the rural poor. His plan for CRLA had several noteworthy features:

- Ten regional law offices would be established in rural parts of the state and be manned by approximately 20 lawyers at salaries of $14,000 a year. The advantages claimed for a statewide program included greater ability to serve migrants, economies of scale, easier recruitment of well-qualified lawyers, and more independence from local community pressures.

- The problems of farm workers would be emphasized by CRLA, although other poor persons living in rural areas would also be served.

- A small research staff would be created to study major problems particularly affecting the rural poor. The duties of this staff might include the drafting of legislation and the preparation of trial and appellate briefs.

- An educational program would be developed to train the program's attorneys and lay assistants. Various social and legal problems relating to rural poverty would be addressed.

Lorenz's proposal was submitted to OEO in March 1966. It was supported by a number of liberal, farm labor-oriented groups, including the Mexican American Political Association, the Community Service Organization, and the Emergency Committee to Aid Farm Workers. In April, however, the Board of Governors of the California State Bar Association adopted a resolution in opposition to the proposal. The State Bar condemned the departure from "the concept of neighborhood legal services offices established and operated by residents of local communities" and CRLA's intention to provide "its services to political and economic groups as well as individuals." The State Bar's resolution went on to charge:

The proposal is basically one of militant advocacy on a statewide basis of the contentions of one side of an economic struggle now pending. Ostensibly designed to furnish only legal services to the poor, the proposal also encompasses the furnishing of political and economic aid.

Despite the State Bar's opposition, OEO's Office of Legal Services recommended that the CRLA proposal be funded. Clinton Bamberger, Director of Legal Services, remarked at the time that "advocacy of the contentions of one side of an economic struggle now pending" was the best one-line definition of the War on Poverty he had heard. In May, Sargent Shriver, Director of OEO, approved a grant to CRLA of $1.3 million—the largest grant OEO had made to any legal services program. Before he announced the grant, Shriver called the President of the California State Bar, James Hemphill. When Hemphill complained that the poor might use the CRLA lawyers in suits against the growers, Shriver replied: "Look, I'll make an agreement with you. If you will agree that no lawyers in California will represent the growers, I will agree that no legal services people will represent the pickers." That ended the argument.

As with all OEO programs, the grant specified standards that determined who was eligible to receive services from CRLA. The eligibility standards limited CRLA to representing persons who earned less than $2200 per year plus $500 per dependent. Like other OEO grants, the one to CRLA could be vetoed within 30 days by the governor of the state. A gubernatorial veto was subject to override only by the Director of OEO.

Under the standard conditions applied to all OEO grants, CRLA would be prohibited from engaging in partisan political activities. In addition, OEO placed several special restrictions on this grant, including:

- CRLA could not undertake or sponsor activities to encourage the formation of the poor into collective bargaining units (but it could represent persons satisfying the program's eligibility requirements who requested assistance regarding their legal interests, including interests relating to labor relations).

- CRLA was prohibited from acting as legal counsel or supplying legal representation to any labor union or political organization.

At Shriver's insistence, the CRLA office proposed for Delano—Cesar Chavez's union headquarters—would instead be located seven miles away in McFarland.

Getting Started

Bellow, Lorenz, Jensen, and Clark devoted a great deal of time during the fall months to hiring lawyers. By late November a full staff of 24 lawyers was in place, and CRLA reported in its refunding application to OEO:

When we first drafted this program, we felt that our greatest problem would be attracting able, energetic lawyers to work in outlying rural areas. . . . Nevertheless we have been able to hire an extremely capable and diverse group of attorneys. Four of our attorneys were rated first or second in their law school classes. Two graduated summa cum laude and at least twelve graduated magna cum laude or cum laude from their colleges. Almost the same number were Phi Beta Kappa.

Their backgrounds are as varied as the regions which the program serves. Included in their number is the former manager of a furniture store in Santa Maria; a leading civil liberties lawyer in San Francisco; the Deputy Director of the Washington, D.C. Poverty Program and a noted lecturer on poverty law; a trial attorney for the Internal Revenue Service; an administrative assistant to a State Senator in Sacramento; a trial attorney for the Justice Department in Mississippi; a criminal defense lawyer in Washington, D.C.; a member of Oakland's Legal Aid program; chief corporate counsel for a large California dairy; a Deputy Attorney General of California; a draftsman of one of the two federal civil rights bills proposed for 1965; a Deputy District Attorney of Imperial County; and a Deputy County Counsel of Tulare County. Six have worked as seasonal agricultural workers and one raised corn and pigs as a farmer in Iowa. Five are bilingual in English and Spanish. And, we should not neglect to state, three are women.

Early in August, we decided that if we had to choose between attorneys of energy and ability and attorneys with great experience, we would choose the former. We succeeded in getting a staff which was capable, but young. The average age of our attorneys is 30.5 years. The Directing Attorneys of the regional offices have been in private practice for an average of more than four years. . . . Due to the inexperience of some of our attorneys, some mistakes may occur. Nevertheless, it is our strong belief their flexibility, ability to learn, diligence, character, and intelligence will be more important in the long run in ensuring that the rural poor are forcefully, persuasively, and imaginatively represented.

Fully staffed, a regional office (of which there were to be ten) ypically consisted of a directing attorney, an associate attorney, two egal secretaries, one or two community workers, and a clerk-typist who lso served as the receptionist. The job of the community workers was) make contacts for the lawyers and to give them legitimacy among the farm workers. The community workers often had experience in social work and were hired for their knowledge of and standing within the community. The legal secretaries, on the other hand, were normally hired from outside the local community since this helped to ensure that CRLA's activities and its clients' problems would be kept confidential.

From the start, the CRLA staff held frequent meetings and conferences. One objective of these meetings was to build spirit and cohesion. But the meetings were equally important as a means of training the staff. Training was needed not only by the community workers and the secretaries, but also by the attorneys. Bellow and Lorenz knew that only a few of the program's attorneys were experienced in legal services work. The rest had excellent credentials, but little knowledge of poverty law and its applications. To remedy this deficiency, Bellow set up meetings at which he and the other experienced attorneys helped to teach their colleagues about legal problems they could expect to encounter in their work, including welfare regulations, landlord-tenant relationships, employment law, family law, consumer protection, and civil rights.

Although this training seemed to be successful as far as it went, Bellow soon realized that it was not meeting the lawyers' most urgent needs. As of November, Bellow concluded that the training "didn't produce what we thought it would produce—it didn't produce a political perspective in our lawyers. They functioned as lawyers handling rules, and they rarely went to court." Bellow wanted the lawyers in the regional offices to be more active in seeking ways to use their skills to aid organizational efforts. For example, if a lawyer is presented with a case of eviction:

> the lawyer should say to himself: "What are the politics of that eviction? What is there in the eviction that I can get or that will start producing political forces to change it?" For example, if a public housing tenant is being evicted, it may turn out that the real lever to get at a public housing project is the matching funds from the federal government. And what you want the lawyer to do is not only to defend the eviction, but also to bring an action to cut off or control those funds in some way that guarantees that no one gets evicted.

Bellow decided that many of the program's lawyers suffered from two basic problems: they had not mastered the nuts and bolts of being a lawyer—things like how to interview a client, how to take a deposition, how to file a suit—and they were tending to "lawyerize" issues. He began to realize:

[We] had enormously underestimated what law school training
meant. Our lawyers were not going to court and not engaging
in political activity because they were afraid or felt incompetent to do either. And to say to them, of all things, that they
should not only go to court, but go to court with a challenge to
the welfare department, as distinguished from a divorce case—
which was an injunction action and involved much more complicated legal mechanics—was just beyond them. And we had
just assumed that if you get the best lawyers, they are going to
be able to do legal work. We had also underestimated the
degree to which they separated their role as lawyers from their
political views. When we talked to them, they could talk
about it easily and see the connection. But when they went to
those offices, they practiced law. We couldn't budge them.

After lengthy discussions among themselves and with several other
members of the staff, CRLA's directors settled on a strategy for dealing
with this problem. They shifted the emphasis of the training sessions
away from topics in poverty law and concentrated more heavily on the
mechanics of lawyering. They also decided to use the rising tensions
between the program's lawyers and its community workers in an effort
to change the lawyers' approach to their job. They planned a conference of the lawyers and community workers for early December so that
the intra-office antagonisms could be brought into the open and discussed. They hoped that this open discussion would start to increase
the lawyers' sensitivity to the community workers and, by extension, to
the Chicano community as a whole.

These hopes were frustrated. The conference was much more
emotional and bitter than anyone had predicted. A deep rift appeared
between the lawyers and the community workers. Aroused community
workers voiced their feelings about the salaries and prerogatives of the
lawyers, suggesting that the Anglo lawyers were racists. The lawyers
criticized the community workers in turn for having unreasonable
expectations and failing to understand the problems and constraints
inherent in legal practice. Emotions became so hot during the conference that Lorenz and Bellow let the community workers go home on
schedule and kept the lawyers around for an extra day. Tempers
cooled slowly as the lawyers talked things over among themselves, but
many people still left the conference "angry, and bitter, and questioning." CRLA had been severely shaken, but it did not collapse.

For Gary Bellow, the conference had been an agonizing personal
experience. Despite his great sympathies for the community workers,
he ultimately had felt compelled to side with the lawyers as the only
way to hold the program together. He saw the conference as touching:

on all those issues of class and caste and race that dominate our society anyway. And how far are you from the truth when you get a bunch of white guys who have not really had this kind of experience before? All of us who have done this work have had to work through that racial hang-up, and I don't believe any of us have fully worked it out. You know, it gets to be breast beating. But it's there! And you can't be brought up in this society without being aware of it.

Relationship with Cesar Chavez

The racial tensions within CRLA were especially troublesome considering Bellow's objective of having CRLA work closely with Cesar Chavez and the National Farm Workers Association (NFWA); the tensions added a personal impediment to a relationship already constrained on paper by CRLA's funding grant. At the time CRLA was starting up, Chavez's union, the NFWA, was engaged in a major strike against the Di Giorgio Fruit Corporation, one of the largest agribusiness corporations in California. The NFWA had already achieved several victories on behalf of its members and was the object of nationwide attention. It launched a national boycott of Schenley wines and liquors in December 1965. Four months later, Schenley, the second largest grower in the Delano area, agreed to recognize the NFWA as the sole bargaining agent for all of its farm workers in the counties surrounding Delano.

Chavez's parents were migrant farm workers, and he learned to be an organizer from Fred Ross of the Community Service Organization (CSO), an outgrowth of Saul Alinsky's Industrial Areas Foundation. In 1952, Chavez accepted a job organizing CSO chapters throughout California. Rising rapidly in the organization, he was appointed director of the National CSO in 1960. However, he became disenchanted with the organization as it prospered and seemed to lose touch with the people it was designed to serve. Chavez explained:

> As the organization grew, we found ourselves meeting in fancier and fancier motels and holding expensive conventions. Doctors, lawyers, and politicians began joining. They would get elected to some office in the organization and then, for all practical purposes, leave. Intent on using the CSO for their own prestige purposes, these "leaders," many of them, lacked the urgency we had to have. When I became general director I began to press for a program to organize farm workers into a union, an idea most of the leadership opposed. So I started a revolt within the CSO. I refused to sit at the head table at meetings, refused to wear a suit and tie, and finally I even refused to shave and cut my hair. It used to embarrass some

of the professionals. At every meeting I got up and gave my standard speech: we shouldn't meet in fancy motels, we were getting away from the people, farm workers had to be organized. But nothing happened. In March of '62 I resigned and came to Delano to begin organizing the Valley on my own.

How the union was started is now a legendary story that Chavez has been called on to repeat many times:

> By hand I drew a map of all the towns between Arvin and Stockton—86 of them, including farming camps—and decided to hit them all to get a small nucleus of people working in each. For six months I traveled around, planting an idea. We had a simple questionnaire, a little card with space for name, address and how much the worker thought he ought to be paid. My wife, Helen, mimeographed them, and we took our kids for two or three day jaunts to these towns, distributing the cards door-to-door and to camps and groceries.

> Some 80,000 cards were sent back from eight Valley counties. I got a lot of contacts that way, but I was shocked at the wages the people were asking. The growers were paying $1 and $1.15, and maybe 95 per cent of the people thought they should be getting only $1.25. Sometimes people scribbled messages on the cards: "I hope to God we win" or "Do you think we can win?" or "I'd like to know more." So I separated the cards with the pencilled notes, got in my car and went to those people.

> We didn't have any money at all in those days, none for gas and hardly any for food. So I went to people and started asking for food. It turned out to be about the best thing I could have done, although at first it's hard on your pride. Some of our best members came in that way. If people give you their food, they'll give you their hearts. Several months and many meetings later we had a working organization, and this time the leaders were the people.

The union grew slowly through 1963 and 1964. Chavez established a Farm Workers Credit Union, a small Farm Workers Cooperative (to purchase automotive supplies for NFWA members), a Farm Workers Press (which published a bi-weekly newsletter), and a service center that helped members with welfare and legal problems. He and NFWA vice president Maria Sanchez lobbied California state legislators for the extension of disability and unemployment benefits to farm workers. By August 1964, the NFWA had 1,000 member families spread over seven counties. NFWA's membership voted in November 1964 to give

Chavez a salary of $40 per week, making him the first farm labor organizer in history to be supported by the workers themselves.*

Encouraged by its growing strength, NFWA engaged in two small, local strikes around Delano in the summer of 1965. The major issues in both strikes were wages and union recognition. NFWA also organized a rent strike and protest march when the Tulare County Housing Authority announced plans to raise rents at two of its labor camps; state and county authorities investigated and the Authority rescinded the rent hikes.

While the NFWA was meeting with some success in its battles, CRLA was winning some battles itself. Among the most publicized legal battles that CRLA won in its early years were those that:

- forced Governor Ronald Reagan to restore $200 million that he had cut from the State's Medicaid program;

- brought about the complete overhaul of a municipal water system;

- enabled citizens who were literate only in Spanish to vote in California elections;

- liberalized the state's welfare requirements.

All of this, of course, hardly began to solve the farmworkers' array of serious problems. One of the most pressing from both NFWA's and CRLA's perspective was the bracero issue.

The Bracero Lawsuit

For many years prior to 1967, California's agricultural growers had imported braceros to help harvest their crops. This practice had a significant impact on the farm labor market since the existence of a pool of Mexican nationals willing to work for low wages undercut the position of domestic farm workers. In 1964, Congress repealed the law under which the bracero program had been authorized, but this action did not end the use of braceros. There remained several complicated ways in which Mexicans could be brought in legally to work in California fields. One of the least complicated and therefore most commonly used ways was provided by the Immigration and Nationality Act. In accordance with this act, the Secretary of Labor had promulgated regulations under which the Bureau of Employment Security (BES)

---

* Chavez placed great stress on his union being self-supporting: "One of the first things I decided was that outside money wasn't going to organize people, at least not in the beginning. I even turned down a grant from a private group—$50,000 to go directly to organize farm workers—for just this reason. Even when there are no strings attached, you are still compromised because you feel you have to produce immediate results. This is bad, because it takes a long time to build a movement, and your organization suffers if it gets too far ahead of the people it belongs to."

could authorize the issuance of temporary entry permits to Mexican farm workers after determining that a sufficient number of domestic workers was not available at fair pay and working conditions. The regulations further provided that a request for braceros "should be filed at the local office in sufficient time to allow the BES 30 days to determine the availability of domestic workers, in addition to the time necessary for the employer to secure foreign workers by the date of need if the certification is approved."

The bracero program had long been opposed by persons and organizations concerned with the plight of domestic farm workers, especially the United Farm Workers Organizing Committee (UFWOC), which was the product of the August 1966 merger of the NFWA and the Agricultural Workers Organizing Committee (AFL–CIO). The UFWOC was worried about the potential use of braceros as strike-breakers, hindering attempts at union organization. Moreover, American workers were being hurt by the growers' deliberate efforts to foster a shortage of domestic labor to meet the legal criteria for certifying braceros. The growers had at times used their political and economic influence to deny housing to local workers, to pressure county welfare agencies into cutting off benefits for unemployed workers, and otherwise to drive away unemployed farm workers prior to harvest time.

CRLA's action on the bracero issue began to become serious in the spring of 1967. Jason Smith, Directing Attorney of CRLA's Modesto office, and George Fernandez, a young Chicano lawyer, became interested in braceros because of another case they were working on. At about the same time, Jim Lorenz and Gary Bellow (who was about to take charge of the McFarland office) decided that CRLA should give the bracero question a high priority during 1967. Getting in touch with Jason Smith, they agreed that the Modesto office would undertake a major investigation to be directed by George Fernandez under Smith's supervision. They would assign extra community workers to Modesto to interview farm workers. Because the standards set by the Department of Labor (DOL) were far in excess of the growers' existing practices, they anticipated little difficulty in proving the growers' failure to comply with DOL's criteria.

The Modesto office proceeded with its investigation during the spring and summer. Early in the summer, CRLA's Salinas office also began to study the bracero issue. Lee Reynolds, Directing Attorney in Salinas, and Denny Kalb, his close friend and colleague, became interested in the bracero problem because of two cases they had pending. In both cases, CRLA was representing farm workers who had been fired in violation of the California Labor Code for alleged union activities. The defendants were growers and grower associations that normally used bracero labor during the harvest. In fact, one of the defendants was the largest single user of braceros in California. Reynolds and Kalb wanted to prevent the growers from receiving certification for braceros until their clients' cases were settled. They planned to rely on the DOL regulations providing that no employer in violation of state labor laws or involved in a labor dispute could use braceros.

The Modesto and Salinas offices conducted their investigations independently through July and August. Both offices contacted James Nottingham, Regional Administrator of BES in San Francisco, and elicited a promise that he would notify them and allow them to present their evidence before BES certified any request for braceros. Fernandez and Kalb checked periodically with Nottingham as the weeks passed to remind him of this promise. In the meantime they worked on their respective cases. Fernandez began to prepare a set of pleadings with guidance from Jason Smith, who had much greater experience as an attorney. Smith left most of the work to Fernandez because he was immersed in a major suit to enjoin Governor Reagan's reduction of Medi–Cal benefits for the indigent.

At 4 p.m. on Thursday, September 7, Nottingham announced the certification of 8,100 braceros for the tomato harvest. The CRLA attorneys were notified of his action by the press. This sudden action provoked a swift reaction from CRLA. Denny Kalb and Lee Reynolds spent most of the night putting the finishing touches on their brief. During this time they received a call from Jim Lorenz, who had been talking with Robert Blake, the regional representative for the Secretary of Labor. Blake had remarked about how bad it would be for one arm of the government to be suing another, and he implied that CRLA would jeopardize its funding if it sued DOL. Despite this threat, Lorenz did not discourage Kalb and Reynolds from pursuing their case.

The next morning, Reynolds and Kalb appeared before Judge Chapman in San Jose to ask for a temporary restraining order (TRO). They realized that BES's sudden action had put CRLA at a disadvantage. Now that BES had announced the certification, the Mexican authorities would begin immediately to arrange for the braceros. Busloads of farm workers would soon arrive at the border. Most judges would be more reluctant to intervene in the process at this point than at an earlier stage. Moreover, Denny Kalb was forced to admit under questioning from Judge Chapman that few domestic workers were available to help with the harvest. Kalb explained that most farm workers had left the Salinas area a few weeks earlier because of the growers' failure to advertise and to guarantee the workers adequate employment at fair pay. In spite of these adverse factors, Kalb and Reynolds were still hopeful. They were somewhat surprised when Judge Chapman refused to issue a TRO. Instead he simply scheduled a hearing on the suit for the following Friday. By then the braceros would be at work in the fields.

Without knowing what had happened in San Jose, Jason Smith and George Fernandez presented their suit to Judge Jewett in San Francisco. Jewett turned out to be receptive, and he acceded to Smith's request for a TRO. However, Jewett then learned from the U.S. Attorney about Judge Chapman's denying a TRO on a similar case only hours earlier. Furious, he chewed out Smith, accusing CRLA of trying to whipsaw the courts. Smith tried to explain that these were two distinct and separate cases, but he knew too little about the Salinas office's case to make the point convincingly. Judge Jewett finally calmed down long enough to transfer the Modesto office's case to Judge Chapman to be consolidated with the other CRLA case and heard on the following Tuesday, September 12. At least CRLA now had a TRO so that no braceros could cross the border before the 12th.

By this time Smith himself was thoroughly angry. Later, leaving court, he was quick to let Reynolds and Kalb know that they had fouled up the case completely. They had miscalculated about which judge would be more favorable to CRLA's arguments, and now the more favorable judge had washed his hands of the case. He, Smith, had obtained the TRO; they had failed.

Apprised of the tense and confused situation, Jim Lorenz tried to mediate. On Friday evening he called Lee Reynolds and Denny Kalb and persuaded them to extend a peace offering to Smith. Reynolds and Kalb agreed to go to Modesto the next morning to plan a strategy for the court hearing, which was only four days away.

The Saturday meeting was attended by Lee Reynolds, Denny Kalb, Jason Smith, George Fernandez, and Jim Lorenz. Gary Bellow kept in contact by telephone. Before the meeting, Reynolds and Kalb patched up their differences with Jason Smith, at least superficially. They also took their first look at the affidavits that George Fernandez had collected during the preceding months. They found the affidavits related primarily to working conditions and pay; not much had been done to show the growers' failure to advertise for workers. Kalb and Reynolds decided the affidavits were sloppily drawn and could be torn apart by a clever lawyer. In their view, Fernandez had merely catalogued abuses, not tied them to specific times, places, and growers.

The meeting started with a comparison of the two suits. There were differences in the clients and in the kinds of violations cited, as well as obvious differences in style. The Salinas brief was tightly written, while the Modesto brief "read like a novel," to use Denny Kalb's description. But for all practical purposes, the amount of proof CRLA would have to supply was the same for both cases. In either case, CRLA would have to establish a clearly discernible pattern of practices that injured their clients.

The meeting then turned to strategy. The possibility of getting an out-of-court settlement was raised. George Fernandez protested against any negotiations with the DOL, but the others finally persuaded him that "it won't hurt to talk." No one was sure whether DOL's lawyers would be inclined to settle the case. Lee Reynolds saw a good chance that they would give CRLA a favorable settlement since they could not be sure how strong CRLA's case was. He said that government lawyers were often penalized for losing cases, but never for settling out of court. Also, the DOL was undoubtedly embarrassed by BES's handling of the bracero certification and would want to avoid public exposure. Gary Bellow, on the other hand, believed the DOL would be intent on fighting CRLA in court; they could hardly afford to back away from such a direct challenge. Although they did not resolve this issue, they did agree upon a plan of action. Bellow and Fernandez would prepare for the court hearing on Tuesday. In the meantime Kalb and Reynolds would negotiate with the government's lawyers to see if a settlement was possible. Jason Smith would help Kalb and Reynolds prepare for the negotiations, then return to working on his Medi–Cal suit.

The negotiations began in San Francisco on Sunday, continued all day on Monday, and extended into the early hours of Tuesday morning. The parties reached agreement on the basic terms of a settlement around four in the morning on Tuesday, September 12. At Lee Reynolds's insistence, the government lawyers called Secretary of Labor Willard Wirtz at his home in Washington and obtained his approval of the terms. Then the government lawyers—most of whom were older men—went to their hotel to get some rest. Reynolds and Kalb were left to work out the exact wording of this agreement and to have it typed.

The agreement represented a remarkable victory for the CRLA lawyers. A seven-member panel was to be set up to study the certification procedures for foreign farm-workers; CRLA was to nominate three of the members. Every applicant for farmworkers from Mexico would have to swear under penalty of perjury that he had complied with a set of criteria promulgated by the Secretary of Labor. The regional administrator of the DOL was committed to investigate violations of the Secretary's criteria at any time upon request by an aggrieved party, giving all interested and affected parties an opportunity to present evidence. No braceros would be certified sooner than seven days after the DOL received a request for foreign workers asserting that no domestic farm workers were available. During this period any interested party would have an opportunity to present evidence of non-compliance with the Secretary's criteria as to what wages and conditions of employment had to have been offered earlier in an attempt to employ domestic workers. There were specific requirements as to advertising for workers in both Spanish and English, and there was more.

While Reynolds and Kalb were typing up the agreement in San Francisco, Bellow and Fernandez were in San Jose preparing to go into court. They were accompanied by a group of farm workers led by Maria Sanchez, Deputy Director of UFWOC. At about 10 a.m., Bellow received a phone call from Denny Kalb telling him about the proposed settlement. Bellow asked if the farm workers would have an opportunity to present their grievances publicly before the braceros were admitted. Kalb assured him that the Department had agreed to hold a public hearing at which CRLA and the farm workers could testify and present their evidence. Bellow then told Kalb not to sign the agreement yet, that he had to talk with the people who were with him, and that he would call back shortly.

When informed of the proposed settlement, George Fernandez was vehemently opposed to it. He protested on principle to any compromise. Maria Sanchez was not unalterably opposed to a settlement, but she was skeptical about whether the DOL would live up to its bargain. Bellow concentrated on selling the agreement to her. He used two main arguments:

- If the DOL did not abide by the agreement, nothing would be lost. CRLA could go back to court and would stand an even better chance of winning its suit because of the Department's demonstration of bad faith.

- UFWOC would get much more publicity out of an administrative hearing in San Francisco than from a court hearing in San Jose. CRLA could bring farm workers to the hearing to testify and present its evidence without being subject to the rigorous cross-examination of a court proceeding.

Sanchez accepted Bellow's arguments, and with some effort she and Bellow persuaded George Fernandez to go along. Bellow then called Denny Kalb and told him to sign the agreement as long as CRLA was assured of a public hearing by the DOL.

After the signing, the government lawyers returned to their hotel for more sleep. Because the agreement provided for the dismissal of CRLA's suit, they saw no reason to drive to San Jose. Instead they left it to Kalb and Reynolds to take the agreement to Judge Chapman, though they insisted that the agreement be shown to the judge in chambers. When Kalb and Reynolds arrived in San Jose, however, Judge Chapman was outraged that the DOL's lawyers had not bothered to come. He made a caustic remark about the unwillingness of government officials to leave San Francisco, then he ordered Denny Kalb to present the settlement in court. Kalb agreed—not reluctantly, to be sure—and he read the agreement to the large crowd of farm workers, growers, and reporters who were gathered in the courtroom. Kalb placed great stress on all the things the growers and the government would be required to do. While this was going on, Lee Reynolds prepared a press release that suggested the agreement was a major victory for CRLA and the farm workers. In speaking to reporters, he called the pact a "Magna Carta for the domestic field worker."

CRLA immediately turned its attention to the public hearing the DOL scheduled for Friday, September 15, in San Francisco. But on September 14 the Department abruptly declared that all news media would be barred from the hearing. Robert Blake, Wirtz's representative on the West Coast, said that the hearing would be closed because accusations would be made that "may or may not have any merit." He claimed that his department "never contemplated anything but a private meeting" and that the scope of the hearing had been "blown out of proportion." James Nottingham added that "investigative processes are never conducted in an open arena." Reacting quickly, CRLA announced that its witnesses would not participate in any "secret meeting." Although the wording of CRLA's agreement with the DOL was ambiguous, CRLA claimed that its understanding with the Department had been that the hearing would be public. Since neither side was willing to budge, they cancelled the hearing.

Now CRLA faced a critical decision: should it stick with its existing agreement with the DOL, or should it go back into court on the grounds that the Department had broken its pledge? This question was hotly debated within CRLA, with emotions running high on all sides. Action would need to be taken at once. On Sunday, September 17, Kalb, Reynolds, Smith, and Fernandez met with Jim Lorenz to decide the issue. Gary Bellow was in Washington preparing to testify before a congressional committee, so he participated in the discussion by phone. The positions the participants in this meeting took are summarized below:

Denny Kalb argued that CRLA would risk all the benefits that its clients had won through the agreement if it went back to court. Fernandez's investigation had been entirely inadequate and the affidavits were next to useless. No one could show a pattern or practice on the basis of this evidence, so CRLA had little choice but to sit tight and stick with the original settlement. If CRLA tried to fight in court, it would almost certainly lose, and this would have severe repercussions. Looking grossly incompetent in court would seriously undermine CRLA's leverage in future dealings with the DOL and other powerful groups. It would also give credence to opponents' charges that CRLA was harassing government agencies.

Lee Reynolds' views paralleled Denny Kalb's. CRLA had a professional responsibility to the farm workers it was representing, and the existing agreement was the best they could hope for. He doubted that the courts were prepared to question seriously the actions of a federal agency. They were demanding evidence beyond a reasonable doubt even at the preliminary injunction stage. In any event, no judge was going to let the crops rot in the fields. CRLA should not risk exposing the weakness of its case in court. That would be "grasping defeat out of the jaws of victory." CRLA's "aura of invincibility" would be undermined. And UFWOC would lose the favorable publicity that the settlement had generated. This publicity could be a valuable organizing tool since it showed farm workers that the DOL recognized their rights and power.

Jason Smith was not as pessimistic as Kalb and Reynolds about the prospects for winning if CRLA went to court. While acknowledging the technical deficiencies of the affidavits, he contended that they still provided a damning expose of the DOL's failure to follow its own regulations. He agreed, however, that a judge would be reluctant to let the crops rot in the fields. On balance he thought CRLA should try to make the best of the existing agreement. They would be in a good position to resume the attack on the bracero program in 1968.

George Fernandez was still angry about the criticism of his investigation and about the fact that his case had been taken away from him. He charged Kalb and Reynolds with having no guts and with knowing nothing about the wishes of Mexican–Americans. He felt emphatically that CRLA should fight down to the wire. He believed he had "got the goods" on the DOL, and that CRLA would win if it went back to court.

Discussion Questions

1. To maintain funding for CRLA Gary Bellow and Jim Lorenz needed the support of the California Bar Association and the American Bar Association. Governor Reagan was a determined opponent of the program and could muster substantial influence with Congress. Lyndon Johnson's OEO would necessarily be concerned about congressional reactions to such a prominent program. But the support of the American Bar Association, which had urged federal funding for legal services programs from 1965 on, would provide a guarantee that OEO could and would continue to fund CRLA, despite its bold strategy and the Governor's hostility.

To maintain that crucial support of the California Bar Association and the American Bar Association, Bellow and Lorenz had to depict CRLA as a law office doing traditional lawyer's work on behalf of individual clients with only one major difference: these clients were too poor to afford to pay for legal services and thus to choose their own lawyers. In everything they did, including such managerial decisions as the recruitment and selection of lawyers, Lorenz and Bellow were careful to convey the impression that what they were creating was a superior but traditional law firm. Understandably, the lawyers they recruited thought of themselves in this way and were anxious to bring and win big cases. The bracero case and its settlement must have looked like a triumph of lawyering to Kalb and Reynolds.

At the same time Lorenz and Bellow believed that no real progress could be made by lawyers who concentrated on individual cases or even major class actions or law reform-type litigation. Is there any answer to the arguments that Bellow sets out for favoring an organizing model, if one's objective is to improve the political, economic, and social position of the poor and the powerless? White middle-class lawyers with traditional legal training could hardly be expected to spearhead the organization of Hispanic migrant farmworkers. Therefore Lorenz and Bellow saw their role as providing support in a number of ways to the organizing activities of Cesar Chavez.

It is worth considering how the activities of an organizing lawyer differ from those involved in more traditional trial and appellate work. In a matter like the bracero case, the organizing model would look for ways to reveal the plight of farm-workers to the public, to encourage a sense of community and a belief in the efficacy of organization among migrant workers, and to maintain the centrality of the political organizers, Cesar Chavez and his colleagues. Announcing that federally funded lawyers had won a great victory for farmworkers without the assistance of the union is hardly helpful to organizing and would tend to undermine trust between Chavez and CRLA. This is particularly true because Bellow had all but given his word to Maria Sanchez, Deputy Director of the UFWOC, that farmworkers would have the politically important opportunity to present their grievances publicly. To accept the negotiated settlement would be to accept the DOL's unwillingness to have any such public hearing.

CRLA would hardly look like a reliable ally if it ignored Bellow's understanding with Sanchez or seemed to lack heart for a fight with the DOL. On the other hand, renouncing the settlement, returning to court, and organizing around the DOL's "betrayal" might well further the union's organizing efforts.

What would you do if you were Lorenz or Bellow in this situation? Would you stand by the settlement, which represented a triumph of good lawyering? That is the kind of law you had suggested to the American Bar Association you would be practicing. And how could you explain a contrary decision to your attorneys if that decision were going to deny them the success of a legal triumph of the very sort that had caused them to leave more comfortable and lucrative surroundings for CRLA? Or would you renounce the settlement and show that you stood for the only model of legal services that seemed to promise long-term benefits to the poor and the powerless: the organizing model? Could you explain to Sanchez or Chavez that this was too much of a triumph of good lawyering to warrant taking the chance of renouncing the settlement?

Do you think the dilemma in which Bellow and Lorenz found themselves is accidental or is it, in some sense, deeply rooted in the problem of trying to use federal funding and the legitimacy, in the United States, of a claim of the importance of access to lawyers to accomplish something as politically controversial and socially revolutionary as a major shift in political and economic power through organizing migrant farmworkers? Is there any other way, apart from legal services, by which Lorenz and Bellow could have brought federal assistance to the effort to organize migrant workers? Is there any way in which federal assistance could have been obtained without suggesting strongly that it was to provide the same type of lawyering that middle-class individuals and corporations enjoy? Is the organizing model one that the federal government will knowingly support?

2. Another way to state the problem of choice facing Lorenz and Bellow is to look at a number of their more discrete objectives. They want to serve the welfare of migrant farmworkers. They want to demonstrate the efficacy of the organizing model, a new concept of legal services. They want to preserve and strengthen CRLA, the organization they head, at least to the extent that the other two objectives depend upon its continued viability and vitality. Is accepting the settlement better or worse for the welfare of migrant farmworkers? the effort to show the viability of the organizing model? the health of CRLA as an organization? Is it possible to reach firm conclusions about what should be done in these terms?

3. Can Lorenz and Bellow ignore the strength of Fernandez's feelings as they reach a decision? Fernandez is one of the few Mexican–Americans who are working as lawyers for CRLA. The organization is already riven by a dispute between the lower paid, lower status community workers who are largely Mexican–Americans, and the attorneys. In each office the community workers have the politically crucial role of making contact with migrant farmworkers and organizing groups but they are subject to the direction of the attorneys who play a central role in more traditional litigation. Resentment between the two groups has been high. In addition to their personal commitment to racial justice, which is considerable, Bellow and Lorenz have to be concerned about the impact of charges of bias or insensitivity on their ability to carry out their chosen objectives among migrant farmworkers and in cooperation with the UFWA.

Assume that Fernandez felt he had been patronized and insulted by Kalb and Reynolds, who had severely criticized the quality of his work, and that he also believed that this was a crucial test of the willingness of CRLA to stand by its commitment to fight for migrant farmworkers. There is a real risk that Fernandez will quit the organization and bring charges of discrimination if the case is taken out of his hands and left to the settlement Kalb and Reynolds negotiated. Should this affect the decision to be made by Lorenz and Bellow? How serious would charges of discrimination against Mexican–Americans be in terms of the objectives discussed in Question 2? Does your answer depend upon how strong a rebuttal Bellow and Lorenz can make—and how quickly and how persuasively they can make this rebuttal to OEO, Cesar Chavez, and Mexican–American groups?

4. Questions 1, 2, and 3 assume that Bellow should make his decision by considering what would be best for legal services, or for his CRLA organization, or for the migrant farmworkers. However, the general understanding within the legal profession—including legal service lawyers—is that lawyers must serve the interests of their *clients*.

For instance, Professor Derrick Bell, in an influential article about the professional responsibility of civil rights attorneys [1] wrote: "[S]ome civil rights lawyers, like their more candid poverty law colleagues, are making decisions, setting priorities, and undertaking responsibilities that should be determined by their clients and shaped by the community. It is essential that lawyers 'lawyer' and not attempt to lead clients and class."

Who is California Rural Legal Assistance's client in this case—the named individuals or Chavez and his union? What would it mean for Bellow to do what his client wanted? Should it make a difference if the individual client was only picked to bring this case?

Would it be proper for Bellow, either alone or through Chavez and his union, to "persuade" the client to make this crucial decision the way he wants it to be made? In other words, within what limits can a lawyer properly seek to change the client's view of his or her interests in order to work toward some larger goal that the lawyer has in mind? The status and wisdom of the lawyer and the importance of Chavez are powerful factors that are likely to be influential with a poor, Spanish-speaking farmworker unless they are held carefully in check. Should Bellow and Chavez unleash their influence?

On the other hand, is there any moral justification for allowing the interests of one "client," chosen as a representative of a group, to control litigation strategy that may affect hundreds or thousands of similarly needy people?

To what extent can the traditional responsibility of the lawyer—to serve the client's interests—truly apply in this type of situation?

Epilogue

California Rural Legal Assistance decided to stick with its settlement. It did not go back to court against the U.S. Department of Labor. In fact the agreement imposed substantial restrictions on the flow of braceros into the fields. Still, the United Farm Workers union was not happy with that result and the loyalties it reflected. Relations between CRLA and UFWOC cooled, although Bellow retained close personal ties to the union and Chavez.

The organization came under heavy political attack in Congress in the fall of 1967 when three separate investigations were launched and Governor Reagan threatened to veto the organization's 1968 funding. The program survived all these threats with the help of the organized bar, and it continued to bring major cases and attract considerable attention. Still, some would say it became more restrained in response to these battles. It slowly ceased to focus on the organizing model.

---

[1] Bell, *Serving Two Masters: Integration Ideals and Client Interests in School Desegregation Litigation,* 85 Yale L.J. 470, 512 (1976).

Fernandez resigned a few months after the decision described in the case. His resentments helped rekindle racial tensions. The organization was also called upon by Mexican–American groups to defend its openness to Chicanos. In part in response to this, in part because they felt they had done their part, Lorenz and Bellow decided early in 1968 to step down in place of a Chicano director. They left in early 1969.

B. Lawyers for Ordinary People

The Law Offices of Lewin & Associates *

Elizabeth Lewin, managing partner of The Law Offices of Lewin & Associates, was concerned. It was January 1983 and business was in a precarious state for one of the largest law clinics in the United States. Four of the firm's 18 offices in the large midwestern city of Lakeshore were losing money, and two more were financially marginal. Altogether, the firm was losing somewhere around $15,000 per month. Over the next two months, Lewin and her associates needed to agree on a plan to increase the number of cases per office and to improve office efficiency.

The Firm

The Law Offices of Lewin & Associates (L & A) was founded in 1978, growing out of a long-held concern of Elizabeth Lewin with the limited accessibility of legal services. Lewin, then aged 33, was a graduate of the Stanford Law School who had worked in government agencies as well as for a major law firm in downtown Lakeshore. She believed strongly in the need for a full-service law firm devoted to handling the legal problems of middle-income people at affordable prices. Other investors, including several lawyers, accepted her invitation to invest capital in the new firm that she decided to found. It was agreed that only Lewin, who was named managing partner, would be involved in the day-to-day administration of the firm.

The partners sought to achieve economies of scale by modeling the new organization after successful retail chains. They intended to achieve these economies by:

- Opening a significant number of small neighborhood offices, to increase clients' accessibility to the firm.

- Creating a system of standardized forms and procedures for handling personal legal problems to achieve more efficient processing of clients' cases.

- Delegating routine administrative tasks to secretaries so that the more highly paid lawyers would be available for client

49

consultation and for handling those tasks which only they were qualified to perform.

- Centralizing and computerizing the administrative functions, such as accounts payable, purchasing, and personnel.

- Concentrating the work of attorneys on a limited number of recurring legal needs to take advantage of economies of scale and learning curve effects.

- Utilizing specialists who served more than one office to enable the firm to offer a broad product line.

The firm sought to target two very large market segments: (1) middle-income people who patronized traditional law firms, but could be served equally well through the new firm's less costly system; (2) people who did not use legal services as often as they needed them because the services were too expensive or inaccessible.

Lewin selected a product line that was general in that it covered every kind of personal legal service and specialized in that not all L & A lawyers handled all types of legal cases. For complex problems ranging from bankruptcy to consumer law, the firm had specialists located in various offices to whom its other lawyers referred these problems. This system enabled L & A to serve all clients and yet achieve the learning curve effects that occurred when a lawyer handled many similar cases. As one of the firm's attorneys said: "We are in law what family practitioners are in medicine."

Lewin spent her first six months preparing for the simultaneous opening of nine offices in October 1978. She noted that there were economies of scale involved for furniture and equipment purchases. "More important, though," she added, "it was the only way to make advertising economical." The firm's rapid development precluded any formal planning. "In general," Lewin said, "our offices were located with a view both to the population and a sense of the neighborhood we'd be serving." Offices were established in commercial buildings, shopping centers, and malls in downtown Lakeshore and its suburbs. Five offices were on the ground floor of the buildings they occupied, but this location did not seem to bring in more clients than offices situated on higher floors.

By late 1981, the firm had expanded to 11 offices. Lewin then arranged to open seven offices in the Valu–Rite chain of discount retail stores, which sold household items and clothing. The firm needed more suburban offices in Bulbeck County, south and west of Lakeshore, to spread advertising costs and to maximize advertising potential. Valu–Rite customers were the group at which L & A was aiming. "Putting offices in a chain store has great potential," said Lewin. "It offers us a convenient location and a captured client." Some L & A employees thought that the Valu–Rite image was negative; they were also concerned that the new offices were too near several existing offices and competed directly with them. Exhibit 1 summarizes information on each of the 18 offices operated by Lewin & Associates in January 1983.

The Changing Face of the Legal Profession

According to a 1971 article in the *American Bar Association Journal,* approximately 70% of the U.S. population lacked access to needed legal services because they had too little money to afford the services yet too much to qualify for free legal aid. It was estimated that one-third of all adults had never consulted an attorney and that less than one in five used attorneys to resolve consumer problems.

A number of legal clinics were established to remove some of the mystique from the law and to make legal services more accessible and affordable. However, a 1977 survey found that, of 33 legal clinics throughout the U.S., eleven were insolvent, five relied on subsidies to fund losses, fourteen were solvent, and only three could be described as prospering. Part of the problem was that state bar associations prohibited lawyers from using advertising to solicit professional employment. This barrier was eliminated in mid–1977, when the United States Supreme Court ruled in *Bates v. State Bar of Arizona,* 433 U.S. 350 (1977), that lawyers had a constitutional right to advertise. Associate Justice Blackmun wrote:

> Since the belief that lawyers are somehow above trade has become an anachronism, the historic foundation for advertising restraint has crumbled . . . (I believe that advertising by lawyers would reduce the cost of legal services . . . without encouraging any more shoddy work than now exists.)

Two months later, the four-office legal clinic of Jacoby & Meyers in Los Angeles became the first law firm to advertise on television. Within 18 months, that firm had expanded to a total of 22 offices. An independent study reported that since the firm began its TV campaign, it had attracted approximately 2,500 new clients each month. By 1983, Jacoby & Myers boasted a total of 63 offices in California and New York. Other multioffice legal clinics expanded rapidly. Hyatt Legal Services, based in Kansas City and affiliated with the H & R Block chain of income tax preparers, operated 114 offices in 14 states and Washington, D.C.

The Lakeshore Area Legal Market

Although there were no other chains of legal clinics or law offices in the Lakeshore area, Elizabeth Lewin had noted increased television and newspaper advertising by law partnerships and solo practitioners.

Most of these solo practitioners specialized in a particular area of law, such as personal injury, immigration, or bankruptcy. A few had formalized referral services from other attorneys on a statewide basis and offered a toll-free number for initial consultation. The *Lakeshore Area Yellow Pages* featured 30 pages of listings under the category of "Lawyers," including separate listings grouped by type of practice and by location of practice. There were a number of eye-catching display advertisements for lawyers in the *Yellow Pages,* including one for Lewin & Associates.

Consumer Use of Legal Services

A telephone survey of randomly selected Lakeshore area residents commissioned by Lewin found that fewer than half of the respondents had previously used legal services. These users were more likely to be middle-aged, male, white, with above-average incomes, and professionals or managers. Half of these individuals had used legal services at least twice before. The most frequent case types were business, real estate, personal injury, and divorce (Exhibit 2).

When previous users were asked how they chose their attorney, they listed, with equal frequency: quality, reputation, and fees. Among nonusers, the most cited criterion for future selection was fees. The survey revealed that 65% of respondents (mostly previous users) would refuse to consult a lawyer whose office was located in a department store. Eighty-nine percent of respondents said they did not believe that a price-quality tradeoff existed. The survey also asked what sources people would consider most helpful in finding an attorney: 76% of respondents cited referral from a friend or relative, 16% listed word-of-mouth, and 5% mentioned the *Yellow Pages.* However, combined mentions of all other media totalled only 3.5%. More than half the respondents said they would not feel comfortable consulting an attorney who advertised on television or in a newspaper. This feeling was unrelated to prior experience with lawyers. Aversion to advertising generally increased with income level and correlated with refusal to consult an attorney whose office was in a department store or shopping mall.

In contrast to the profile of the "typical" Lakeshore legal client, L & A records showed that the firm attracted a larger proportion of clients who had a below average income, were black, or aged between 25 and 35. Each of these groups was more receptive to legal advertising. Although half of the firm's clients had used an attorney before, only 3% had consulted L & A previously—a fact that Lewin attributed to the firm's relative youth. Some clients wanted a "second opinion" on a matter about which they had already consulted another attorney.

The most frequent type of case brought to L & A was divorce (Exhibit 3).

When asked how they chose their attorney, L & A's clients most frequently cited fees (61%), personal attention (44%), and convenient location (36%). Those who listed fees were most likely to be young and white; there was no correlation between fee sensitivity and income level. Almost three quarters of the firm's clients had learned of L & A through TV advertisements, which emphasized fees and personal attention. Only 13% heard of the firm from a friend. Another 15% learned of L & A through the *Yellow Pages*. About 70% of clients came to the firm's offices directly from their homes; more than half of this group of clients lived 2 to 10 miles from the office in question.

Competition Among Providers of Legal Services

Providers of legal services in the Lakeshore area ranged from prestigious firms in downtown office towers to neighborhood solo practitioners. Lewin & Associates competed primarily with solo proprietorships, local partnerships, legal clinics, and do-it-yourself legal kits. Within this group it did not provide the lowest-priced services (Exhibit 4). Rather, it served those clients who could not or did not want to pay the high-priced prestige firms, yet did not seek out the lowest fees available.

The firm had had some difficulties with the organized bar. One attorney observed: "We're not well liked by the legal community because we take business away from the little guys. And judges have a bone to pick with Lewin & Associates from time to time. They see our ads on TV and become suspicious that the level of service is not what it should be." Lewin acknowledged that her firm was encroaching on the turf of solo practitioners, but emphasized that L & A had tried to avoid antagonizing the bar through advertising:

> We try to make our ads as informative as possible. We try to stay within all the guidelines that are required. And if something is potentially controversial, we'll analyze it and decide whether we think we're justified in trying it. There's no reason to make the legal community angry with us. We try to do things professionally.

Organization and Management

Lewin & Associates had developed a two-tiered system of management. Certain administrative functions were handled centrally. Individual offices were headed by a managing attorney who both practiced law and supervised office personnel and financial matters.

The head office employed six administrators. Two of these, Elizabeth Lewin and Gordon Kane, were attorneys. The major functions of the head office were pricing decisions, monitoring of office management, quality control, and attorney hiring, training, and compensation. It collected business statistics from the individual offices, handled client complaints, and coordinated advertising efforts with the firm's advertising agency. Excluding advertising costs, Lewin estimated that head office expenses consumed about 25% of the firm's total earnings. Lewin took responsibility for office locations and attorney incentive and compensation plans. She participated with her financial partners in decisions regarding financing and future growth strategies. Kane handled personnel hiring and supervision of individual offices.

Pricing

Each attorney had a fee manual that listed categories of cases, covering nearly every option a client might need, and identified the appropriate fees in each instance. Lewin determined the fee based on the dollar and cents costs of running the business and an evaluation of what the market would bear. The goal was to set a price in advance, rather than to charge on an hourly basis. L & A was not the cheapest legal service in the Lakeshore area. For example, the firm offered to undertake an uncontested divorce for $328 plus court costs; individual practitioners charged from $100 to $700 (Exhibit 4). Kane trained new attorneys to use the fee manual. He went over fact patterns or situations that might be encountered, and demonstrated how that case should be categorized.

On arriving at an L & A office, a new client was requested to complete a brief form and pay a $25 consultation fee. The client then met with an attorney for approximately 30 minutes to discuss the problem. After analyzing the case, the attorney selected the appropriate fee category, gave the client a written estimate, and sent a copy to the main office. Approximately one consultation in three resulted in a client's retaining L & A to handle the case.

For the estimated fee, the client would receive a certain number of the attorney's hours, at a rate averaging more than $100 per hour. If the required time exceeded that included in the fee, the client was charged for the balance at an hourly rate of $85, which approximated the actual cost to L & A of providing legal services. Lewin claimed that her firm's more efficient procedures enabled it to offer clients greater value for their dollar than conventional law firms.

If the nature of the case changed—for example, if an uncontested divorce became contested—the attorney had to file a case-type change form to adjust the fee as appropriate. Certain cases, such as legal name changes, were charged at a flat rate regardless of the amount of time spent. Wills were priced as loss leaders. Although fees on a few cases, such as contested divorces or felony charges, could be as high as $3,000 or more, the average case at L & A yielded fees to the firm of about $350.

There was still some variability in fee quotes. Kane explained that the difference could arise if one attorney was more optimistic about settling the case through negotiation while another foresaw lengthy litigation. In 1981, a disguised visit to two L & A offices by a reporter for the *Lakeshore Tribune* revealed a $600 variance in fee estimates to do a contested divorce. Kane believed that training had narrowed such differences. Fees were usually changed once a year. The situation would be reviewed if attorneys complained that a fee was too high and that they were not retaining clients or if they claimed that a fee was too low for the time required. Proposed revisions were submitted to attorneys for comment.

Recruitment

Most attorneys at Lewin & Associates came to the firm from their own practice or from a small law firm. L & A's official qualifications were five years of general practice experience for a managing attorney and one to three years for an associate. Each attorney had a personnel handbook that outlined basic firm policies such as working hours and dress codes. Practicing law on the side was strictly forbidden. When Kane interviewed an applicant, he looked for attorneys with a broad base in general practice and experience in dealing with people:

> I look for someone with the ability to elicit facts from clients expeditiously and to tell clients what to expect in terms of representation and fees. I look for someone who is generally well-organized and has the ability to follow up, because what we are looking for is a solo practitioner in a sense.

Applicants who passed Kane's screen were then sent to visit managing attorneys of offices to which they might be assigned. The managing attorney determined whether the applicant would be able to retain clients and do a reasonable share of the work. About 30% of the firm's attorneys were women, none were black. There was a scarcity of black attorneys, Lewin explained, and most of them went to work for large firms.

Monitoring Office Management

Each office called head office daily with figures on the number of appointments kept, the fees collected the previous day, and the number of appointments booked for the present day. Monthly rankings were assigned to each office based on number of clients, rate of retention, and profitability. Kane visited all offices periodically. Those with new attorneys or poor statistics were visited more frequently—for example, once a month—whereas a more established office might not be visited more than twice yearly. By 1983, each office had enough of a track record to allow Kane to know if it should be doing better. He reviewed files to ensure that cases were being moved along expeditiously. Depending on the office, 50 to 150 files would be open at any one time. A file might remain open for anything from two weeks to as long as two and a half years. The average uncontested divorce case file remained open for 16 weeks.

L & A's policy required offices to call and confirm appointments, but not to call and inquire about an already missed appointment. "People feel that's a little too aggressive and pushy," said Lewin. To minimize the number of missed appointments, L & A policy required that offices schedule appointments at the earliest possible date, preferably the same day that a client called. Lewin commented:

> We have trouble with this. The attorneys in the offices don't really believe it, but the faster you get clients in after they phone, the less likely they are to be no-shows. Offices can be really lax about this sometimes. You can understand the tendency to say, "Oh no, another client—book them tomorrow, book them Wednesday." But that's not good for business.

When Kane had finished reviewing files at an office, he sat down with the managing attorney to discuss his impressions and to make suggestions on how to manage the case load more efficiently. "One of the things I tell the attorney," he said, "is that we're a 'pay-as-you-go' law firm. The faster the work can be accomplished, the sooner the file can be closed and the better off that office is economically."

The firm had an of counsel [1] litigation specialist, whom Lewin urged the attorneys to use since she felt litigation was disruptive to an office. The more experienced attorneys, she said, would handle a case up to trial before turning it over to the specialist.

Both Lewin and Kane described the task of evaluating the quality of service as a matter of judgment. Kane observed that one of the most direct ways of evaluating an attorney's advice was being in the office frequently. "You have to have a feel for what goes on in an office: how does it look, how does the attorney handle his staff, how does he greet the client, how does he behave with the client?" The firm also relied on client complaints to alert it to problems, which Kane then investigated.

---

[1] An of counsel attorney is neither a partner nor an employee of the firm. He or she maintains a relationship not unlike that of a consultant, providing assistance to the firm on some matters, but working independently on others.

Every year, L & A reviewed the performance of each office and each attorney; this review was based on Kane and Lewin's impression of the office, and the office statistics. The results helped the firm decide on salaries and on whether an attorney should stay with the firm.

Not all attorneys felt that the administrators were able to control quality effectively. Said one: "The administrators say they ensure consistency because of the forms, training, hiring process. But not really. They find out when there's a problem. They have carried some people for a long time when they've known the attorney had problems, when the problems were pretty consistent." Another attorney agreed that the firm's quality control was not that effective but felt, in general, that the attorneys had been good and hard working.

Attorney Compensation

After some experimentation, L & A had adopted a compensation formula whereby each office was assigned a certain gross earnings target per month, such as $12,000 for a one-attorney office. The attorney was paid a salary plus 10% of anything the office earned over that gross amount. The annual salary, including bonus, for a managing attorney ranged from $27,000–$45,000; for an associate, it was between $17,000 and $22,000. The additional cost to L & A of benefits and payroll taxes amounted to about one fifth of the salary totals.

Lewin was still unsure whether the compensation scheme provided enough incentive for the attorneys "to go that extra mile which you really need to make these offices very effective." It appeared that the stronger offices were carrying the weaker, and Lewin felt that many managing attorneys had lost all sensitivity to the cost of their offices. She was not happy with the plan, stating that she wanted to see some change:

> This kind of firm really needs an entrepreneurial type of attorney. It's a retail business. You've got to be out there hustling. You've got to be on top of your office. It's a nickel and dime business in a way, with lots of small cases. So unless attorneys really feel they're going to be getting something out of the office, you're going to have a situation where you're not getting the maximum amount you can from each operation.

Monetary compensation was an especially important incentive since L & A attorneys could not look forward to rising in the firm's ranks. Lewin had no plans for taking on new partners nor additional executive personnel. One managing attorney described his probable career path as: "Associate, manager, out. . . . I don't see my future with L & A. I can see myself opening a competitor and becoming an

entrepreneur. I'm not crazy about the practice of law. I'd rather be
the owner." The turnover rate was described variously by attorneys as
"extremely high" and "not as high as you'd think."

Individual Offices

The typical L & A office was staffed by a managing attorney and a
paralegal secretary. Where the volume of cases warranted it, an
associate attorney and additional secretarial help were hired. Secretaries were paid, on average, $320 per week. Benefits and payroll taxes
added another 21% to these wage costs. Most offices were small,
ranging in size from 700 to 1000 square feet. Annual rental costs
averaged $15 per square foot. Miscellaneous office expenses, such as
supplies, copying, electricity, heating or cooling, telephone, etc.,
amounted to around $280 per week for the average office.

The managing attorney was responsible for office management and
for compliance with firmwide policies with regard to the keeping of
statistics, fee quotes, and appointment booking procedures. He or she
also had full responsibility for handling the case load and supervising
the associate attorney. The firm was considering extending office
hours (currently Monday–Friday, 9:00 a.m.–5:30 p.m.) into two evenings
each week and opening for a full day every fourth Saturday.

L & A offices were simple and unpretentious. The firm accepted
credit cards. Wherever possible, all brochures and written materials,
including legal documents, were prepared in straightforward language.
Attorneys were encouraged to be direct and matter-of-fact in their
dealings with clients.

The Market Street Office in Lakeshore

Four blocks from Union Station, across from a coffee shop and
wedged between two banks, was the L & A office managed by Steven
Farmann, who worked with an associate. Serving a substantial area of
mid-town Lakeshore, it had been one of the firm's highest revenue
offices, averaging a gross of about $19,600 per month with a record high
month of $26,000 and a record low month of $14,000.

Farmann had held a responsible position in a family sportswear
company before graduating from Illiana Law School. After passing the
bar, he opened his own practice in a suburban town 20 miles from
Lakeshore. For 10 months he worked as an attorney during the day
and as a waiter at night for additional income. When he decided to
marry, Farmann began applying for jobs in Lakeshore and joined
Lewin & Associates.

The work itself could be repetitive, Farmann felt. What made it
interesting was the variety of people: "At the bottom end, I see an

alcoholic postal worker who wants a divorce. At the top end, I see a psychiatrist at a major hospital. I also see nurses, middle managers—mostly women—people who work for Blue Cross and in health-related fields." They came to Lewin & Associates, he thought, because they didn't know any lawyers, and had seen the firm's advertisements. Due to the nature of the cases—predominantly divorce—there was little repeat business from the same clients.

In summarizing his role, Farmann said:

> Once I became managing attorney, it became a challenge to bring the office from an average of $12,000 or $13,000 per month up to $20,000 or $21,000. So that's where I put all my energy. I got a paralegal who was like a diamond in the rough. She got so good at her job that I could give her verbal instructions and half an hour later something would be completed on my desk. This gave me time to sit with clients. L & A can succeed only if an attorney is in the office a maximum number of hours. An attorney can't afford to go to court to answer motions, go to trials, do real estate closures, because time is precious and should be spent in the office.

However, Farmann did not turn down cases involving court time: "I can't turn down clients because I have to make the money. It's all about making the money. I have a second attorney, so if I go to court, there's coverage here." He estimated that he spent only 5% of his time in court.

Despite Farmann's efforts, business during the third quarter of 1982 had not been good. The office scheduled as many appointments as possible, but there was an exceptionally high rate of missed appointments. Lewin estimated the firmwide average at 35%. Farmann attributed the increase in no-shows to the firm's austerity program under which radio spots replaced TV advertisements when the cost of television spots rose seasonally. He felt that radio advertising attracted a different kind of client, who was surprised, on calling for an appointment, to learn that the firm charged an initial consultation fee and who was less likely to keep an appointment.

Farmann had other concerns about the firm:

> The organization is so unusually informal that each office basically is fairly autonomous. The manual with fee schedules dictates the policies of the firm. But, whether we follow it closely varies office by office. There's no strict monitoring like Kentucky Fried. Lots of things go by the board here because we don't have the time.

> Beth Lewin feels that if attorneys have direct control over costs, offices will be more profitable. But she needs to put

more time into sitting down with the attorneys and figuring out what it is about their offices that isn't profitable in terms of time and consultation management. Most office expenses are fixed. The only thing to maximize is performance of individual attorneys and the head office administrators have us pigeonholed in such a way following their procedures that they lose a lot of people along the way. They've tried to standardize and make the operation so uniform that they don't take attorney preferences to heart. We're not pushing lingerie over the counter. I like to think of myself as a professional, not a retail store operator, and this as a law firm, not Valu–Rite or Sears.

In November 1982, about a month after making these observations, Farmann resigned to go back into private practice. Lewin remarked that she and Kane had not regarded Farmann as a good manager. The new managing attorney appointed to Market Street had taken the initiative in establishing a better work flow, thereby lowering costs, while also moving aggressively to increase revenues. The net result had been a significant improvement in profitability of this office, which had hitherto been operating at close to break-even.

The Nuffield Street Office in Broadmoor

The Nuffield Street Office was located on a side street just off a busy and colorful shopping street in Broadmoor, an old neighborhood just west of central Lakeshore. It was on the top floor of a three-story building populated by small retail businesses and fast-food chains. There was a family dental practice on the second floor. The waiting room had the same utilitarian carpeting found in nearly all L & A offices. Brochures were available on a small table. A receptionist sat behind a glass window. Hanging on the wall was a framed quotation from Abraham Lincoln. It read: "A lawyer's time and advice are his stock in trade."

Martha Ross was managing attorney at this office. She was also the firm's bankruptcy specialist. Ross, a graduate of Ohio State Law School, had worked for legal aid in Cleveland for two years, and then for a two-person firm in Lakeshore before joining Lewin & Associates in 1980. She had left the small firm because she felt she was being exploited, "doing 75% of the work for 25% of the income," as she put it. Discussing her work at L & A, Ross commented: "I kind of enjoy what I do. It really is my own office. I feel fairly entrepreneurial. I do basically what I want within certain guidelines which are rational, so there's no reason to argue." Six months had gone by since Lewin or Kane had been out to check on her office.

Ross supervised one general practice attorney, two bankruptcy attorneys (located in other offices), and three paralegal secretaries (two of whom worked in other offices). By early 1983, she was spending 75% of her own time on general legal work, the balance on bankruptcy work. The typical bankruptcy client had been out of work for six months and had just become employed again. Most had fallen in arrears on their mortgage payments and faced foreclosure, but given time, they would be able to pay off their debts. Chapter 13 of the Bankruptcy Code allowed them three years. Ross preferred to see as many first-time clients as possible, believing that she was best able to evaluate a case, establish a fee, and make referrals where necessary. She remarked:

> I do virtually no routine work. The secretaries do all the routine work, all the pleadings, papers, simple matrimonials. I quickly skim it before it goes to court. Basically, it's all done by the secretaries. They've done it countless times, they're perfectly competent. When I have a question I ask them.

Three-quarters of the business that came into Ross's office consisted of matrimonial and family court cases. The rest included bankruptcy, real estate, and wills. Criminal cases were referred to the firm's criminal law expert in the First Avenue office. Ross remarked:

> I don't turn anything down. The head office may encourage it indirectly. I think they're concerned about people getting caught in cases that are going to require a lot of time and take them out of the office. I wouldn't like what I'm doing if I was turning down everything that was a little complex and therefore interesting, leaving myself only uncontested divorces.

The area where Ross worked was largely populated by blacks. This was reflected in her client mix. Many clients worked for Lakeshore Transit, Henderson's Department Store, Union Electric, and the Illiana Telephone Company, all of which had offices nearby. Most clients' incomes ranged from $15,000 to $30,000. Many had pensions, some had credit union accounts, fewer than half owned homes.

Ross kept a record of the time she spent on each case on strips of paper attached to the side of her desk. Like the firm's other attorneys, she worked with L & A's standard fee schedule, but noted:

> I tend to give higher fee estimates than indicated by the schedule because experience tells me that it's really hard to explain to someone that what you said would be $1,000 will now be $4,000. If there's a real problem paying, I take less money up front. The general policy is to take at least half the fee in advance. I may take a quarter. Still, there are billing collection problems. Five percent, maybe, are bad debts.

Communication Efforts

L & A's business was heavily dependent on advertising. Lewin estimated that the firm spent 12% of every dollar earned to cover advertising expenses. The firm's advertising agency selected advertising media by comparing efficiencies. The goal was to reach the largest number of potential clients for the least cost. Advertising was bought on a quarterly basis, with the same amount of money budgeted for each quarter. During the first and third quarters of the year, television advertising was relatively cheap, and so L & A ran about fourteen 30–second TV spots per week. During the second and fourth quarters, when TV advertising was seasonally more expensive, the firm switched to 60–second radio spots. Several attorneys noted a drop in business during the second and fourth quarters.

Lewin & Associates did not advertise on transit vehicles or on billboards. In 1978, the firm had run some full-page advertisements in the *Lakeshore Examiner,* a large circulation daily newspaper; these showed a man with a mask over his eyes saying, "The way lawyers charge, there ought to be a law." The advertising did not generate many calls to L & A offices. It did, however, offend many members of the legal community. Lewin remarked;

> We have not done print advertisement on a consistent basis. I think there might be some print opportunities we haven't taken advantage of. On the other hand, it's expensive and we face a lot of competition. Every other lawyer who advertises in print quotes specific fees. We don't want to do that. We're usually more expensive.

Community Contacts

Lewin said she would like to see her attorneys taking out local advertisements, joining more local neighborhood activities, and putting up billboards near their offices. However, she wanted to retain control over their efforts. One managing attorney observed that if the office were his own, he'd be out in the field more, making contacts and trying to get referrals. "I want to know why L & A has no community-based contacts and why they rely strictly on advertisements," he said.

Another attorney said he would not invest in local print advertising because it was expensive and not cost effective. He had thought about giving seminars on common legal problems for employees of major businesses in the area, but was not sure how to go about this. It had occurred to him to give discounts to members of large groups; this would require Lewin's approval and he had never pursued his idea so far as to ask for that.

A third L & A attorney said he had no time to organize meetings with local clubs and churches. "If the firm took one month's worth of advertising money," he remarked, "they could get a PR person for 12 months, but they think each individual attorney has enough time. An organization with these resources should do a lot more local PR."

The Partners Deliberate

After Lewin had summarized the firm's difficult economic situation, she and her financial partners considered possible solutions. One was to reduce the number of offices. However, the tension level among employees was rising as word spread that drastic changes were in the offing. Lewin worried about the impact of office closings on attorney morale. Reducing the number of offices would also increase the burden of advertising expense on the remaining offices.

The partners next considered changing the compensation plan to a 50–50% split of gross income between the managing attorney and the head office, with a guaranteed minimum salary of $2,000 per month. According to this plan, the managing attorney would be required to pay all office expenses out of the 50% share, including the salary of the associate attorney, if the office had one, and that of the office secretaries. The managing attorney would then take home whatever was left over as salary. Lewin felt that this arrangement would give the attorneys an incentive to keep office costs down. Any office which was not able to meet its expenses out of its 50% would be closed.

But the partners foresaw several problems. New offices would need to be carried until they could establish themselves. Moreover, the gross income of some offices was highly variable from month to month; employment contracts, hitherto unused at L & A, might be necessary to give attorneys the security they required. The location of new offices would become extremely important since these might dilute business at existing offices if established nearby. Further, the fee-sharing arrangements between the general practice attorney and the specialist might have to be changed.

The partners also considered providing additional services to increase volume. Tax service was one possibility. As Lewin perceived it, the problem with this option was that L & A's image would then become blurred, and expensive changes in the advertising would have to be made. In addition, L & A personnel lacked the necessary expertise for complicated, specialized areas of the law, such as tax.

Exhibit 1
THE LAW OFFICES OF LEWIN & ASSOCIATES
Location and Characteristics of Lewin & Associates Offices in Lakeshore Area, 1983

Location	Neighborhood	Employees	Type of Client	Average Consultations Per Month	Average Monthly Income
Market Street Lakeshore	Business	Atty. 2 Secy. 2	Mixed ethnically Status: Professional	145	$19,600
1st Avenue Lakeshore	Business Residential	Atty. 2 Secy. 2	Mixed ethnically Status: Middle management	108	$17,800
15th Avenue Lakeshore	Business Residential	Atty. 1 Secy. 2	Mixed ethnically Status: Middle management	49	$11,400
Broadmoor	Residential	Atty. 2 Secy. 2	Black Status: Blue collar	97	$18,000
Royal Highway	Residential	Atty. 2 Secy. 2	White Status: Blue collar	87	$26,000
Town Park	Residential	Atty. 1 Secy. 2	White Status: Blue collar	75	$20,900
Logan	Residential	Atty. 1 Secy. 2	Mixed ethnically Status: Blue collar	66	$10,500
Green Lake	Residential	Atty. 1 Secy. 1	Black/Hispanic Status: Middle management	98	$ 8,400
Black Plains	Residential Business	Atty. 2 Secy. 1	Mixed ethnically Status: Professional	112	$10,500
Arlmont *	Residential	Atty. 1 Secy. 2	Black Status: Blue collar	35	$ 7,900
Georgeville *	Residential	Atty. 1 Secy. 1	Black Status: Blue collar	75	$11,200
Fittburg *	Residential	Atty. 1 Secy. 1	White Status: Blue collar	129	$12,400
East Bulbeck	Residential	Atty. 1 Secy. 1	White Status: Middle management	29	$ 7,400
Bulbeck Center *	Residential	Atty. 1 Secy. 1	White Status: Blue collar	103	$13,100
Vienna *	Residential	Atty. 1 Secy. 2	White Status: Blue collar	119	$16,800
Petit Lac *	Residential Business	Atty. 1 Secy. 2	White Status: Middle management	71	$ 9,000
Plymouth	Business	Atty. 1 Secy. 1	Mixed ethnically Status: Middle management	32	$ 6,000

* Denotes unprofitable or financially marginal office (note: Vienna and Fittburg were located in Valu–Rite stores).

Exhibit 2
THE LAW OFFICES OF LEWIN & ASSOCIATES
Types of Legal Needs Encountered Among Residents of Greater Lakeshore

Type of Case	% of Total Cases Reported
Business	22.9
Real estate	20.0

Type of Case	% of Total Cases Reported
Wills	15.9
Other	11.3
Personal injuries	8.7
Divorce	6.1
Criminal	3.8
Workers compensation	3.2
Estate	2.6
Motor vehicle	2.0
Landlord/tenant	1.2
Immigration	1.2
Malpractice	0.9
Social Security	0.6
Adoption	0.3
Employment	0.3
Name change	0.3
Guardianship	0
Bankruptcy	0
Unemployment	0

Source: Telephone survey of 402 randomly selected residents of L & A's service area, 1982.

Exhibit 3
THE LAW OFFICES OF LEWIN & ASSOCIATES
Composition of the Firm's Caseload, Fall 1982

Type of Case	Proportion of Total Cases
Divorce	33.4%
Criminal	10.7
Money claims	7.3
Landlord/tenant	6.9
Wills	6.6
Bankruptcy	5.9
Real estate	5.5
Business	5.4
Personal injuries	3.4
Employment	2.0
Dept. of Motor Vehicles	1.9
Adoption	1.8
Name change	1.6
Immigration	1.2
Social Security	1.0
Workers compensation	0.8

Type of Case	Proportion of Total Cases
Guardianship	0.7
Other	4.0

Source: Company records.

Exhibit 4
THE LAW OFFICES OF LEWIN & ASSOCIATES
Comparative Fees for Different Types of Cases

Type of Case	Lewin & Assoc.	Solo Practitioners	Legal Clinic	D–I–Y Legal Kit
Uncontested divorce	$328	$100–700	$250–350	$99–150
Simple bankruptcy	459	500–750	350–550	N/A
Real estate closing	1% of value *	250 or 1% of value *	250 or 1% of value *	N/A
Legal name change	250	200–250	200–350	N/A
Wills				
—single	60	0–200**	40–100	N/A
—reciprocal	110	0–300**	80–300	N/A

Note: Fees cited exclude court costs (where applicable).

* That is, 1% of the selling price of the property.

** Some practitioners made no charge for a will in expectation of subsequently handling the estate work.

Source: Company records plus local research in Greater Lakeshore.

Discussion Questions

1. This case describes L & A as a business venture. An earlier version of the study was in fact prepared for use at the Harvard Business School. Thus the focus of the discussion is on the entrepreneurial challenge of managing the provision of legal services. Access to the legal system is a serious problem for ordinary working people, as well as for the poor. Efforts to deliver high quality legal services efficiently and economically are of primary importance to the fairness of the legal system. The market for legal services supplies information about the representation people need and how much they are willing to pay for it. L & A is an organization testing the market for gaps and opportunities.

2. Consider the market in which L & A is competing. One study shows that the average American uses legal services about twice in a lifetime for real estate acquisitions, about once for a divorce, and almost one-and-a-half times for estate planning.[1] L & A could seek to expand this market, to get a larger share

---

[1] B. Curran, *The Legal Needs of the Public,* (ABA 1977).

of it, or to do both. One way to expand the market is by competing through efficiency and reasonable cost. Assuming that most of L & A's competitors are small offices with one or a few lawyers, what are the steps that L & A takes in its effort to increase efficiency? In addition to cutting costs, L & A seems to focus on an effort to provide something that is missing in the present market: a qualitative advantage for consumers at roughly the same cost for services. What is the organization offering in the way of a superior product? By offering either lower prices or a superior product, L & A could achieve a larger share of the existing market, even if there was no substantial increase in the number of people going to lawyers. A third way of seeking a larger share of the existing market is reliance on better ways of making contact with clients. What is the strategy of L & A in this regard? Can you imagine better ways to accomplish any of the objectives of lower cost, a better product, or better access to clients?

3. Does L & A's story suggest that more elaborate and valuable personalized service costs more to deliver than middle-class families are willing to spend? If that is true, legal services to working-class and middle-class people will not be a growing market in the U.S. Should it be? For transactions that involve relatively small stakes to the individual client, there is no point in paying more than the amount of the stake. Similarly, if there are alternatives to legal services as ways of dealing with the problem presented by the event or transaction—alternatives such as self-help or recourse to such institutions as an insurance company or a bank—the use of more expensive legal services may be pointless. As to many of the types of problems for which L & A provides legal services, efforts are under way to simplify procedures and to reduce the need for lawyers. Examples include no-fault auto insurance, no-fault divorce, and standardized will forms. Should society attempt to make lawyers unnecessary for these transactions or to increase the supply of legal services?

4. Some new legal services ventures offer more limited assistance than L & A supplies or offer their services without out-of-pocket costs to clients. Telephone consultation services can be delivered at a very low fee to subscribers to a pre-paid plan. What are the limits of this device? Far more extensive services are offered under other pre-paid plans, often furnished by unions or other organizations. The cost may not be less per transaction than L & A charges, but it is spread over a sizable number of people, most of whom will not need legal services in any particular year. Insurance plans for legal services can provide the same benefit. The contingent fee is a major device for financing the costs of legal services to those injured by accidents or misdeeds. Because of the availability of contingent fee services to tort plaintiffs, such cases form only a small part of the workload of L & A and are often excluded from the coverage of pre-paid plans.

5. If there will be a growing market, is L & A a good development for servicing it? L & A is not noticeably less expensive than its neighborhood competitors. Rather than cutting prices, L & A promises a dependable product at a surprise-free price in a setting that does not intimidate an ordinary person. Advertising communicates this product. Thus L & A sells two things. One is routinized performance of certain tasks. Here the development of computerized software may hold great potential. If L & A can create high-quality software for estate planning, divorce pleading, landlord-tenant transactions,

and so on, and an efficient process of plugging individual circumstances into the standard forms, perhaps it can deliver a needed service at low cost. Second, L & A sells labor: the work of young professionals. Its challenge is to hire those professionals at low salaries, train them well, keep them motivated, supervise them to limit errors, and separate them when it is efficient to replace them with younger talent. What impediments does L & A face as an employer of professional talent?

6. Would you like to work at L & A? Does a job there look like professional work, or like being a cog in a big machine? The lawyers who supply the service must avoid excessive commitment to clients, stick mostly to routine work, and accept as salaries only part of the gross receipts attributable to their work. Does that make them the equivalent of the young associates in large law firms serving corporate clients—but without the possibility of professional development into important and well-paid partners? Do L & A and the large corporate law firm both represent the transformation of a profession into a business? What is lost? Is the development inevitable? Desirable? How does L & A compare as a place to work with a job as a public defender, see p. 49, or a position with Raul Lovett, see p. 258, or the role of Joan Kiladis in a legal services office, see p. 2?

7. Discussion of the asserted tension between "profession" and "business" is often unspecific. Consider the issue in the L & A context. Can an L & A lawyer be loyal to clients? Can that lawyer protect confidences and avoid conflicts of interest? Can he or she tailor service to individual needs or provide zealous advocacy in a criminal defense? L & A must structure its operations to achieve economy through standardization, centralization, and incentives for lawyer productivity. Will the client inevitably lose something? Is the answer that the client ought to be able to choose whether to pay for more elaborate and expensive legal service?

C. Lawyers for Criminal Defendants

Notes of a Public Defender *

My name is Randy Bellows. I am a public defender and this is my story or, more precisely, a collection of my stories. It is all true, with the following caveats: I have changed the names of all my clients and the names of certain other individuals. Where necessary to protect attorney-client confidences, I have changed material and immaterial facts. In a few instances, I have felt it necessary even to change the nature of the crime with which my client was charged. This article is based upon a review of my files and upon my memory. The former is almost always accurate, the latter is only usually so.

Since October 1979, I have been employed as a staff attorney at the Public Defender Service (PDS) in Washington, D.C., an office consisting of approximately 50 attorneys, several social workers, and a staff of professional and student investigators. PDS represents less than one-quarter of all defendants charged with crimes in the Superior Court of the District of Columbia. The rest of the cases are handled by private attorneys, appointed by the Court and paid out of public funds. PDS represents more than 60 percent of those individuals charged with homicide offenses and a large percentage of individuals charged with armed robberies, rapes, and other serious felonies.

* * *

This is the story of David Keith and a marriage that was almost broken.

David Keith was charged with four brutal murders of elderly men and women in a once-peaceful Southeast Washington neighborhood. Murder by strangulation and asphyxiation. Murder by stomping. Murder by concussion/shock/fear. Several of the elderly women had also been raped. One morning, my co-counsel and I trekked over to the medical examiner's office and reviewed color glossy photographs of the carnage. Long after the case was over, long after the Keith case was replaced in the newspaper by other rapes and other robberies and other murders, I would remember the photograph of a sneaker print on the head of an 87–year–old man.

David Keith was just 18 years old, a veteran of the juvenile justice system. He had escaped several years earlier from a juvenile detention facility and had not been apprehended. He seldom lived at home.

---

* Randy Bellows wrote this account of his work as a public defender in 1983.

Much of the time, he would stay in condemned apartments, smoking reefer, getting high.

The police were led to David after he was caught in possession of a car stolen in one of the robberies. At the time of arrest, 4:00 a.m., he was tired, high, and scared. Sometime during the next seven hours he signed a nine page, single-spaced confession, admitting to dozens of different crimes, including the murders.

Defending David Keith was a pungent experience. Indelible. Even, in its own way, profound. I remember it well.

I remember visiting David at the jail, an unnerving experience. Sometimes, David was cocky and filled with bravado. But sometimes he was moody, alternately subdued then angry then subdued again, like a 200-watt light bulb which keeps flicking on and off and on and off. Watching David fidget was like watching a volcano and wondering when it was due to erupt. And worrying how far the lava would flow this time.

I try hard, when I visit my clients, to ignore the crimes with which they are charged, to give them my own presumption of innocence. But when I would go to see David, particularly when I was the emissary of bad news, I would think of John Daniels, whose head had been stomped in two dozen times. I would think of 65-year-old Rita Davis, who had been raped and strangled and left to rot under a mound of her own clothing. Visiting David was not really a lot of fun.

I remember the cross-examination of the homicide detective. David had decided that he stood nothing to gain from pleading guilty to multiple life offenses. It was not an inappropriate decision. As we prepared for trial, it became readily apparent that the only conceivable defense, in light of the nine page confession, was that the confession itself was a fraud.

I did not personally know the detective responsible for the confession. And that was a good thing. Because those colleagues of mine who did know him considered him to be one of the most honorable, decent, honest, and compassionate men on the police force. As one of my colleagues said, "If I murdered someone, he's the guy I'd want to confess to." It was my job to convince the jury that this man was not worthy of their trust, that it was really the detective, not David, who had composed the confession, that it was really the detective who had included all the voluminous details that gave it authenticity. It was my job to convince the jury that David had signed this document, not out of guilt and remorse, but as the last desperate act of a tired and strung-out youngster who had been questioned from 5:00 a.m. to noon and who just wanted to be left alone.

I cross-examined the detective for hours. The questioning was harsh, unfriendly. I intentionally sought to come across as hostile and disbelieving. I could not expect a jury to find this detective guilty of the malevolence with which I was charging him if it did not appear that I was angry, incensed by his conduct. When it was over, I did not really feel very good about the whole thing. I did what I had to do. I did not regret it then and I do not regret it today. But I had tried to make an honorable man appear dishonorable. And that is a sad thing to have to do, even if you are a public defender and even if that is your job.

I remember my closing argument, which was written from 10:00 p.m. one Friday night until 11:00 a.m. the next morning and which was rehearsed in front of a dozen PDS lawyers sitting in a jury box. When I finally gave it to the real jury, I felt like the whole argument took just 10 minutes. In fact, I talked for almost two hours. I did everything in my power to make David the victim and the detective his assailant. I argued until I was hoarse. I savaged the so-called confession, arguing that it was authored by the police to justify David's arrest and thereby, at least momentarily, squelch the public clamor for an end to the crime spree. I poked holes in all the other evidence: an inconclusive fingerprint, an ambiguous shoeprint, a weak identification.

Finally, it was over. The jury retired to deliberate. The next day they returned with a verdict. David was acquitted of every offense in which the sole evidence of guilt was the confession. He was convicted of every offense in which there was other evidence—like the fingerprint—to corroborate the confession. He was acquitted of a lifetime of offenses. Unfortunately for David, he was also convicted of a lifetime of offenses. And, so, he was ultimately sentenced to life in prison.

David Keith was a watershed case in my life as a public defender. It also turned out to be a watershed in my marriage.

Barbara had encouraged me to be a public defender. It sounded idealistic. It certainly sounded more idealistic than being a prosecutor. I would be a latter-day Atticus Finch. Instead, I was representing rapists and robbers, many of whom were obviously guilty, and many of whom would certainly pillage again upon release. Worse still, I was working feverishly to free these guys, even acting sometimes like this was not a job but a holy mission. And did I really have to help these people on Sundays, too? Did I have to work all night and get sick from lack of sleep? This was incomprehensible to her. These men were evil. What in hell was I doing working desperately to free them? Intellectually, Barb understood all the rationales and was tired of them. This was not law school, where we had stayed up late into the night talking abstractly about justice. This was for real. I was for real helping child molesters go free. I was for real getting stick-up men out on technicalities. Barb began to wonder if the man she was married to was not unwittingly serving evil. He certainly was not serving justice.

Even worse, I had not seen the signs of disenchantment coming. I continued to bring home the horrendous war stories that float around PDS like helium balloons. And when Barb came to the office to pick me up, she heard a great deal more. One of the reasons that PDS is a jewel of a place to work is that we not only care about our clients, we care about each other. We know that our clients do horrible things. We know that we are required to advocate positions which are personally abhorrent. We know how wrenching it is to be hard on witnesses for whom you really feel pity. So when we get out of court we unload on each other. We tell sick jokes to ease the tension. We share the grimy, gritty details, as if to exorcise ourselves. The more Barb heard, the more depressed she got, the more fixed she became that this was not Atticus Finch at all. This was just bad. Maybe even immoral, certainly amoral.

And then came David Keith, sort of a distilled nightmare, all the gruesome crimes that had come down the pike rolled into one neat indictment. And Barb could not get away from it. Not only was she hearing about it from me. She was reading about it in the newspaper and on television. Her teacher colleagues were asking whether that was her husband they had read about and, if so, how could he possibly be representing an animal like that? Barb had no answer to give them.

For a while, and long after the Keith case was over, things were touch-and-go at home. Ultimately, we worked out a fragile compromise. I stopped telling her about my bad clients and she stopped thinking about them. When I did talk about PDS, it was about our friends who worked there. When I did talk about my clients, I tip-toed, limiting myself to those innocent or innocuous clients about whom one could easily feel good.

It has worked. We no longer fight about PDS. We were eyeball to eyeball. To preserve our love, and out of our love, we both blinked.

*   *   *

Life at PDS. First, let me put things in perspective. Nothing compares to the recent birth of the cutest little girl to come out of Virginia in a long, long time, who just learned to say Da–Da. But PDS ain't bad.

How many places can you be a lawyer and wear jeans to work? For people like myself, who bought their first three-piece suit for interviewing season and hope never to buy another one, that is of no mean significance. I keep four suits at work and change into them only when I have to go to court. I suppose it says something about my suits that, in an office where nothing is safe if it is not bolted down, none of my suits has ever been ripped off.

The best thing about PDS is its people, an eclectic lot whose only common denominator is a commitment to providing quality legal representation to poor persons. Our attorneys range from the ideological (who view their work at PDS as part of the class struggle and who cannot conceive of any of our clients going to prison) to the merely idealistic to the bemused to the cynical. We have attorneys who are brilliant on paper but not in court and attorneys who are the reverse. We have been blessed with a few attorneys who are all things to all people: shining in court, incisive on paper, persuasive with clients.

If we have an ethic, it is mutual support. We attend each other's closing arguments, cross-examine one another's clients, handle court appearances for colleagues, commiserate, shoot the bull, and nibble at each other's food.

We have no more or less stress than anyone with two or three trials set a week, a case load of 30–45 cases, and the constant, unyielding, wearying pressure of having six court appearances in four different courtrooms, all set for 9:00 a.m. Sentencings. Pleas. Trials. Important stuff. Stuff you cannot ever afford to screw up. Not if you want to walk out of that courtroom with a client in tow. We swallow Extra Strength Tylenol as if they were gum drops. With no better results. And, still, the pressure keeps on coming. Appearing before judges who you know, who you just know, are waiting at the edge of their seat for the opportunity to explode; seeing pleas blow up in your face when your client cannot muster the courage to admit his guilt (and knowing it is your own damn fault for not preparing him well enough to suffer through the *mea culpa*); putting your heart and soul into a sentencing and watching the judge, often as troubled as you, lock your client up anyway. By the end of the day, you are spent. Physically, emotionally, on empty. You trudge back to PDS and drop into your chair. It all begins again tomorrow.

* * *

If you were to come to PDS today, you would spend your first six weeks in training, learning how to advocate and learning enough law to know what to advocate. After that, it is on to juvenile court for nine months. Then you would move into misdemeanors and minor felonies. Sometime during your second full year, you would begin picking up serious felonies. Before that point, you would have co-counselled a number of major felonies with senior attorneys. During your first three years, you would have a supervisor to provide guidance and support and sometimes to bop you on the head for rank stupidity. After that, you would be on your own.

A PDS attorney has total control over his or her caseload and over the individual management of a case. You take on only as many cases as you feel you can handle competently. For me, that was 30–35 cases. Other attorneys took on 50.

While you and your client make all the decisions in any particular case, you are crazy if you do not take advantage of the ready willingness of virtually every attorney in the office to help you wrestle with dilemmas. When you feel you need expert witnesses, you go out and you hire your own shrinks, your own fingerprint examiners, your own handwriting analysts, your own pathologists or, in one case of mine, your own arborist. When you need help in a hurry, when you need moral support in court, when you need judges to know that your office is behind you 100 percent, the leadership is there.

No institution which handles 5,000 cases a year is perfect. But if there is a better place to be a public defender, I cannot imagine it. It is that simple.

*   *   *

One of the most wonderful things about being a public defender is the enormous number of opportunities you have to help your clients (and make yourself feel good to boot). You can get their cases dismissed pre-trial. You can extract fantastic plea offers from the government. You can keep your clients on the street pending sentencing. You can write wonderful sentencing letters that just bowl the judge over. You can get your clients out on probation. And, of course, you can win jury trials. Even if none of these things is possible, you can at least treat your clients with respect and with dignity. If they have been through the criminal justice maze before, they will not be expecting it.

*   *   *

It is an axiom of criminal defense practice that you represent your guilty clients as zealously as you do your innocent ones (not that you can always tell the difference). Inevitably, though, a client who you really believe is innocent sets your innards churning in a way that no other client does. It does not happen very often. In fact, it happens rarely enough to be considered remarkable. One of the awkward truths about being a public defender is that you are in the practice of representing people who are, indeed, guilty as charged. We may cut spectacular deals with the government, obtain sentences which are absurdly light, and get cases dismissed for want of prosecution. But that does not change the facts: your clients are usually guilty. (Even the ones who get acquitted are often guilty.) And that is all the more reason why representing a client who you really believe to be wholly innocent is a nerve-wracking experience.

Putney Simpson was 19 years old, thin, unassuming, with a pleasant, almost gentle look on his face. He had never been arrested before and here he stood, in a courtroom, charged with armed robbery, armed burglary, and assault with a dangerous weapon.

A man had broken into the dwelling of an apartment rented by a woman who knew Putney slightly. The burglar was wearing a mask which showed only his eyes. The man ransacked the apartment, robbed it of jewelry, and beat up the woman. The victim immediately told the police that, based on the man's eyes and voice, she thought it was Putney Simpson. The police arrested Putney and placed him in a lineup where all the participants donned ski masks. The victim picked Putney out.

From the beginning, I was convinced of Putney's innocence. He was employed by a fast-food restaurant and had just gotten paid that day. In fact, he had spent a considerable portion of his salary buying an exotic bird and spent the evening getting acquainted with his new pet. As a prelude to a brutal armed robbery, the facts just did not fit. On top of all of this, armed robbers do not pop up out of thin air. They usually have track records, often beginning as juveniles, and work their way up to such sophisticated stuff as burglaries and robberies. Putney, in contrast, had never been in trouble before.

Finally, Putney had an alibi, not an iron-clad alibi but not tin-clad either. Putney lived with a co-worker who remembered him coming in at about 9:00 p.m. and being there the next morning at 6:00 a.m. (The robbery took place at 2:00 a.m.) Putney's girlfriend spent the night with him and swore that he did not leave the bed. The alibi suffered from what most 2:00 a.m. alibis suffer from: the people who are with you in the middle of the night are not likely to be priests or judges or neutral bystanders.

The victim would not talk to my investigator. We talked to her neighbors but learned nothing more. We could find no reason why this woman would want to get Putney. Meanwhile, the better I got to know Putney, the more convinced I became that he could not possibly have committed this robbery.

At this point, I knew that I might win and I might lose a jury trial. The government had a firm identification by the victim. For my part, I had the fact that the culprit wore a ski mask and that there was nothing remarkable about Putney's voice or eyes; I had the fact that Putney could testify convincingly; I had his alibi; and I had the fact that the police had no other evidence—such as the ski mask or proceeds of the crime—to connect Putney to the offense. Although I was confident that I could win the case, I decided to try once more to convince the government it was making a mistake. I had tried before, without success.

A new prosecutor had been assigned to the case. To my surprise, he shared my reservations about Putney's guilt and suggested a polygraph.

Unbeknownst to the government, I had already hired a polygrapher and Putney passed unequivocably. I had been saving the results for just the right moment. I requested a meeting with the prosecutor and his supervisors to go over the case. I laid out everything I had, knowing that if the government did decide to go forward with the case I would be damaging my chance of ultimately prevailing. I also arranged for my polygrapher to meet with the police department's polygrapher and go over my client's charts. The police expert agreed with my expert. Putney was not lying.

There is no dramatic end to this story. The government sat on the case for a month or so, mulling it over, and then, shortly before the trial date, dismissed all charges against Putney. As we left the courtroom, Putney gave me a big bear hug, a huge grin on his face. Every now and then, being a public defender pays off in a sublime moment of joy. This was one of those moments.

* * *

It is minutia and frustration that fill my days, not passionate closing arguments. It is getting a client to court on time. It is finding student investigators to go out and get statements. It is training those investigators so they do not get you disbarred on their first day out. It is dialing the same probation officer, day after day, and finally concluding that he does not exist. It is duty day, a day spent fielding phone calls from the public and praying that this is not the day that all the fugitives decide to surrender. It is getting cops to return your calls. It is subpoenaing unfriendly witnesses. It is seeing that they get paid so they will come back next time. It is preparing for trials that never take place.

It is always waiting for a photocopying machine to be fixed, and developing mechanical prowess you thought you never had when it breaks down again. It is getting supplies from a stockroom perennially oversupplied with rubberbands and paper clips but often—amazing as it may seem—bereft of pens, legal pads, and scotch tape. How can you practice law without a yellow pad?

It is becoming an expert typist, churning out briefs that would not be filed on time if you did not type them yourself. Most of the secretaries are wonderful. But they have too much to do too much of the time. The last major pleading I filed was 106 pages. I typed the last 80. No doubt it showed.

It is a meager, beleaguered library, where books are everywhere but on the shelf, where it is a cause for celebration when you actually find the volume you need. It is coming in on weekends in winter and having no heat. It is working in a building with so little security that pocketbooks and wallets are ripped off routinely. The cops probably find it ironic filling out theft reports involving PDS lawyers.

It is having no one cooperate with you, not the police, not the judges, not the clerks, not the D.A.'s, not even your typewriter, which decides that you do not really need the letter "t".

Minutia and frustration. Words, I might add, which I could not use during several t-less weeks.

* * *

Jerold Gilford was charged with armed rape. Our first line of defense was misidentification, although the police artist's sketch, created immediately after the rape, bore a striking, even astonishing resemblance to our client. And there were not many folks who looked like Jerold Gilford, what with his full beard, distinctive nose, and bulbous face. Coupled with the facts that he was arrested in the neighborhood of the assault and that he was carrying the same type of hawkbill knife used during the assault, a misidentification defense was a thin reed indeed.

We put a great deal more faith in our second approach: the insanity defense. Jerold really did have a bizarre personality disorder. Doctors called it "episodic dyscontrol" or "disassociative reaction," sort of a Dr. Jeckyl/Mr. Hyde, with Mr. Hyde having a proclivity for rape.

Jerold had no recollection of the rape. Even the doctors hired by the government believed him. His personal history was tailor-made for an insanity defense. He had seen the first of several psychologists in the fourth grade; he was beaten as a child; he had an abnormal electroencephalograph (EEG); his behavior at home was strange in the extreme (he would walk for hours and hours all through the night; he would hang out with stray mongrels; he would spend days alone in his basement room; he would communicate with his family through notes).

Early on in the case, we obtained a crucial ruling from the court. The trial would be bifurcated. First, there would be a guilt/innocence phase which would deal solely with whether Jerold had committed the rape. If found guilty of the rape, we would immediately select a new jury and enter into the insanity phase. This way, the first jury, evaluating our misidentification defense, would not be swayed by the knowledge that Jerold was, to put it mildly, clinically weird.

After a week and a half of trial, we had managed to convince ourselves that maybe there was something after all in this misidentification defense. Unfortunately, we did not convince the jury and they

found him guilty of armed rape. The insanity phase began immediately. We put two psychiatrists on the stand and showed the jury large
blowups of Jerold's abnormal EEG. The government came back with
three doctors of its own who pooh-poohed our EEG and suggested that
Jerold knew exactly what he was doing when he committed the rape.

For me, it was a memorable trial for many reasons. It was my first
serious adult trial and I did it with one of the finest trial lawyers in (or
out) of our office. For the first time I realized how impossibly hard it is
to be a trial lawyer, let alone a competent one. During the government's direct exam, you must listen to what the witness is saying; take
copious notes; make objections before—not after—the answers are
given; refine and re-plan your cross-examination; and watch the jury's
reaction. I repeatedly found my mind wandering and had no idea what .
the witness had said. When I did focus carefully on what the witness
was saying, I forgot to make objections. When I managed to listen and
make objections, I found that I had taken no notes (and thus had only
the vaguest recollection of the testimony). Witness by witness, I did get
better. But it would take several more trials before I began to feel
comfortable and (relatively speaking) in control.

But there was another reason why this trial became a memorable
experience or, more correctly, an emotionally wrenching (and retching)
experience. On the day before I was supposed to give the opening
statement in the insanity phase of the trial, on the day before I was to
make a pitch to the jury that my client should be excused after having
raped this woman, a close family relation was robbed and raped at
knifepoint. She called us at 5:30 a.m. and we rushed to D.C. General
Hospital. There, we gave her what little comfort we could. After all,
what can you really do for someone who has just been to Hell? Then I
put on my tie and rushed to court. There was a knot in my stomach. I
felt like throwing up. What in God's name was I doing here representing this rapist? What was I about? If Jerold was a Dr. Jeckyl/Mr.
Hyde, what kind of split personality did I have? How could I be on
both sides of this bloodied, tear-streaked fence?

Since I had drafted and prepared the opening statement, and since
I had nurtured and prepped the key defense psychiatrist, I stayed on
the case. I gave the opening, we both handled direct and cross-
examination, and my colleague gave a stunning closing. The jury
returned a verdict of not guilty by reason of insanity and my client was
sent to Saint Elizabeths Hospital, where he is today.

For a long time after the case was over, I wondered if I really could
continue being a public defender. I wondered if I really could handle
another rape case. How would I know my client was not the same
person who had raped a member of my family? And, beyond this, if I
could not represent the man who had raped a member of my family,

how could I represent the man who raped a member of someone else's family?

The first question was easier to answer than the second. A man was caught who police believed had committed the rape of my relative, although they would never be able to prove it in court. The man was sentenced to a very, very long prison term on other sex offenses, and I stopped worrying about him showing up on my docket one day. The second question was much more difficult, at least if you believe in the family of man. Eventually, I arrived at an uneasy resolution and handled many, many rape cases after Jerold Gifford's. I concluded that, at a certain point, emotion simply overwhelms logic. I can believe in the adversary system as if it were a religion, but I still could never represent someone who hurts someone I love. I loathe that person; I want him punished; I want no escape routes to grace his path. On the other hand, if the victim is unknown, if the suffering is not focused upon, then it is possible to do my job.

Thus, I try not to think about victims too much. The more I think about them, the more difficult it is to represent my clients. And, of course, sometimes victims are not victims at all. Sometimes victims are liars, fabricating incidents that never occurred; sometimes victims are really assailants who have managed to cloak themselves in innocence; sometimes victims pick the wrong man and your client becomes a victim too. But often it is none of those things. A victim is a victim is a victim and your client a victimizer. Those are the cases where I try hardest not to think of the victim.

To represent a client properly, you have to be able to develop an enormous amount of empathy. You have to be able not only to advocate, but to advocate passionately. Thus, again and again, I found myself becoming almost overwrought at sentencings, pleading for one more chance, pleading to keep families together, pleading for a judge to reach out to my client, pleading for freedom. At a few sentencings I nearly cried and, as I stood there awaiting pronouncement of sentence, I felt transfixed, as if it were my life and liberty hanging in the balance.

This kind of intense involvement is a necessity. If you care about your client, maybe, just maybe, the judge will care about your client. But if you do not care, if you feel no bond to your client, that fact will be so obvious to the court that all your carefully architectured blandishments will go unheeded. The same is true, only more so, with a jury. If the jury senses that you do not like your client, that you just do not care if he goes down the drain, sure as anything they will flush him.

Ideally, feelings of empathy toward your client are a natural product of a good lawyer-client relationship. As I get to know my clients and they come to see me as someone genuinely trying to help them, warm strong feelings emerge.

While it is often impossible not to feel sympathy for the victim, this is not an emotion you can afford to nurture or encourage. To put it simply, it is not easy to develop warm feelings when your focus is on the devastation which your client has left in his wake. It makes a difficult job nearly impossible.

Occasionally, however, it does become impossible. In one case, for example, my client was charged with robbery. I was told in discovery that my client had robbed a pregnant woman, threatening to kick the woman in the stomach if she did not turn over her purse. At the time, my wife was six months pregnant. At the first opportunity, I pulled out of the case.

* * *

Nothing in life, except maybe labor, compares with awaiting a jury's verdict. Life takes on a surrealistic flavor. You go about your business mechanically, with no real idea what you are doing. The clock has stopped and will not start moving again until the note—"We have reached a unanimous verdict"—comes in. And then you are standing there with your client, waiting for the foreman to announce the verdict. Waiting, praying to hear the word "Not." I could swear my heart stops. I know I stop breathing. And then, suddenly, it is over. Your client is either with you in the hallway, awash with relief. Or in the cellblock, dazed. Once again, I ask myself: How many more of these moments can I stand?

* * *

Michael Walker was charged with first degree murder while armed. A roofer by trade, with no prior record, he was charged with shooting down a security guard during a liquor store holdup. His arrest was based on an affidavit by a detective who reported that some unidentified person had overheard Walker and his co-defendant talking about how they had committed this robbery.

The first major battle in the case occurred almost immediately— getting Walker out of the overnight lockup. In a first degree murder case, there is almost a presumption in favor of incarceration pending trial. But here we had a man with a stable job, a stable residence, family in court, and no prior record. The court released him.

It is one of the curiosities of criminal practice that your relationship with a client can be made or broken on the first day. If you get your client out of jail, particularly if this has been his first exposure to being locked up, your relationship is golden. As far as he is concerned, you can do no wrong and he will follow your advice unerringly. On the other hand, if you fail to get him released—even if release is a virtual impossibility—some clients will hold you responsible for their incarceration. Some will assume that you do not care what happens to them. Some will even figure you want them locked up. And once your client has soured on you, resurrecting the relationship is difficult and, often, impossible.

In any case, Walker was out and our investigation began. I was lucky to have two fresh investigators, both college students trying to decide whether they wanted to be lawyers and spending a semester at PDS. During the next two weeks, they spent night and day in the neighborhood where my client lived and the offense occurred.

It did not take long to learn that the unidentified person who had told the police that she had overheard my client talking about the crime was Margaret Drew: none other than my client's very estranged (and very strange) girlfriend. Drew, it emerged, had a history of psychiatric disorders and had actually shot a prior paramour. Most recently, she had bashed out the window of my client's car and poured sugar in his gas tank.

My investigator went out to see Drew. She appeared to be nervous and preoccupied. She said she never would have told the police about overhearing the conversation involving Walker and the co-defendant if she thought it was going to result in his being charged with murder. More significantly, she added an astonishing twist to her story: she had not overheard Walker talking about having committed the robbery; rather, all she had heard was Walker discussing the fact that the liquor store had been robbed and the guard shot. This was a piece of dynamite; it would severely undermine her credibility at trial.

I gave the co-defendant's lawyer Drew's home address and he sent out an investigator to interview her as well. By this point, Drew was in a frenzy. She confessed to the investigator that she had made the whole thing up. She said she was mad at Michael Walker and had lied to the police in order to hurt him.

Once we shared the fruits of our investigation with the government, all charges were dismissed. The last I heard, the government had launched an investigation to determine whether to charge Margaret Drew with perjury.

*   *   *

It has always amazed me how cavalierly some prosecutors press judges to lock up my clients. It is as if they do not take prison seriously, as if they do not know what a dirty hole prison can be, as if they have never even seen the inside of a prison. And that is the problem: many have not. A D.C. prosecutor can pass through his whole career and never visit the D.C. Jail or Lorton.

A public defender has no such luxury. We go where our clients go. And our clients go to jail. And they go to mental wards. And, of course, they go to prison. And so because our clients are locked up we get ourselves locked up, if only for a few hours.

It is the least enjoyable part of the job, yet it is also the most rewarding part of my job. Being in a tiny glass booth behind three locked doors spending hours on end is the pits. Yet my clients receive me so warmly; they are so happy that I have come. I am tangible evidence that someone is trying to get them out of there.

An incarcerated client is filled with anxiety. And why not? Here he is completely dependent on his public defender lawyer, someone he does not know and did not hire. The jail abounds with stories about clients being screwed by their lawyers. About incompetent lawyers. About lazy lawyers. About lawyers who just do not care. Am I the one who is going to sell him down the river? Is it really true that PDS stands for Plea Delivery Service? Visiting a client in jail, in and of itself, cannot possibly amelioriate all this anxiety. But it is a beginning.

Arriving at the jail, unfortunately, is only the first step in actually getting to see a client. Sometimes it seems like the entire bureaucracy of the Department of Corrections has coalesced around the goal of ensuring that you spend no less than four hours in their custody. Watching the guards process the visitation forms is like watching a movie, frame by frame by frame. Clients are sent to the wrong floor or not even called out of their cells. Visiting rooms are filled to overflowing. And then there is the count, the bane of every lawyer who has ever gone to the D.C. Jail. Every few hours, apparently designed to coincide with your arrival at the jail, a count is made of all jail residents. While the count is on, all movement ceases. If the count does not jibe with jail records, there is a recount and, if necessary, another recount and so on and so on for hours and hours and hours. *The Executioner's Song,* one of Mailer's longer tomes, was begun and finished during jail counts.

Next to the D.C. Jail is a place called the Ugast Pavilion, a dark, dingy place, vaguely smelling of urine. The Ugast Pavilion is where many of the mentally ill male defendants are sent for psychiatric evaluation. A disturbed environment for disturbed persons. If they are not clinically depressed when they arrive, they ought to be when they leave. I get in and out of Ugast as seldom and as fast as I can.

In contrast is the John Howard Pavilion at Saint Elizabeths Hospital. This is where some of our clients go before trial to have their heads examined and this is where they go when they are found not guilty by reason of insanity. Seeing a client at John Howard is almost (though never quite) pleasant. You get in without a wait, the personnel are friendly, you are escorted to your client and you meet with him in a private room.

Finally, there is Lorton Reformatory, an aged, barbed wired enclosure which no one could mistake for anything other than a maximum security prison. Lorton looks like a movie set for one of those cruel prison dramas. Except it is real. Like an ugly wart, Lorton mars the face of a fertile, rolling countryside, cows grazing on one side, men vegetating on the other.

I go to Lorton to meet with clients for whom I am doing postconviction relief or for whom I am drafting appeals. My visits are only occasionally substantive. Really I am there to give cautious little slivers of hope. Maybe there are grounds for appeal. Maybe this issue is a winner. Maybe the Supreme Court will grant cert. In a place filled with life sentences, in a place filled with people who have exhausted their appeals and have no straws left to grasp, a little bit of hope is a lot.

I always get depressed when I go to Lorton. In my mind—in fact, in my heart—I know that many of these people deserve to be there. Still, it is so sad, such an admission of failure on so many different levels, to see people locked up behind barbed wire. And it is even sadder when the backdrop is acres of farm land stretching into the distance.

On my way out, when I pass through the final locked gate, I always feel a palpable sense of relief. It is so good to be free.

* * *

Margarita Lyden was another client who made only occasional visits to the planet Earth. She had been nabbed by a police decoy squad. One police officer, acting drunk, curled up on the ground with a wallet and a dollar bill sticking out of his pocket. Other police officers hid nearby, waiting for a sucker to come along and pick the wallet. Margarita obliged.

When I first met Margarita, she gave me a warm smile. Quietly, almost conspiratorially, she informed me that she had a third eye in the middle of her head, had a close, if not intimate, relationship with a 14th Century monk, and saw pyramids everywhere. What this had to do with pickpocketing was not immediately discernible. But it was clear that Margarita lived in a world all her own.

I called all the women's shelters in town and, for the first time, I learned that Margarita was not unknown in the community. They flatly refused to have her back. Margarita had no family to rely upon, no place to live, and no visible means of support. The judge ordered her held in jail. To my surprise, she was not the least bit distressed at the prospect of jail. She had been living on the street. At least in jail she would have regular meals and a warm bed.

Several days later, I visited Margarita at the jail. I started asking her about her past, about past psychiatric hospitalizations. She began to fidget and grew increasingly uncomfortable. Finally, she jumped up and began screaming "I know who killed Martin Luther King" over and over and over. As the guard led her away, and I shakily prepared to leave, I began to wonder if I somehow lacked the finesse appropriate to dealing with the mentally ill.

I visited Margarita again not long afterwards. She could not have been more pleasant this time. She patiently went through her whole life story. Abandoned as an infant, she was raised by a gentle aunt who exercised no control over her. Margarita went off to college where she fell in love with a ne'er-do-well who introduced her to drink.

Within a few months, Margarita had quit school and was drinking full time. She and the ne'er-do-well married and he proceeded to beat her frequently. She finally set fire to his house, effectively ending that relationship and leading Margarita to her first encounter with the law. Five admissions to psychiatric hospitals followed. Eventually I pieced together the history of a person who had spiraled ever downward into mental illness. Initially diagnosed an alcoholic, years later she was termed a borderline psychotic and, finally, a full-fledged paranoid schizophrenic.

Despite her ever-present delusions, I was able to do something with Margarita—bring her down to Earth for a sufficient period of time to realistically apprise her of her options. One of the greatest frustrations of working with mentally ill clients is that they are often too out of it to make appropriate (or even inappropriate) decisions. For example, one time I had a client who had walked away from a halfway house without permission. He was clearly guilty of prison breach, a five year felony. The government offered a plea to a six month misdemeanor. My client had already been locked up for eight months and so would be released the moment he pled guilty. My client adamantly refused to accept the plea (as he had refused to accept my business card). Ultimately, I discussed the situation with the judge and, having obtained a tiny window of lucidity from my client, we did the fastest plea in history.

In contrast, Margarita was able to listen to what I was telling her and understood what it meant. The bottom line was this: if we pled not guilty and went to trial, she would certainly be convicted. More-over, she was not charged just with robbery but with assaulting a police officer while armed. It seems that Margarita had compounded her troubles by attacking the arresting officer with a butcher knife. She faced life in prison. On the other hand, if we could pull off an insanity defense, she would go to the mental hospital and could be out in a few years. She eagerly chose the latter approach.

I hired two psychologists. One of them agreed that Margarita was mentally ill but found no link between the crime and the illness. The other psychologist found her crazy in all respects and drew a straight line through her third eye, the pyramids she kept talking about, her friendly monk, and the pickpocket/assault on the police officer.

A trial is always a crapshoot and even strong cases get lost for mysterious reasons. So, before committing myself to an insanity trial, I tried to convince the prosecutor assigned to the case that Margarita was crazy and there was no need for a contested insanity trial. The prosecutor said he would leave the decision up to the psychologist who had been hired by the government to see Margarita. I contacted this psychologist and sent him every tid-bit of craziness I could lay my hands on. I talked to him more often than the prosecutor did. After meeting her twice, he agreed that Margarita was crazy and that she was in the midst of a delusional state when she pinched the wallet. We did an uncontested insanity defense. My client admitted guilt for the crime and the government conceded that she was not guilty by reason of insanity.

A few months ago, I spoke to Margarita. She is happy at Saint Elizabeths Hospital. She gets three good meals a day; she likes her room; she tells me that they treat her nice; and, best of all, she tells me they are helping her.

Margarita is an exceptional case. Usually, a client's mental illness is not so pronounced that it becomes the number one item on the agenda. Generally, mental problems, when they afflict our clients, are less acute. They flavor, they distort, they occasionally pervert the lawyer-client relationship; they do not prevent one entirely. That is not to underestimate the headache potential of representing a disturbed client. Everything is harder. Harder to explain court proceedings. Harder to make decisions. Harder to reach agreement. Harder to remember yesterday's meeting.

Whenever I think of disturbed clients, I think of Monica. Monica would call me from the jail every few days. I would know it was she because she would begin each call, in her low rumbling voice, with "Hey . . . Bellows . . . what's going on?" On several occasions, when she felt she was not getting enough attention, she would call up and say she was about to commit suicide, her favorite technique being chewing glass. You can never, never ignore a suicide threat and so, each time she would do this, I would start a long chain of court orders, psychiatric exams, suicide precautions, etc. One time, I barged in on the Chief Judge to get an emergency writ to get Monica over to Saint

Elizabeths Hospital for treatment. Once there, she immediately called me and told me that she liked the jail better and wanted to go back.

On another occasion, I made the horrendous mistake of getting Monica released into my personal custody so that she could be interviewed by a rehabilitation program. When it came time to return to court, she refused to go back. Several hours of cajoling and pleading ensued. Finally, she relented. Monica was the first—and last—client I arranged to have released in my personal custody.

Even with those clients who see the world and their options realistically, being a public defender is a tough job. When clients see life at an angle, particularly at a bizarre angle, legal skill is almost irrelevant. Your capacity as a social worker and psychiatrist—and your capacity as a patient, tolerant, listening, caring human being—is far more important. An interesting job, this public defending, almost an art form.

*   *   *

I spent six months in Juvenile Court, a frustrating and only occasionally rewarding experience.

Some of my juvenile clients:

Darlene, for whom I obtained a pain-free dismissal after she was arrested for shoplifting. It was her first offense. It was only later that I realized that, by helping her get off so easily, I was making it almost inevitable that she would be back again.

Michael, who was a dream juvenile client. He and his brother had, in a fit of exuberance and stupidity, reached into a parked car and pulled out several pieces of luggage. Perhaps they expected jewels; all they received were old clothing and a term on probation. I knew I would never see Michael again. He was just too embarrassed.

Daniel, whose father was a police officer, a man who arrested other men's sons but could not control his own. We got Daniel into counseling. Maybe it helped. Maybe not. I never heard from him again.

Allan, a sad youngster, smoking marijuana constantly, beyond control of his family, driving his mother to an early grave (she was dead before the case was over). Allan ended up being committed to the juvenile authorities. I did not help him one bit. I did not know how to help him.

Debra, a wild young woman who had socked a security guard in the face at a fast food restaurant. A tough young lady, she walked out of the courtroom without a scratch. She, too, would probably be back.

I disliked Juvenile Court. Adult clients were simple. Their needs were simple. They needed to get out of jail. That I understood. That I could help them achieve. My juvenile clients needed much, much more. They needed fathers and mothers who cared. They needed friends who would not lead them astray. They needed discipline and counseling and remedial reading and a thousand and one other things I could not give them. I was not trained to be a social worker, yet so much of Juvenile Court is social work.

With juveniles, there was always the hope of change, a mending of ways. And that was the problem. When you represent a guilty adult client and get him off, you have succeeded. You have done what you were appointed to do. But when you represent a guilty juvenile client, and get him off, what have you done except convey the message to him that a sharp-talking lawyer is all he needs? Certainly, you have given him no cause to change his behavior. He got off this time, he will get off next time. Only it does not work that way. Later he will learn that sharp-talking lawyers only work some of the time. And so, five or ten years from now, there he will be, in the chow line at Lorton, facing ten or twenty or thirty years.

When I first came to PDS, I was told that there is a rule of thumb that applies to Juvenile Court practice: your prime legal goal in most cases is to get your clients back out on the street. Certainly, that is your client's prime goal and, after all, you are his lawyer. Moreover, the juvenile commitment facilities, in many respects, are just junior versions of Lorton. But I sure did not help Raymond Walker much when I got him back out on the street on probation after committing a robbery. He was arrested six months later on a charge of armed rape—and this time he was charged as an adult. Maybe he needed a junior version of Lorton.

* * *

Clients who have earned a spot in my mind (and, occasionally, in my heart):

Angela, one of a host of clients who could be termed uncooperative. She would not keep appointments; she would give me non-working phone numbers; she would show up for court an hour late, with me having spent that hour begging forgiveness from the judge; she was into denial, denial that someday she would have to pay the piper, denial that having had the case continued for one year, she could not have it continued for another. Our relationship was stormy. At one point, she threatened to go out and get herself another lawyer (which I would have welcomed).

In the end, Angela—charged with a ten year felony, and having a murder conviction in her past—walked out of court on probation. At that point, I was the greatest lawyer she had ever known. A real honey of a lawyer. Had the judge locked her up, she would have spit in my face.

Ramon, a client who would have made a brilliant lawyer. Charged with a burglary he actually may not have committed, he dreamed up one spectacular strategy after another. He would call me virtually every day, assuming that since I was his only lawyer, he must be my only client. He would give me my marching orders, who I should interview that day, what investigation we should do before noon, how I should handle the cross-exam. He was impossible to ignore because he was almost always right. After representing him for three months, I was exhausted. So was the prosecutor, to whom I had conveyed what seemed like volumes of discovery and suppression motions.

Trial began with the government's key identification witness, a woman who made it obvious that she would rather be anywhere than on the witness stand. She answered the prosecutor's questions grudgingly. When I began to ask questions, she put her head down, and bluntly told the judge that she had said all she was going to say. The government dismissed the case.

Two weeks later, Ramon was back, asking me to take over another case which had been pending. I refused. I could represent him or I could carry a caseload of 35 misdemeanors and felonies. I could not do both.

Thomas, one of the few clients who actually fooled me. Charged with robbery, he had everything going for him: a look of innocence that would melt a juror's heart; a good job; a spotless record; a minister who swore to his good name; a loyal and loving family; a victim whose own brushes with crime—not to mention his status as the neighborhood hooligan—would make him a poor choice for jury sympathy; the sheer inconceivability that a nice young man like this would commit a crime like that; and, last but certainly not least, an impressive and convincing denial by Thomas himself. I was so certain that the government had really botched it that I hired a polygrapher, intending to use the results in lobbying for dismissal.

He flunked. Not only did he flunk, he even confessed.

I was stunned. Generally I am not shocked or surprised when my clients lie to me. Why shouldn't they? They do not know me from beans; they do not trust anyone who works in the court system; I am white and they are usually black; they are not paying me a dime and since when does that get you anything; even worse, they know that the people who are paying me are the same people, more or less, who pay the cops and the D.A.'s. So, when a client like Thomas lies to me, I am not offended or angry. What did get me angry is that I fell for it.

Andrew, an unusual client: candid, straightforward, practical (he did not hesitate to rat on his good buddy in order to avail himself of a sweetheart deal), and absolutely truthful with himself. He knew what he had done (an armed robbery); he knew what his options were; and he knew exactly what he wanted in terms of a deal.

More significantly, he knew exactly how to get the most out of his lawyer. He was polite, respectful, grateful whenever I would go and see him at the jail, and understanding of the other demands on my time. I loved him for it. A man can be a mass murderer but if he treats me nice, if he is decent and friendly and respects my advice, I will usually feel good about representing him.

It is a fact of life that all clients are not treated equally. The ones you like—the ones you look forward to visiting at the jail—inevitably get a slight, though probably only a slight, edge in service. On the "big ticket" items—like investigation or trial preparation—it makes no difference. But on small matters, like calling a client's mother to say that her son has run out of cigarettes at the jail, it makes a big difference.

Andrew never ran out of cigarettes.

* * *

You begin with gentle persuasion. But if it become necessary, you wheedle, you cajole, you twist arms, you harangue, you bring in reinforcements. The one thing you do not do is let a client reject a plea which is inescapably in his best interest. Not, at least, until you both drop from exhaustion. Pleading guilty to murder, pleading guilty to robbery, pleading guilty to offenses which can cost your client 10 or 20 years of his life is one of the most difficult things you can ask another human being to do. But seeing a client flush himself down the drain, seeing a life sentence imposed which did not have to be, is so, so much worse. More than in any other sphere, our office shines in the way we handle our pleas.

The possibility that your client may need to plead guilty makes the need for quickly establishing trust of overarching importance. Plea offers come and go like meteors. If your client does not trust you until a plea has expired, you have failed. You have quite simply screwed your client. You have got to show your client immediately that you care—whether it consists of three visits to the jail in a week or overwhelming him with all the investigation you have already done. Somehow, you must break through the wall of distrust that defendants have of lawyers in general and appointed lawyers in particular.

Some lawyers think it's macho to go to trial, that their clients will not respect them if they push a plea. Well, the same client who demanded a trial—despite the certain likelihood of conviction—will have years of solitude in which to ponder his choice. And as for the lawyer who so easily acceded to his client's bravado, he will just go on his way, onto new clients whose lives he can ruin.

The very first step in the plea process is investigation. A lawyer who tells his client to plead guilty—or not to plead guilty—without proper investigation of the facts is a charlatan. So fundamental is the fact that, on one occasion, our normally mild trial chief threatened to fire any lawyer who pled his client guilty without doing adequate investigation. You cannot rely on what the police or prosecutors tell you. They see things through their own tinted glasses. You must do it yourself. Go to the scene. Have your investigator take signed statements from the complainant and eyewitnesses. Interview the arresting officers. Talk to potential alibi witnesses. Using the facts, build a defense and see how it stands. If it topples, build another one. Can you win this case? If so, can you lose it too? What are the odds?

Once you have investigated the case and your client authorizes plea negotiations, seek to negotiate from strength, even if it means turning down an offer (with your client's consent) if you are confident that a better offer lies down the road. Once you have tried—and won—a bunch of cases, the D.A. will know you are not chicken. The D.A. will know that if you appear to be eager for trial, it may be time for him to reevaluate his case. Sometimes, wonderful plea offers disappear, never to be seen again. But sometimes, they first appear on the eve of trial. It is your job to know the difference.

Plea negotiation and decision making requires experience and judgment. Share your dilemma with every one in sight. I have sometimes talked to over a dozen attorneys about a plea offer. What sentence do you think this judge will impose? Is the D.A. good in trial? Does the judge care about legal issues? Can a better plea offer be extracted?

In the end, though, it is your case and you are the lawyer and you have to make up your own mind. Other lawyers cannot make it for you. And, certainly, your client cannot make it for you. He will make the ultimate decision. He will choose what he thinks is best for himself. But how can you help him make an informed decision if you have not first made your own judgment about what is best?

If you decide that your client needs to accept a plea offer, sell it to him as if your life depended upon it. His does. Do what it takes to convince him, whether it is making pro-con charts of the facts, having him talk to other lawyers in the office, or even having him cross-examined by another lawyer so that he sees his defense demolished.

Say a client is charged with armed robbery. The government's case is strong and there is a high likelihood of conviction. The offer is to attempted robbery. Life vs. three years. Many defendants, particularly novices, figure they can bluff their way through a trial and, unfortunately, there are too many lawyers who just do not care enough, or who do not feel it is their job, to persuade them otherwise. If the client wants a trial, so be it. It is no skin off their back. PDS, in contrast, has an ethic which rejects this approach. We consider ourselves obligated to see that, if our client can do three years instead of the life sentence he may get if he goes to trial, he chooses to do the three years. If you know what your client should do, you push it even if your client initially believes you are selling him a rotten fish. If you have got a trust relationship, trust will pull you through.

Sometimes, it does not work. You have pushed so hard, you pushed your client right out of the relationship. He loses all faith in you. At that point, you get out. You have done everything your education and intuition and training taught you to do. And it did not work. You lost the plea. And you lost the client.

Yet this happens remarkably rarely. Certainly, clients often reject plea offers against advice. But if you have built up trust, your client will usually see that you have been aggressive because you care, because you value his life and the years he may have to spend behind bars.

The other half of persuading a client to plead guilty is the obligations that come with success. Clients plead guilty because of your predictions. Will they get locked up pending sentencing? Will they get probation? Will the sentence be light? I never make promises but I certainly make predictions. And then I sweat bullets making sure that my predictions come true.

Take the case of Gary Brown. Gary was charged with second degree murder. At 3:20 one morning, Gary killed a man. The facts were these:

Gary had been job hunting all day. When he got home, he was tired, demoralized, and had a splitting headache. As usual, his elderly roommate, Ben, was asleep in front of a blaring television set. An empty jug of wine sat on the floor and Ben reeked of alcohol. Gary woke him up, shut off the set, and asked him to clean up the mess he had made.

Gary went downstairs to his bedroom and fell asleep. An hour later, around 3:00 a.m., he was startled to hear that the television was on again and someone was banging around in the kitchen. He trudged upstairs and told Ben that, if he did not pipe down, Gary would throw him out of the house and he could spend the night outside. Ben refused. Gary grabbed him, dragged him to the door, and threw him out on the porch.

The porch was cement and Ben landed on his head. Gary heard a loud crack, then nothing. He tried to revive Ben, pouring water on his head, trying CPR. Nothing worked. Ben, in fact, had died instantly.

Gary called an ambulance. He then called the police and reported that
he thought he had killed someone. Within an hour, Ben was at the
Medical Examiners and Gary was at the Homicide Squad. Gary gave a
detailed, signed confession and was arrested.

In my initial conversation with Gary, he insisted that he acted in
self-defense, asserting that Ben had threatened him. And anyway, he
argued, he had never meant to kill Ben. It was just an accident. The
self-defense claim was a joke. No jury would find that Gary Brown, a
muscular, 26–year-old man, was in legitimate fear of a 65–year-old man
with a blood alcohol level three times the amount that will get you
arrested for drunk driving.

Gary had intentionally thrown Ben out on the porch. While that
did not make him guilty of murder, he certainly was guilty of manslaughter—an offense which, in the District of Columbia, requires no
more than the intentional doing of an act which results in another
man's death. Thus, an accident defense would not work either. It was
no accident that Ben was tossed outside.

The plea offer was to manslaughter, which carries a 15 year
maximum penalty. Gary rejected it. He was not going to plead guilty
to anything that might result in a 15 year prison term.

Gary had good cause for apprehension. A man died and a price
would have to be paid. Furthermore, Gary had two prior convictions,
including one for robbery. And, to top it off, he had been given
probation before and failed to complete a course of psychiatric counseling.

I put it to Gary this way: if he pled guilty he had a very slight
chance at probation. If he did not plead guilty he had no chance at
probation and he might even get the maximum sentence. Gary was
adamant. He rejected the plea offer. He figured that once he told his
story to the jury, he would be acquitted.

There was another matter at issue as well. Gary had a right to
testify before the grand jury and there was an outside chance that the
grand jury might choose not to indict him. At my request, a colleague
spent most of an hour grilling Gary. When he was done, Gary realized
that his self-defense claim and accident defense had virtually no chance
of success. He would be indicted. And if he went to trial, he would be
convicted.

After several more weeks of wrangling, Gary gave in. He would
plead to manslaughter and place all of his chips on the thin possibility
of probation. As if it was not clear to me already, he told me that the
only reason he was doing this was because I recommended it and he
knew I would do everything I could to get him probation. Gary, in his

own way, wanted to make sure that I knew where the responsibility lay for what would either be a dazzling success or a smashing failure.

Several weeks later—after intensely lobbying the probation officer writing the pre-sentence report, after obtaining a sympathetic psychological evaluation, after putting together a collection of wonderful letters from Gary's family, his employer, and his minister, and after drafting a fairly emotional letter of my own—we appeared before the judge for sentencing.

Gary was placed on probation. Being a public defender does have its moments of glory and this was surely one of them. Later, I met with Gary and he told me that his friends and family had encouraged him to fire me when they heard that I was pushing a plea. He had rejected the advice and now he wanted me to know that he felt he made the right choice.

I was not surprised. After all, we were meeting in my office. Not at Lorton.

*   *   *

Allen Graham was charged with three separate acts of sexual assault, each of which also involved an allegation of burglary. In the first case, he was supposed to have attacked a young woman in the laundry room of her apartment building. In the second case, an 81–year-old woman was attacked in her basement stairwell. In the third case, a young woman was attacked in the ladies room in the professional building where she worked.

Legally, Graham's cases were fascinating. The government sought preventive detention of Graham pending trial. A part of me—the part of me with a mother, wife, and daughter, the part of me with a relative and a friend who have been raped—considered the request eminently reasonable. The part of me that labored in court fought desperately against preventive detention. I sent my investigator out to get a statement from the 81–year-old victim. He came back with a statement that astonished me: not only did the victim repeatedly cast racist slurs at the defendant and black persons in general but, contrary to the government's papers, the victim denied ever having identified my client as the culprit. I used the statement to convince the judge that I had a right to call the complainant as a witness. Since the government was unwilling to have me cross-examine their complainant at such an early stage of the proceedings, preventive detention was denied. It was an empty victory, however. Graham remained locked up on a high money bond.

As the trial approached, the legal maneuvering went into high gear. I filed a severance motion, certain that if I had to try all three cases before the same jury, the jury would convict Graham on the notion that "where there's smoke, there's fire." The severance motion was granted.

The government elected to try, as its first case, a sexual assault which took place in an affluent Washington apartment building. My client was caught two blocks from the scene of the assault, bleeding profusely from the spot on his arm where the victim had cut him with a piece of glass. I recognized immediately that there was virtually no chance of convincing the jury that this was a case of misidentification. Rather, I argued that my client may have been guilty of simple assault and unlawful entry (misdemeanors) but he was not guilty of assault with intent to rape and burglary (15 year felonies). My defense depended upon convincing the jury that my client had erroneously believed that the victim was coming on to my client and, based on that belief, my client had approached her. One thing led to another, things got out of hand, and next thing you know my client was running down the block with his arm slashed.

In my own mind, I thought this defense was unlikely to succeed (to say the least), but it was the only one we had. Not for the first time, nor for the last, I subjected the victim of an alleged sexual assault to lengthy and probing cross-examination.

I know many wonderful attorneys—whose advice I seek and with whom I socialize—who can cross-examine rape and sexual assault victims without blinking an eye. For me, it is always difficult and unpleasant, one of the major reasons why being a public defender can be an emotionally trying experience.

Nevertheless, I cross-examined her as aggressively as I could without generating a backlash of sympathy. I need not have worried. The victim came across as cold, even contemptuous, condescending, and uncooperative. Furthermore, the jury was apparently willing to suspend its disbelief and consider the scenario I had suggested. Following lengthy closing arguments—with me passionately asserting my "understandable misunderstanding" theory and the government ridiculing it—the jury acquitted my client of the assault with intent to rape and burglary charges, finding him guilty of simple assault and unlawful entry. Instead of 30 years in jail, he faced just a year and a half.

Two months later, we were in trial again, this time involving the sexual assault on the elderly woman. She had repeatedly used the term "niggers" during her interview with my investigator and her identification of my client was somewhere between shaky and non-existent. Our defense here was misidentification, the only problem being that my client's fingerprint was allegedly found at the scene of the crime. I tried to convince the jury that the fingerprint examiner was wrong, that it was not really my client's fingerprint, and that anyone could look at the fingerprint blow-ups and discern numerous discrepancies between the known fingerprints of Graham and the one found on the scene. Thankfully, the jury and not a judge was making the decision. A judge would have laughed at this defense. The jury, on the other hand, was open to all possibilities. The other half of my defense was to destroy the victim's identification of my client, an identification which had firmed up considerably in the intervening months before trial. Cross-examining an 81–year-old woman, particularly one who bore a faint resemblance to my grandmother, was not a great way to spend an afternoon. Even though the court prohibited me from going into the racial slurs and bias of the victim, the jury apparently decided that it was not wholly convinced of my client's guilt. He was acquitted of the assault with intent to rape charge but convicted of the burglary charge. The verdict is utterly inconsistent, but it did save my client 15 years in prison.

Ultimately, my client entered a plea of guilty to several misdemeanors involving the third sexual assault and felony charges were dropped. Had my client been convicted of all charges, he could have been given a maximum sentence of 90 years. He will now be eligible for parole in seven years—and that is assuming he does not prevail on appeal.

Two of Graham's alleged assaults occurred in the same neighborhood in upper Northwest Washington. My wife and I lived in that neighborhood. We do not anymore.

* * *

Michael Woodruff was charged with simple assault and possession of a prohibited weapon, the weapon being an ax handle. Michael was, not to put too fine a point on it, a drunk. He lived with several other individuals of similar persuasion in a boarding house. One day, he and his roommate got into a squabble and, both having consumed more than their daily allotment of cheap wine, fell to blows. The roommate used a bat and Michael used the ax handle. Michael, it must be admitted, clearly got the better of his roommate. His roommate, however, found the police first and Michael ended up being the one arrested.

Michael decided he wanted his day in court and we prepared for trial. We made as big a production of it as possible: diagrams, color photos, investigative statements, suppression motions, etc. Just as we were to begin to select the jury, the government dismissed the case. The prosecutor never told me why he did so but I suspect that, in a marginal misdemeanor case like this one, the prosecutor decided it just was not worth the trouble.

This dismissal may have had something to do with the fact that misdemeanor prosecutors do not generally find it difficult to win their convictions. One of the most shocking things I found as a public defender—shocking due, apparently, to my naivete—was the inadequacy of many of the criminal defense lawyers who represent clients in misdemeanor cases in the District of Columbia. Many of these lawyers, working for the paltry sums paid by the court for appointed cases, simply do not care. They do not investigate. They do not file motions. They do not talk to their clients. They do not think through a defense, prepare an opening statement, subpoena witnesses, or do any of the other myriad tasks necessary to adequate representation. Sometimes, on the day of trial, they cannot even recognize their clients. For a prosecutor, trying a case against one of these lawyers is like shooting fish in a barrel. Thus, when these same prosecutors face lawyers who prepare their misdemeanor cases as if they were serious felonies, they are frequently caught entirely off-guard.

Coupled with this is the fact that any given misdemeanor case is just one of 100+ misdemeanors on the prosecutor's calendar. While I know my case inside out, have interviewed all my witnesses, and have been to the scene of the crime, the prosecutor may have only the most cursory understanding of her case. In fact, one of the reasons many misdemeanor cases are dismissed on the day of trial is that the prosecutor, having finally interviewed her witnesses, realizes her case is a bust.

Once I had a client who was charged with assaulting another young lady with a stick. The prosecutor had never spoken to his own complainant. On the day of trial, he spent a half-hour talking to her, came out with a sheepish expression, and announced that, while he still thought my client's story was a crock, his complainant, as he delicately put it, lacked something in credibility. This case had dragged on for almost two years. I had repeatedly tried to persuade prosecutors to drop the case. But it was not until the day of trial, with all my witnesses in court, with my color glossy prints in hand and my suppression motion about to be heard, that the government threw in the towel.

Felony practice is much, much different. Prosecutors often have case loads smaller than the ones we carry. They have grand jury transcripts in which they have deposed not only their own witnesses but many of mine. They have experienced, conscientious detectives doing their legwork. And they have the seasoning of 15 or 20 misdemeanor trials.

Sadly, many of the same incompetent attorneys picking up misdemeanor cases are also picking up felonies. Remarkable as it may seem, individuals with life offenses are often represented by lawyers who have done negligible preparation. It is fair to say that many individuals are now at Lorton Reformatory who, but for their attorneys, would not be there. This is not to say that these individuals are innocent, although a few probably are. It is to say that competent lawyers—who put on credible defenses, who prepare their witnesses to testify, who prepare their clients to testify, who subpoena defense witnesses, who file obvious and meritorious motions, who file sentencing memoranda with imaginative alternative sentencing schemes—often keep their clients on the street, clients who would be locked up had the luck of the draw given them one of these inadequate lawyers.

I became a public defender because I believe passionately in our system of justice, in the adversary system. Without a lawyer fighting with all of his strength to advocate for his client, without a lawyer as competent and able as the prosecutor, the system simply is not legitimate. I help make it legitimate and that is why I do what I do. Lawyers who do not care about their clients, who do not represent them competently, who do not provide even a shadow of effective assistance of counsel render the system null and void. They are an obscenity.

* * *

I am leaving PDS. I need more money to raise a growing family. (Have you not heard that refrain before?) I find myself burned out, a syndrome which I thought afflicted only other lawyers. I am tired of being a public defender. I am sick of representing so many bad people, though I will certainly miss the many good people I have helped. I am sick, in particular, of representing rapists. I am sick of being afraid to walk in my own parking lot yet helping people who mug citizens in other parking lots. I have lost much of the empathy I once had for my clients. It is time to go.

I also leave because I want to be a prosecutor. There are people in my office who could no more conceive of themselves as prosecutors than they can conceive of themselves as police officers. They consider prosecutors persecutors and could not possibly picture themselves trying to get someone locked up. I can. It is an imperfect world with imperfect solutions. Lorton is one of them.

I want to be a prosecutor because I want to be in a position where I can do good more of the time. As a public defender, I do good when I represent innocent persons. I do good when I represent guilty men who deserve a break. But I do not do good when I help bad men go free— except, that is, in the broad, philosophical sense that I have vindicated the judicial system and upheld our constitutional principles.

I am at a point right now where I need more than a philosophical construct, even one as noble as the Sixth Amendment. I want direct, not circumstantial, evidence that I am doing good, that I am doing justice.

I am not naive about being a prosecutor, though certainly I probably sound it. In my four years at PDS, I did as much prosecutorial
misconduct litigation as any attorney in the office. I know that
prosecutors sometimes mess up. So do public defenders. I know that a
prosecutor's obligation—to insure that justice is done to both victims
and defendants—is occasionally honored in the breach. On my book-
shelf, I count at least a half-dozen well-thumbed books in which prosecutors are charged with overreaching. In my own career at PDS, I
have seen prosecutors who were more interested in a conviction than in
doing justice and who were not beyond pulling a fast one.

But far more often, I have found my adversaries to be good and
decent men and women, genuinely trying to be fair. I have seen
enough to convince me that it will be an honor to be a prosecutor, that
representing the United States will be as great a privilege as it has
been to be entrusted with the representation of my clients.

*   *   *

Last week, I packed up my boxes, the last act of leave-taking.

Box upon box upon box, my own little cardboard monument to the
lives I have touched. I have represented a lot of people, hundreds and
hundreds and hundreds of them. And these people were not calm
when I knew them. They were desperate, in extremis, often hysterical,
though often numb. If you really want to know what it is like to be
needed, to be needed passionately, be a public defender.

My clients would not be stars in any solar system. But they were
stars in their own families; they were stars on the block. They were
the most important people they knew. And, either by a quirk of fate or
an act of faith, their lives were in my hands.

There are lawyers who draft billion-dollar contracts and there are
lawyers who breathe life into failing companies. There are lawyers
who negotiate for GM and there are lawyers who advise the President.
But none do more important work than a public defender. Because we
deal in liberty. And, more specifically, we deal in the liberty of our
clients. To our clients, we are a lifeline, a road to freedom. If we
screw up, if we are lazy, they lose and they lose big.

Before I came to the Public Defender Service, I worked in a public
interest law firm. I worked on huge, ambitious projects, projects that
affected whole states, projects that affected the country. It was good
work, work that needs to be done. But I rarely had that sense of
individual impact; I rarely had that sense that there was some one
person out there who was desperately depending upon me. For whom I
really, really counted. And that is why I came to PDS. To count. To
make a difference in individual lives. And maybe, if I was lucky, to be
able to say when I was through that I had saved some lives.

I am through now, and I can say it: I saved some lives. Of course, that is only part of the story. Many lives I did not save; many lives I could not save. But I did save some lives.

I kept a number of innocent men and women from going to prison. Will I ever do anything more significant than that? I helped people who needed help, people who *had* committed the crimes they were charged with but who did not deserve to go to prison or who did not deserve to spend the rest of their lives in prison. I earned the trust of men for whom trust comes hard.

But now it is over. I am leaving. As I packed up my boxes, I saw names that I had not thought about in years. Some names had innocently flitted from my mind; other names had been banished, the names of difficult and unpleasant clients whom I would not miss. I saw names that made me chuckle and names that made me feel good about myself and names that left me wondering wistfully what happened after we parted.

Some of my clients had more than one file. For a few clients, a point was reached where they began to view me as their in-house counsel. At that point, I would usually end the relationship. I would be no one's consigliere. I would be no client's insurance policy. But it was more than that. It was also the fact that, occasionally, you just burn out on a client. You burn out on particular clients long before you burn out on public defending. How many times can you ask the same judge to give the same client the same break? Maybe you can do it forever. But not forever with vigor, not forever with conviction and feeling. So, sometimes, I tell my clients, "This time I'll help you and that's it. You're no good for me but, more importantly, I'm no good for you." These are almost always the clients who once meant the most to me, for whom I shed blood, for whom I sweated. But that is just it: there is no more blood; there is no more sweat; certainly, there are no more tears. The well has run dry. Someone else will have to replenish it.

*   *   *

The saddest files were those of my juvenile clients who graduated, not from high school but from Juvenile Court, their adult files silently mocking my Juvenile Court efforts. Some files, after all, were testaments to failure.

As I packed up each box, I saw exactly where the last four years of my life had gone. I saw David Goldblum, an engaging kind of rogue, mortally offended at being arrested, charged with stealing a typewriter and fencing it. For more than 40 years, he had been buying and selling office equipment, a marginal sort of existence but probably legitimate. The arrest was an embarrassment. The best thing about David was his mother, a gentle, sweet old lady who insisted on splitting her tuna sandwich with me during the trial "to keep up your strength." Before the trial, David would call me almost daily for months on end, each day a new outrage on his mind. He would rail against the government, against the complainants, against the District of Columbia itself. He would make preposterous suggestions about his defense and threaten to get himself another lawyer if I would not go along with them. Repeatedly, I challenged him to do just that. He would calm down and we would begin anew. I liked David. He was filled with bluster but, really, he was just an anxious, frightened old man.

I saw Henry Goring. I spent a solid month of my life writing a brief for Henry which sought to convince the D.C. Court of Appeals that a moped was not a motorcycle under the unauthorized use of a vehicle statute. All things considered, a rather curious use of one's limited time on Earth. (Particularly since we lost.)

I saw Gary Hadley. Gary had repeatedly tried to convince me that the cashier had just handed him $50 for no reason at all and therefore he should go to trial on his robbery charges. I would not bite and, eventually, he concluded that no jury would either.

I saw Mack Kendricks, who was charged with the armed robbery of a man who had once been his friend. In the third day of trial, the case was mistried after I discovered that the complainant had been repeatedly paid witness fees illegally. Ultimately, the case was dismissed with prejudice. Mack was one nice guy, almost certainly innocent, almost certainly the victim of a falling out with the complainant. Getting him off was a pleasure.

I saw so very many clients in those boxes. Clients like Andy, whom I took with me on my first solo flight through a jury trial. He was acquitted (in spite of, not because of, me). Clients like Robert, a heroin addict for the past 20 years, who managed to get himself arrested, like clockwork, every few months on narcotics charges. I represented Robert for several years in a row. Our last meeting was in the cellblock. I had finally run out of rehabilitative programs. I had finally run out of arguments. Robert was a realist. He knew he would have to do some time. Over the years, I had saved him a lifetime of prison sentences. I could not save him this time.

And clients like Stanley Severn. I spent two weeks in trial with Stanley. I prepared him repeatedly to testify and put on a whale of a defense. Unbeknownst to me, my client was lying. He lied to me and he lied on the stand. And he was caught in his lie by a sharp prosecutor. Would you believe it, he was acquitted anyway.

Two days later, I was back before the same judge for another trial involving the same client. The judge was astonished to see my client again before him. I asked the court for a few weeks continuance. I wanted a jury panel which did not know Stanley and did not know the extent to which he was contributing to court congestion. The judge agreed to the continuance. As we began to leave, he drily noted that my client had made a wise decision in insisting on a trial by jury instead of a trial by judge.

* * *

I finished packing. The files will go to Suitland, Maryland, where they will be stored permanently. Some will be retrieved when my clients get arrested again. Most will never be seen again. That is strange in a way. Those files represent thousands of hours of work. And no one will ever look at them again. But, after all, why should anyone want to?

Nor will I ever see most of these clients again. For a brief period of time, I touched their lives and they touched mine. I am glad it happened. And I am glad it is over.

Discussion Questions

1. Randy Bellows describes occasions on which a defense attorney's investigation or cross-examination or argument to a complacent prosecutor or judge achieves a more just outcome than would result from a less adversarial system. But he also describes more troublesome aspects of the role of zealous advocate. Like most defense attorneys, he believes the adversary system requires:

    (a) trying to convince a jury that a police officer of fine reputation has fabricated a false confession and perjured himself to convict a man he knew might be innocent;

    (b) attempting to show by vigorous cross-examination and by direct testimony of the defendant that a woman who has probably been the victim of a vicious attempted rape had in fact, purposely or unconsciously, conveyed her consent to the defendant; and

    (c) making arguments to a jury about a quasi-scientific issue—the likelihood that a fingerprint found in the home of a victim was not that of the defendant—which a judge would find laughable.

Should a lawyer do these things?

2. Bellows discusses repeatedly and at length the decision whether the client should plead guilty or go to trial. But he never suggests an unwillingness to take a client he believes is guilty to trial. He tries to show clients how foolish their alibis will look on cross-examination. But he does not question the right of a client to present a story the attorney finds ridiculous. He acknowledges a tendency to work harder for the client he believes is innocent but regrets that tendency. Do you question any of these judgments? If so, on what basis?

3. On the other hand, Bellows does not give unlimited sway to the client's autonomy. He urges bringing pressure to bear on a client who, in the attorney's better informed view, is rejecting a desirable plea. He describes the

PDS ethic as an obligation to see that the client chooses the better deal when a favorable plea has been offered.

(a) How free does a client feel to reject strong persuasion by his attorney?

(b) What forms of self-interest can enter into the attorney's judgment and how serious are they for a large, well-run office? For a sole practitioner?

(c) What values is the defense attorney serving by taking this position and at what cost to other values?

4. Bellows expresses his increasing discomfort with the defense attorney's determined—and he believes wholly proper—effort to free dangerous people who may well do great harm again. Why does someone become a criminal defense attorney?

In an article entitled "Defending the Guilty,"[1] Barbara Babcock, a professor at Stanford Law School and a former public defender, offers five reasons:

The Garbage Collector's Reason. It is dirty work but someone must do it. We cannot have a functioning adversary system without a partisan for both sides. The defense counsel's job is no different from, and the work no more despicable than, that of a lawyer in a civil case who arranges, argues, and even orients the facts with only the client's interests in mind. . . . The civil libertarian tells us that the criminally accused are the representatives of us all. When their rights are eroded, the camel's nose is under and the tent may collapse on anyone. In protecting the constitutional rights of criminal defendants, we are only protecting ourselves.

The Legalistic or Positivist's Reason. Truth cannot be known. Facts are indeterminate, contingent, and in criminal cases, often evanescent. A finding of guilt is not necessarily the truth, but a legal conclusion arrived at after the role of the defense lawyer has been fully played. The sophist would add that it is not the duty of the defense lawyer to act as factfinder. Were she to handle a case according to her own assessment of guilt or innocence, she would be in the role of judge rather than advocate. Finally, there is a difference between legal and moral guilt; the defense lawyer should not let his apprehension of moral guilt interfere with his analysis of legal guilt. The example usually given is that of the person accused of murder who can respond successfully with a claim of self-defense. The accused may feel morally guilty but not be legally culpable. The oddsmaker chimes in that it is better that ten people go free than that one innocent be convicted.

The Political Activist's Reason. Most people who commit crimes are themselves the victims of horrible injustice. This statement is true generally because most of those accused of rape, robbery and murder are oppressed minorities. . . . Moreover, the conditions of imprisonment may impose violence far worse than that inflicted on the victim. A lawyer performs good work when he helps to prevent the imprisonment of the poor, the outcast, and minorities in shameful conditions.

---

[1] Babcock, *Defending the Guilty,* 32 Clev.St.L.Rev. 175, 177–78 (1983).

The Social Worker's Reason. Those accused of crime, as the most visible representatives of the disadvantaged underclass in America, will actually be helped by having a defender, notwithstanding the outcome of their cases. Being treated as a real person in our society and accorded the full panoply of rights and the measure of concern afforded by a lawyer can promote rehabilitation. Because the accused comes from a community, the beneficial effect of giving him his due will spread to his friends and relatives, decreasing their anger and alienation.

The Egotist's Reason. Defending criminal cases is more interesting than the routine and repetitive work done by most lawyers, even those engaged in what passes for litigation in civil practice. The heated facts of crime provide voyeuristic excitement. Actual court appearances, even jury trials, come earlier and more often in one's career than could be expected in any other area of law. And winning . . . has great significance because the cards are stacked for the prosecutor. To win as an underdog, and to win when the victory is clear—there is no appeal from a "Not Guilty" verdict—is sweet.

Which, if any, of these reasons do you think are valid? Which trouble you? Why?

5. Charles Ogletree, a defense attorney who worked with Randy Bellows in the Washington, D.C., public defenders office, shares some of Babcock's perspectives but focuses on two reasons why lawyers go into criminal defense work.

First, some people become criminal defenders because they love the challenge, are competitive by nature, and have unusual personal curiosity. They like the idea of representing the underdog, where the scales are tipped against them, the prosecutor has all the resources, and they have virtually none. They want to change the world. They are result oriented. Ogletree says that when these people begin to lose cases, as they inevitably do, they tend to blame their clients for the convictions, become "burned out," and look for other work.

Second, many people who go into criminal defense work are more oriented to process. They believe that the public defender plays an important role in the criminal defense process—that the criminal defense attorney is necessary to preserve our system of government and our civil liberties. These lawyers are motivated by a belief in their clients' rights, do not prejudge their clients, push the government as far as possible, and are satisfied with the result if the cases were adequately prepared and presented. At that point the lawyers have made the government "keep its promises," and have done the system a service.

Professor Alan Dershowitz of Harvard Law School echoes Ogletree's perspective. He sees the role of a criminal defense attorney as crucial to our system of justice and civilized government. In his book, *The Best Defense,* Dershowitz asserts that "[p]art of the reason we are as free as we are, and why our criminal justice system retains a modicum of rough justice despite its corruption and unfairness, is our adversary process: the process by which every defendant may challenge the government. . . . [D]efending the guilty and the despised—even freeing some of them—is a small price to pay for our liberties."

Both Ogletree and Dershowitz stress the first reason given by Babcock for protecting the rights of the accused: that we must protect their rights in order to protect our own civil rights and liberties. Most of us would agree with that perspective, especially when combined with the argument that every person who is potentially innocent has a right to be defended, no matter how small the probability of innocence.

There is another way to make this point. The attorney who feels sure her client is guilty is generally basing that judgment either on evidence that will be available to the jury or on revelations produced by inviting the trust in confidentiality of the defendant and his friends. (Sometimes, far more rarely, the defense attorney will simply discover relevant facts that the prosecution overlooks.) Without more than what the jury will know, there is no justification for the attorney "second guessing" the jury; but using the defendant's invited trust to the disadvantage of the client without prior warning is a flagrant betrayal on which we should not base our system. The only defensible choice is zealously to defend those the attorney believes or even knows to be guilty or else to warn each suspect not to rely on the attorney preserving his confidences. The latter alternative would bring about a frightening change in relations between citizens and the state.

Why then, does Bellows have such ambivalence about his work?

6. Ogletree argues that the work of criminal defense attorneys is no different from that of corporate defense counsel who defend companies such as Union Carbide in the Bhopal case (thousands of innocent people were killed from a chemical leak at the Union Carbide plant in Bhopal, India) and SmithKline (it marketed the anti-hypertensive drug Selacryn without reporting deaths and adverse reactions among patients who took the drug during experimental trials; at least 34 deaths and more than 500 cases of severe liver and kidney damage were attributed to the use of the drug).

Is there a difference between criminal and corporate defense attorneys? Is it the fact that in criminal defense work the crimes are generally intentional and in corporate defense cases such as the two described above the alleged wrongs are "merely" negligent? Is it the nature of the act itself, i.e. the face-to-face, direct confrontation of an aggressor with his victim which occurs only with the street criminal? Is it the fact that we can identify more closely with the corporate executives at Union Carbide and the four middle-aged doctors at SmithKline than we can with the typical defendant in a criminal case? Or is it that we think that street criminals are more likely to repeat the offensive action while we think that corporate executives, once shown the error of their ways, will reform?

7. The real dilemma for Randy Bellows centers on this last difference between corporate and criminal defense work: Bellows finds poignantly real the notion that these people are inherently dangerous and that by getting them "off," criminal defense attorneys are putting them back on the street where they can commit new crimes.

Alan Dershowitz does not apologize for (or feel guilty about) helping to let a murderer go free—even though he realizes that some day one of his clients may kill again. He analogizes the role of a criminal defense attorney to that of a surgeon who saves the life of a patient who recovers and later kills an innocent victim. Is the analogy appropriate?

The dilemma faced by Bellows demonstrates that society pays a price in security for its insistence that the government prove its case beyond a reasonable doubt. The person who is expected to exact that societal price is the criminal defense attorney. The problem for a young lawyer considering a career in defense work is how to reconcile a professional life that may involve trying day after day to win freedom for defendants he or she believes are dangerous with a personal life in which friends, relatives, and law abiding fellow citizens are potential victims of the defense attorney's success.

8. Bellows finally concludes that "I want to be a prosecutor because I want to be in a position where I can do good more of the time." Is this a matter of personal preference—of comfort and discomfort of the attorney—or is it an argument about who contributes more to the social good? If the latter, is the argument correct?

D. Lawyers for Wall Street

M & A: The Conoco Takeover *

If anyone had told Martha Solinger the day she graduated from Georgetown University Law Center in 1980 that in less than one year she would play an active role in one of the world's largest corporate takeovers, she would have doubled over with laughter. And if that prescient someone had informed the 25–year–old graduate that she would labor 45 out of 47 straight days her first "real" summer at a New York law firm on securities litigation—and love every minute of it—her smiles would have flashed to a look of skepticism, if not outright scorn. "I had that liberal orientation, you know, same as lots of others at law school," she says now from her quarters at Dewey, Ballantine, Bushby, Palmer & Wood. "I thought all of this corporate litigation was a lot of crap." Outside of a course in corporations and another in tax, until she came to Dewey, Ballantine, her only knowledge of Wall Street came from a subway map of Lower Manhattan.

So when she entered her office that early day in May 1981, Martha Solinger did not automatically turn to the back section of *The Wall Street Journal* to scan for "tombstone" ads, those squared-off bits of somber block print that serve as the corporate world's billboard of just-hatched deals. If she had, she might have spotted one curious notice. A pipsqueak Canadian oil company named Dome Petroleum Ltd. announced that it was attempting to buy a piece of the ninth largest U.S. oil concern, Conoco, by purchasing some of the company's common stock. Maybe it is just as well that her mind was not drawn. For all but a handful of cognoscenti, the offer seemed absurd, sort of like Calgary declaring war on the United States and demanding Washington, Oregon, and the rest of the Great Northwest, not a battle you expected to hear a lot from that summer—let alone be inducted to fight in.

Dome, after all, had made it known that it was not really trying to buy Conoco. It just wanted to twist Conoco's arm into surrendering its Canadian subsidiary, Hudson's Bay Oil & Gas, to Dome. But in corporate takeover wars, looks beguile. The Dome offer signaled the beginning of a fight that would eventually conscript 300 lawyers, spill millions of dollars in legal fees, and crunch hundreds of thousands of billable hours before it would come to a truce at the end of the summer.

---

* This case is based on journalistic accounts of the Conoco takeover dispute and on interviews with some of the lawyers who participated.

How did the fate of a company with 41,000 employees worldwide and $18 billion in revenues come to rest in the hands of people like first-year associate Solinger and other associates and partners at law firms around the country? That is one question this case study seeks to answer. Along the way the case looks for answers to a few other questions, including: (1) What exactly do lawyers do—and not do—in these takeovers? (2) Does anyone benefit from their frantic activities? (3) Are they worth the fees these companies lavish on them?—and perhaps the most important, considering the broken evenings, canceled dinners, littered vacation plans, sleepless nights, and tension-filled days, all for the bidding of large corporations—(4) why do so many do it, and do it so proudly?

Long Hot Summer

The last thing Conoco Chairman Ralph Bailey wanted to do that May day was sell to the upstarts from Dome a big piece of the company he had spent his life helping to build. But unlike all other decisions he had reached over the years involving Conoco's assets, he knew this one might not be his to make. By offering to buy up some of Conoco's stock at a premium, a sum higher than the current market price, Dome was bypassing Bailey's authority over Conoco and appealing directly to the company's shareholders.

Wall Street professionals dub this move a "hostile" tender offer. The term, however, refers only to relations between the chief executives of the predator and prey. If you happen to own Conoco shares when the company is trading at $49.875, as it was that day, you probably do not harbor much hostility toward someone who offers to pay you $65 for some of those very same shares. Most stocks move up or down in quarter- and eighth-of-a-dollar increments. The Dome offer represented a chance to make a quick 30 percent killing for all stockholders, especially the pension and mutual fund managers who, through their investments in Conoco common stock, were the real majority "owners" of the company. For most shareholders, who bet on a company's stock the way touts wager on horses—trying to pick the one with the best possible payoff, not the one that is the prettiest, or the most kindly managed—"hostile" certainly is a misnomer.

But that is not the way Conoco executives viewed it. Until May 6, the company's status as a publicly held corporation meant little more than having to pay lawyers to file reports to the Securities and Exchange Commission, hosting a noisy shareholder meeting once a year, and sending out a batch of splashy yearbooks annually. Executives answered only to each other and to the board of directors.

After May 6, the roles suddenly changed. Everyone from the widows and orphans who had held the stock for years to the quick-buck speculators who had snapped up Conoco on takeover rumors before the offer was made became the real decision-makers. It is as if army generals suddenly faced elections for the first time, and the other side was offering privates money to vote against them.

Company officers who work their way up the corporate ladder may meet this kind of challenge to their authority once in their lives, if ever. They cannot turn to their in-house counsel. Their lawyers may be schooled well in oil and gas, as were Conoco's, but they know little about takeovers. So executives must turn to outsiders, corporate lawyers and investment bankers, to figure out what to do.

There were more than 650,000 lawyers and 14,500 banks in the United States, but only a handful of each knew enough about corporate mergers to be of use to Conoco's management at that moment. Chief executives know all about this scarcity. About 300 of them, including at that time Conoco, pay one law firm, Skadden, Arps, Slate, Meagher & Flom, a retainer of between $25,000 and $150,000 per year just to be sure the New York law firm will be on their side if an offer strikes. So Bailey's first move, naturally, was to call Joseph Flom, Skadden's leader and one of the best-known merger and acquisition (M & A) specialists in the country. The 60–year–old lawyer agreed to meet with Conoco's management the next day.

Besides Skadden, Conoco turned to its regular counsel, Dewey, Ballantine, which had performed the large bulk of Conoco's corporate work over the years. Leonard Larrabee, a 53–year–old senior partner at Dewey, and Conoco's attorney at the firm, learned of the troubles facing his largest client when Conoco's in-house counsel phoned him at the Yale Club in midtown Manhattan, where he was attending the firm's monthly dinner.

Larrabee knew that Conoco had retained Skadden. But in takeover situations the usually resolute lines between the personnel of each firm blur into one united team. Larrabee instantly realized that Russel "Cap" Beatie, Jr., a fiery securities litigation partner, might spur some creative thinking. "I left the firm dinner, came back to the downtown office, picked up my papers and got hold of Cap," recalls Larrabee. "I had to track him down at a Ranger hockey game." Both agreed to journey to Conoco's Stamford, Connecticut, headquarters for the next day's meeting.

Legal takeover specialists work in tandem with investment bankers in corporate merger practice. These bankers do not solicit deposits or handle checking accounts, like savings and loans or commercial banks. They help companies raise money by structuring and selling a company's stock and bonds. Only about a half-dozen firms, all in New York, have carved out expertise in large scale M & A work. Like law firms, top M & A talent is scarce. Conoco chose Morgan Stanley, Conoco's regular investment banker for a host of financings in past years. Morgan Stanley, as is the custom in all takeovers, immediately called in its own regular counsel, Davis Polk & Wardwell, to advise the firm on the matter. Davis Polk's Peter Bator, until his death in 1984 one of the firm's leading corporate lawyers, was dispatched to Stamford to join Morgan's, Skadden's, and Dewey's representatives.

In an era when it seems that no company is too large to be swallowed and the likes of U.S. Steel and Texaco are taking buyout precautions, it is difficult to imagine now what that first meeting between Conoco and the experts must have been like. Even as recently as 1981, executives of companies on the scale of Conoco did not worry about golden parachutes, shark repellants, and all the other merger paraphernalia that make up take-over defense. Conoco's brass did not suspect that Dome's offer to buy 20 percent of its shares through a tender offer would amount to much. And they certainly figured that at least one of the hired guns in the room would be able to shoot down Dome's offer before it did any damage. But that judgment, recalled Bator in an interview shortly before his death, is precisely what lawyers and investment bankers get paid to worry about.

From the beginning, Morgan's corporate finance people, who, as part of their job, try to predict how shareholders will react to the prices of different offers, feared that Dome's offer might provoke disaster for their client. They fretted even though Dome's stated goal was the much less ambitious plan to swap a piece of Conoco for its real target, Conoco's Canadian subsidiary.

"Morgan Stanley advised us that unless something else happened, something unforeseen, then Dome Petroleum was likely to get far more of Conoco's stock than was subscribed for," Bator recalled. "There was a great deal of skepticism about that advice in Conoco headquarters that day. There was general disbelief in those circles that Morgan could be right in its evaluation. They [Conoco's managers] couldn't believe that they would be held in such low esteem by their stockholders. They still suffered from a romantic illusion that they had loyal institutional shareholders. They had wined and dined them, even taken them out on fishing trips, and, on the whole, they had done a very good job at shareholder relations. They assumed that people wouldn't tender for less than the value of the company"—a value Conoco's management pegged at much higher than the current market price and substantially higher than Dome's $65 offer.

Nor could the lawyers gathered that day allow Conoco's management to believe that even the best of hired guns would necessarily

triumph over their rivals, especially if the shootout were to take place
in a federal court. "In tender offer litigation, members of the target
company invariably sue with the hope that it will strike a quick death
blow to the potential acquirer and win the whole deal," said one of the
key litigators on the case. "But anybody with any brain at all advises
the board that the likelihood of winning a knockout punch is negligible.
Having given them that advice, you go forward and do your best."

With that sobering wisdom dispensed, the lawyers dissolved their
own firm allegiances and re-combined in corporate and litigation ranks,
with Skadden's Flom heading up the former, and Dewey's Beatie
running the latter. Both teams shared one goal: keeping Conoco
independent by finding a way to beat back Dome's 20 percent offer.
Each used his respective tools honed through years of practice. For
Flom, that meant trying to negotiate, perhaps with another Canadian
company that might be interested in purchasing Conoco's northern
subsidiary, or, if things proved as dire as Morgan Stanley's prognosis,
with Dome itself, trying to hammer out better terms than Dome had
offered already. For Beatie, that meant suing to stop the offer, not so
much to defeat Dome in court, but more to buy time for the investment
bankers to create a better deal.

These attorneys approach their work differently. Flom is solitary.
Other than Bator, a self-described sounding board for Flom's ideas
during all of the Conoco events, and Robert Greenhill, the senior
Morgan managing director on the deal, Flom tended to seek his own
counsel. "I operate a little peculiarly," says Flom about his methods.
"I go to these meetings by myself. I don't bring along a lot of others."
How does he communicate information back to other members of his
firm, let alone with teammates from other firms on deals? "Badly," he
says with a laugh. "But people here have a way of finding out what is
going on. It filters down." The loner approach is not all Flom's doing.
Corporate work on large mergers at first entails concentrated meetings
either with high-level executives in individual strategy sessions or in
large board meetings. Neither lends itself to armies of associates, says
Flom.

But litigation, on the other hand, is exactly the opposite: it is
people intensive. Staffing a big securities law case excites Cap Beatie,
who has since left Dewey to open his own firm. He likes to choose and
discard associates as if he were in an aggressive schoolyard pick-up
game. For this matter Beatie drew on some of his more experienced
associates and, as he remembers now, he decided to dip deep into the
ranks, all the way down to a first-year associate, someone who had
already showed sparkle on two earlier assignments: Martha Solinger.

A Game of Low–Percentage Arguments

Solinger's view from the bottom up provides a unique vision of what a junior litigator can—and cannot—do in a takeover battle. No matter how savvy a first-year associate may be, her role is decidedly small-picture. For example, Solinger knew from the beginning that she would not be the lawyer who would depose Dome's flamboyant chairman, Jack Gallagher, with the hope of tripping him up, getting him to spill out something that could later come to haunt him in court. That assignment, grilling the top manager of the acquiring firm, perhaps the most coveted in a takeover battle, typically goes to the partners in charge of litigation, as it did here. Nor would she necessarily be deciding which arguments would be made, once they got into court. That would be the province of Beatie, with input from Flom.

But finding the right court to sue Gallagher—that is a matter that fits an associate's research skills. Beatie asked Solinger to find out which state, of all the states in which Conoco operated, would have the most favorable anti-takeover statute. There they would make their first stand. "We knew that most of the states' statutes wouldn't be upheld if Dome were to challenge them," she says now. "They would probably be found to be unconstitutional or to be preempted by federal law. But I started reading all of the statutes, and you could tell that some looked better than others for us. I thought the statute in Louisiana (where Conoco had a large refinery) looked particularly good because, unlike most of the vague anti-takeover statutes of the day, this one was specific, and it was directed at natural resources, oil and gas, an area traditionally regulated by states. That was perfect for us, and it gave us hope."

Solinger informed the higher-ups of the good news and got to work plumbing what Conoco would need to fight Dome's preliminary injunction motion (which, if granted, would block Conoco's efforts to utilize the state's anti-takeover statute) in Louisiana federal court. She produced a discussion level draft that was considered by mid-level associates and partners at both Skadden and Dewey.

All agreed that they needed more information, and Solinger arranged with Kurt Koegler, a Skadden partner, to fly to New Orleans to meet with state regulators to find out if their reading of the statutes was correct. "They had spoken together constantly by phone all week," recalled one lawyer who knew both attorneys. "But it wasn't until they got on the plane together that day that Kurt learned that Martha was only a first-year associate, just out of law school. He just fainted dead when he learned she was so young. But they worked great together."

Solinger said that after their day-long meetings they returned and decided to write two briefs, one saying that they were right because of the law and the other saying they were right because the regulators agreed with them. They found they needed additional support for their arguments and jetted back to Louisiana for more affidavits. They ended up going back to Louisiana not just once but twice that week. "I went back three times in five days altogether," she recalls. It was all for naught. Conoco lost the motion to block the merger—Dome's motion to dismiss was granted.

In most legal disputes, when a federal judge boots you out of court summarily, you have to question whether it is not worth caving in and telling your client to forget it. But, as one defense litigator explained, this defeatist attitude does not even get an airing in takeover battles. "From the viewpoint of the target, this is a life or death situation. People who run companies in these situations will pay anything to anyone who can give them hope. Chief executive officers see this as a fight to the death. Consequently, anything with even the most remote chance of success is done." Takeover litigation, the lawyer said, "is not a game of high percentage arguments. Don't get me wrong. It is not that you are filing totally idiotic lawsuits. It is just that you are more likely to make an argument that would not hold up in some other situations."

That logic brought Conoco's lawyers to the next confrontation—Oklahoma, another state with massive Conoco operations and one in which Conoco's defenders were hoping to find a judge who would be open-minded about enjoining a takeover for disclosure reasons, a plea judges in the securities-litigation-weary northeast look upon with increasing skepticism.

This time Solinger was assigned a question that read like something out of a corporations class hypothetical. She was asked to research why Dome should be allowed to purchase 20 percent of Conoco, become its largest shareholder, and then act contrary to its newfound fiduciary responsibilities to Conoco's shareholders by cutting a deal that benefitted only Dome's interests. Did Dome owe a fiduciary duty not to act in its self-interest by foisting its opinions on the rest of Conoco's shareholders?

"It was like *Perlman v. Feldmann*," * she says, citing that venerable corporations class warhorse. "We ended up phrasing it in disclosure language, saying that the deal would not be arms-length. Dome had a particular intention, but had not disclosed it. It was sort of a bizarre claim," she says. And for that reason it was not pushed hard by local counsel in court and merited only a couple of pages in the brief.

---

* *Perlman v. Feldmann,* 219 F.2d 173 (2d Cir.1955), *cert. denied,* 349 U.S. 952 (1955).

Instead, Conoco pushed arguments questioning Dome's ability to pay for the acquisition without running afoul of Federal Reserve margin rules. "We proved pretty conclusively that Dome's debt would increase dramatically, and the company wouldn't be able to handle it," one of the defense lawyers said. Nevertheless, none of the arguments found favor with Oklahoma federal judge Lee West, and he sent everyone packing to New York in a hurry. It was a judgment that still has a key defense litigator stewing. "The trial judge took what I consider to be a knee-jerk attitude of many federal courts these days and said, 'We don't want to interfere with tender offers. Let the shareholders vote and just tell me if there is anything grossly misleading. If not, so long.' "

Another defender pointed out that Conoco's arguments that day have been borne out by subsequent events. "At the time the company was practically insolvent, but its bankers kept saying 'how much more money do you want?' " the lawyer said. Those optimistic bankers and heady talk of oil cascading to $40 or $50 a barrel on new shortage fears had Dome's stock selling for about $20 a share at the time. Not much after the Conoco deal, Conoco lawyers' doomsday scenario came true for the Canadians. The company went broke, could not meet its interest payments, and the stock plummeted to $3. Dome exists now only because of Canadian government intervention. "I feel vindicated about it everyday," says Solinger.

Meanwhile, the corporate team was faring no better. "Because Conoco's management was skeptical about the Dome thing as a major threat, I am not sure that efforts to find an alternative solution were pursued as hard as possible," recalled Bator. "Our activities at this stage were basically sitting in on the councils of war, seeing what interest could be elicited in finding a buyer for Hudson's Bay," he continued. "I spent a lot of time in Canada doing a lot of work with oil companies, hoping to interest them. We looked at the obvious [acquirers], anyone who could have an interest, and made presentations to them. But Conoco wanted too much from any prospective buyer. All that can be said of these efforts now is that they were too little, too late. We saw it is a real threat that Dome could buy 25 to 30 percent of Conoco. And if the offer was oversubscribed, then Gallagher would reserve the right to acquire real control of the company. The scarey part of all of this is that Dome was riding terribly high at the time. I thought fair warning had been given, but it was not really believed. Conoco, in other words, was on the thin edge of being bought by Dome Petroleum."

The Seagram Caper

Morgan Stanley's view of what shareholders would do, and not that of Conoco's management, proved prescient. When the tender expiration date was reached, Dome, which had set out to acquire only 20 percent of Conoco, ended up with 52.9 percent of the company's shares, an amount equal to control. But because of the structure of its offer, Dome would have to revise its agreement before it could begin to purchase any of the tendered shares in excess of 20 percent. As the bad news set in with Conoco's management, the lawyers and bankers reached the conclusion that it was time to make a deal with Dome.

Speed was paramount, because the over-subscription of Dome's offer left 32.9 percent of Conoco's stock floating free, available for anyone who was willing to offer a price slightly higher than Dome's. That loose block could be used as a start to buy up the rest of Conoco before Dome could arrange the credit to do so itself.

At any given moment there are lots of companies with millions of dollars in cash that managers do not want to pour back into their own companies or disburse as dividends to their shareholders. Often it is because they feel they can get a better return on their money from an investment in another industry.

Joseph E. Seagram & Sons, a behemoth Canadian distiller, was one of those companies. Flush with $2.3 billion in cash from the disposition of an oil and gas property, it was prowling for coal companies when Dome's all-too-successful bid was made. Seagram's management moved swiftly to find out if Conoco would make a deal with them rather than Dome. And so the second round, "the Seagram Caper," as Bator called it, began.

It is not easy to reconstruct what happened next, not because no one remembers, but because everybody remembers differently, and many remembrances are couched in bitterness. Several points, however, are clear.

The first is that Seagram came to Stamford at the end of May with the idea of making some sort of deal to purchase a substantial block of Conoco shares directly from Conoco or from the market. The offer was meant to be "friendly," in the merger sense of the word, meaning not unilateral, but with the blessing of Conoco management. We are sure of that, in part, because Seagram hired Goldman, Sachs & Co. as its investment banker for the negotiations and Goldman is the only investment bank with a stated policy against doing hostile takeovers. We also know, however, that at the same time Conoco was sitting down in discussions with Seagram, Conoco's officers were also dealing with Dome and a third company, Cities Service, which it hoped to acquire so as to make Conoco too big to be taken over.

Seagram, on Saturday, May 30, proposed that it buy 35 percent of Conoco's stock, and agreed not to purchase any more—a standstill agreement—for a set number of years. Conoco countered that perhaps 25 percent was a more suitable figure. Before an agreement could be reached, Bailey suspended discussions until the next day. Unbeknownst to Seagram, Bailey then flew to Cities Service headquarters in Oklahoma to prospect for a better deal with that midwest oil company. "We knew that Ralph Bailey—apparently on his own—was playing footsie with Cities," says Bator. "But it was fairly clear that if Dome stayed around, then Seagrams would too."

With Friends Like These . . .

On Sunday, May 31, Seagram's officers were ready to make a deal. So were the officers of Dome. Bailey, who flew back late the night before, placed Seagram's officials in one room and Dome's in another. Flom and Greenhill worked the two different rooms, moving quickly from one prospective suitor to another. The halls between the two suites were lined with associates, both lawyers and bankers, most of whom remained in the dark about the discussions that surrounded them.

"You could tell that Flom and Greenhill were doing a tag-team," said one associate who spent the weekend waiting for board meetings to break up. "But you didn't have much of an idea of what was going on." While Conoco officials debated the very existence of their corporation, the associates outside did their very best to stay awake and beat the tedium. "We played endless hours of liars' poker," said one, referring to a makeshift poker game based on the serial numbers of dollar bills. "We would do anything to keep ourselves busy while we waited for these people to reach a decision."

The hold-up? As Bator explains, "The basic problem was schizophrenia in Conoco on the whole relationship with Seagram. They were needed and essential if Dome stayed in and tried to buy. But if [Conoco] could get rid of Dome as a stockholder, then obviously Seagram's role as a preferred majority shareholder didn't seem that marvelous."

The resolution came later that Sunday when Conoco agreed to trade its subsidiary to Dome in return for the 20 percent of the stock Dome had acquired and $245 million in cash. The move immediately cooled negotiations between Seagram and Conoco about the remaining large block of shares up for grabs.

Seagram still put forward its friendly standstill offer. But with the Cities option maturing, Conoco could afford to put Seagram on hold. When, two weeks later, the Cities deal became a real possibility, thus freeing Conoco from its schizophrenic paralysis, the Conoco board of directors rejected the Seagram bid. At the same meeting Conoco's board took action to protect Bailey's job with a golden parachute. No matter what happened to Conoco, Bailey would get his current annual salary of $637,766 until 1989. But if he decided he could not work well with whoever his new boss might be, he could walk out of his job and get all of the money due—$5 million—in one chunk.

After the Seagram rejection, Dewey partner Larrabee recalls: "We began working around the clock to hammer out the Cities Service matter." But they misjudged Seagram's response to their actions. One day after its rejection at the hands of Conoco's board, Seagram began buying Conoco's stock in the open market. Trading activity was so great that, on Friday June 19, the New York Stock Exchange stopped trading and demanded that Conoco offer an explanation about what was going on with its stock.

The company complied with a bland statement explaining that it had received an offer from a U.S. subsidiary of a foreign corporation to purchase its shares, and that it was holding preliminary discussions about a possible merger with a "major corporation." Neither Seagram nor Cities Service was mentioned.

Cities and Conoco steamed toward a deal that night. Both sides agreed to a stock-for-stock swap with the arrangement hinging on the companies' current stock prices the next day. As the finishing touches were being applied, Seagram struck like a lightning bolt. "I was working on the press release to announce the merger," recalls Larrabee, "when someone rushed in with the news from the stock ticker that Seagram was making a hostile bid for Conoco." Conoco's stock price jumped immediately in reaction to the news, thus scuttling the Cities deal because the stock for stock pricing ratio was now hopelessly distorted. "It got put on the sideburner," said Larrabee. And it never moved to the front again.

There is still much speculation about why Seagram took its unilateral plunge. It had pledged not to go hostile to both Conoco and its investment banker, who subsequently resigned from the deal in accordance with its policy not to do hostile takeovers. One reason given at the time was that Seagram's management felt taken in by Conoco's behind-the-back negotiations with Cities. Board meeting minutes released later as part of discovery reflected that sentiment.

Bator, for one, says he felt that the lawyers and bankers on his side simply played too much hardball. "I think Seagram was pressured too hard," he recalled. "If Seagram hadn't been strung along, would they have considered an unfriendly tender? That's relatively unlikely. They were played for a chump. The terms Conoco wanted were simply too onerous. It would have been a nonsensical deal for [Seagram]. I believe now that if Seagram had not been pushed to extremes in the deal then [they] wouldn't have acted like this. Clearly it's the biggest single reason why Conoco was unable to stay independent."

Flom quickly dismisses Bator's history of the event. He notes one unassailable truth: Seagram would later agree to the same sort of deal that Bator said was too tough for them to accept with Conoco. "It was the Conoco directors that didn't want to do it," Flom reminds about the breakdown that led Seagram to go hostile.

Conoco's March to the Sea

Up until Seagram's surprise attack, Conoco's defensive team had waged a restrained war, reflecting the client's belief that the 25th largest industrial concern in the country ultimately would not succumb to an acquirer. But Seagram's $2.5 billion bid to purchase 35 million Conoco shares at $73 per share (approximately 40.7 percent of all shares outstanding) changed all that. Now the defenders were unleashed, and younger lawyers got to see first-hand why companies fall over one another to retain Joe Flom.

With lawyers from Dewey and Skadden waiting for orders, Flom ticked off idea after idea about how Conoco could either stop Seagram or temporarily derail the company until Morgan Stanley's people could come up with a more friendly suitor. Some of the more promising tactics that came to Flom's mind immediately, associates say, included:

- possible violations of state statutes that forbid wholesale liquor sellers such as Seagram from owning alcoholic beverage retailers, such as Conoco, which sold liquor at some of its gas stations;
- possible damages to Conoco's extensive network of foreign oil contracts because of a merger with Seagram (Seagram's chief business, liquor, found no favor with abstinent Moslems, and Seagram's boss, Edgar Bronfman, was president of the World Jewish Congress and a long-time supporter of Israel); and
- congressional disapproval of a transaction that would allow Canadians to raid American natural resources while the Canadians were erecting barriers to American entry into their markets.

How did these ideas, normally the product of several days of thinking, germinate so quickly in Flom's mind? "First of all," he answers, "those ideas don't come from the sky. I've got a little bit of experience and I do a lot of listening to clients. The clients, you see, know their businesses far better than you will get to know them during the short time you are on these matters. So if you listen to them—

instead of them just listening to you—they will tell you what you can use. You don't know all of the implications of the merger like they do. You find out some of your best ideas from them. But not one of these is like an apple that falls from the sky and hits you on the head. That's not the way it works." Anybody, he insists, can come up with winning ideas in a short time. But in takeovers, the winners "come up with them in 15 minutes."

Flom's quarter of an hour's worth of ideas did not take long to put in place. Within a short time, *The Wall Street Journal* ran a story about letters from the governments of Dubai—an oil-rich state in the United Arab Emirates—and Norway containing threats of oil supply cutoffs if Seagram were to take an interest in Conoco. Hearings soon opened in the House of Representatives about Canadian ownership. Representatives questioned whether Canadians should be allowed to bid on federal leases.

Meanwhile, Skadden and Dewey people went to work trying to employ "tied house" statutes—state laws designed to keep wholesalers from competing with retailers—to stop Seagram. Finding out which states had the strongest tied-house statutes was a perfect assignment for an eager associate, and once again Solinger drew it. "There were at least 20 states to start," she says. Once they were isolated she and other associates corralled local counsel in each state to check up on the possibilities. "Many statutes fizzled out quickly, as the local lawyers said, 'forget it, they won't hold up,'" she says. But five states looked good: Florida, Alabama, Iowa, Missouri, and North Carolina. Solinger took charge of keeping track of the potential litigation or regulatory activity in each state.

While Conoco's defense team was placing these indirect roadblocks, the litigators also attacked Seagram's hostile move head-on in a federal district court in New York. Before Judge Edward Weinfeld, Conoco sought $1 billion in damages and a temporary restraining order blocking Seagram from purchasing any shares. Beatie pressed three contentions: Seagram broke its word by going hostile; the Canadian company's actions caused Conoco to lose a good business opportunity in its scuttled merger with Cities Service; and a Seagram takeover would raise various disclosure claims, including the fact that Seagram had not informed shareholders that its move would violate the tied-house statutes in states across the country.

Shopping the Company

At the same time Beatie was preparing to file his suit, efforts by the corporate half of Conoco's defense team were beginning to bear fruit. From the moment that the Conoco fracas began brewing, Morgan Stanley people started doing what they do best: valuation studies of the company's worth. Most companies fighting hostile bids hope things never get to the stage where these studies have to be used. A company must lay its soul bare to the investment bankers, only to have the information turn up in the hands of any company, including rivals, that might have an interest in purchasing the target.

The value study had another purpose, more central to law than to business. It is the document that corporate directors rely on when they assess the price of a tender offer with an eye toward its possible endorsement or rejection. For directors, who are the natural targets of suits by disgruntled shareholders if they reject a potential acquirer's price as too low, the valuation study and the quality of the name on that survey may be the only protection against a lawsuit. Conoco's board members knew that they had to be sensitive to such charges. Even though 11 out of 15 of the board members were "independent" (they had other jobs and were not salaried executives of Conoco), so many executives fight scorched earth battles to stay in office that almost all directors are wary of simply rejecting an offer with the usual "not in the shareholders' interests" excuse.

The valuation study showed that, without much doubt, the value of Conoco's assets exceeded $100 per share. Thus, even though Seagram's $73-a-share offer might look good to shareholders who bought in at a much lower price, the offer looked much too low to Conoco's directors. Morgan's study also showed another problem: the fine print of the offer. As is the case with most tender offers, the actual share price bandied about—in this case $73—had little to do with what shareholders might get after the smoke cleared. Seagram was not offering to buy all of the shares, just 41 percent, enough to get control of the company and no more. If Seagram were offered everybody's shares, all stockholders would have their shares "pro-rated," meaning that Seagram would purchase only 41 percent of their shares. The rest would be returned to the market, at who knows what price—certainly much lower than the $73 premium Seagram was willing to pay, and possibly as low as the pre-Dome price of $50. That boded poorly for the 600 institutions that owned 62 percent of the company's stock, and it was those stockholders, among others, that the directors were paid to protect. With this information in hand, the Board again rejected a Seagram offer.

With that turndown, Morgan's people were free to "shop the company," Wall Street parlance for a corporate firesale. Despite Conoco's giant size, investment bankers know that there is almost always a buyer for a profitable company. Morgan had shopped enough companies in the past to know that it must do it scientifically so as not to overlook potential buyers. Using a sophisticated computer filled with information from just about every company in the world, Morgan analysts began winnowing. Which companies had enough assets to command a credit line big enough to swallow Conoco? Plug in a minimum asset number. Which companies would not suffer from earnings dilution if they printed up stock to make the purchase? Plug in earnings per share data. Which companies had such strong cash flow that they would not blink at shelling out billions? Insert a cash flow. Once programmed with these kinds of data, the computer can spit out a list of potential buyers. Morgan's people could then pitch Conoco in the same way that any salesperson offers his or her wares— except this purchase would come with a multi-billion dollar pricetag.

At the same time Morgan was drawing up its list, Conoco's chairman was getting discreet inquiries on his own. One of them, according to a prospectus filed later, was from the chairman of Du Pont, the nation's largest chemical company and an industrial concern with assets about equal to Conoco's. Du Pont said it just wanted to know if Conoco needed help. It was the beginning of a $7.54 billion shotgun marriage.

The Best Seat in the House

July Fourth weekend for most is a celebration, three days of picnics, barbecues, and fireworks in the midst of a hot summer. Unless you worked on Conoco. During those three days, meetings often began before 8 a.m. and never quit before midnight. Beach plans, summer houses, and in Peter Bator's case even his own birthday party became casualties (although the *Journal* reported several days later that Bator had managed to drop in to the festivities for ten minutes). The only concession to the holiday: "we got to wear jeans," says Solinger.

As if the near round-the-clock Conoco dealings were not enough for most mortals, the irrepressible Flom was negotiating another acquisition simultaneously, as counsel for Texasgulf in its talks with acquirer Société Nationale Elf Acquitane. Fortunately, the shuttle was not too arduous; Texasgulf shared the same industrial park quarters with Conoco.

And the spirit of the Fourth was not totally missing. "I had the best seat in the house for the Macy's fireworks," says Skadden partner Richard Easton. Unfortunately for him, it was from the 57th floor of One Chase Manhattan Plaza, in the offices of Cravath, Swaine & Moore (representing Du Pont), where he was holed up all night with five lawyers.

Once Du Pont declared its intentions, negotiations centered on three points: (1) developing a financial package that would allow Du Pont to afford Conoco without destroying its balance sheet, (2) structuring a merger proposal that pleased Du Pont's shareholders while winning over Conoco's in the face of competing tenders, and (3) finding a way to steer its offer through government shoals and put it into effect on time.

The first two points were largely the province of Cravath and First Boston—the new investment bankers on the scene, Du Pont's selection—with a team headed by M & A specialists Joseph Perella and lawyer-turned-banker Bruce Wasserstein. In a situation with a competing offer, the two most important considerations are mastering the maze of federal takeover laws that govern the time periods for the offers and gauging what might look attractive to investors. The first, obviously, was Cravath's job. Investment bankers know the second because, in addition to their function as deal makers, they also, through their large institutional trading desks and sales forces, know what buyers want. Together, Cravath and First Boston hammered out a complicated agreement that would give shareholders an option to take cash, or stock if they wished the tax-free status that comes from a stock-for-stock swap. Shareholders tendering to Du Pont would get $87.50 in cash for 40 percent of their stock and 1.6 Du Pont shares for the rest, the stock valued at $82 on the day of the announcement. It was a combination with parts borrowed from a host of previous deals but, taken together, was quite novel.

Friendly deals may insure the cooperation of the target's management. But when management does not wield a large portion of a company's shares, as was the case with Conoco, that friendliness may not be enough to sell the deal to the market. So, as a security blanket, the lawyers and bankers devised an option for Du Pont that would allow the chemical company to buy 15.9 million unissued Conoco shares, also at $87.50 each. No other suitor would have such an option. However, with an offer that was $9 higher than Seagram's at the time, such an option seemed to be an excess of caution.

The third key factor, the speed of the deal, is solely the work of lawyers. Well-run companies like Du Pont, with a solid credit status, can line up $7 billion over a weekend, even when it is a national holiday. But when it comes to filing a complicated registration statement and getting SEC and antitrust approval, lawyers must compress what would normally take several months of work into just a few days.

The job of creating this registration statement and shepherding it through all the relevant agencies fell to Skadden, Dewey, Ballantine, and a team of lawyers from Du Pont's counsel, Cravath, Swaine & Moore. Meanwhile, it was, once again, the job of Dewey, Ballantine litigators to buy time, as these corporate lawyers went to work.

Registration statements take on larger-than-life proportions during takeovers because, besides being necessary for SEC clearance, they act as fodder for opposing litigators to create deal-threatening problems. As Dewey's Larrabee explains: "You can't bring frivolous suits, but these tender offer documents are sometimes put together in tremendous haste and sometimes they turn out to have information that is not correctly stated. So, first you decide if the tender offer price that is being offered is too low. Then you climb all over the other guy's documents." To the trained eye, the document's mass can be filled with 10b–5 actions for fraud and manipulation.

Patience, Humility & Caffeine

Much gets written about powerhouse corporate lawyers who, as dealmakers, play a role in determining which companies live or die. Most corporate lawyering is not as glamorous. Work on the Du Pont registration statement typified what it takes to be a great corporate lawyer: care, writing skills, patience, humility, and an ability to go without sleep for long periods of time without complaining. How else could eight to ten people work together around-the-clock to write a 191–page book that contains fluid prose, no typos, and no credit for its authors?

Partner Alan Stephenson served as the lead lawyer for Cravath in negotiating and structuring the registration statement issues, coordinating all of the parties, and making sure that the statement fairly represented the wishes of everyone involved. Colleague and partner George Lowy did the actual drafting. The group worked almost non-stop for two straight weeks. Rich Easton, the Skadden partner, who was at that time an associate, cannot recall having dinner with his wife during the whole period, and more than once he would trudge home to Larchmont as dawn emerged, not to catch a few hours of sleep, but to take a cold shower, button down a new shirt, and head back to the office.

At 6 a.m. on the morning of July 15, just two weeks after Du Pont came in, Lowy, the oldest attorney on the deal, was the only one still standing—and still drafting. He had included several dozen chapters with information ranging from the nature of the offer to the size of the fees the investment bankers would receive. After he put the finishing touches on the document, he decided to file it personally at the SEC in Washington. Luckily he did. Upon arrival, he was told by the clerk that the filing fee check was $1.71 shy of the mark. "I had to take it from my pocket," says Lowy. "I even had to borrow a penny from the clerk."

Lowy stayed in Washington for some time, shooting down red flags raised ostensibly by the SEC's Corporate Finance Division but provided principally by Seagram's lawyers, who were climbing all over the statement. The registration process is wide open, with the SEC not only tolerating comments from opposing lawyers but seeking them out to aid disclosure. The Seagram people wanted the SEC to raise eyebrows about the so-called "lock-up" option, allowing Du Pont to buy 15 percent of Conoco's not-yet-minted shares. But Lowy reminded the SEC's staff that it recently had embraced that type of arrangement. He made sure to secure a waiver from the division for the option. With a document chock full of red marks, Lowy bounded back to New York for a few more tense nights at the printer, making revisions and having them proofed by associates, a common task for bleary-eyed junior people. But through Cravath's efforts, the SEC approval was achieved.

When Friendship Is Not Enough

Despite the euphoria of the initial filing commencing Du Pont's offer, discouraging news seemed to lurk everywhere. First, while Du Pont was filing, Seagram upped its bid to $85 a share, signalling its intention to remain competitive with Du Pont. Du Pont immediately countered to $95 a share and bumped up the back end of its deal to 1.7 Du Pont shares. But its stock price was sagging badly, bringing down the value of the whole offer.

Second, the federal rules involving merger waiting periods had an inexplicable quirk that clearly favored Seagram's type of bid. To let the government, either through the Federal Trade Commission or the Justice Department's Antitrust Division, study the anti-competitive nature of cash tender offers, the Hart–Scott–Rodino Act of 1978 provides that one or the other agency has 15 days to approve the bid, with a proviso that ten more days can be added if additional information is needed.

But if your offer contains a mixture of stock and cash, as did Du Pont's, the approval period doubles in length to 30 days. Seagram filed its Hart–Scott application June 22, and was approved for purchasing stock on July 8—the same day that Du Pont began the filing process. However the Williams Act, which regulates tender offers, states that companies that bump up their offers must wait an additional ten days after each bump before they can purchase shares. Seagram's raise thus set back its bid ten days in its race with Du Pont. But unlike Seagram, Du Pont faced antitrust questioning under Hart–Scott. For an energy-intensive company like Du Pont, buying Conoco would mean potentially violative vertical integration.

A dizzying flurry of events soon followed. First, Judge Weinfeld dealt Du Pont's attempt a severe setback on July 16 when he angrily dismissed Conoco's action against Seagram. It was just one in a series of 12 defeats the defense team suffered that summer, but it was a bitter one. One of the litigators later reflected on how defensive takeover litigation has fallen into disrepute with judges and academics. "It's easy for some airhead to say that the litigation we filed is stupid and counterproductive and if it has no chance then why bother to file it. They tell you they would be embarrassed to file some of this stuff. But if you would only litigate those matters you were absolutely certain you would win, you would be a pisspoor litigator." As for the skein of defeats on behalf of Conoco, the lawyer said: "I look at it this way. I was shot at 12 times, got a dozen bullet holes in me and I still lived to fight again."

The day after Weinfeld's dismissal, Mobil, the second largest U.S. oil company, which had been rumored to be interested in Conoco from the moment Seagram surfaced, struck with a $90 a share cash offer for 50 percent of the company. The offer was lower than most Wall Street analysts expected. However, because it was a cash deal, it could be approved under Hart–Scott in 15 days, thus potentially freeing Mobil to purchase shares on July 31, a week before Du Pont would be able to buy. Of course, such a short period would be relevant only if Mobil could clear all antitrust objections; otherwise, Mobil could be stuck with an additional information request, keeping Mobil's bid back for another ten days.

Then, on July 23, Seagram raised its bid to $92 in cash and announced it would begin purchasing shares tendered on July 31, also a full week before Du Pont could hope to begin buying its tendered shares.

At this point, with all the offers on the table, the fight moved from the legal and financial spheres to the world of public relations. Each offer had its strengths and weaknesses. It was now up to lawyers on each side to exploit them.

When Joe Flom talks about what it means to be a good business lawyer, he frequently cites three qualities that all must have: good legal sense, some business savvy, and a flair for public relations. "Takeover work is multi-disciplinary," he says. "All of these things are mixed together." Flom's firm started its public relations campaign against Mobil with an all-out attack on the antitrust implications of merging the nation's number two and number nine oil companies. The campaign was designed only in part to scare the Justice Department into action. The real goal was to make the large institutional holders wary of tendering to Mobil and then ending up with nothing if the government were to clamp down on that merger.

Skadden filed a private antitrust suit in Washington against Mobil, figuring correctly that Mobil would have to waste a day removing the case to New York. "We were hoping that it might throw Mobil off-guard to file down there," says antitrust partner William Pelster, who headed up Skadden's foray. "We also wanted out of the Southern District where we had already lost once before. It bought time. We had to do that because we were not yet up to speed on the oil industry."

Pelster used the time to set up a ten-attorney drafting crew. The hours were incredible. "Let's see," says Pelster, leafing through his red lawyer's diary for the period, "hmmm, Saturday, 18 hours; Sunday, 19 hours; then 18, 20, 21, 21. It did go on like that for a long time." The going was not easy because Mobil's lawyers put up a stonewall to discovery attempts. "We asked for a bunch of specific documents, and all we got back were 10-k's, which contain information no different from Mobil's annual reports. Pelster quickly broke down the antitrust issues into coal, pipe-line, refining, jet fuel, and retail gas overlaps. Partners then divvied up all of the areas except one, coal, which went to Robert Zimet, a senior associate with much securities litigation experience.

Zimet does not deny that for an associate just a few months away from a partnership decision, getting the coal draw was a good sign. But it was not the first time he had been given large responsibility for an important discrete matter, and he approached it as an old hand.

Zimet immediately secured the talents of the two associates who worked next door to him and went to work researching everything he could find out about coal. "It didn't look like it going in, but there were significant overlap issues involving coal," he recalls. "It was fascinating for me because it was a lesson in business. I got to learn about an industry that I knew absolutely nothing about before I went into this. I hadn't studied anything about coal since junior high, when you find out the difference between anthracite and bituminous."

After that Zimet focused on formulating a discovery strategy. He noticed the depositions of those in coal from Mobil and he defended Conoco's coal people. Then he scouted the country for experts in the field. It was a process he had done many times before but, he points out, the skills needed are not taught in law school. "You can only learn this by observing what lawyers more senior to you and their adversaries do," he says. "You learn from their successes and their failures. You learn how to look at annual reports and spot the problem areas. You learn how to track down the experts. You develop a sort of mental checklist, a cookbook on how to approach each of these."

Zimet says that despite some of the longest days he has spent at the firm, he felt "galvanized" by the activity. "You want to be involved in

all phases of one of these big cases," he says. "You want to find out
what is going on at all times. You wander into other lawyers' offices,
just to try to get an awareness. You bump into partners and ask what
is happening." Zimet finished up his section of the brief on time. He
says he felt "very proud" of both his team and the final product, even
though his section, along with almost all of the other antitrust issues,
never got an airing in court.

With the brief writing underway, Pelster turned his attention
toward smoothing any government objections to Du Pont's merger and
creating a few for Mobil to deflect. "We were trying to agitate," he
recalls. At that moment the Federal Trade Commission and Justice
were locked in a turf war over which department should scrutinize the
cases. FTC had built up expertise in the oil business over the years,
but William Baxter, then the new antitrust division chief, was eager to
assert his authority and stamp Justice with his philosophy. He
grabbed the matter.

At first, Skadden people thought such interest on the part of a
Justice official boded poorly not only for Mobil but for Du Pont itself.
Negotiations for Du Pont's antitrust clearance centered on a Conoco
joint venture agreement with Monsanto, Du Pont's archrival in the
chemicals business. Surprisingly, the staff talks, also attended by a
Covington and Burling attorney, went exceptionally well. Justice
seemed to be willing to accede to the merger if Du Pont bought out
Monsanto, thus ending the joint venture.

So Skadden turned its attention toward warning Justice of the evils
of a merger between number two and number nine. Skadden bolstered
its ranks by adding William Mulligan, an antitrust expert and former
federal district judge turned Skadden partner, to the negotiations. And
it brought in Harvard antitrust professor Philip Areeda as a paid
consultant. A meeting between Baxter and these experts was arranged.

"At first he just glowered a lot," says Pelster of Baxter at the
meeting. He kept saying "show me, show me," after everything Skadden's team said would be anticompetitive. Areeda discussed some
foreign supply restrictions, but Baxter did not seem bothered. He then
raised some extensive joint venturing problems, pointing out that the
oil market was less competitive than it looked. Baxter expressed some
interest and acted a trifle concerned. But Pelster did not think the
session went very well. "It was a depressing meeting," he would
summarize later.

Nevertheless, the next day, Justice approved Du Pont for immediate clearance, provided it would work out the Monsanto problem. But
it asked for additional information from Mobil. The effect on Mobil's

bid was devastating. Even though it seemed that Mobil would probably get through clearance in the next ten days, there were no guarantees. The offer lost credibility. It seemed that everything that Skadden had been saying all along about the antitrust hang-ups of Mobil's offer had been right. Mobil's bid suddenly had too much risk in relation to its reward. Although Mobil raised its price to $105 right before the call for additional information, the largest player was looking more and more like Goliath to Seagram's David.

Six Packs and Crown Sevens

While Du Pont's effort to show antitrust violations in a Mobil–Conoco merger was building to a climax, Seagram was within days of being able to begin purchasing the shares tendered to its offer. No one was sure how many shares had already been attracted to Seagram. But the opportunity for a quick pay-out—Seagram was readying checks to be sent out Saturday night—was a terrific lure. What Du Pont needed was some sort of last-minute impediment to Seagram's cash-on-the-barrelhead campaign. It got its wishes with the now-ready tied house litigation.

Solinger, charting the progress of the tied house suits, was in constant contact with local counsel. "Our Florida attorney told us they had a good chance of prevailing there, so our Florida lawyers drafted papers for state court. Our lawyer chartered a plane that Thursday afternoon from Miami to fly to Tallahassee. He would call me from each place, you know, 'Now I'm at the airport. Now I am at the court house.'" The Miami lawyer, from the Florida office of Stroock & Stroock & Lavan, convinced state judge John Rudd in an ex parte discussion in chambers that the $7–billion merger should be put on hold because Conoco sold six packs at Florida gas stations. But because the Florida lawyer needed time to post the necessary bond for the suit, Solinger said the announcement of Conoco's sub rosa victory had to wait until the next day, Friday—the day before Seagram would be allowed to purchase shares.

It came as a crucial blow to Seagram. Their attorneys were enraged by the ex parte action and lashed out that Friday morning to Judge Weinfeld, imploring him to overturn the Florida ruling. Weinfeld, too, was livid. But he cautioned that he could not touch a Florida state court's judgment. He did, however, warn that he would not tolerate further secret actions on behalf of clients. The warning came too late. As Seagram's people that afternoon convened an open hearing in Florida and got Judge Rudd to recant his TRO, the exact same scenario was unfolding in North Carolina. A state court judge once again blocked the Seagram purchase plan because Conoco sold liquor in his state's gas stations. "By the time they found out about it," says

Solinger "the judge was on a boat somewhere in some North Carolina river."

Seagram's people, however, were up to the challenge. As the American Lawyer later reported, an associate at Simpson, Thacher & Bartlett, Seagram's attorneys, had taken the precaution of incorporating both in New York and Delaware the Seagram paper subsidiary doing the bidding, just in case diversity would be needed down the road against a suit by Conoco, a Delaware company. That shrewd precaution gave Seagram the right to take the matter to the emergency federal judge who is always available on a 24–hour basis in each district. Seagram prevailed later that evening, but once again not before Du Pont could create uncertainty and confusion about Seagram's offer. The TRO was not lifted until long after the close of Friday's market. Most Wall Streeters had already fled their offices for the weekend without considering whether to deliver their shares to Seagram because they presumed that the North Carolina order would last at least until Monday, and no checks would be sent out Saturday night.

Robert Myers, a litigation partner at Dewey, defended the ex parte dealings in this fashion: "Whether you are required or not to notify opposing counsel about such discussions is only a matter of state law. Sure, it was an elbow in the eye and probably does not meet everybody's expectation of what a good guy is. But these two companies were in a life and death struggle. From our standpoint, we did nothing inappropriate. I'm friends with a lot of lawyers from Simpson Thacher, but that doesn't mean they are going to get special consideration."

Where Wall Street Hits Madison Avenue

With investors now facing all three competing bids, all with confusing deadlines and prices that seemed to change with every day of trading, the contenders took to the newspapers to wage a war of words. Within one page of each other, in *The Wall Street Journal* and *The New York Times,* giant full-page ads appeared stating each company's case. "Seagram is paying $92 in cash. Quickly," screamed the ad for the distiller. "No Maybes." Mobil's advertisement urged all Conoco shareholders: "You must act now."

But it was Conoco's ad, in the form of a letter from Chairman Bailey, with simple "Important" stamped where the letterhead should be, that would prevail. It ticked off reason after reason why Du Pont made the most sense politically, economically, and legally. To highlight the antitrust hazards of the Mobil offer, Conoco switched to bold print to say that possible intervention by the government "makes it questionable whether the Conoco shareholders would ever get paid under the Mobil offer." It also noted in boldface that "All Conoco directors have tendered or are tendering their shares to Du Pont," in an attempt to show institutions that Du Pont was the favored hand. While the letter bore Bailey's signature, most of the input was Flom's. "Looking back, I would have to say the thing I was most proud of in Conoco was the ad," he said. "It was the best thing I did on the deal. It hit a lot of themes, and I think it was most effective. The public relations people, they hardly changed a word, maybe just a line or two," he says with a smile.

Whether it was the ad campaign or the lawsuits or just Conoco's antitrust baiting, the message was working. By the time Seagram began mailing checks that weekend, Du Pont could lay claim to 48 million shares, about 56 percent of those outstanding. By contrast, Seagram had pulled in about 17 million shares, mostly those of the arbitrageurs, quick-trading specialists who buy shares on news of a takeover and then tender to whoever pays the quickest and most sure profit. Often these "arbs," as they are known, can hold hostage a whole deal because they represent such a large part of the pool of outstanding shares by the time the final bidding begins. But here the pool was simply too great, drowning the arbs in a sea of more important institutional holders—all of whom seemed smitten by Du Pont's bid.

At that point, however, because tendering is not synonymous with purchasing, the war could not be considered over. Because of the quirk in the federal timing rules, shareholders who had tendered to Du Pont could still withdraw their shares from Du Pont's pool if another bidder pleased them more.

With the price of Du Pont's stock eroding almost daily, because of fears of what Du Pont's increased debt and diluted stock would do to the company's future earnings-per-share figures, the back end of Du Pont's offer—the exchange of stock—was looking more and more dubious. At one point it was possible to take Seagram's $92 and go out and buy two shares of Du Pont's stock, far better than the 1.6 shares you would get if you held on for some indefinite period of time before Du Pont could begin purchasing.

I Will Sue You and Raise You Twice

For Mobil, Du Pont's late purchase date was enough of a hope to merit one last chance at Conoco. On Monday August 3, Mobil raised its bid to $115. The bump was vital; Mobil had only gotten 2 million shares so far, way below its rivals, even with its higher offering price, because institutions feared possible antitrust action. Mobil also tried one last legal foray.

Michael Mitchell, a 46–year–old Skadden litigator, remembers well how things unfolded. He had been brought into the case one week

before, to help defend depositions of high-level Conoco officers. At
around lunch time he had begun the defense of Chairman Bailey when
he learned that Mobil had just gone into federal court in the Southern
District to seek a temporary restraining order to block Du Pont's bid.
The application ostensibly represented Mobil's counter-claim to Du
Pont's antitrust case, but it was obviously a last ditch attempt to stop
Du Pont from its imminent purchase of the shares in its pool. At 5
p.m., Mitchell found himself standing before Federal District Court
Judge Lawrence Pierce, prepared to defend Du Pont against anything
that Mobil could throw at him.

A transcript of the hearing shows that the judge must not have
read a newspaper, or at least the financial pages of one, anytime during
the summer. He admitted being unsure of who brought the case and
even who the parties involved were. Sanford Litvack, a partner at
Donovan, Leisure, Newton & Irvine, the New York law firm that
represented Mobil, tried to explain that he thought Du Pont should be
restrained because its lock-up option was manipulative. He urged that
the deal be put on ice for a few days—just long enough to get Mobil out
of the clutches of Justice's Antitrust Division, so both could be considered equally.

To an uninitiated judge, Litvack had one compelling argument on
his side. It did not seem right that Du Pont should be offering roughly
$1 billion less than Mobil and yet still be able to walk off with the prize.
What he did not know was, judging by the way the market was acting,
Mobil could be offering double what Du Pont was prepared to pay and
nobody would be nibbling as long as the antitrust hold-up lurked.

Mitchell stuck to the facts and the law, explaining why they were
in court in the first place and how Mobil had had plenty of time to
press its action before that crucial moment. Further, he pointed out
that not a single case supported Mobil's position. Thomas Barr, a
Cravath litigator, followed up, again trying to answer a bewildered
judge's questions about how the federal takeover rules interacted with
the suit.

A victory was imperative for Du Pont. "It would have been like a
bank panic if that judge had said, 'Maybe let's take a week and decide
this thing,'" Cravath's Stephenson said later. "The capital at that
point just runs to the safest offer, whether it be $92 or $95, anything
just so it works."

A look at Pierce's opinion issued the next day shows that the
Conoco litigators had prevailed—the opinion matched almost word-for-
word Mitchell's brief filed earlier that day. Pierce found that Mobil
had failed to show that a TRO refusal would harm Mobil more than a
TRO would damage Du Pont. "Mobil entered the bidding contest for

Conoco knowing that it would be subjected to waiting periods," he noted. The next day, August 4, Mobil breathed two more gasps: raising its bid to $120 and filing an appeal. Both were for naught. Du Pont announced it was moving its bid up to $98 a share and that it had reached agreement with Monsanto to buy out that chemical firm's end of the joint-venture agreement, thus clearing away any Hart–Scott problems and allowing it, at last, to close the gate on the millions of tendered shares.

Champagne corks popped that night for 200 lawyers, investment bankers, executives, chauffeurs, typists, and messengers at Du Pont's Wilmington, Delaware, headquarters. The next day Du Pont purchased 55 percent of Conoco's shares and exercised its option for 15.9 million others, giving it 62 percent of Conoco. Mobil threw in the towel, directing its shares to Seagram, and the Canadian liquor company in turn swapped its 27,885,000 Conoco shares for 20 percent of Du Pont. This time, Seagram signed the standstill agreement and consented to sit, docile, on Du Pont's board. Three months and $7.54 billion later, the deal was over.

Characters

Martha Solinger—Associate, Dewey, Ballantine

Ralph Bailey—Conoco's Chairman

Joseph Flom—Partner, Skadden, Arps

Leonard Larrabee—Partner, Dewey, Ballantine

Russel "Cap" Beatie—Partner, Dewey, Ballantine

Peter Bator—Partner, Davis Polk

Robert Greenhill—Senior Managing Director, Morgan Stanley

Jack Gallagher—Dome's Chairman

Kurt Koegler—Partner, Skadden, Arps

Richard Easton—Associate, Skadden, Arps

Joseph Perella—Investment Banker, First Boston

Bruce Wasserstein—Investment Banker, First Boston

Alan Stephenson—Partner, Cravath, Swaine & Moore

George Lowy—Partner, Cravath, Swaine & Moore

William Pelster—Partner, Skadden, Arps

Robert Zimet—Associate, Skadden, Arps

William Baxter—Assistant Attorney General for the Antitrust Division

Robert Myers—Partner, Dewey, Ballantine

Michael Mitchell—Partner, Skadden, Arps

Discussion Questions

1. Does the Conoco story show you a sensible system for deciding the ownership of Conoco's assets? If we accept the basic idea of capital markets, then the proper questions involve how informed, fair, and vigorous the bidding is for Conoco's shares. In that light, are the lawyers somehow helping to create a more competitive market for Conoco's shares or are they working to exclude competitive offers? They seem to be doing both. On what occasion does their activity seem to further a competitive market? Which actions seem designed to prevent its operation?

2. The lawyers are hired to represent the participants' interests, not to further the interests of an abstract "market." There is no reason to think those participants are naive when they hire lawyers. They know the services they will receive and the prices they will pay. So why does the Conoco story give us the sense the lawyers are not playing a proper role? If the vigorous representation of all interests does not produce a competitive market for Conoco's shares, surely that is not something for which the lawyers should be blamed.

One reason is that we may be concerned about who the lawyers represent. Conoco's lawyers are paid by the corporation, but in this case the managers and the shareholders do not have entirely parallel interests. An exceptionally attractive "hostile" offer may make the shareholders rich at the same time it deprives the current managers of their jobs. Did Conoco's lawyers think they were working for the shareholders, although they were hired and directed by the current managers? A widow's pension may be at stake in this dispute. Was any of the high-priced legal talent in fact working for that widow? Indeed the conflict may involve the law firm itself. Would Mobil or Seagram have kept Dewey, Ballantine as the counsel for Conoco if they had been successful in their takeover efforts?

Can Conoco's lawyers defend a wholehearted effort to help the current management retain control? How much of the shareholders' assets is it proper for those lawyers to spend on this effort? In the final days of the merger, Mobil lawyer Sanford Litvack argued that if Judge Pierce would simply delay Du Pont for a few days, the Justice Department might find that Mobil had no antitrust problems, with the result that the shareholders would receive one billion dollars more. Who was Michael Mitchell, the Skadden litigator, representing when he fought that alternative in the name of Conoco?

If it is a regular practice for a company's lawyers to be responsive to current management, it may not be possible for a single lawyer or firm to ignore that practice. Assume that you are a lawyer for a medium-sized company that is the target of a takeover. Suppose your attitude is that you work for the shareholders, you think the market should have its way, and you will not file lawsuits solely to delay. Is it your duty to tell the company president that this is your attitude? What if a company executive retains you, asking, "If we are the subject of a takeover, will you use all the traditional weapons of defense?" What institutional changes can you suggest that might deal with this problem?

3. Is there also a serious problem of abuse of the law and the legal process in this story? Bar association rules forbid bringing frivolous suits (see When to Give Up a Lawsuit: *Davidoff v. Meyerson* at page 336), yet proceedings were regularly brought that were thought to have a slim chance of success. At one point Conoco's lawyers had lost twelve times. Yet each suit distracted or delayed the opponent, interfering with the opponent's ability to make a persuasive offer to shareholders. Was this useful to the client? Was it consistent with the disciplinary rules? Is it wrong to obtain an ex parte order from a judge who then goes out fishing if it is likely the order will be overturned or rescinded forty-eight hours later? Even if those forty-eight hours may make a big difference to the outcome?

Rule 3.3(d) of the ABA Model Rules of Professional Conduct provides: "In an ex parte proceeding, a lawyer shall inform the tribunal of all material facts known to the lawyer which will enable the tribunal to make an informed decision, whether or not the facts are adverse." This rule is intended to ensure that a "substantially just result" is achieved even where the adversarial system is not operating. Was the result of the ex parte proceeding in this case "substantially just"?

4. One of the things for which takeover lawyers are hired is public relations skills. Is there anything wrong with calling to the attention of the Arab countries who sell oil to Conoco that Seagram was headed by a long-time supporter of Israel? With inciting congressional hostility towards the effort by a Canadian company, Seagram, to buy American natural resources? Were these reactions that would have occurred anyway, although at a later date, like the assistance Conoco's attorneys provided to the government's attorneys raising doubts about the antitrust implications of Mobil's offer?

5. In his 1981–82 annual report, Harvard President Derek Bok wrote: "Not only does the law absorb many more young people in America than in any other industrialized nation; it attracts an unusually large proportion of the exceptionally gifted. . . . [F]ar too many of these rare individuals are becoming lawyers at a time when the country cries out for more talented business executives, more enlightened public servants, more inventive engineers, more able high school principals and teachers." James Vorenberg, Dean of Harvard Law School, responded as follows: "I believe that the central work of lawyers—representing clients in matters of deep importance to them—is demanding and calls for people of the highest talents." Is this story evidence for the Bok or the Vorenberg view?

Epilogue

Since Du Pont swallowed Conoco in 1981, "The Deal" has been knocked out of the record books first by Texaco–Getty and then by Socal–Gulf. But for many of those involved, that torrid summer epitomized all that is exciting about the practice of law. As Dewey partner Myers put it: "There were some who might have had qualms about working so hard, but there is only one Conoco in people's lives. Each morning you would pick up the *Times* and read about something you were working on." This kind of work, he says, "is not the kind of thing where people want to sneak off and play golf. We were at the heart of it. It was a once in a lifetime experience."

Solinger agrees, even though she spent 45 out of 47 days in June and July at the office, billing about 300 hours a month. She says she would not have had it any other way. Although she was often the only woman in the room for much of the Conoco negotiations, the ratio did not bother or intimidate her. She laughs now at some of the more blatant forms of sexism she saw and heard during the deal, including constant apologies for the use of four letter words in her presence. She says she never felt excluded from any of the hard work or the camaraderie.

Was it all worth it? For the lawyers, the payoff, besides psychic rewards, was handsome. Skadden reportedly received $4 million for its efforts, the top draw of all the law firms. Such a sum, however, is much smaller than the fees the investment bankers racked up for their work. Unlike lawyers, who bill by the hour, the bankers can command a percentage of the deal. Thus First Boston, which came in more than a month after Skadden, got .2 percent of the deal for its work: $15,080,000. Morgan Stanley made about the same from Conoco. Neither firm employed one-fourth as many professionals as Skadden.

Are these fees justified in relation to the spoils of the lawyers who toiled side-by-side with them throughout the period? To Solinger, an associate who got her regular first-year salary whether she billed 300 hours or 150, the sums seemed outrageous. "I can't see why they are able to draw 10 times what we earn," she says.

But Cravath's Lowy says he is not cynical about the differences. "We get paid what I think we should get paid. What is just is what the market will bear," he says. "Perhaps lawyers are undercompensated, but I think we make out well enough. I know that First Boston's contribution was absolutely critical, at least as critical as any lawyer's role." Flom agrees: "We do fine." Bankers, he says, have a lot more overhead, including a much larger support system than lawyers have. "And," he adds, "their risk opinions (analyzing the pluses and minuses of making deals) are very meaningful."

For Du Pont, the results of the merger are mixed. On the one hand, oil prices, far from shooting up, have leveled off, making the purchase appear expensive compared to where oil prices seemed to be heading at the time. On the other hand, Du Pont's stock has performed well since the merger relative to other chemical companies, so the market perceives the merger to have made some sense.

How about the shareholders who ended up paying those fees? Do they benefit from the thousands of hours put in by these firms? Du

Pont's shareholders saw their stock fall rapidly but then retrace its steps to wind up at around pre-Conoco merger levels. But how about the shareholders of Conoco whom the rules are designed to protect? One defense lawyer, who prefers to stay anonymous, thinks they made out the best of all. "One of the worst of the arguments I hear from airhead academics is that litigation hurts shareholders. Well, if we hadn't filed all of those suits, then Conoco would have gone for $65 a share instead of $98. Some ass on your law review wrote soon after that there should be no resistance attempts once an offer is made, because that is what is supposed to be best for shareholders. That guy doesn't have the first idea of what he is talking about."

Sure, the lawyer admits, there must be a better way to settle these fights. But all ways he can think of would interfere with the ultimate rights of the shareholders to get the best price. Until a better method is created, he says, the Conoco way will be the standard. Do you agree?

E.   Lawyers for Government

The Case of the Segregated Schools *

The brief had to be submitted. William Bradford Reynolds, head of the Justice Department's Civil Rights Division, and Charles Cooper, his special assistant, had already signed it. The case, *Bob Jones University v. United States,* had stirred national controversy when the Reagan administration decided to abandon its support of the Internal Revenue Service's authority to deny tax exemptions to segregated schools.

The government rarely filed a brief with the Supreme Court that was not signed by a member of the Solicitor General's Office. Rex Lee, the Solicitor General, had disqualified himself from the *Bob Jones* case because of a conflict of interest arising from his prior private representation of religious schools in their challenge of tax exemption denials. The task of signing the brief then fell to Deputy Solicitor General Lawrence G. Wallace, the senior career lawyer in the office.

Wallace had supervised the *Bob Jones* case for the government long before the decision to reverse positions took place. He had signed an earlier brief in which the government had argued that the tax laws "do not countenance Federal tax benefits to organizations operated for educational purposes that discriminate against students or applicants on the basis of race." He had also argued strongly within Justice for a brief on the merits that contained the same message. He remained convinced that his position was right, and that the government's new stance enjoyed, in his words, "no support" in the law.

In the previous eight weeks, Wallace had witnessed an extraordinary sequence of policy commitments and retreats, political maneuvering and public uproar. Now he was called upon to approve the administration's new brief, produced in large measure by political appointees in the Justice and Treasury Departments. Wallace reviewed the history of the case in his mind.

Legal Background

The controversy over tax exemptions for segregated private schools first arose in the wake of *Brown v. Board of Education.*[1] As desegregation efforts expanded, hundreds of all-white "segregation academies"

---

* The House Ways and Means Committee investigated these events. *Administration's Change in Federal Policy Regarding the Tax Status of Racially Discriminatory Private Schools,* 97th Cong., 2d Sess. 1 (1982). This case study is based on the committee report.

[1] *Brown v. Board of Education,* 347 U.S. 483 (1954).

sprang up. Although the Civil Rights Act of 1964 prohibited government assistance to segregated schools, it did not mention tax exemptions. As a result, segregated private schools sought and received federal tax exempt status; in August 1967, after a two-year freeze on suspect exemption applications, the IRS announced that it would continue to grant exemptions to such schools because it lacked "legal authority to deny [them] the usual charitable deduction."

In 1969 the Lawyer's Committee for Civil Rights brought suit on behalf of several black parents and their children attending public schools in Mississippi. The suit challenged tax exemptions to private segregated schools in Mississippi as a violation of the equal protection clause. The federal government initially opposed the suit. On January 12, 1970, a three-judge panel of the U.S. District Court for D.C. issued a preliminary injunction ordering the IRS to withhold tax exemptions from private segregated schools in Mississippi.[2]

Meanwhile, however, an advisory committee, established at the IRS even before the initiation of *Green*, concluded that denial of tax exempt status to racially discriminatory private schools was "compelled by law." After deliberations that included Treasury, Justice, HEW, and the White House, the IRS recognized that it "could not attribute to the Congress an intent to violate the Constitution, and thus felt compelled to search for a reasonable construction of Section 501(c)(3) [of the Internal Revenue Code, dealing with tax exempt institutions] which would avoid a constitutional confrontation." Furthermore, attorneys at Justice advised the IRS that the United States would probably lose the *Green* case on the merits. Accordingly, on July 10, 1970, the IRS adopted a new policy of denying exempt status to all segregated schools nationwide.

One year later, the *Green* court unanimously held that the Internal Revenue Code did not permit exemptions for racially discriminatory private schools.[3] The court first observed that under common law an organization whose activities were illegal or contrary to public policy was not entitled to privileges and immunities ordinarily afforded to charities. Thus, the court noted, "if we were to follow the common law approach," the tax code would be interpreted to deny exempt status in the case of segregated schools. Second, the Internal Revenue Code "must be construed and applied in consonance with the Federal public policy against support for racial segregation of schools, public or private." The numerous "sources and evidences of that Federal public policy" included the Thirteenth and Fourteenth Amendments, *Brown* and its progeny, and the 1964 Civil Rights Act. Third, any other

---

[2] *Green v. Kennedy*, 309 F.Supp. 1127 (D.D.C.1970).

[3] *Green v. Connally*, 330 F.Supp. 1150 (D.D.C.1971).

construction "would raise serious constitutional questions" and "it would be difficult indeed to establish that such [tax] support can be provided consistently with the constitution."

Parents of white students attending private segregated schools in Mississippi appealed the *Green* ruling to the Supreme Court. As a result of the IRS policy shift, the government opposed the appeal. The Supreme Court unanimously affirmed in a short, unsigned opinion.[4]

Later, in a 1973 ruling, the Supreme Court cited the *Green* case approvingly, noting the government's "constitutional obligation to steer clear . . . of giving significant aid to institutions that practice racial . . . discrimination."[5] In addition, numerous other courts also subsequently endorsed the *Green* opinion. However, in 1974, the Supreme Court, in a footnote in *Bob Jones v. Simon,* observed that the *Green* case "lacks the precedential weight of a case involving a truly adversary controversy." In explanation, the court noted that the government had "reversed its position while the case was in appeal. . . ."[6] Yet the appeal in *Green* had been taken not by the government but by white parents whose children attended segregated private schools.

Over the next few years, Congress appeared to give tacit approval to the *Green* decision. In 1976, it enacted Internal Revenue Code Section 501(i), which denied tax exempt status to social clubs that discriminated. The new law was intended to reverse an earlier district court ruling that discriminatory social clubs were not subject to the same exemption rules as segregated private schools. As the Court of Appeals for the D.C. Circuit later noted, "[T]he Senate Report on the private club provision cites *Green* as the leading case on tax exempt status under section 501(c)(3) for educational institutions, and reflects an understanding that race discrimination disqualifies private schools from obtaining or retaining tax exemption." Moreover, when Congress in 1979 enacted two appropriations riders which restricted the use of funds to enforce or formulate certain new IRS guidelines on grants of exempt status, senators and congressmen commonly assumed or asserted the power of the IRS to deny exemptions because of racial discrimination. For example, Senator Jesse Helms said:

> Mr. President, the purpose of this amendment is quite simple: it places a 1–year moratorium on the ability of the Internal Revenue Service to establish new procedures—and I emphasize the word "new"—regarding the termination of the tax-exempt status of private schools. . . . The IRS may still move to

---

[4] *Coit v. Green,* 404 U.S. 997 (1971).

[5] *Norwood v. Harrison,* 413 U.S. 455, 467 (1973).

[6] *Bob Jones University v. Simon,* 416 U.S. 725, 740 n. 11 (1974).

withdraw the tax-exempt status of a school which [discrimi-
nates].

The Bob Jones Case

Established in 1927 and located in Greenville, South Carolina, Bob
Jones University taught fundamentalist Christian doctrine. The school
enforced strict social rules. Women had to wear skirts to the middle of
the knee; no slacks were allowed; men were required to wear ties and
jackets in the dining room. Public displays of affection were banned;
rock and roll was forbidden along with movies, television, and dancing.

The school was also firmly committed to what it understood to be a
biblical injunction against mixing the races. As one student put it,
"The Lord established differences, and it's not man's place to go around
and say, 'God, you didn't know what you were doing when you made us
different, and so we're going to erase those differences.' "

Before 1971, Bob Jones University excluded blacks entirely. From
1971 to 1975, married blacks and members of other minority groups
were not excluded from enrollment, but Bob Jones continued to deny
admission to unmarried blacks unless the applicant had been a staff
member at the university for at least four years. In response to court
rulings, Bob Jones revised its admissions policy to permit unmarried
blacks to enroll. However it continued to exclude any applicant known
to be a partner in an interracial marriage. Further, under express
policies, it would expel any student who (1) was a partner in an
interracial marriage, (2) was affiliated with an organization that advocated interracial marriage, (3) engaged in interracial dating, or (4)
encouraged others to violate the rules against interracial dating.
While the university refused to keep records on the races of its
students, its president, Bob Jones, acknowledged in 1982 that a *New
York Times* estimate that fewer than 12 of the school's 6,300 students
were black might be correct.

The IRS moved to revoke Bob Jones's tax exempt status in 1971.
After a long legal challenge to the revocation, which included Supreme
Court review in 1974 (the university's claim was rejected on procedural
grounds), the revocation became final in 1976. The university then
returned to the courts, seeking reinstatement of its exemption and
refund of taxes paid. The Justice Department defended the IRS revocation.

The district court ruled for Bob Jones, finding that Section 501(c)(3)
did not endow the IRS with the authority to discipline wrongdoing or to
engineer social policy. The Fourth Circuit reversed, rejecting the
district court's hypothesis that all "religious" institutions qualify for a
tax exemption as a "simplistic reading of the statute" that "tears

section 501(c)(3) from its roots." The court of appeals found that in order to qualify for an exemption, an institution "must be 'charitable' in the broad common law sense, and therefore must not violate public policy." Because Bob Jones University's racial practices violated clearly defined public policy, rooted in the Constitution and case law, it was not entitled to an exemption under the statute.

In the summer of 1981, the Justice Department and the IRS agreed to urge the Supreme Court to review the *Bob Jones* case. The case presented an opportunity to obtain a definitive ruling on the authority of the IRS when faced with a religious school, with its First Amendment protections, that practiced racial discrimination. Lawrence Wallace filed the government's acquiescence to Supreme Court review in September, and on October 13, 1981, the Court agreed to hear the case.

A few weeks later, on October 30, Representative Trent Lott, a Republican from Mississippi, wrote to Solicitor General Rex Lee—with copies going to President Reagan, Treasury Secretary Donald Regan, Attorney General William French Smith, and IRS Commissioner Roscoe Egger, Jr.—to express his displeasure at the government's position in the upcoming Supreme Court case (i.e., its support for the IRS's authority to withhold tax exempt status from segregated schools). Arguing that the government's stance "ignores Congressional interest," Lott took issue with the common law argument that, to qualify for an exemption, institutions must be "charitable" and, hence, compatible with public policy. Lott wrote:

> Section 501(c)(3) of the Code plainly defines exempt organizations to include bodies "organized and operated exclusively for religious, charitable, scientific, testing for public safety, literary, or educational purposes." "Charitable" is merely one of those purposes, as are "religious" and "educational." Nowhere does the statute require a religious or educational organization to be "charitable" in order to qualify for a tax exemption. If the statute is read this way, then organizations must also be "scientific" and test for public safety.

Further, Lott claimed, the government had distorted its reading of congressional intent in section 501(c)(3) by referring to "subsequent unrelated Congressional actions against racial discrimination." The IRS's action in revoking the tax exempt status of schools like Bob Jones was, Lott concluded, "peculiarly reminiscent of the federal bureaucracy's activism and usurpation of power during the previous Administration. Mississippians and many other of their fellow citizens supported President Reagan simply to end this kind of unwarranted interference." (See Exhibit 1 for the full text of Lott's letter.)

Response at Justice

At Treasury, Lott's letter was treated as a routine legislative inquiry and was forwarded to the department's legislative affairs branch, but the congressman's complaint found a more sympathetic hearing at the Justice Department, where Attorney General William French Smith had already made known his views on judicial activism. In an October 1981 speech before the Federal Legal Council, Smith had decried what he termed the "judicial policy-making" of the federal courts and vowed that, during his tenure, the Justice Department "will focus upon the doctrines that have led to the courts' activism. We will attempt to reverse this unhealthy flow of power from state and federal legislatures to federal courts. . . ."

These sentiments were later echoed by Associate Deputy Attorney General Bruce E. Fein, in a memo to his boss, Deputy Attorney General Edward C. Schmults, which he wrote in preparation for a December 8 meeting at Justice on the *Bob Jones* case. Fein's memo reviewed the history of the legal rationale behind the IRS's denial of the tax exemption; he also noted that the IRS's authority to deny had been initially endorsed by the Nixon administration and that incumbent IRS Commissioner Egger had not "expressly voiced any objection to maintaining those regulations [regarding denial of tax exemption to segregated schools]." Furthermore, Fein acknowledged, "to alter the government's position in *Bob Jones* and *Goldsboro* [a companion case] would be viewed by some as a retreat from the Department's commitment to protect civil rights." Nevertheless, hearkening back to the Attorney General's views on judicial activism, Fein maintained that there was "a convincing argument against interpreting [section 501(c)(3)] to exclude private schools practicing racial discrimination." Among other points, Fein noted that section 501(c)(3) had been enacted in an era "rampant with racial discrimination," and it seemed "unlikely" that Congress intended to "endow courts with authority to strip" discriminating schools; Congress, wrote Fein, "traditionally has been most reluctant to divest itself of authority over policies of taxation." Furthermore, the logical extension of the current IRS interpretation of the statute was "daunting": "It would support judicial decisions denying tax exempt status to institutions that did not accommodate the handicapped, the aged, women, and other groups currently favored in federal statutes on the ground that a tax exemption would be inconsistent with national policy." (See Exhibit 2 for Fein's memo.)

Despite Fein's efforts, the December 8 meeting at Justice did not give serious consideration to a possible change in policy. Deputy Solicitor General Larry Wallace and John Murray of Justice's tax division outlined the government's position on the *Bob Jones* case and left with plans to complete a draft brief (in support of denying the exemption) in the next two weeks. About a week later, Schmults wrote to Lott to inform him that the Justice Department "has been unable to conclude that abandonment of the legal position in defense of the [IRS] Commissioner's regulations in *Bob Jones* and *Goldsboro* would be expedient." Later, Schmults explained that he had sent the letter because "we were still representing the views of our client, the Treasury Department and the IRS, and there had been no other decisions made."

Still, there were signs of dissatisfaction with the status quo at Justice. Schmults himself (although termed by some conservatives "a typical establishment Republican who is weak on the Reagan agenda") was an adherent of the Attorney General's views on judicial policymaking; commenting later on his own position on the tax exemption, he remarked: "The law is the law. If we want to change the law, we ought to make Congress change it." Also lukewarm to the government's official position on *Bob Jones* was Ken Starr, the Attorney General's counselor, who had attended the December 8 session. On the day of that meeting Starr (and Bruce Fein) had received copies of two statements sent by Carolyn Kuhl, the Attorney General's special assistant. The first, from a Reagan/Bush campaign position paper, stated that Reagan "opposes the IRS's attempt to remove the tax-exempt status of private schools by administrative fiat"; the second, from the 1980 Republican platform, promised to "halt the unconstitutional vendetta launched by Mr. Carter's [sic] IRS Commissioner against independent schools."

Response at Treasury

In the meantime, at Treasury, IRS Commissioner Roscoe Egger had prepared a response for Secretary Regan to send to Representative Lott, stating that "all private schools, including church-related schools, must be operated on a racially non-discriminatory basis to be tax exempt." While acknowledging that the *Bob Jones* case raised important issues about the scope of religious liberties, Egger concluded that "[t]hey have been squarely presented to the Supreme Court and should be decided by that body."

Regan did not send Egger's letter, instead inviting the commissioner to join him at a meeting with Lott scheduled for mid-December; however, due to a hospitalization, Regan was unable to keep his appointment. On December 21, 1981, Lott again wrote Regan about the *Bob Jones* case and enclosed a copy of a page from President Reagan's log, which contained a summary of Lott's October 30 letter ("Indicates that the Supreme Court has now agreed to review [*Bob Jones*] . . . and urges you to intervene in this particular case"); next to the summary, the President had written the words, "I think we should." (See Exhibit 3.)

When the letter arrived at Treasury (a copy also went to Justice), Deputy Secretary of the Treasury R.T. McNamar asked Treasury General Counsel Peter Wallison to write a memo on the matter in preparation for a meeting the next day with White House Counsel Fred Fielding. In his memo, dated December 22, Wallison reviewed the history of the tax exemption issue, the common law interpretation of "charitable," and the legal rulings that had upheld the IRS's authority to deny a tax exemption to racially discriminatory schools. Unlike Fein and others at Justice, Wallison found the common law basis for denying the exemption "not unreasonable"; but he did acknowledge that "it must be recognized that once this principle is adopted it is difficult to find a stopping point." However, Wallison argued, given the current make-up of the Supreme Court, a decision in favor of the IRS would most likely be based on "narrow grounds" and would "emphasize that the *Bob Jones* case is unusual in that the school practiced racial discrimination openly and as a matter of policy." Wallison concluded:

> Thus . . . the case is unlikely to lead to substantial litigation over the revocation of tax exemptions unless the organizations involved practice racial discrimination as a matter of policy. If *Bob Jones* is viewed in this way, it will still provide a useful Supreme Court determination as to whether schools which discriminate on racial grounds are entitled to tax exemption, but will not provide a rationale for aggressive IRS action against tax exempt organizations on other theories or on other fact patterns.

Finally, Wallison predicted that an administration decision not to pursue the *Bob Jones* case in the Supreme Court would be seen as a "significant retreat" from past policies. He warned: "The explanation of the Administration's position—that the tax laws are not the proper vehicle for pursuing racial discrimination—would be lost in the ensuing outcry." (See Exhibit 4 for the full text of Wallison's memo.)

A Harder Line From Justice

Wallison's arguments notwithstanding, proponents of a policy shift began to press their views within the administration. Along with Bruce Fein, William Bradford Reynolds, assistant attorney general in charge of the Civil Rights Division, emerged as a strong advocate of abandoning support for the IRS's position on withholding tax exempt status. In Reynolds's opinion, nothing in the language of Section 501(c)(3) denied exemptions to segregated private schools. Even if an institution could not be "charitable" if it discriminated, he reasoned, it could nevertheless be "educational." The statute mandated exemptions to institutions that were "charitable" or "educational" or "scientific." Furthermore, Reynolds argued, the Civil Rights Act of 1964 prohibited only government *assistance* to private institutions that discriminated; nowhere in the law was there language indicating that exemptions were considered a form of assistance. To hold that an exemption constituted assistance would assume that the government in some way exercised prior ownership of private property—an intolerable assumption. As he put it later to the *New York Times,* "I think that the head of the Civil Rights Division ought to be applying the laws as they are written, and that's precisely what I'm doing and intend to keep doing. I don't think Congress has yet passed legislation that requires taking away tax-exempt status from a school that racially discriminates."

Reynolds and Fein met several times with Deputy Attorney General Schmults, and succeeded in convincing him that the present position could not be sustained. They also found an ally in the Treasury Department in Deputy Secretary McNamar, who was dissatisfied with the draft brief on the *Bob Jones* case (in support of the IRS position) which he had received from the Solicitor General's office on December 23. Like Schmults, McNamar was concerned about the lack of a limiting principle in the arguments set forth in the brief. As Schmults later explained, "Let us assume that the Internal Revenue Service today may, without congressional authorization, determine on the basis of what it genuinely perceived as national policy considerations that tax-exempt status should be denied to private schools that discriminated on grounds of race. Tomorrow, the tax exemption could well be eliminated by the Service, again without congressional action, for private schools that enroll only males or females. Presumably, hospitals that either do or do not permit abortions would be equally vulnerable to the taxing decisions of the IRS on the basis of its perception of national policy in this area at any given time." As a result, Schmults and McNamar agreed to send the brief back for further work to state more precisely the "legislative basis" for IRS authority.

About a week later, the Solicitor General's office delivered the second draft brief. According to McNamar, the brief

> was still based on the theory that the Service could determine that certain federal public policies could be used as a precondition for obtaining and retaining tax-exempt status. Given two tries, there apparently was no legal theory that would permit the Service to deny tax exemptions on the basis of racial discrimination without also giving the authority to deny or revoke exemption on other grounds. I, therefore, concluded that the Treasury could no longer support the IRS on this matter because the government would be required to take a

position in the Supreme Court that we simply did not regard as being either supported by statutory authority or adequately determined by the relevant case law and appropriate policy.

Deputy Attorney General Schmults reached the same conclusion. As he later put it: "After reviewing [the second draft brief], Mr. Reynolds, I and others remained unpersuaded by the legal arguments advanced. It was our opinion that such arguments were not sufficient to justify denial of tax exemptions because of race discrimination without also empowering the Internal Revenue Service to deny exemptions for a host of other policy reasons." At Treasury and at Justice, the decision had been made.

Involving the White House

Up to this point, the White House had been only peripherally involved in the debate. On December 18, Kenneth Cribbs, aide to presidential counselor Edwin Meese, had alerted Meese about the debate in Treasury and Justice on the *Bob Jones* case, and indicated that White House mediation might be needed. (Treasury General Counsel Peter Wallison had urged Donald Regan to raise the issue in the White House before the government had to file its brief in the Supreme Court.) Several days later, White House Counsel Fred Fielding briefed Meese on *Bob Jones*. Fielding recalled that he warned Meese that "you have to bear in mind that this could be interpreted as helping people who discriminate." He said he also warned that other groups of questionable legitimacy might seize upon the precedent to seek tax exemptions. Meese asked to be kept informed.

On December 28, Donald Regan met with McNamar, who told the Treasury Secretary that the tax exemption policy should probably be changed. Regan assented, but said McNamar should talk with Meese before making a decision. Later that day, McNamar phoned Meese and expressed his readiness to recommend a policy change. Meese then asked him, "How comfortable are you with the law"? McNamar replied that the law supported his position, but that he was concerned about possible political repercussions. Meese simply repeated, "Are you sure you are comfortable with the law?" Two days later, Fielding met with Schmults, Reynolds, and McNamar, who informed him of their decision to withdraw administration support of the IRS position. Fielding said he would check with Meese, and would get back to them if Meese raised any objections. Later, Fielding spoke with Meese, who approved the decision.

On the following day, New Year's Eve, Schmults and McNamar held a meeting with IRS Commissioner Egger and IRS Counsel Gideon. Schmults and McNamar outlined their decision, and asked them to be prepared to implement the policy shift. Egger and Gideon argued for retaining the current stance and letting the matter be resolved by the Supreme Court. They believed the draft brief, written by the Solicitor General's office, presented a sound, defensible position. It argued that the purpose of tax exemptions historically was to recognize the special benefits society reaped from organizations that were "charitable" in the broad common law sense. The brief cited numerous legal authorities for the proposition that the enumeration in the statute—charitable or educational or religious—simply detailed the kinds of organizations that were charitable in the broader common law meaning. Thus, they concluded, to qualify under the statute, an organization must not violate clearly defined public policy.

Besides, Egger and Gideon pointed out, all of the circuit courts that had ruled on the issue had decided in favor of the IRS position; in fact, the IRS was still bound by the *Green* injunction that forbade granting exemptions to segregated private schools in Mississippi. To reverse the policy without cover from a Supreme Court ruling could therefore precipitate a clash between the authority of the executive and the judiciary.

Schmults, Reynolds, and McNamar were unmoved. By this time, their beliefs were deeply established; in fact, a news release reflecting their position had already been prepared. No one at the meeting—or at any of the meetings in those weeks—represented minority interests. Traditionally, the head of the Civil Rights Division would serve this function, but Reynolds viewed the issue in terms of statutory interpretation and judicial power. In addition, the civil rights community had been unusually quiet during the first year of Reagan's term. The Civil Rights Division's reversals (under Reynolds' direction) on busing and affirmative action had raised no outcry. According to one official, "There was a belief that the great liberal age had expired. No one expected a great uproar in response to the *Bob Jones* reversal." To the extent that public disapproval was anticipated, the decisionmakers said later, they believed their cause to be worth the price. Schmults told a Senate committee a month later: "When confronted with the identical politically expedient issue in 1970, the Nixon administration succumbed to the pressure of public opinion and allowed the IRS to proceed down a path that was politically palatable but legally unjustified. This administration . . . [has] declined to operate on such a basis. The President has time and again demonstrated his commitment to principle over political expediency."

Other people who might have questioned the political wisdom of the decision—officials from public affairs or congressional liaison—were not consulted. Larry Wallace was not invited to any of the policymaking meetings; the Solicitor General's office was considered outside the policymaking circle at the Justice Department.

Final Steps

After the long New Year's weekend, Bruce Fein drafted a "confession of error" for the Supreme Court. (See Exhibit 5.) In that document, Fein argued that, historically, when Congress wished to use the tax code to "foster civil rights policies," it had been "unequivocal and explicit" in its intentions. In the absence of "any civil rights purpose in the explicit language and legislative history of Section 501(c)(3)," therefore, the federal government "confesse[d] error in its previous interpretation of the Internal Revenue Code as investing the Commissioner of Internal Revenue with authority to declare ineligible for tax-exempt status organizations that engage in racially discriminatory practices." The IRS intended, the document continued, to grant tax exempt status to Goldsboro Christian Schools [the companion case to *Bob Jones*] and reinstate tax exempt status for Bob Jones University.

Fein forwarded the confession of error to Larry Wallace to file with the Supreme Court, but Wallace refused to sign the document, asserting that his prior submissions to the court upholding the IRS position represented his view of the cases. In notes to Fein, Schmults, and Ken Starr, he attached documents bolstering his argument that Congress had ratified the IRS practice in its 1976 social clubs legislation. He also observed that the footnote from the 1974 Supreme Court case (which Reynolds used to attack the *Green* precedent), asserting that the *Green* appeal was non-adversarial because the government had switched sides, was factually wrong. Wallace noted that the appeal was indeed adversarial, because it had been taken by parents of students attending segregated schools.

In response to Wallace's refusal to sign the confession of error, administration officials considered an alternative approach. They would persuade the Commissioner of Internal Revenue to reverse the IRS policy through administrative action—i.e., to change the regulations on tax exempt status. In that event, Wallace would merely have to file a straightforward statement informing the Supreme Court that, due to pending revisions in IRS regulations, the *Bob Jones* and *Goldsboro* cases were now moot. Since such a document did not require him to argue that past IRS practices had been illegal, Wallace acquiesced and drafted a short memorandum. The motion he drafted merely noted the steps being taken by Treasury to grant tax exempt status in both cases at issue and to "revoke forthwith the pertinent Revenue Rulings that were relied upon to deny petitioners tax exempt status under the Code." Accordingly, the draft memorandum concluded, "the

United States therefore asks that the judgments of the court of appeals be vacated as moot."

On January 6, 1982, Attorney General William French Smith gathered together all the principles from Justice, Treasury, and the Solicitor General's office. After 2½ hours during which the participants presented the legal arguments for and against the claimed IRS authority, the Attorney General gave his final approval to the policy reversal. In Schmults's terms, "It was determined that the Department of Justice should advise the Department of the Treasury that our legal analysis led us to conclude that the IRS practice lacked statutory authority."

That evening, Smith mentioned the decision to James Baker, the White House Chief of Staff, during a phone conversation. Baker, who had not heard about the issue before, brought it up at a White House senior staff meeting the next morning. Meese and Fielding explained the decision, presenting it as a fait accompli. (Several high-level officials there received the erroneous impression from them that the administration had lost the appellate cases.) Meese also presented the decision as a reversal of a Carter policy, apparently repeating the error committed by the Republican platform. Michael Deaver, Deputy Chief of Staff, later recalled, "I just heard that it was a reversal of a Carter policy, and at that point I tuned out." Another official present said, "One left the senior staff meeting thinking that it wasn't about much of anything. It was a pending Carter regulation that needed to be overturned, on which Justice and Treasury agreed."

That evening, or the morning of January 8, Meese and Baker informed President Reagan of the decision and the impending announcement. Meese said later that the President "was advised as an information matter. I don't remember any statement [from Reagan]. I don't think it was asked in that way. I think it was just given to him for information." (Reagan later told a *Washington Post* reporter, "I didn't know at the time there was a legal case pending.")

IRS Counselor Gideon and Commissioner Egger—not wanting to take responsibility for a decision from which they dissented—insisted that McNamar order them in writing to reverse the IRS exemption practice. Accordingly, on Friday, January 8, McNamar issued a memo to Egger directing him "to take the necessary steps to reverse the previous decisions of the [IRS] in denying tax-exempt status to Bob Jones University and Goldsboro Christian Schools, Inc." That same day, the motion to vacate the *Bob Jones* and *Goldsboro* cases was filed with the Supreme Court. (See Exhibit 6.)

Also on that day, the Treasury Department issued a press release, with the headline "Treasury Establishes New Tax–Exempt Policy."

(See Exhibit 7.) As he had done internally in recent weeks, McNamar put forth the argument that the IRS did not possess authority "to decide . . . whether private organizations conform with fundamental national policies. The Treasury Department has concluded that this kind of judgment—which may mean life or death for certain organizations—is fundamentally a question for Congress. . . ." The news release went on to announce the IRS's intention to restore the tax exemption of both Bob Jones and Goldsboro.

Backlash

It was immediately clear that the opposition had been severely underestimated. A firestorm of protest came from all fronts: the press, congressional leaders (Democrats and Republicans alike), and civil rights leaders. On Saturday morning, Michael Deaver awoke to realize what had been done. "I don't know why we did that," he told an aide. "It's the wrong signal to be sending, especially at this time." Baker and Deaver were variously described as "genuinely upset," "frustrated," "angry," "livid," and "worked up" because Meese had not discussed the issue with them earlier and more fully. Baker was especially disturbed because Fred Fielding, who officially reported to him, had worked with Meese on the issue without mentioning it.

Deaver, a trustee of Howard University, a leading institution in black education, took control on Monday morning. He engineered the administration's modification of its position, and arranged for three black leaders to meet with President Reagan to express their outrage at the new policy. Later on Monday, David R. Gergen, White House Director of Communications, was given the job of writing a statement repudiating the policy. That statement, a one-page document worked on by a group of 14 presidential advisors, was issued the following day. (See Exhibit 8.) In it, the President asserted that his administration's opposition to "administrative agencies exercising powers that the Constitution assigns to the Congress" had been the "sole basis" for Treasury's decision on *Bob Jones*. Expressing his "regret" about the "misunderstanding" that had ensued, Reagan stated that "the right thing to do" would be to enact legislation prohibiting tax exemptions for racially discriminatory organizations; and he announced his intention of submitting such legislation to Congress. Several days later, on January 18, he sent the proposed legislation to House Speaker Thomas P. O'Neill, Jr. As expected, the bill denied tax exemptions to racially discriminatory schools and deductions for contributions to such institutions; the measure would be retroactive to 1970, to prevent law suits for tax refunds. (See Exhibit 9 for full text of the proposed legislation.)

In his letter of transmittal for the bill, President Reagan announced that the IRS would postpone any action on granting exemptions to segregated private schools until Congress acted. At the same time, however, the IRS proceeded with the reinstatement of tax exempt status for Bob Jones University and Goldsboro Christian Schools; the administration felt that its Supreme Court submission, representing the cases as moot, constituted a "pledge" to grant the exemptions. (The IRS first had to check whether the schools qualified in all other respects for exempt status, a process which was expected to take about a month.)

Despite the administration's efforts, the furor over the tax exemption issue continued. During a news conference held the day after the legislation was submitted, Reagan was subjected to close questioning on the *Bob Jones* affair. (See Exhibit 10.) More grilling was in store during the first week in February, when Congress opened hearings on the administration's tax exemption measure. Congress gave the bill an icy reception: liberals and moderates believed the IRS already had the authority to bar tax exemptions, while many conservatives felt the proposal betrayed the President's campaign promise.

At the Senate Finance Committee hearing, Democratic Senator Spark M. Matsunaga remarked to Reynolds:

> Somehow it bothers me that you seem to place so much emphasis on statutory basis as opposed to legal basis. You know as well as I do, having been in the legal profession I'm sure for years now, that there are rulings based on legal bases which need not be statutory, such as in the *Brown v. Board of Education*. And if you are seeking a legal basis, which you ought to be seeking, I would think that the *Green* case does provide sufficient legal basis on which the IRS could act.

Senator David L. Boren took issue with Schmults's and McNamar's notion that a limiting principle could not be found to justify the IRS policy:

> I want to say candidly that I have great difficulty following the logic of some of the analogies that have been used, for example the Sierra Club analogy. [McNamar had contended that under IRS's rationale in *Bob Jones,* the Sierra Club could have its exempt status revoked for actions contrary to the "national policy to encourage domestic energy production."] Certainly the Chairman and I agree there ought to be [domestic energy production], and it's sound public policy, but it is not constitutionally mandated public policy. Nowhere have we had a constitutional mandate from the courts that women would have to be ordained as priests, or other things that have been mentioned, or energy would have to be produced domestically. We have had a constitutional mandate from the courts for

equal educational opportunity without regard for discrimination by race.

If the Senate hearings were inhospitable, the House Ways and Means hearings three days later were, at times, downright hostile. Harvard Law Professor Lawrence H. Tribe opened the hearings calling for formal censure of the Reagan administration. He testified, "What is absolutely clear is that the executive branch isn't supposed to take the law into its own hands and just shovel it away and not proceed with a pending case in the Supreme Court to test its legal themes." Representative William M. Brodhead of Michigan, calling the administration's testimony "the shabbiest, most incredibly unbelievable crap," berated the government witnesses: "It is the administration here which has acted by executive fiat and attempted to change the law. This administration needs to be reminded that it is the province of the court, not the executive, to interpret the law. The courts have interpreted the law. The courts have spoken. The law is clear, and this administration simply would not follow it, and I'm appalled."

With the administration bill in disfavor, the IRS in a holding pattern, and the *Bob Jones* case apparently mooted (the Supreme Court had not yet ruled on the motion to dismiss), the controversy seemed to have become so tangled that there could be no easy escape. As *New York Times* reporter Stuart Taylor, Jr. observed, "The paradox is that, although the Administration and a clear majority in Congress now agree that there should be a law against granting exemption to racially discriminatory schools, and the Federal courts have ruled that there is already such a law, none of the three branches of Government may be willing or able to do what each agrees should be done." The longer the stalemate continued, the more likely it was that the administration would have to grant exemptions, at a heavy political cost.

The Reagan administration found an unlikely rescue in the activism of the U.S. Court of Appeals for the District of Columbia Circuit. That court was hearing a nationwide class action suit brought by black parents seeking to invalidate the administration's plans to grant exemptions to segregated schools. On February 18, the court enjoined the IRS from granting or restoring such exemptions. In response, a White House official commented, "Legally at this point we cannot do what we told the Supreme Court we intended to do. It might provide us with the opportunity to have the Supreme Court litigate the issue, since Congress itself has obviously shown no inclination to resolve it." A week later, the administration seized the opportunity. It filed papers with the Supreme Court asking for leave to argue the case in support of Bob Jones University on the issue of whether the IRS had statutory authority to revoke the exemptions. At the same time, it maintained its position that the Congress could, consistent with the First Amendment, act to deny tax exemptions to segregated schools. Justice asked the court to appoint counsel to argue the opposing side on the issue of statutory authority.

Wallace's Dilemma

In preparation for the Supreme Court case, the Solicitor General's office was sent a brief which incorporated much of an "alternate" brief composed earlier at Reynolds's direction by his aide, Charles Cooper, and Attorney General Smith's aide, Carolyn Kuhl. Not surprisingly, the arguments differed radically from the draft brief Larry Wallace had submitted back in December. The new brief stated, for example, that the 1970 reversal of IRS policy (resulting in denial of tax exempt status to racially discriminatory schools) had "no support in the language of Section 501(c)(3), or in its legislative history." Further, the brief stated, "We do not find sufficient evidence of affirmative action by Congress since 1970 to warrant the conclusion that the I.R.S. practice now under attack [by Bob Jones and Goldsboro] has received legislative ratification. Thus the denial of tax exemptions to Bob Jones University and Goldsboro Christian Schools is, we submit, unauthorized agency action that should not, in the absence of Congressional action, be countenanced."

The Solicitor General's office had a long tradition of viewing its first duty to be to the Supreme Court or, in an alternate formulation, to the overall development of the law in the United States. Erwin N. Griswold, Solicitor General in the Johnson and Nixon administrations, once observed:

> The Solicitor General has a special obligation to aid the Court as well as to serve his client. Moreover, since his client is always the United States government or its officers or agencies, the loyalties are not as easily defined as they generally are in private practice. The Solicitor General's client in a particular case cannot be properly represented before the Supreme Court except from a broad point of view, taking into account all of the factors which affect sound government and the proper formulation and development of the law.

In obedience to these ideals, past Solicitors General had at times refused to do the bidding of the administration in power. When, for example, President Eisenhower's first Solicitor General, Simon E. Sobeloff, was handed *Peters v. Hobby*,[7] in which the government had taken the position that an accused man could lose his job without having the right of confronting his accuser, he refused to argue the case

---

[7] *Peters v. Hobby,* 349 U.S. 331 (1955).

or sign the brief—perhaps at the cost of a future Supreme Court appointment.

Now Wallace found himself in a similar situation. The marked differences in this new brief from his earlier filings brought into sharp relief his own personal and professional disagreement with the administration's position. He recalled his earlier confrontation with the Attorney General's office over the proposed "confession of error." Now he had to decide what he would do with the brief.

EXHIBIT 1

Letter from Trent Lott to Solicitor General Rex Lee

TRENT LOTT
7th District, Mississippi

REPUBLICAN WHIP

RULES COMMITTEE

ADMINISTRATIVE ASSISTANT
TOM M. ANDERSON, JR.

Congress of the United States
House of Representatives
Washington, D.C. 20515

October 30, 1981

The Honorable Rex Lee
Solicitor General
United States Department of Justice
Washington, D.C. 20530

Dear Mr. Solicitor General:

I am sure you are familiar with my correspondence earlier
this year with the Attorney General and the Deputy Attorney
General regarding the many pending cases concerning the tax
exempt status of church schools. I was disappointed to learn
that you will not be involved in Bob Jones University v. United
States and, indeed, that no Reagan appointee will play a major
role. Please pass my concerns along to whoever is handling
these consolidated cases.

I am delighted that the Administration encouraged the
Supreme Court to resolve these issues. However, I am more than
a little disturbed that the United States has taken a position
on the merits which plainly conflicts with Congressional intent
and with a specific pledge of the President's platform. I
strongly encourage your office to reconsider your position.

The Government's position ignores Congressional intent.
Section 501(c)(3) of the Code plainly defines exempt organizations
to include bodies "organized and operated exclusively for religious,
charitable, scientific, testing for public safety, literary, or
educational purposes." "Charitable" is merely one of those purposes,
as are "religious" and "educational." Nowhere does the statute
require a religious or educational organization to be "charitable"
in order to qualify for a tax exemption. If the statute is read
this way, then organizations must also be "scientific" and test
for public safety. Since the plain language of the statute fore-
closes the construction urged by the Government, ordinary rules
of construction preclude looking behind the language to the
legislative history.

The Government does not even bother to look at the history
of this particular section as it was adopted in 1938. Rather,
the United States derives its construction from subsequent unrelated Congressional actions against racial discrimination. Ordinarily, committee reports and floor remarks made long after the
fact are completely irrelevant in determining the intent of a
previous Congress. Furthermore, these later Congressional actions
were responsive to other problems and there is absolutely no

Exhibit 1 (continued)

Page Two
The Honorable Rex Lee
October 30, 1981

indication that Congress intended these relatively recent
actions to be read into an unrelated statute passed in 1938.

If subsequent actions are relevant, then the Government
should focus upon expressions of Congressional intent on this
very issue. The Ashbrook Amendment to successive Treasury
appropriations prohibits absolutely the use of federal funds
to "cause the loss of tax-exempt status to private, religious,
or church-operated schools under section 501(c)(3) of the
Internal Revenue Code of 1954." Congressional intent could
not be clearer. Therefore, if the Government insists on
defining Congressional intent by later actions, then certainly
that intent is most clearly reflected by the Ashbrook amendment.

The Internal Revenue Service's action in revoking the tax
exempt status of these schools is peculiarly reminiscent
of the federal bureaucracy's activism and usurption of power
during the previous Administration. Mississippians and many
of their fellow citizens supported President Reagan simply
to end this kind of unwarranted interference.

The last time I read the Constitution, it provided that
the Congress is to make the laws--not appointed officials.
The people across the country whose lives are directly affected
are entitled to have the decision of their elected Representatives
respected and followed by the Government. Congress has spoken,
and its message is clear. It is up to the Government to enforce
what Congress has done. I expect your office to reconsider its
position and to report its decision to me.

With kind regards and best wishes, I am

Sincerely yours,

Trent Lott

TL/mbv

cc: Hon. Ronald Reagan
    Hon. Donald Regan
    Hon. Roscoe Egger, Jr.
    Hon. William French Smith

EXHIBIT 2

Memorandum from Bruce Fein to
Deputy Attorney General Edward Schmults

Office of the Deputy Attorney General

Washington, D.C. 20530

December 7, 1981

MEMORANDUM FOR: Edward C. Schmults
                  Deputy Attorney General

                                                    BEF

FROM: Bruce E. Fein
                  Associate Deputy Attorney General

SUBJECT: Meeting on Justice Department Briefs
                  in Bob Jones University v. United States
                  and Goldsboro Christian Schools v. United
                  States

                  (Tuesday, December 8, 11:00 A.M. with
                  Messrs Larry Wallace, Ken Starr, and John
                  Murray; Rex Lee is recused from the case)

The purpose of this meeting is to alert you to the legal doctrines that the Tax Division and the Solicitor General currently intend to champion in the above-captioned Supreme Court
litigation to determine whether they may be inconsistent with
the litigating policies recently elucidated by the Attorney
General and yourself. If you believe that there is a discre-
pancy, you may find it expedient to suggest a legal approach
different from the one currently endorsed by the Tax Division.

The controlling issue in Bob Jones and Goldsboro is whether
Congress intended §170 of the Internal Revenue Code to exclude
private schools from eligibility for tax exempt status if they
practice racial discrimination. An affirmative answer was
given by a three judge district court in 1970 and the U. S.
Supreme Court summarily affirmed. The Supreme Court has explained that summary affirmances have little doctrinal value.

Briefly stated, the legal rationale advocated by the Tax Division to justify denial of tax exempt status to private schools
practicing racial discrimination is as follows:

Exhibit 2 (continued)

−2−

1. Congress intended in enacting §170 some sixty years ago
tacitly to bestow on federal courts authority to deny
organizations that fell within the ambit of §170 tax
exempt status if, after surveying contemporary national
social, economic, and other policies, the courts determined that the applicant organization engaged in a practice
in conflict with any such policy.

2. Although §170 was passed when both public and private
racial discrimination was the norm, national policies
have evolved since that time to make racial discrimination anathama to federal law. Congress, it is contended,
intended to invest the federal judiciary with responsibility for detecting such a change in national policy and
to alter pro tanto, the ambit of §170 in accord with
contemporary national mores.

3. The Tax Division claims that the federal judiciary in these
cases properly exercised a roving commission to examine
all potentially eligible tax exempt schools to determine
whether any should be ousted from §170 because practicing
a policy that the judiciary found at odds with an over-
riding national policy. This expansionist view of §170,
if accepted, would reflect an unprecedented entrustment
of policymaking power from Congress to the judiciary.

In support of the Tax Division's views, it should be noted that
they were initially endorsed under the Nixon Administration, that
they are incorporated in outstanding regulations of the Internal
Revenue Service, and that the incumbent Commissioner of Internal
Revenue has not expressly voiced any objection to maintaining
those regulations. Furthermore, to alter the government's
position in Bob Jones and Goldsboro would be viewed by some
as a retreat from the Department's commitment to protect civil
rights.

On the other hand, the legal theory advanced by the Tax Division
seems to conflict with the Attorney General's view that the Department should discourage rather than encourage judicial activism and policymaking, except when clearly mandated by statute
of the Constitution. The Attorney General has stated, as you
know, that the Department would not deviate from its litigating
policies simply to obtain an advantage in a particular case.
There is a convincing argument against interpreting §170 to
exclude private schools practicing racial discrimination:

1. The statute was enacted during an era rampant with
racial discrimination. It seems unlikely that the
enacting Congress intended to endow courts with
authority to strip schools of tax exempt status upon
a finding that racial discrimination was no longer
nationally acceptable. Congress, as you know, traditionally has been most reluctant to divest itself
of authority over policies of taxation.

Exhibit 2 (continued)

- 3 -

2. No substantial constitutional question would be
   raised by permitting private schools practicing
   racial discrimination to claim the exemption offered
   by §170. The Supreme Court has ruled that granting
   tax exempt status to churches or church property
   does not violate the First Amendment, and that
   offering institutions liquor licenses or similar
   benefits that do not actively encourage private
   race discrimination is constitutionally acceptable.
   There is thus no need in these cases to strain the
   interpretation of §170 to avoid a constitutional
   encounter.

3. The consequences of accepting the Tax Division's
   legal theory are daunting. It would support judicial
   decisions denying tax exempt status to institutions
   that did not accommodate the handicapped, the aged,
   women, and other groups currently favored in federal
   statutes on the ground that a tax exemption would be
   inconsistent with national policy. This exercise of
   judicial power would represent a sharp deviation from
   traditional congressional resistence to regulating
   comprehensively the affairs of nonprofit and other
   small entities.

The briefs in the Supreme Court are scheduled for filing in
approximately one week, although it might be possible to obtain
an extension. If you believe at the conclusion of the meeting
that there is any merit to altering the Department's litigating
position, then further consultation with the Attorney General
and our client agency in the matter, the Internal Revenue Service,
would be necessary.

EXHIBIT 3

Excerpt from Presidential Log

PRESIDENTIAL LOG OF SELECTED HOUSE MAIL

SUBJECT	CONTENTS

EXPRESSES STRONG SUPPORT FOR THE EXTENSION
OF THE TARIFF ON IMPORTED FASTENERS

. B. JINGELL
ALSO SIGNED BY:
   PHILIP R. SHARP

COMMENDS THE ADMINISTRATION FOR NOT
SUPPORTING ANY FURTHER WAIVERS OF LAW FOR
THE ALASKAN NATURAL GAS TRANSPORTATION SYSTEM

TRENT LOTT

WRITES REGARDING PENDING CASES CONCERNING
THE TAX EXEMPT STATUS OF CHURCH SCHOOLS.
INDICATES THAT THE SUPREME COURT HAS NOW
AGREED TO REVIEW THE CASE OF "BOB JONES
UNIVERSITY V. UNITED STATES," AND URGES
YOU TO INTERVENE IN THIS PARTICULAR CASE

J. KENNETH ROBINSON
ALSO SIGNED BY:
   JOHN M. ASHBROOK
   ROBERT MCCLORY
   G. WILLIAM WHITEHURST
   C. W. BILL YOUNG

EXPRESS THEIR SUPPORT FOR THE PROPOSED
EXECUTIVE ORDER ON INTELLIGENCE, AS WELL
AS THEIR CONCERN OVER THE MISLEADING STORIES
IN THE PRESS. IN PROTECTING OUR NATIONAL
SECURITY INTEREST CONSISTENT WITH THE
EXECUTIVE ORDER, SUGGESTS THAT CERTAIN
MODIFICATIONS OF EXISTING STATUTES MAY BE
REQUIRED, PARTICULARLY IN REGARD TO THE
LIMITS IMPOSED BY THE FOREIGN INTELLIGENCE
SURVEILLANCE ACT

EXHIBIT 4

Memorandum from General Counsel Peter Wallison to
Treasury Secretary Regan

Noted by DTR

81-19464

Inter-Office Memorandum

□ ACTION   ☒ BRIEFING   □ INFORMATION

Date: December 22, 1981

For: SECRETARY REGAN

Thru: R. T. McNamar

From: Peter J. Wallison
General Counsel

Subject: Treasury Position on Bob Jones Case

     In an earlier memorandum to you, I discussed in summary
fashion the kinds of questions which Congressman Trent Lott
would be likely to raise concerning the Bob Jones case and the
related case of Green v. Regan. Further review of these issues
within Treasury suggests that they are significant enough to
raise at the White House level now, so that the Administration's
position can be finally settled before the Justice Department's
brief is filed in the Supreme Court on December 31.

     The brief-filing requirement provides a good reason for
raising this issue at the White House as soon as possible,
and would also place us in a position to respond to Congressman
Lott without substantial additional delay.

     As noted in my earlier memo, the Service and the Justice
Department have taken the position that a tax exempt religious
school must be "charitable" in the broadest sense in order to
be entitled to retain its tax exempt status. Thus, the mere
fact that the school is a bona fide religious organization does
not entitle it to a tax exemption, even though § 501(c)(3) of
the Internal Revenue Code lists religious organizations as one
of the categories of groups which are entitled to tax exempt
status. The Service contends that in enacting Section 501(c)(3)
of the Code, Congress intended to provide tax exemption only to
those organizations which were "charitable" within the broad
meaning of that word as used in common law. This means that
the organization cannot pursue practices which are inconsistent
with the most fundamental public policies of society, and in
particular may not practice racial discrimination.

Exhibit 4 (continued)

-2-

In its most general terms, the question here is whether any organization which is <u>bona fide</u> religious or educational is entitled to a tax exemption no matter what its practices.* Some people are very comfortable with the proposition; others believe that Congress could not have intended to provide the significant benefit of tax exemptions to organizations which practice racial discrimination.

In the <u>Bob Jones</u> case, the Service encountered an institution which, although tax exempt and <u>bona fide</u> religious, overtly practiced racial discrimination because of its fundamentalist reading of Scripture.

That the Service has the authority to revoke the tax exemption of organizations which practice racial discrimination has been upheld in the <u>Bob Jones</u> case by the United States Court of Appeals for the Fourth Circuit and, in another case, by a three-judge panel of the Federal District Court for the District of Columbia. Indeed, it does not seem unreasonable that an organization which discriminates on the basis of race is not "charitable" in the broadest sense and therefore should not be entitled to the benefits of tax exemption.

On the other hand, it must be recognized that once this princip is adopted it is difficult to find a stopping point. With a broad enough decision in <u>Bob Jones</u>, the Service could challenge a range of private schools for enforcing racially discriminatory policies <u>de facto</u> -- even though the distinctive feature of Bob Jones is that it established its discriminatory rules overtly. Moreover, a far-reaching decision of the Supreme Court could conceivably form the basis for other challenges to tax exempt organizations which are engaged in practices which arguably are not "charitable" -- <u>e.g.</u>, churches which will not perform ceremonies in which members marry outside the faith. This, in my judgment, is the most serious objection to the principle articulated by the Service in the <u>Bob Jones</u> case.

However, given the current composition of the Supreme Court, I think it is possible that any endorsement of the Service's position will be based on narrow grounds. Such a decision would hold that the Service may revoke the tax exemption of a school

---

*. It should be noted that the beliefs or ideas which are inculcated or taught at the school or other organization are not the issue; the issue is the school's <u>practices</u>. The tax exemption of Bob Jones University was revoked not because it teaches that Scriptur requires separation of the races but because it implements that belief by discriminating on the basis of race.

Exhibit 4 (continued)

- 3 -

which is not "charitable" because it practices racial discrimination, but the Court's opinion would emphasize that the
Bob Jones case is unusual in that the school practiced racial
discrimination openly and as a matter of policy. In the ordinary
case, the Service must present some evidence of discrimination
in order to prevail, and this is difficult to obtain without
the unusual facts of Bob Jones.

Thus, even if the Service wins Bob Jones, the case is
unlikely to lead to substantial litigation over the revocation
of tax exemptions unless the organizations involved practice
racial discrimination as a matter of policy. If Bob Jones is
viewed in this way, it will still provide a useful Supreme Court
determination as to whether schools which discriminate on racial
grounds are entitled to tax exemption, but will not provide a
rationale for aggressive IRS action against tax exempt organizations on other theories or on other fact patterns.

At the same time, one must consider the politics of a change
in the Administration's policy with respect to Bob Jones at this
point. The case was commenced during a Republican Administration
in 1970 and carried through a successful appeal to the Fourth
Circuit Court of Appeals. This suggests that the Service's
position is neither frivolous nor the implementation of the social
policies of the IRS bureaucracy. If the Administration were now
to take the position that the case should not be pursued before
the Supreme Court, that view would be read as a statement by the
Administration that overtly discriminatory practices are not
objectionable, and as a significant retreat from the past policies
in this area of both Republican and Democratic Administrations.
The explanation of the Administration's position -- that the tax
laws are not the proper vehicle for pursuing racial discrimination -- would be lost in the ensuing outcry.

To summarize, then, the Bob Jones case is not in my view
troublesome if it upholds the authority of the Service to
challenge tax exemptions for private schools which discriminate --
as in Bob Jones -- as a matter of policy. At the same time, I
believe in the Administration's support for the Service's position
in the Bob Jones case could be very troublesome -- with the
political benefits heavily outweighed by the political liabilities.

a change

EXHIBIT 5

Confession of Error, drafted by Bruce Fein

CURRENT
PROPOSED (5)
TO BE FILED
WEDNESDAY

Nos. 81-1 and 81-3

IN THE SUPREME COURT OF THE UNITED STATES

OCTOBER TERM, 1981

GOLDSBORO CHRISTIAN SCHOOLS, INC., PETITIONER

v.

UNITED STATES OF AMERICA

BOB JONES UNIVERSITY, PETITIONER

v.

UNITED STATES OF AMERICA

ON WRITS OF CERTIORARI TO
THE UNITED STATES COURT OF APPEALS
FOR THE FOURTH CIRCUIT

MEMORANDUM FOR THE UNITED STATES

Exhibit 5 (continued)

604

This Court granted writs of certiorari in the above-captioned cases and ordered consolidation on October 13, 1981. Petitioners seek reversal of the Court of Appeals' decision upholding Internal Revenue Service regulations that were applied to deny them tax-exempt status as "religious" or "educational" institutions under Section 501(c)(3) of the Internal Revenue Code of 1954 and sister Code provisions regarding federal social security taxes (Section 3121(b)(8)(B) of the Code), federal unemployment taxes (Section 3306(c)(8) of the Code), and the deductibility of charitable contributions (Section 170(a) and (c) of the Code) because of certain racially discriminatory practices of petitioners. In the courts below and in our Memorandun in opposition to the petitions for writs of certiorari, the United States argued tht the Commissioner of Internal Revenue acted within his statutory authority in determining that Congress intended to deny petitioners tax-exempt status under the Internal Revenue Code. After closely reexamining the challenged regulations and the Internal Revenue Code provisions cn which the regulations are based, the United states has concluded that this position and the Court of Appeals' decision were in error.

605

Generally speaking, Congress employs the Internal Revenue Code for revenue raising or other fiscal purposes. On rare occasions, Congress has employed the Code to foster civil rights policies that it has established in a comprehensive network of civil rights laws. Congress has been unequivocal and explicit, however, when it has taken this course, as in denying tax-exempt status to social clubs that practice racial discrimination. (cite).

Exhibit 5 (continued)

Congress has addressed problems of racial and other forms of discrimination in a networks of laws providing both public and private remedies for violations. For example, Congress has in various statutes invested private individuals with power to challenge acts of racial discrimination practiced by private institutions such as petitioners. See, for example, 42 U.S.C. §1981-1982; Jones v. Mayer; Runyon v. McCrary. The United States, however, has concluded that the absence of any civil rights purpose in the explicit language and legislative history of Section 501(c)(3) of the Internal Revenue Code demonstrates the lack of authority in the Commissioner to unilaterally impose nondiscrimination requirements on organizations that would otherwise qualify as tax-exempt under that statute. Whether or not such nondiscrimination requirements should be engrafted onto Section 501(c)(3) is a question entrusted by the Constitution to the Congress.

606

Accordingly, the United States hereby confesses error in its previous interpretation of the Internal Revenue Code as investing the Commissioner of Internal Revenue with authority to declare ineligible for tax-exempt status organizations that engage in racially discriminatory practices. The Commissioner intends to grant petitioner Goldsboro tax-exempt status under Section 501(c)(3) of the Code, and will refund to it federal social security and unemployment taxes in dispute. The Commissioner also intends to reinstate tax-exempt status under Section 501(c)(3) of the Code to petitioner Bob Jones, and will refund to it federal social security and unemployment taxes in dispute. Finally, the Commissioner has instituted procedures to revoke the regulations (26 C.F.R.) that were employed to deny petitioners tax exempt status under the Code. Accordingly, the United States suggests that the cases in Nos. 81-1 and 81-3 be dismissed as moot and that the judgments of the Court of Appeals be vacated.

EXHIBIT 6

Memorandum from R.T. McNamar to IRS Commissioner Roscoe Egger

MEMORANDUM FOR COMMISSIONER EGGER

Subject: Tax-Exemption for Bob Jones University
             and Goldsboro Christian Schools, Inc.

    This memorandum is to confirm the Department's direction to you to begin the process of granting Bob Jones University and Goldsboro Christian Schools, Inc. tax-exempt status under section 501(c)(3) of the Internal Revenue Code.

    After much consideration and having the benefit of discussions with you and the Department of Justice, I have decided as a policy and legal matter that the Internal Revenue Service is without legislative authority to deny tax-exempt status to otherwise eligible organizations on the grounds that their policies or practices do not conform to notions of national public policy.

    Therefore, I am directing you to take the necessary steps to reverse the previous decisions of the Internal Revenue Service in denying tax-exempt status to Bob Jones University and Goldsboro Christian Schools, Inc. It is my understanding that in order to accomplish this, you will also have to revoke the applicable revenue rulings under which you denied these institutions tax-exempt status and refund to them Federal social security and unemployment taxes. These steps should be taken as soon as legally possible.

R. T. McNamar

EXHIBIT 7

Treasury News Release

TREASURY NEWS

Department of the Treasury ● Washington, D.C. ● Telephone 566-2041

FOR IMMEDIATE RELEASE   Contact: Marlin Fitzwater
Friday, January 8, 1982   (202) 566-5252

TREASURY ESTABLISHES NEW TAX-EXEMPT POLICY

The Treasury Department announced today that without further
guidance from Congress, the Internal Revenue Service will no
longer revoke or deny tax-exempt status for religious,
charitable, educational or scientific organizations on the
grounds that they don't conform with certain fundamental public
policies.

"In the past," said Deputy Treasury Secretary R. T. McNamar,
"the IRS has revoked the tax exemptions of organizations which,
did not adhere to certain fundamental national policies, such as
those forbidding discrimination on the basis of race, even though
this requirement is not explicitly stated in the Internal Revenue
Code except in the case of social clubs."

"Whether or not the Treasury Department or this
Administration agrees with the position of the IRS in particular
cases is not the issue," McNamar stated. "The question is
whether the IRS is required under the Code as enacted by Congress
to decide -- as a condition to granting or continuing tax-exempt
status -- whether private organizations conform with fundamental
national policies. The Treasury Department has concluded that
this kind of judgment -- which may mean life or death for certain
organizations -- is fundamentally a question for Congress; and if
the authority to make this judgment is given by Congress to an
administrative agency it should be done in explicit terms and
subject to specific guidelines."

As a consequence of this decision, the IRS will restore the
tax exemption of certain organizations which had previously been
revoked. In particular, the appeal of Bob Jones University,
and the Goldsboro Schools, which are currently before the Supreme
Court will be rendered moot.

Exhibit 7 (continued)

-2-

"In taking this action," McNamar stated, "we are attempting
to protect the independence of all private tax-exempt
organizations -- many of which may follow practices and adhere to
principles with which we disagree. But before the government
gets into the business of deciding which organizations are worthy
of tax exemption and which are not, we want Congress to fully
consider the implications of such a course."

The Treasury Department decision reflects the advice of the
Department of Justice that the authority which the IRS previously
had been asserting as its basis for revoking the tax exemptions
in question is not supported by the language of the Internal
Revenue Code or its legislative history. The Internal Revenue
Code provides tax exemptions for "Corporations (or other
organizations) organized and operated exclusively for religious,
charitable, scientific ... or educational ... purposes ...." IRC
Section 501(c)(3), 26 U.S.C. Section 501(c)(3). The Justice
Department has advised that both the language of Section
501(c)(3) and the statute's legislative history provide no
support for the statutory interpretation adopted by the
Commissioner in 1970. Thus the IRS is without legislative
authority to deny tax-exempt status to otherwise eligible
organizations on the grounds that their policies or practices do
not conform to notions of national public policy.

This new policy is reflected in a motion filed with the
Supreme Court today by the Justice Department to vacate a case in
which the Internal Revenue Service revoked the tax-exempt status
of Bob Jones University and Goldsboro Christian Schools. IRS
revoked the Bob Jones University tax exemption in 1970 on the
grounds that the school's racial policies violated Federal
policies on racial discrimination. This decision was nullified
by the U.S. District Court in South Carolina on June 30, 1971.
However, the lower court's decision was reversed by the 4th
Circuit Court of Appeals on December 30, 1980.

Similarly in 1974 the IRS determined that Goldsboro
Christian Schools Inc. did not qualify for an exemption on the
grounds that it maintained a racially discriminatory admissions
policy. On May 7, 1980 the District Court for the Eastern
district of North Carolina upheld the IRS decision. On
February 24, 1981 the Court of Appeals for the 4th Circuit
affirmed this judgement period.

Both schools appealed the Circuit Court decision to the
Supreme Court which accepted their petitions for certiorari on
October 13, 1981.

EXHIBIT 8

Statement By President Reagan

THE WHITE HOUSE

Office of the Press Secretary

For Immediate Release   January 12, 1982

STATEMENT BY THE PRESIDENT

This issue of whether to deny tax exemptions to non-profit, private, educational institutions raises important questions and sensitive policy considerations.

My administration is committed to certain fundamental views which must be considered in addressing this matter:

— I am unalterably opposed to racial discrimination in any form. I would not knowingly contribute to any organization that supports racial
   discrimination. My record and the record of
   this administration are clear on this point.

— I am also opposed to administrative agencies
   exercising powers that the Constitution assigns
   to the Congress. Such agencies, no matter how
   well intentioned, cannot be allowed to govern by
   administrative fiat. That was the sole basis of
   the decision announced by the Treasury Department
   last Friday. I regret that there has been a
   misunderstanding of the purpose of the decision.

I believe the right thing to do on this issue is to enact legislation which will prohibit tax exemptions for organizations that discriminate on the basis of race.

Therefore, I will submit legislation and will work with the Congress to accomplish this purpose.

###

EXHIBIT 9

Proposed Legislation to Amend Internal Revenue Code

97th Congress, 2d Session - - - - - - - House Document No. 97–132

TAX-EXEMPT STATUS OF CERTAIN SCHOOLS

COMMUNICATION

FROM

THE PRESIDENT OF THE UNITED STATES

TRANSMITTING

A DRAFT OF PROPOSED LEGISLATION TO AMEND THE IN-
TERNAL REVENUE CODE OF 1954 TO PROHIBIT THE GRANTING
OF TAX-EXEMPT STATUS TO ORGANIZATIONS MAINTAINING
SCHOOLS WITH RACIALLY DISCRIMINATORY POLICIES

JANUARY 25, 1952.—Referred to the Committee on Ways and Means
ordered to be printed

U.S. GOVERNMENT PRINTING OFFICE
89–011 O   WASHINGTON : 1982

Exhibit 9 (continued)

THE WHITE HOUSE,
Washington, January 18, 1982.

Hon. THOMAS P. O'NEILL, Jr.,
The Speaker,
The House of Representatives, Washington, D.C.

DEAR MR. SPEAKER: As you are aware, the Department of the Treasury announced on January 8 that the Internal Revenue Service would no longer deny tax-exempt status to private, non-profit educational organizations that engage in racially discriminatory practices but otherwise qualify for such status under the present Internal Revenue Code. That decision reflects my belief that agencies such as the IRS should not be permitted, even with the best of intentions and to further goals that I strongly endorse, to govern by administrative fiat by exercising powers that the Constitution assigns to the Congress.

I share with you and your colleagues an unalterable opposition to racial discrimination in any form. Such practices are repugnant to all that our Nation and its citizens hold dear, and I believe this repugnance should be plainly reflected in our laws. To that end, I am herewith submitting to the Congress proposed legislation that would prohibit tax exemptions for any schools that discriminate on the basis of race. This proposed legislation is sensitive to the legitimate special needs of private religious schools.

I pledge my fullest cooperation in working with you to enact such legislation as rapidly as possible, and urge that you give this matter the very highest priority.

I have been adivsed by the Secretary of the Treasury that he will not act on any applications for tax exemptions filed in response to the IRS policy announced on January 8, until the Congress has acted on this proposed legislation.

I believe the course I have outlined is the one most consistent both with our mutual determination to eradicate all vestiges of racial discrimination in American society, and with a proper view of the powers vested in the Congress under our constitutional system.

I feel this legislative action is important to and desired by all citizens of this great Nation; I am confident that you will give this issue the prompt attention it deserves.

Sincerely,

RONALD REAGAN.

JANUARY 18, 1982.

TAX EXEMPTION BILL SUMMARY

The proposed legislation being submitted by the President to the Congress will, for the first time, give the Secretary of the Treasury and the Internal Revenue Service express authority to deny tax-exempt status to private, non-profit educational organizations with

(1)

Exhibit 9 (continued)

2

racially discriminatory policies. The legislation recognizes and is sensitive to the legitimate special needs of private religious schools.

Section 1 of the bill adds to section 501 of the Internal Revenue Code a new subsection that expressly prohibits granting tax exemptions to private schools with racially discriminatory policies, notwithstanding that such schools otherwise meet the tests for exemption presently listed in section 501(c)(3).

Religious schools of all faiths are permitted to limit, or give preferences and priorities, to members of a particular religious organization or belief in their admissions policies or religious training and worship programs. However, the bill expressly provides that a tax exemption will not be granted if any such policy, program, preference or priority is based upon race or a belief that requires discrimination on the basis of race.

Section 2 of the bill amends several sections of the Internal Revenue Code dealing with deductions to provide, consistent with the exemption provisions of the new law, that no deductions will be allowed for contributions to a school with a racially discriminatory policy.

A BILL To amend the Internal Revenue Code of 1954 to prohibit the granting of tax-exempt status to organizations maintaining schools with racially discriminatory policies

Be it enacted by the Senate and House of Representatives of the United States of America in Congress assembled,

SECTION 1. DENIAL OF TAX EXEMPTIONS TO ORGANIZATIONS MAINTAINING SCHOOLS WITH RACIALLY DISCRIMINATORY POLICIES.

Section 501 of the Internal Revenue Code of 1954 (relating to exemption from tax) is amended by redesignating subsection (j) as subsection (k) and inserting a new subsection (j) reading as follows:

"(j) ORGANIZATIONS MAINTAINING SCHOOLS WITH RACIALLY DISCRIMINATORY POLICIES.—

"(1) IN GENERAL.—An organization that normally maintains a regular faculty and curriculum (other than an exclusively religious curriculum) and normally has a regularly enrolled body of students in attendance at the place where its educational activities are regularly carried on shall not be deemed to be described in subsection (c)(3), and shall not be exempt from tax under subsection (a), if such organization has a racially discriminatory policy.

"(2) DEFINITIONS.—For the purposes of this subsection—

"(i) An organization has a 'racially discriminatory policy' if it refuses to admit students of all races to the rights, privileges, programs, and activities generally accorded or made available to students by that organization, or if the organization refuses to administer its educational policies, admissions policies, scholarship and loan programs, athletic

Exhibit 9 (continued)

3

programs, or other programs administered by such organization in a manner that does not discriminate on the basis of race. The term 'racially discriminatory policy' does not include an admissions policy of a school, or a program of religious training or worship of a school, that is limited, or grants preferences or priorities, to members of a particular religious organization or belief: *Provided*, That no such policy, program, preference, or priority is based upon race or upon a belief that requires discrimination on the basis of race.

"(ii) The term 'race' shall include color or national origin.',

SECTION 2. DENIAL OF DEDUCTIONS FOR CONTRIBUTIONS TO ORGANIZATIONS MAINTAINING SCHOOLS WITH RACIALLY DISCRIMINATORY POLICIES.

(a) Section 170 of the Internal Revenue Code of 1954 (relating to allowance of deductions for certain charitable, etc., contributions and gifts) is amended by adding at the end of subsection (f) a new paragraph (7) reading as follows:

"(7) DENIAL OF DEDUCTIONS FOR CONTRIBUTIONS TO ORGANIZATIONS MAINTAINING SCHOOLS WITH RACIALLY DISCRIMINATORY POLICIES.—No deduction shall be allowed under this section for any contribution to or for the use of an organization described in section 501(j)(1) that has a racially discriminatory policy as defined in section 501(j)(2)."

(b) Section 642 of such Code (relating to special rules for credits and deductions) is amended by adding at the end of subsection (c) a new paragraph (7) reading as follows:

"(7) DENIAL OF DEDUCTIONS FOR CONTRIBUTIONS TO ORGANIZATIONS MAINTAINING SCHOOLS WITH RACIALLY DISCRIMINATORY POLICIES.—No deduction shall be allowed under this section for any contribution to or for the use of an organization described in section 501(j)(1) that has a racially discriminatory policy as defined in section 501(j)(2)."

(c) Section 2055 of such Code (relating to the allowance of estate tax deductions for transfers for public, charitable, and religious uses) is amended by adding at the end of subsection (e) a new paragraph (4) reading as follows:

"(4) No deduction shall be allowed under this section for any transfer to or for the use of an organization described in section 501(j)(1) that has a racially discriminatory policy as defined in section 501(j)(2)."

(d) Section 2522 of such Code (relating to charitable and similar gifts) is amended by adding at the end of subsection (c) a new paragraph (3) reading as follows:

"(3) No deduction shall be allowed under this section for any gift to or for the use of an organization described in section 501(j)(1) that has a racially discriminatory policy as defined in section 501(j)(2)."

SECTION 4. EFFECTIVE DATE.
The amendments made by this Act shall apply after July 9, 1970.

○

Exhibit 10

During a January news conference, Sam Donaldson of ABC News asked President Reagan about the January 8 decision on tax exemptions.

TAX-EXEMPT STANCE

Q. Mr. President, on Jan. 8, the Justice Department announced a decision concerning tax-exempt status for certain schools that clearly gave aid and comfort to racial discrimination. Then in subsequent days you began a series of steps to sort of go back from that. My question is, what happened? Are you responsible for the original decision, or did your staff put something over on you?

A. Sam, no one put anything over on me. No, Sam, the buck stops at my desk. I'm the originator of the whole thing and I'm not going to deny that it wasn't handled as well as it could be. But I think that what we actually saw was confusion, and it was rather widespread and encouraged, about what - we had not anticipated the reaction because we were dealing with a procedural matter. And it was interpreted by many of you as a policy matter, reflecting a change in policy. And then therefore, when we went forward, you said well then this was another change back in policy.

What we were trying to correct was a procedure that we thought had no basis in law, that the Internal Revenue Service had actually formed a social law and was enforcing that social law. And we think that that's a bad precedent and it's a bad thing to do. And so we-- there was no basis in the law for what they were doing. So what we set out to do was to stop - to change that procedure and stop - the Internal Revenue Service from doing this and then to have Congress implement with law the proper procedure.

I am opposed at every fiber of my being of discrimination, and to have set in law the fact that tax exemptions could be denied to schools and educational institutions that

practiced discrimination. Now, as I say, it probably
wasn't handled as well as it could because it being
in our minds a procedural matter - and in my mind
certainly - we didn't anticipate that it was going
to be as misinterpreted as it was. And we since -
what we have accomplished with what we did was
we've prevented the I.R.S. from determining national
social policy all by itself. It'll now be by elected
officials, the Congress. We'll continue to prohibit
tax exemptions for schools that discrimination and
for the first time that will be the law of the land.
And we helped to reserve the rights and liberties of
religious schools as long as they don't discriminate.

Q. But, sir,if I may, in your original Jan. 8 decision,
you didn't ask for legislation, you simply said unless
Congress acted. It wasn't until the firestorm that you
then asked for legislation.

A. No, because we went right ahead. I was having talks with
Senators about this. Maybe we didn't act as swiftly as
we could have - and, as I say, I'm not defending that
we proceeded on a course that was as well planned as it
might have been. And just - so we were mistaken in that
regard. But don't judge us by our mistakes - I'm
probably going to make more of them. But judge us
how well we recover and solve the situation.

EXHIBIT 11

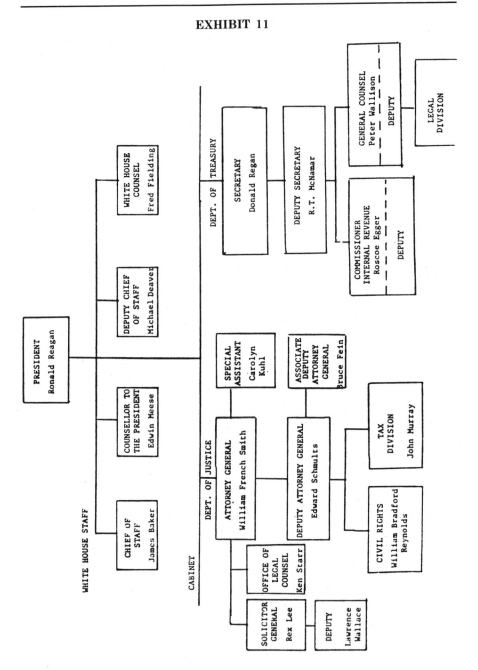

Discussion Questions

1. As this story ends, what do you think Larry Wallace should do? He has a good sense of what the Supreme Court is likely to think of the legal dispute. As a member of the Solicitor General's office, which presents the federal government's position in all cases before the Supreme Court, he has

become an expert on the Court's processes and views. Wallace presumably expects a large majority to adopt the position that the Commissioner of Internal Revenue had authority to interpret the provisions for charitable deductions and exemptions so as to exclude schools that segregate or otherwise discriminate on the basis of race. Traditional deference to the Commissioner, the special position in our jurisprudence of racial equality and steps to abolish discrimination, the repeated instances of acceptance of the Commissioner's position by the Congress, and the uniform executive branch interpretation until now all point in that direction.

But Wallace is not being asked to predict or announce what the law will be or is. He is being asked to argue a position as a career government attorney, in the Solicitor General's office, under the Administration of Ronald Reagan. He may have an obligation to the Administration he serves to urge even implausible or unlikely interpretations of precedent, statute, or the Constitution in order to further the policies of the President. And the Attorney General may have a view of what the law "really" is which is different from the interpretations adopted by the Supreme Court—a view which he and the President are entitled to have urged upon the courts.

2. Is it at least clear that when a government attorney recognizes that any of several positions that could be taken before the courts is defensible, he is obligated to follow the policy views of those appointed by the President? If Wallace thought that the views of Reynolds and Fein were about as likely to prevail as those of Egger, could he refuse to follow the Attorney General's decision to come down on Reynolds's side simply because, if he were a judge, Wallace would decide otherwise?

A closely related question is presented if one puts oneself in the position of either Reynolds (head of the Civil Rights Division) or Egger (Commissioner of Internal Revenue). Is it appropriate for each of these, at least when he can picture defensible arguments on both sides of an issue, to forget what he would do as a judge and simply choose the position he wants the government to adopt in terms of policies he believes are desirable and the implications of the position he chooses for his organization and the President? In arriving at their positions in this case, would it be appropriate for Reynolds and Egger to consider what the President had said during his campaign and the promises of the Republican platform, the views of their staffs and the traditions of their organizations, their judgments about segregation and the mechanisms of tax policymaking?

Is it only appropriate to consider such factors and is it only clear that a government attorney should take the position politically appointed or elected officials urge where what the courts will do is subject to legitimate dispute (or at least where there is a presentable view of what the law "is" to support the political position)?

One possible argument is that the government is free in litigation to take any position on this issue that it wishes—i.e., that prior decisions or arguments about law do not control the government's position before the courts and so the government's position can be freely chosen as a matter of policy. Then, the argument goes, the court decides what the law is. Do you agree? Or is the government, i.e. the Attorney General's Office, limited, even in the positions it takes in litigation, by legal precedents?

A new President has the public's endorsement, and arguably its mandate, to make certain policy changes, some of which require changes in the law. Does this mean the government's lawyers can or should then be ordered to argue the view of what the law "really" means, at least as espoused by the President in his campaign? Or does the view of the law as interpreted by the Attorney General have an independent force upon which even the President should not intrude?

Some would argue that the issue is not whether or not the President can urge his army of attorneys to argue for certain interpretations of the law, but rather that the issue is one of honesty. In those cases where the President's position is not in line with existing law, how frank must the administration be about this fact? Can the administration attempt to argue that the desired policy outcome is dictated by law or must it be more forthright and argue that existing law is wrong and should be overruled? Does the Attorney General's Office have a political or moral obligation to admit that the desired policy goal is outside the boundaries of existing law (as it has been interpreted judicially) and that the existing law should be overruled?

Acknowledging frankly that a position is being urged for policy reasons and that it involves a change in law is likely to make the position less palatable to the courts. In addition, there is sometimes a political cost to forthrightness. The present case provides a dramatic example. President Reagan plainly did not want his personal views or his administration's policies portrayed and understood as in favor of segregation or even of the freedom of private schools to segregate. He wanted the result of granting tax deductions and exemptions to schools that discriminate on the basis of race only if that result could persuasively be characterized as a result dictated by law, not chosen as a matter of administration policy. Did Deputy Attorney General Schmults or Attorney General Smith understand this? Was there any way that they could have successfully argued that the result which they wanted—that the IRS did not have the authority to deny tax exempt status to educational or religious institutions that discriminated—was required by existing law? Would the policy, as opposed to the legal, basis of the position have been more apparent or better hidden if they had instead simply changed the IRS regulations which denied tax benefits to these schools?

3. Attorney General Smith and his successor, Attorney General Meese, apparently believed that the courts are, in their decisions, ignoring what the law "really means" and requires. The President shared that view, which urges a more limited judicial role and a greater attention to the "original intent" of legislators and the framers of the Constitution. Is there anything wrong with an administration pressing its view of how courts should interpret "the law," even though its views are plainly inconsistent in important ways with the views of the courts? President Reagan ran, in part, on a platform of reining in the courts. When a new President who has made such positions part of his campaign takes office, does he have a mandate to seek to change the way the courts interpret the law?

Does this mean that government lawyers such as Wallace can or should be ordered to argue the view of what the law "really" means that the President and the Attorney General have adopted, even though it is contrary to the views of the courts in which they are representing the government? Is there any obligation in this situation for the government attorney to be frank about the fact that the views of the law he is setting forth would, if adopted, amount to a significant change in the broad jurisprudence of the Supreme Court or the lower courts? Would this be obvious in any event to the court before whom the government attorney appears? Is what is at stake, then, simply a question of what credibility the courts will accord to the views of the government attorney in the future?

Is there also a significant issue as to the effect on public acceptance of the obligations of legality when the executive branch urges a quite different view of the broad nature of "the law" from that adopted by the courts? Does the President's constitutional obligation to enforce the law commit him to a greater loyalty to the law as interpreted by the courts? Is it politically acceptable for a President to admit openly that he is refusing to accept the Supreme Court's interpretation of the law, even if the refusal amounts to nothing more than taking a different position openly in arguing before that Court?

4. Even if Wallace had decided that as a government attorney he had an obligation to limit his arguments to those that are in some sense "defensible" in terms of the prior or predictable decisions of the Court, at least unless there is some effort to be frank about urging a departure from established judicial interpretation, Wallace would still have a difficult decision. Whose responsibility is it to decide whether an argument is sufficiently based in existing law or is outside any reasonable interpretation of the law? When there is disagreement between a career attorney who is the government's representative in court in the matter and one of his superiors, appointed by the President, whose views should be given greater weight?

In most cases there is an easy answer: the attorney need not personally say to the court what she does not believe to be correct, but her superiors can ask another attorney to represent the administration's views before that court. Would Wallace have had any basis for objecting if the Attorney General decided to file a brief under his own name with the Supreme Court? If that were to happen, neither the integrity nor the reputation of Wallace or the Solicitor General's office would be at stake. As subordinates of the Attorney General can they really argue that he is not entitled to ignore their views?

The difficulty with this solution is that the Attorney General would fear the consequences of filing a brief that was not signed on behalf of the Solicitor General's office. The Supreme Court would regard the absence of the regular and familiar role of the Solicitor General's office as a significant signal that what was being set forth was not the view of that office, on which the Court has come to rely, about the law. If the Attorney General wants to insist on Wallace's participation for this reason, can he at the same time argue that his judgment, rather than Wallace's, should be controlling, on whether an argument is sufficiently based in existing law, as it is understood by the Supreme Court, to be urged on that Court?

5. In his book Kennedy Justice, Victor Navasky describes the position of Solicitor General:

The Solicitor General is the third-ranking officer in the Justice Department, but he is traditionally autonomous. . . . [He] can conduct and argue any case in which the government has an interest. No appeal is taken by the government in any appellate court or to the Supreme Court without his authority. The Solicitor General's office argues over 60 percent of the cases the U.S. Supreme Court hears. He is in fact what the Attorney General is in name—the chief legal officer of the U.S. Government as far as the courts are concerned. Nowhere is the tension, the institutional pull between law and policy, greater than that between the Solicitor General's office and the Attorney General's office. The Attorney General is adviser to the President, and the Solicitor General is adviser to the U.S. Supreme Court. It is in the nature of things that the Attorney General focuses on short-range political results and the Solicitor General focuses on long-range constitutional-law implications. . . . The nine lawyers in his office—most of whom have clerked for a Supreme Court Justice—regard themselves as the elite, the creme de la creme of the legal profession. "When you enter the Solicitor's office, you join one of the most exclusive clubs in America" is the way one alumnus put it.

The tension between law and policy is inherent in the Solicitor General's office. Navasky describes such a conflict between Archibald Cox and Attorney General Robert Kennedy over the meaning of "state action" under the Fourteenth Amendment:

Ever since the landmark case of *Shelley v. Kraemer,* 334 U.S. 1 (1948) . . . liberals and judicial activists were engaged in an effort to expand and crystallize the categories of discriminatory actions which the Supreme Court might declare unconstitutional and/or unenforceable. [The argument centered around the definition of "state action" necessary to bring an action under the Fourteenth Amendment. Archibald Cox came to the position of Solicitor] with a generally Frankfurterian approach to the matter, believing that "state action" was roughly coterminous with official action, that it wasn't the court's job to legislate morality and that it wasn't the Department's job to push the court further than its own words had already taken it. The liberal view, put forth by men like Jack Greenberg, the . . . chief counsel of the NAACP Inc. Fund . . . was that in today's complex world it made little sense to talk about "state action" in the narrow meaning of that term. . . . [Greenberg felt] that regardless of what one believed to be the better theoretical position, the law was in flux and therefore the Solicitor should not decide such an issue on the basis of legal theory but rather on the basis of departmental policy. Greenberg, who had been invited to the Justice Department to air his opinions on the state-action issue, once told Cox, "If you believe your position, write it up for the *Harvard Law Review.* But now you're the Solicitor General of the United States, and it is the policy of the Kennedy Administration to oppose discrimination wherever it can."

Do you agree with Greenberg? Is this conflict any different than that between Wallace and Fein?

6. In 1986, Senator Humphrey of New Hampshire proposed legislation that would deny tax exempt status to hospitals and other charitable institutions that perform or finance abortions. A group of experts on tax law opposed this statutory change, arguing that the proposal "to use tax provisions to promote controversial social policy runs directly counter to the salutary concept of tax neutrality that fuels the current Congressional tax reform endeavor." They also said that the proposed amendment "would embroil the tax law and the Internal Revenue Service in matters that properly are the business of neither, and would thus provoke disrespect for both."

Could someone consistently support denial of tax exempt status for Bob Jones University yet argue that some general principle of "tax neutrality" is offended by denying tax exempt status to hospitals that perform abortions?

Epilogue

Wallace filed a brief setting forth the views of the Attorney General and the Reagan Administration but attached the following footnote to his statement of the questions presented:

> This brief sets forth the position of the United States on both questions presented. The Acting Solicitor General fully subscribes to the position set forth on question number two, only. [The U.S. position on question two was that Bob Jones University's First Amendment right to the free exercise of religion would not insulate it from a valid IRS rule denying charitable status to institutions that practice racial segregation.] His views on question one are set forth in the Brief for the United States filed in this Court in September 1981 in response to the petitions for certiorari in these cases. Those views are more fully developed in a draft brief on the merits which was ready to be printed for timely filing in early January 1982. Copies of that draft brief were furnished by the Department of Justice in late January 1982, pursuant to request, to the Senate Finance Committee and the House Ways and Means Committee, along with other documents requested by those committees.

The Supreme Court was faced with the problem of deciding *Bob Jones University v. U.S.* without an advocate for the position the United States had taken until the Reagan Administration changed sides. The Court appointed William T. Coleman, Jr., a Washington lawyer who had been Justice Frankfurter's law clerk and President Ford's Secretary of Transportation, as "amicus curiae in support of the judgment below." After receiving briefs and hearing oral arguments, the Court affirmed, holding that nonprofit private schools that enforce racially discriminatory admission standards on the basis of religious doctrine do not qualify as tax-exempt organizations under the Internal Revenue Code. Only Justice Rehnquist dissented.[8]

When the Court decision was issued, Attorney General Smith said the Court's ruling made it "clear that additional legislation is not needed" and that the I.R.S. should enforce the law. President Reagan commented, "We will obey the law."

Rev. Bob Jones, president of the university founded by his father, said in a sermon in the school chapel: "We're in a bad fix when eight evil old men and one vain and foolish woman can speak a verdict on American liberties." At the Justice Department, some lawyers in the Civil Rights Division greeted news of the Supreme Court decision with what the *New York Times* called "backslapping elation."

---

[8] *Bob Jones University v. United States,* 461 U.S. 574 (1983).

III. Lawyer Responsibilities in the Adversary System

A. Zealous Advocacy

1. Client Fraud

OPM Leasing Services, Inc.*

In December of 1982, Myron S. Goodman and Mordecai Weissman pleaded guilty and were given prison terms of twelve years and ten years respectively for their roles in one of the largest corporate frauds in American history. Goodman and Weissman founded OPM Leasing Services, Inc. in 1970, and during the next decade built it into a leader in the computer leasing field. Throughout this period, they used OPM to defraud banks and other lenders—and, ultimately, those institutions' depositors and shareholders—of more than $225 million. For the success of this scheme, Goodman and Weissman relied extensively upon their relationship with OPM's general counsel, the law firm of Singer Hutner Levine & Seeman.[1]

The Participants

Goodman and Weissman

Goodman and Weissman had long been close personal friends. They knew each other as children, they went to the same yeshiva in Brooklyn, they attended Brooklyn College together, and their wives were sisters. Weissman started OPM (short for "other people's money") in 1970 and brought in Goodman a few months later by giving him half the business. They split the duties, with Weissman being responsible for marketing and Goodman taking control of the finances.

OPM

OPM's business involved borrowing money to purchase computers and other business equipment that it then leased to corporate customers at a rate high enough to service its debt and provide it with a profit. OPM financed these transactions with funds provided by large banks, insurance companies, and other financial institutions, many of them

---

* This case is based on information drawn from J. Hassett, Trustee, and Wilmer, Cutler & Pickering, Washington, D.C., Special Counsel, *Report of the Trustee Concerning Fraud and Other Misconduct in the Management of the Affairs of the Debtor* (April 25, 1983), and Taylor, *Ethics and the Law: A Case History,* The New York Times Magazine, January 9, 1983.

[1] In considering the role of Singer Hutner in this course of events it is essential to know the ethical rules applicable to lawyers in such situations. These are set out at the conclusion of the case study.

recruited by Lehman Brothers, the company's investment banker. These lenders secured their money with the lessee's obligations to make lease payments and with the value of the computers themselves. OPM obtained additional financing by selling legal title to the computers to individual investors in search of tax shelters.

With the company purchasing multi-million dollar computers from manufacturers such as I.B.M. and leasing them to such respected corporate customers as AT&T, Revlon, and Polaroid, this business arrangement proved lucrative. By the late 1970's OPM had become one of the nation's five largest computer leasing companies, with 250 employees, eleven offices across the country, and a controlling interest in a Louisiana bank.

Singer Hutner

OPM first retained Singer Hutner in 1971 and kept the firm as its general counsel until late in 1980. OPM was initially attracted to Singer Hutner due to the personal ties between Goodman and Andrew B. Reinhard, a Singer Hutner associate who had grown up in the same neighborhood in Brooklyn as Goodman and was the older brother of one of Goodman's boyhood friends.

In the early years, the services Singer Hutner performed for OPM constituted only a small part of its legal business. Between 1971 and 1975, OPM's operations were limited to leasing minicomputers and other small equipment, and Reinhard handled the company's legal needs with minimal assistance from other Singer Hutner lawyers. These needs included improving OPM's lease forms, representing OPM in several equity transactions, litigating claims against defaulting lessees, performing general corporate and tax services, and advising Goodman and Weissman on estate planning matters.

This relationship changed in 1975 when OPM moved into the more lucrative mainframe computer market. As OPM's transactions increased in complexity, so did its demand for legal services. During the latter half of the decade Singer Hutner expanded its operations to accommodate the increased demand and devoted more and more of its legal talent to meeting OPM's needs. By 1980, most Singer Hutner partners spent some of their time on projects for OPM and 10 of the 15 associates in the firm's New York office worked exclusively on OPM matters. Much of the law firm's work centered on complicated OPM leasing transactions. In addition to negotiating, preparing documentation for, and closing OPM's lease financing deals, Singer Hutner also provided lenders with legal opinions regarding the validity of OPM's titles to computers and the legality of OPM's leases.

During the ten years Singer Hutner represented OPM, it grew with the company and, to a significant extent, became dependent on it. Between 1976 and 1980, OPM paid Singer Hutner almost $7.9 million in legal fees, more than sixty percent of the law firm's total revenue for that period.   By 1980, Singer Hutner employed 29 lawyers and had offices in New York and New Orleans.   Moreover, Singer Hutner's relationship with its client became increasingly more intimate.   In 1972, Reinhard was named as one of three OPM directors (the other two being Weissman and Goodman) and several Singer Hutner lawyers served as OPM officers.

> **Questions**   What are the potential problems that might arise where a law firm is dependent upon a single client for more than sixty percent of its business?   Is it really in a position to resist pressure from the client to act in an improper way?   Are there circumstances where the interests of the firm's other clients may be unfairly subordinated?

OPM's Corrupt Business Practices

From its inception, OPM was insolvent and relied for its survival on fraud and bribery.   OPM first turned to questionable practices as a way to obtain new business.   With Goodman's assistance, Weissman routinely paid equipment vendors' sales personnel sizable commissions to induce them to steer customers to OPM.   The company's financing efforts were corrupt as well.   OPM frequently engaged in double and triple discounting, a practice in which the company used a single computer as collateral for two or three loans.   It was also a common practice to inflate the value of a given piece of equipment to obtain larger loans by forging the lessee's signature on altered lease documents before presenting them to financial institutions.   (This practice became known as the "glass table method," in which Goodman would crouch under a glass table with a flashlight and Weissman would trace the signatures.)

To win a place in the competitive computer-leasing market, OPM offered lessees an "early termination" option.   Under this scheme, OPM induced customers to enter into long-term leases by the assurance that they could cancel their contracts if a technological breakthrough rendered their leased equipment obsolete.   For a while this system worked masterfully and was the keystone to the company's spectacular success.   Eventually, however, OPM's bluff was called.   In 1977, I.B.M. announced its new 303X Series that promised to revolutionize the computer business, and OPM customers began to exercise their early termination options.

In 1978, Goodman and Weissman bought a bank in Louisiana. Faced with a severe cash shortage, Goodman used the bank to generate more than $5 million through a form of illegal interest-free borrowing called "check-kiting." Bank officials uncovered this scheme in February of 1979, and in March of 1980 OPM pleaded guilty in federal district court in New Orleans to 22 felony counts and was fined $110,000.

While the guilty plea and the fine might appear severe, the situation could have been much worse. Carl J. Rubino of Singer Hutner persuaded the government not to indict Goodman personally and to dismiss twenty-one additional counts against OPM. When the plea was entered Goodman reportedly became quite emotional. Rubino warned him to conduct himself in the future as "Caesar's wife," and Goodman promised to be "orthodox in every respect." His repentence was short-lived, however. Very soon after OPM's conviction, Goodman began to resort to fraud on a much grander scale.

> **Questions** Should the fact that Goodman and Weissman were willing to violate the banking laws have alerted Singer Hutner that OPM may have been acting improperly in other business dealings? If it did, should Singer Hutner have attempted to find this out and, in effect, police its client's activities?

The Rockwell Fraud

Goodman's illegal activities at this time can be called the "Rockwell fraud" because in perpetrating them he relied almost entirely on leases OPM had with Rockwell International, a huge California aerospace company. At first Goodman and his accomplices simply forged Rockwell signatures on fictitious leases and related financing documents. Later they began creating such materials by removing signature pages from extra copies prepared for legitimate transactions and attaching them to fictitious documents. They also compiled falsified title documents giving OPM ownership in equipment that, in fact, did not exist. To keep Rockwell from discovering these fraudulent leases, Goodman instructed Singer Hutner to institute closing procedures not usually followed in other OPM closings, including the requirements that Singer Hutner channel Rockwell's copies of leases and financing documents through OPM and that the law firm not approach Rockwell directly without Goodman's prior consent.

In late 1979, Goodman switched from creating leases out of whole cloth to altering the terms of genuine Rockwell leases. By making these cover more expensive equipment renting at higher monthly rates for longer periods of time, Goodman could use them as security to obtain larger blocks of financing. For example, in one transaction

Rockwell agreed to pay $6,000 per month on a thirty-six month lease. Goodman doctored this lease so that Rockwell appeared obligated to pay $64,365 per month over an eighty-four month term. He then used the altered lease as security for a substantial loan. To accommodate the lease financing requirement that Rockwell pay rent directly to the lender, Goodman arranged for Rockwell to make the relatively small payments (under the legitimate lease) to OPM which, in turn, used its own funds to make the inflated payments (under the fraudulent lease) to the lender. OPM met the inflated payments by supplementing Rockwell's contribution with funds obtained through other fraudulent financings.

The flurry of illegal activity at OPM did not go entirely unnoticed. By June of 1980, John A. Clifton, OPM's chief in-house accountant, learned of the Rockwell fraud and became concerned that he might somehow be implicated in the scheme if he did not take immediate action. After consulting with his personal lawyer, William J. Davis, Clifton decided to draft a letter detailing his knowledge of the fraud, send it to Reinhard, and then resign.

The June 12, 1980, Meeting at Singer Hutner

On June 12, 1980, Goodman met for several hours with Joseph L. Hutner, a senior partner with Singer Hutner. At that meeting, he confessed that he had engaged in past wrongdoing that he could not remedy because it would take millions of dollars more than he could raise. Goodman refused to reveal any details without an assurance from Hutner that he would not disclose the information to anyone else. Hutner declined to give such an assurance.

At the time of his meeting with Hutner, Goodman knew that Clifton was going to send a letter to Reinhard because Clifton had told him of his intention to do so. During a break in the meeting, Goodman somehow retrieved the Clifton letter. Accounts of how he obtained it differ. Singer Hutner lawyers maintain that Goodman took the letter unopened from Reinhard's hand or from the top of his desk. Goodman claims that this was a story he and Reinhard concocted to cover for the fact that Goodman had found Reinhard reading the letter as he passed by his office. However he obtained it, Goodman took the Clifton letter with him when he left Singer Hutner that afternoon, still refusing to reveal details of his wrongdoing and insisting that it was all in the past.

Questions If all that Singer Hutner knew was that Goodman had been involved in wrongdoing and that some of the details of that wrongdoing were set forth in Clifton's letter, should the law firm have made an effort to learn more about Goodman's acts by insisting that Goodman leave the letter with it? Or was it right to have remained passive and let its client disclose his wrongdoing when he was ready to do so?

Singer Hutner's Meeting With Clifton's Attorney

At Goodman's urging, Hutner met with Clifton's attorney, Davis, on June 13, and again on June 16. According to Davis's account of the meetings, Hutner tried to persuade him to keep Clifton quiet and to convince Clifton to take back his letter. Davis said "he had been prepared to give Hutner a copy of Clifton's letter and would have told him 'as much as he wanted to know,' but that Hutner told him 'he didn't want it, he didn't want to know what was in it.' " [2] Hutner denied these claims.

While a number of facts are in dispute, it is clear that Davis told Hutner and Eli R. Mattioli, another Singer Hutner partner who attended one of the meetings, that Clifton had evidence that OPM had perpetrated a multi-million dollar fraud and that the opinion letters Singer Hutner had drawn up to obtain loans for OPM were based upon false documents. Davis also informed Hutner and Mattioli that it was Clifton's opinion that OPM would probably have to continue the same type of wrongful activity if it was to survive.

Questions From its meetings with Clifton's attorney, Singer Hutner learned three significant facts: (1) that OPM had perpetrated a large-scale fraud, (2) that the law firm itself had contributed to this fraud, and (3) that the fraud was probably ongoing. On the basis of this information alone, should Singer Hutner have demanded, under the threat of resignation, that Goodman disclose the full extent of his wrongdoing? Or should it have waited until its client voluntarily revealed his fraudulent activities?

Davis contends that he was prepared to give Singer Hutner far more information than he did but that the law firm chose not to learn of it. Is Singer Hutner's position that "what I don't know won't hurt me" proper under these circumstances? Should the law firm have adopted an investigative role and attempted to gain information from all possible sources?

Even if Goodman was no longer engaged in fraudulent behavior, the consequences of his past wrongdoing continued. Singer Hutner now knew that OPM had obtained numerous loans based on leases that did not exist. The longer the banks were kept in the dark about the lack of security for these

---

[2] Taylor, *Ethics and the Law: A Case History,* The New York Times Magazine, Jan. 9, 1983, at 33.

loans, the less they would ultimately be able to recover. Should Singer Hutner have been obligated to report the past frauds to mitigate the banks' losses?

The Aftermath of the June Meetings

Following Goodman's initial revelation and the subsequent meetings with Davis, Singer Hutner decided to retain outside counsel to advise it on questions of attorney-client privilege and professional responsibility, and on June 19, Hutner, Mattioli, and Rubino met with Joseph M. McLaughlin, the dean of Fordham Law School and an authority on the attorney-client privilege.[3]

In speaking with the Singer Hutner attorneys it soon became clear to McLaughlin that the law firm's involvement with OPM presented a difficult set of issues about the scope of the attorney-client privilege and the potential conflict between Singer Hutner's duty to its client and its responsibility to the public. He therefore brought in as co-counsel Henry Putzel 3d, an attorney in private practice who formerly had been a federal prosecutor and had taught professional responsibility at Fordham Law School.

On June 20, Hutner, Mattioli, and Rubino met with McLaughlin and Putzel to give them a detailed report of what the law firm had learned from Goodman and Davis. They also told the two consultants of OPM's past practice of double and triple discounting and of the company's check-kiting conviction. At this meeting, "the Singer Hutner lawyers stressed two major points . . .: they wanted to do the ethical thing, and they wanted to continue representing OPM unless they were ethically and legally obliged to quit."[4]

> **Questions** Could Singer Hutner make a decision about whether or not to resign, given how important this client was to the firm? If Singer Hutner had indicated that its primary concern was to act in an ethical manner and that its future relationship with OPM was not to enter the calculus, would the consultants have had a wider range of options to consider?

The Consultants' Advice

In late June, McLaughlin and Putzel presented their recommended course of action to Singer Hutner. Their opinion was predicated on Singer Hutner's statement that they knew of no ongoing fraud, a claim that was itself based on Goodman's repeated assurances that the fraud had stopped.

---

[3] On October 13, 1981, McLaughlin was appointed a U.S. District Judge for the Eastern District of New York.

[4] Taylor, *supra* note 1, at 33.

There were several elements to McLaughlin and Putzel's opinion:

(1) Singer Hutner ethically could continue to represent OPM because it knew of no ongoing fraud;

(2) the law firm could not inform law enforcement officials or affected third parties about Goodman's wrongdoing because this disclosure would violate Disciplinary Rule 4–101(B)(1) of the Code of Professional Responsibility, which provides that "[e]xcept when permitted . . ., a lawyer shall not knowingly: (1) Reveal a confidence or secret of his client;"

(3) Singer Hutner had no duty to withdraw possibly false opinion letters and documents that it had provided to banks to obtain loans for OPM. The law firm had not known at the time that these materials were fraudulent, and leaving the victims of past fraud in the dark is not considered an ongoing fraud;

(4) the law firm was not required to check the authenticity of computer leasing documents with third parties such as Rockwell before closing new loans.

McLaughlin and Putzel also recommended that Singer Hutner take certain steps to prevent OPM from committing any new fraud. First, the law firm was to require that OPM certify in writing that each new transaction was legitimate. Second, Singer Hutner was to prompt Goodman to reveal to it and to Weissman the details of his wrongdoing. With respect to this second factor, McLaughlin and Putzel advised Singer Hutner that it would be unfair to pressure Goodman to give full disclosure that might be adverse to his personal interest without affording him the benefit of independent counsel. Singer Hutner suggested this to Goodman and he retained as his personal counsel Andrew M. Lawler, a former Assistant United States Attorney who was then in private practice.

Singer Hutner's efforts to prevent future fraud proved ineffectual. With respect to the first recommendation, Goodman simply signed certificates of legitimacy that he knew to be false. As to the second, Goodman succeeded in delaying further disclosure of his wrongdoing for a full two months. And Lawler proposed that any disclosure Goodman made be deemed protected by the attorney-client privilege.

The Trustee appointed to investigate OPM's bankruptcy characterized McLaughlin and Putzel's recommendations to Singer Hutner as "in fact the worst possible advice" and asserted that "McLaughlin and Putzel must bear significant responsibility for [Singer Hutner's] conduct." [5] He was also critical of Singer Hutner for failing to determine

---

[5] J. Hassett, Trustee, and Wilmer, Cutler & Pickering, Washington, D.C., Special Counsel, *Report of the Trustee Concerning Fraud and Other Misconduct in the Management of the Affairs of the Debtor* (April 25, 1983), at 410–11.

that the fraud had not stopped and for inadequately recognizing its duties under the civil and criminal law, not just under the Code of Professional Responsibility. The Trustee concluded that "Singer Hutner's failure to deal effectively with Goodman's confessions of massive fraud recklessly and inexcusably resulted in approximately $85 million in further losses to the fraud victims." [6]

Questions Does the consultant's advice appear to have been tailored to Singer Hutner's desire to continue representing OPM? What other routes might Singer Hutner have taken that would have more effectively precluded further fraud?

The consultants formulated their recommendations in reliance on the facts Singer Hutner told them. Singer Hutner, in turn, based its understanding primarily on what Goodman and Davis told it. Was the law firm shortsighted in allowing the consultants to chart its course on the basis of such scant knowledge? Should Singer Hutner have investigated the situation further before choosing a plan of action? Given the surrounding circumstances, should Singer Hutner have been more skeptical about what Goodman told it and about his willingness to conform to its requests?

Events During the Summer of 1980

During the summer of 1980, Singer Hutner noticed several strange events that might have alerted it that OPM was continuing to act improperly. On June 24, Alan S. Jacobs, a Singer Hutner partner who handled OPM's bank financings, discovered what he thought might be false title documents when he was reviewing materials to be used in upcoming Rockwell financings. The invoices and bills of sale in these sets of documents indicated that OPM had recently purchased almost $5 million worth of equipment. However, Jacobs believed that OPM did not have the money to fund these purchases, and when Mattioli reviewed these same title documents he found a vendor's signature that appeared to be in Goodman's handwriting.

Three weeks later, Jacobs found two bills of sale that OPM had given Singer Hutner. Although they were supposed to be for different leases and different bank loans, the equipment descriptions and serial numbers for the two bills of sale were the same. After speaking to Putzel, Jacobs contacted OPM. OPM told him there had been a typographical error and sent him a corrected document. As it turned out, neither the original nor the "corrected" version was legitimate. Meanwhile, Goodman continued to refuse to disclose the details of his

---

[6] *Id.* at 411.

wrongdoing. It was not until September that Goodman finally revealed some of the details of the fraud he had first hinted at in June.

Despite these questionable events, Singer Hutner continued throughout the summer to close loans for OPM without checking the legitimacy of underlying Rockwell leases. Although some of these leases were legitimate, it was later learned that OPM used fraudulent leases to secure loans of $22 million in June, $17 million in July, and $22 million in August.

> **Questions** Given that Singer Hutner's suspicions had already been aroused, were the strange happenings during the summer sufficient proof that the fraud was ongoing? At what point should Singer Hutner have ceased giving OPM the benefit of the doubt?

Goodman's First Detailed Disclosure and Singer Hutner's Phased Resignation

In September, Goodman revealed some of the details of the fraud to Singer Hutner. He told the law firm that the fraud involved Rockwell leases and that Singer Hutner had contributed to the fraud by unwittingly transmitting false documents to financing institutions. However, Goodman insisted that OPM had had no fraudulent dealings after June 11, 1980.

When it learned this information, Singer Hutner decided that it should resign as OPM's general counsel. It approached Putzel about this and, according to the Trustee's Report, he advised the law firm that "under the circumstances, resignation was appropriate, although still not mandatory" because the fraud was not ongoing.[7] Putzel also suggested a phased withdrawal over several months because of the firm's ethical obligation under Disciplinary Rule 2–110(A)(2), which provides that "a lawyer shall not withdraw from employment until he has taken reasonable steps to avoid foreseeable prejudice to the rights of his client, including giving due notice to his client, allowing time for employment of other counsel, delivering to the client all papers and property to which the client is entitled, and complying with applicable laws and rules." He further recommended that during the withdrawal period Singer Hutner should cease relying on Goodman's certificates in OPM's lease financings and should require independent verification of the transaction terms with the lessees. Such verification was necessary, Putzel reasoned, because Goodman had confessed to using Singer Hutner as an instrument of crime by having it transmit false documents to financing institutions.

---

[7] *Id.* at 394.

Singer Hutner accepted Putzel's advice, and on September 23 decided to begin a gradual withdrawal as OPM's general counsel. This phased resignation was finally completed in December of 1980.

Questions Was Putzel under any obligation to disclose his knowledge of the fraud to third parties? Was he prohibited from doing so?

Having decided to resign as OPM's general counsel, Singer Hutner then turned to the question of what to do with the knowledge that OPM had in the past perpetrated a large-scale fraud. Again they consulted Putzel. He advised them that disclosure was impermissible because any information they had obtained from Goodman was confidential. On the basis of this advice, the law firm told nothing to the financial institutions whom OPM had defrauded.

While Singer Hutner refrained from exposing OPM's wrongdoing, Goodman continued unabated. He used Singer Hutner's resignation letter, which characterized the withdrawal as a mutual agreement between attorney and client, as an indication that he had dismissed the law firm. He was thus able to continue to obtain fraudulent loans without alerting business contacts that there might be something awry. He was even able to thwart what little action Singer Hutner did take. The first time the law firm sought to test the legitimacy of Rockwell leases by mailing a verification form to Rockwell in California Goodman arranged to intercept the form and forge the necessary signature.

Questions In light of everything that had happened to this point, was Singer Hutner's trust in Goodman misplaced? Should they have adopted a more skeptical posture and made certain that Goodman complied with their requests? What steps might they have taken?

Should an attorney have responsibility to third parties at all times? At any time? Should an attorney's responsibility to third parties only take effect when the potential damage is substantial? Should such responsibility apply to situations where an attorney has a strong suspicion that his client is acting unlawfully or only where the attorney knows with certainty that his client is breaking the law? Should an attorney be required to investigate the situation to enhance his knowledge?

Singer Hutner's Additional Knowledge

During the course of its phased resignation, Singer Hutner continued to learn more details about OPM's fraudulent activities. On September 29 and 30, Goodman acknowledged that OPM had approximately $90 million in fraudulently obtained loans, an amount almost three times larger than the figure he had confessed to earlier in the month. The law firm also learned, contrary to Goodman's repeated assertions, that the Rockwell fraud had continued throughout the summer.

Even in light of this knowledge, Singer Hutner chose not to notify affected third parties. The firm consulted Putzel and he counseled them that, because Singer Hutner did not learn of the summertime fraud until the fall, such activity was in the past and was entitled to confidentiality. The only affirmative step the law firm took was to prepare a memorandum for OPM's in-house legal staff specifying the due diligence procedures they should follow in all OPM financings. But this step, too, proved ineffective. The firm gave the memorandum to Goodman to edit and, as it might have expected, the final version contained nothing to alert the OPM legal department to potential problems with the Rockwell leases.

> **Questions** Should Singer Hutner have taken whatever steps were necessary to inform OPM's in-house legal staff of its knowledge and suspicions? Would this have involved a breach of Singer Hutner's ethical obligations? Could OPM's own legal department be considered a "third party"?

OPM's Retention of Kaye Scholer

After Singer Hutner announced its resignation, Goodman invited the law firm of Kaye, Scholer, Fierman, Hays & Handler to serve as OPM's new general counsel. In October, Peter M. Fishbein, a Kaye Scholer partner and an old friend of Hutner's, contacted Hutner to ask if there was anything he should be aware of in considering Goodman's invitation. Because Goodman and the law firm had agreed not to discuss the circumstances of the termination with others, all Hutner told Fishbein was that the decision to withdraw had been mutual.

Having no knowledge of OPM's wrongdoing, Kaye Scholer consented to serve as the company's general counsel. Goodman proceeded to use Kaye Scholer as he had Singer Hutner, and OPM obtained loans of more than $15 million in late 1980 and early 1981 based on fraudulent Rockwell leases.

> **Questions** It is not known whether Goodman prohibited Singer Hutner from sharing information with Kaye Scholer. If Goodman neither gave his consent nor prohibited it, was Singer Hutner obligated to share its knowledge with Kaye Scholer? If Goodman did prohibit this, should the client's express wishes be controlling?

Should a distinction be made between disclosing information to Kaye Scholer and disclosing information to the victims of the fraud? Is any such distinction justified?

Should Singer Hutner at least have informed Kaye Scholer of the rule under which it was withdrawing, thus indicating that there were undisclosed reasons for doubting the propriety of OPM's business transactions?

Epilogue

In late 1980, the OPM scam began to collapse. In November, an attorney for Bankers Trust Company, which served as a paying agent in several OPM lease financings, contacted Rockwell to complain about monthly rental payments being made to Bankers Trust by OPM rather than by Rockwell as the closing documents required. During the course of investigating these indirect payments, Rockwell lawyers discovered that the company was paying on two leases for which it had no documentation.

When it contacted OPM and Bankers Trust for copies, Rockwell received two different versions. It later discovered that the copies Bankers Trust submitted to it appeared forged. After further investigation and a series of meetings, lawyers for Rockwell and Bankers Trust provided the United States Attorney's Office in New York with evidence that a number of OPM–Rockwell leases were fraudulent.

On February 19, 1981, a federal grand jury issued a series of indictments arising out of OPM's fraudulent activities. The following month, the company filed for voluntary reorganization under Chapter 11 of the United States Bankruptcy Code. In December of 1982, Goodman, Weissman, and five other individuals pleaded guilty to a variety of charges arising out of their roles in the Rockwell fraud. Goodman was convicted of sixteen counts of conspiracy, mail fraud, and wire fraud, and Weissman was convicted of nine counts of conspiracy, mail fraud, wire fraud, and making false statements to a bank. Although the United States Attorneys Office investigated Reinhard, neither he nor any of the other Singer Hutner lawyers was indicted.

Nineteen of the lending institutions OPM defrauded brought civil actions against Singer Hutner, Rockwell, Lehman Brothers, and two accounting firms for their roles in the fraud. On March 1, 1983, all the civil actions were settled when the defendants agreed to pay a total of $65 million. Singer Hutner contributed approximately $10 million to the settlement.

Singer Hutner has gone through a series of changes since the OPM fraud was exposed. In 1983, Eli Mattioli left to become an associate with the law firm of Wien, Malkin & Bettex. In 1984, Singer Hutner

Levine & Seeman became Singer & Chase. In 1985, Singer & Chase merged with another law firm to form Morrison, Cohen & Singer. As of 1987, Henry Singer, Joseph Hutner, Jay Seeman, and Carl Rubino were members of this firm. Morton Levine, Andrew Reinhard, and Alan Jacobs were in private practice in New York.

Summary of Rules Governing Professional Responsibility

State law in every state provides for the regulation of lawyers. Often rules of professional conduct are in the statutes, and generally the authority to enforce the rules is delegated to the Supreme Court or to some other organization such as an integrated bar.

The first attempt to promulgate national rules was the American Bar Association's adoption of the Canons of Ethics in 1908. Many states made the Canons their law, although certain states varied some of the provisions.

In 1969 the ABA replaced the Canons with the Model Code of Professional Responsibility. The Model Code is divided into three parts: Canons, Ethical Considerations, and Disciplinary Rules. The Code's Preliminary Statement summarizes the distinguishing features of each of these sections as follows:

> The Canons are statements of axiomatic norms, expressing in general terms the standards of professional conduct expected of lawyers in their relationships with the public, with the legal system, and with the legal profession. They embody the general concepts from which the Ethical Considerations and the Disciplinary Rules are derived.

> The Ethical Considerations are aspirational in character and represent the objectives toward which every member of the profession should strive. They constitute a body of principles upon which the lawyer can rely for guidance in many specific situations.

> The Disciplinary Rules, unlike the Ethical Considerations, are mandatory in character. The Disciplinary Rules state the minimum level of conduct below which no lawyer can fall without being subject to disciplinary action.

Versions of the Model Code are in force in most states today, but most states have considered replacing the Code in whole or in part with the 1983 ABA Model Rules, discussed *infra* p. 203.

MODEL CODE OF PROFESSIONAL RESPONSIBILITY

CANON 2

A Lawyer Should Assist the Legal Profession in Fulfilling Its Duty to Make Legal Counsel Available

ETHICAL CONSIDERATIONS

EC 2–32 A decision by a lawyer to withdraw should be made only on the basis of compelling circumstances, and in a matter pending before a tribunal he must comply with the rules of the tribunal regarding withdrawal. A lawyer should not withdraw without considering carefully and endeavoring to minimize the possible adverse effect on the rights of his client and the possibility of prejudice to his client as a result of his withdrawal. Even when he justifiably withdraws, a lawyer should protect the welfare of his client by giving due notice of his withdrawal, suggesting employment of other counsel, delivering to the client all papers and property to which the client is entitled, cooperating with counsel subsequently employed, and otherwise endeavoring to minimize the possibility of harm. Further, he should refund to the client any compensation not earned during the employment.

DISCIPLINARY RULES

DR 2–110 Withdrawal From Employment

(A) In general.

 (1) If permission for withdrawal from employment is required by the rules of a tribunal, a lawyer shall not withdraw from employment in a proceeding before that tribunal without its permission.

 (2) In any event, a lawyer shall not withdraw from employment until he has taken reasonable steps to avoid foreseeable prejudice to the rights of his client, including giving due notice to his client, allowing time for employment of other counsel, delivering to the client all papers and property to which the client is entitled, and complying with applicable laws and rules.

  . . .

(B) Mandatory withdrawal.

 A lawyer representing a client before a tribunal, with its permission if required by its rules, shall withdraw from employment, and a lawyer representing a client in other matters shall withdraw from employment, if:

.   .   .

(2) He knows or it is obvious that his continued employment will result in violation of a Disciplinary Rule.

.   .   .

(C) Permissive withdrawal.

If DR 2–110(B) is not applicable, a lawyer may not request permission to withdraw in matters pending before a tribunal, and may not withdraw in other matters, unless such request or such withdrawal is because:

(1) His client:

.   .   .

(b) Personally seeks to pursue an illegal course of conduct.

(c) Insists that the lawyer pursue a course of conduct that is illegal or that is prohibited under the Disciplinary Rules.

.   .   .

(e) Insists, in a matter not pending before a tribunal, that the lawyer engage in conduct that is contrary to the judgment and advice of the lawyer but not prohibited under the Disciplinary Rules.

.   .   .

(2) His continued employment is likely to result in a violation of a Disciplinary Rule.

.   .   .

CANON 4

A Lawyer Should Preserve the Confidences and Secrets of a Client

ETHICAL CONSIDERATIONS

EC 4–1 Both the fiduciary relationship existing between lawyer and client and the proper functioning of the legal system require the preservation by the lawyer of confidences and secrets of one who has employed or sought to employ him. A client must feel free to discuss whatever he wishes with his lawyer and a lawyer must be equally free to obtain information beyond that volunteered by his client. A lawyer should be fully informed of all the facts of the matter he is handling in order for his client to obtain the full advantage of our legal system. It is for the lawyer in the exercise of his independent professional judgment to separate the relevant and important from the irrelevant and unimportant. The observance of the ethical obligation of a lawyer to hold inviolate the confidences and secrets of his client not only facilitates the full development of facts essential to proper representation of the client but also encourages laymen to seek early legal assistance.

EC 4–2 The obligation to protect confidences and secrets obviously does not preclude a lawyer from revealing information when his client consents after full disclosure, when necessary to perform his professional employment, when permitted by a Disciplinary Rule, or when required by law. Unless the client otherwise directs, a lawyer may disclose the affairs of his client to partners or associates of his firm. It is a matter of common knowledge that the normal operation of a law office exposes confidential professional information to non-lawyer employees of the office, particularly secretaries and those having access to the files; and this obligates a lawyer to exercise care in selecting and training his employees so that the sanctity of all confidences and secrets of his clients may be preserved. If the obligation extends to two or more clients as to the same information, a lawyer should obtain the permission of all before revealing the information. A lawyer must always be sensitive to the rights and wishes of his client and act scrupulously in the making of decisions which may involve the disclosure of information obtained in his professional relationship. Thus, in the absence of consent of his client after full disclosure, a lawyer should not associate another lawyer in the handling of a matter, nor should he, in the absence of consent, seek counsel from another lawyer if there is a reasonable possibility that the identity of the client or his confidences or secrets would be revealed to such lawyer. Both social amenities and professional duty should cause a lawyer to shun indiscreet conversations concerning his clients.

. . .

EC 4–4 The attorney-client privilege is more limited than the ethical obligation of a lawyer to guard the confidences and secrets of his client. This ethical precept, unlike the evidentiary privilege, exists without regard to the nature or source of information or the fact that others share the knowledge. A lawyer should endeavor to act in a manner which preserves the evidentiary privilege; for example, he should avoid professional discussions in the presence of persons to whom the privilege does not extend. A lawyer owes an obligation to advise the client of the attorney-client privilege and timely to assert the privilege unless it is waived by the client.

EC 4–5 A lawyer should not use information acquired in the course of the representation of a client to the disadvantage of the client and a lawyer should not use, except with the consent of his client after full disclosure, such information for his own purposes. Likewise, a lawyer should be diligent in his efforts to prevent the misuse of such information by his employees and associates. Care should be exercised by a lawyer to prevent the disclosure of the confidences and secrets of one client to another, and no employment should be accepted that might require such disclosure.

. . .

DISCIPLINARY RULES

DR 4–101   Preservation of Confidences and Secrets of a Client

(A) "Confidence" refers to information protected by the attorney-client privilege under applicable law, and "secret" refers to other information gained in the professional relationship that the client has requested be held inviolate or the disclosure of which would be embarrassing or would be likely to be detrimental to the client.

(B) Except when permitted under DR 4–101(C), a lawyer shall not knowingly:

    (1) Reveal a confidence or secret of his client.

    (2) Use a confidence or secret of his to the disadvantage of the client.

    (3) Use a confidence or secret of his client for the advantage of himself or of a third person, unless the client consents after full disclosure.

(C) A lawyer may reveal:

    (1) Confidences or secrets with the consent of the client or clients affected, but only after a full disclosure to them.

    (2) Confidences or secrets when permitted under Disciplinary Rules or required by law or court order.

    (3) The intention of his client to commit a crime and the information necessary to prevent the crime.

    (4) Confidences or secrets necessary to establish or collect his fees or to defend himself or his employees or associates against an accusation of wrongful conduct.

(D) A lawyer shall exercise reasonable care to prevent his employees, associates, and others whose services are utilized by him from disclosing or using confidences or secrets of a client, except that a lawyer may reveal the information allowed by DR 4–101(c) through an employee.

CANON 7

A Lawyer Should Represent a Client Zealously Within the Bounds of the Law

ETHICAL CONSIDERATIONS

EC 7-1 The duty of a lawyer, both to his client and to the legal system, is to represent his client zealously within the bounds of the law, which includes Disciplinary Rules and enforceable professional regulations. The professional responsibility of a lawyer derives from his membership in a profession which has the duty of assisting members of the public to secure and protect available legal rights and benefits. In our government of laws and not of men, each member of our society is entitled to have his conduct judged and regulated in accordance with the law, to seek any lawful objective through legally permissible means, and to present for adjudication any lawful claim, issue, or defense.

EC 7-2 The bounds of the law in a given case are often difficult to ascertain. The language of legislative enactments and judicial opinions may be uncertain as applied to varying factual situations. The limits and specific meaning of apparently relevant law may be made doubtful by changing or developing constitutional interpretations, inadequately expressed statutes or judicial opinions, and changing public and judicial attitudes. Certainty of law ranges from well-settled rules through areas of conflicting authority to areas without precedent.

EC 7-3 Where the bounds of law are uncertain, the action of a lawyer may depend on whether he is serving as advocate or adviser. A lawyer may serve simultaneously as both advocate and adviser, but the two roles are essentially different. In asserting a position on behalf of his client, an advocate for the most part deals with past conduct and must take the facts as he finds them. By contrast, a lawyer serving as adviser primarily assists his client in determining the course of future conduct and relationships. While serving as advocate, a lawyer should resolve in favor of his client doubts as to the bounds of the law. In serving a client as adviser, a lawyer in appropriate circumstances should give his professional opinion as to what the ultimate decisions of the courts would likely be as to the applicable law.

Duty of the Lawyer to a Client

EC 7-4 The advocate may urge any permissible construction of the law favorable to his client, without regard to his professional opinion as to the likelihood that the construction will ultimately prevail. His conduct is within the bounds of the law, and therefore permissible, if the position taken is supported by the law or is supportable by a good faith argument for an extension, modification, or reversal of the law. However, a lawyer is not justified in asserting a position in litigation that is frivolous.

EC 7–5 A lawyer as adviser furthers the interests of his client by giving his professional opinion as to what he believes would likely be the ultimate decision of the courts on the matter at hand and by informing his client of the practical effect of such decision. He may continue in the representation of his client even though his client has elected to pursue a course of conduct contrary to the advice of the lawyer so long as he does not thereby knowingly assist the client to engage in illegal conduct or to take a frivolous legal position. A lawyer should never encourage or aid his client to commit criminal acts or counsel his client on how to violate the law and avoid punishment therefor.

EC 7–6 Whether the proposed action of lawyer is within the bounds of the law may be a perplexing question when his client is contemplating a course of conduct having legal consequences that vary according to the client's intent, motive, or desires at the time of the action. Often a lawyer is asked to assist his client in developing evidence relevant to the state of mind of the client at a particular time. He may properly assist his client in the development and preservation of evidence of existing motive, intent, or desire, obviously, he may not do anything furthering the creation or preservation of false evidence. In many cases a lawyer may not be certain as to the state of mind of his client, and in those situations he should resolve reasonable doubts in favor of his client.

EC 7–8 A lawyer should exert his best efforts to insure that decisions of his client are made only after the client has been informed of relevant considerations. A lawyer ought to initiate this decision-making process if the client does not do so. Advice of a lawyer to his client need not be confined to purely legal considerations. A lawyer should advise his client of the possible effect of each legal alternative. A lawyer should bring to bear upon this decision-making process the fullness of his experience as well as his objective viewpoint. In assisting his client to reach a proper decision, it is often desirable for a lawyer to point out those factors which may lead to a decision that is morally just as well as legally permissible. He may emphasize the possibility of harsh consequences that might result from assertion of legally permissible positions. In the final analysis, however, the lawyer should always remember that the decision whether to forego legally available objectives or methods because of non-legal factors is ultimately for the client and not for himself. In the event that the client in a non-adjudicatory matter insists upon a course of conduct that is contrary to the judgement and advice of the lawyer but not prohibited by Disciplinary Rules, the lawyer may withdraw from the employment.

EC 7–9 In the exercise of his professional judgment on those decisions which are for his determination in the handling of a legal matter, a lawyer should always act in a manner consistent with the best interests of his client. However, when an action in the best interest of his client seems to him to be unjust, he may ask his client for permission to forego such action.

DISCIPLINARY RULES

DR 7–101 Representing a Client Zealously

(A) A lawyer shall not intentionally;

    (1) Fail to seek the lawful objectives of his client through reasonably available means permitted by law and the Disciplinary Rules, except as provided by DR 7–101(B). A lawyer does not violate this Disciplinary Rule, however, by acceding to reasonable requests of opposing counsel which do not prejudice the rights of his client, by being punctual in fulfilling all professional commitments, by avoiding offensive tactics, or by treating with courtesy and consideration all persons involved in the legal process.

    (2) Fail to carry out a contract of employment entered into with a client for professional services, but he may withdraw as permitted under DR 2–110, DR 5–102, and DR 5–105.

    (3) Prejudice or damage his client during the course of the professional relationship except as required under DR 7–102(B).

(B) In his representation of a client, a lawyer may:

    (1) Where permissible, exercise his professional judgment to waive or fail to assert a right or position of his client.

    (2) Refuse to aid or participate in conduct that he believes to be unlawful, even though there is some support for an argument that the conduct is legal.

DR 7–102 Representing a Client Within the Bounds of the Law

(A) In his representation of a client, a lawyer shall not:

    . . .

    (2) Knowingly advance a claim or defense that is unwarranted under existing law, except that he may advance such claim

or defense if it can be supported by good faith argument for an extension, modification, or reversal of existing law.

(3) Conceal or knowingly fail to disclose that which he is require by law to reveal.

(4) Knowingly use perjured testimony or false evidence.

(5) Knowingly make a false statement of law or fact.

(6) Participate in the creation or preservation of evidence when he knows or it is obvious that the evidence is false.

(7) Counsel or assist his client in conduct that the lawyer knows to be illegal or fraudulent.

(8) Knowingly engage in other illegal conduct or conduct contrary to a Disciplinary Rule.

(B) A lawyer who receives information clearly establishing that:

(1) His client has, in the course of the representation, perpetrated a fraud upon a person or tribunal shall promptly call upon his client to rectify the same, and if his client refuses or is unable to do so, he shall reveal the fraud to the affected person or tribunal, except when the information is protected as a privileged communication.

(2) A person other than his client has perpetrated a fraud upon a tribunal shall promptly reveal the fraud to the tribunal.

In 1977 the ABA appointed the Commission on Evaluation of Professional Standards. It charged the Commission with evaluating whether existing standards of professional conduct provided comprehensive and consistent guidance for resolving the increasingly complex ethical problems in the practice of law.

The Commission concluded that a new code was needed and commenced a drafting process that produced numerous drafts, elicited voluminous comment, and launched an unprecedented debate on the ethics of the legal profession. The ABA adopted the Model Rules of Professional Conduct in August 1983. By 1985, eight states had adopted the Model Rules in some form.

It is enlightening to follow the changes in successive drafts as earlier versions were subjected to criticism by wider audiences in the bar.

MODEL RULES OF PROFESSIONAL CONDUCT

Proposed Final Draft, Model Rules of Professional Conduct,
May 30, 1981

RULE 1.2 SCOPE OF REPRESENTATION

. . .

(c) A lawyer may limit the objectives of the representation if the client consents after disclosure. If a client insists upon pursuing an objective that the lawyer considers repugnant or imprudent, the lawyer may withdraw if doing so can be accomplished without material adverse effect on the interests of the client or as otherwise permitted by Rule 1.16(b).

(d) A lawyer shall not counsel or assist a client in conduct that the lawyer knows or reasonably should know is criminal or fraudulent, or in the preparation of a written instrument containing terms the lawyer knows or reasonably should know are legally prohibited, but a lawyer may counsel or assist a client in a good faith effort to determine the validity, scope, meaning or application of the law.

(e) When a lawyer knows or reasonably should know that a client expects assistance not permitted by the rules of professional conduct or other law, the lawyer shall inform the client of the relevant limitations to which the lawyer is subject.

ABA Model Rules of Professional Conduct, Adopted August 1983

RULE 1.2 SCOPE OF REPRESENTATION

. . .

(c) A lawyer may limit the objectives of the representation if the client consents after consultation.

(d) A lawyer shall not counsel a client to engage, or assist a client, in conduct that the lawyer knows is criminal or fraudulent, but a lawyer may discuss the legal consequences of any proposed course of conduct with a client and may counsel or assist a client to make a good faith effort to determine the validity, scope, meaning or application of the law.

(e) When a lawyer knows that a client expects assistance not permitted by the rules of professional conduct or other law, the lawyer shall consult with the client regarding the relevant limitations on the lawyer's conduct.

<u>Excerpt from Comment</u>

Criminal, Fraudulent and Prohibited Transactions

A lawyer is required to give an honest opinion about the actual consequences that appear likely to result from a client's conduct. The fact that a client uses advice in a course of action that is criminal or fraudulent does not, of itself, make a lawyer a party to the course of action. However, a lawyer may not knowingly assist a client in criminal or fraudulent conduct. There is a critical distinction between presenting an analysis of legal aspects of questionable conduct and recommending the means by which a crime or fraud might be committed with impunity.

When the client's course of action has already begun and is continuing, the lawyer's responsibility is especially delicate. The lawyer is not permitted to reveal the client's wrongdoing, except where permitted by Rule 1.6. However, the lawyer is required to avoid furthering the purpose, for example, by suggesting how it might be concealed. A lawyer may not continue assisting a client in conduct that the lawyer originally supposes is legally proper but then discovers is criminal or fraudulent. Withdrawal from representation, therefore, may be required.

. . .

Paragraph (d) applies whether or not the defrauded party is a party to the transaction. Hence, a lawyer should not participate in a sham transaction; for example, a transaction to effectuate criminal or fraudulent escape of tax liability. Paragraph (d) does not preclude undertaking a criminal defense incident to a general retainer for legal services to a lawful enterprise. The last clause of paragraph (d) recognizes that determining the validity or interpretation of a statute or regulation may require a course of action involving disobedience of the statute or regulation or of the interpretation placed upon it by governmental authorities.

<u>Discussion Draft, Model Rules of Professional Conduct,
January 30, 1980</u>

RULE 1.7 CONFIDENTIAL INFORMATION

(a) In giving testimony or providing evidence concerning a client's affairs, a lawyer shall not disclose information concerning the client except as authorized by the applicable law of evidentiary privilege. In other circumstances, a lawyer shall not disclose information about a client which relates to the client-lawyer relationship, which would embarass the client, which is likely to be detrimental to the client, or which the client has requested not be disclosed, except as stated in paragraphs (b) and (c).

(b) A lawyer shall disclose information about a client to the extent it appears necessary to prevent the client from committing an act that would result in death or serious bodily harm to another person, and to the extent required by law or the rules of professional conduct.

(c) A lawyer may disclose information about a client only:

. . .

(2) To the extent it appears necessary to prevent or rectify the consequences of a deliberately wrongful act by the client, except when the lawyer has been employed after the commission of such an act to represent the client concerning the act or its consequences;

. . .

Proposed Final Draft, Model Rules of Professional Conduct
May 30, 1981

RULE 1.6 CONFIDENTIALITY OF INFORMATION

(a) A lawyer shall not reveal information relating to representation of a client except as stated in paragraph (b), unless the client consents after disclosure.

(b) A lawyer may reveal such information to the extent the lawyer believes necessary:

(1) To serve the client's interests, unless it is information the client has specifically requested not be disclosed;

(2) To prevent the client from committing a criminal or fraudulent act that the lawyer believes is likely to result in death or substantial bodily harm, or substantial injury to the financial interests or property of another;

(3) To rectify the consequences of a client's criminal or fraudulent act in the commission of which the lawyer's services had been used;

(4) To establish a claim or defense on behalf of the lawyer in a controversy between the lawyer and the client, or to establish a defense to a criminal charge or civil claim against the lawyer based upon conduct in which the client was involved; or

(5) To comply with the Rules of Professional Conduct or other law.

ABA Model Rules of Professional Conduct, Adopted August 1983

RULE 1.6   CONFIDENTIALITY OF INFORMATION

(a) A lawyer shall not reveal information relating to representation of a client unless the client consents after consultation, except for disclosures that are impliedly authorized in order to carry out the representation, and except as stated in paragraph (b).

(b) A lawyer may reveal such information to the extent the lawyer reasonably believes necessary:

> (1) to prevent the client from committing a criminal act that the lawyer believes is likely to result in imminent death or substantial bodily harm; or
>
> (2) to establish a claim or defense on behalf of the lawyer in a controversy between the lawyer and the client, to establish a defense to a criminal charge or civil claim against the lawyer based upon conduct in which the client was involved, or to respond to allegations in any proceeding concerning the lawyer's representation of the client.

Comment

The lawyer is part of a judicial system charged with upholding the law. One of the lawyer's functions is to advise clients so that they avoid any violation of the law in the proper exercise of their rights.

The observance of the ethical obligation of a lawyer to hold inviolate confidential information of the client not only facilitates the full development of facts essential to proper representation of the client but also encourages people to seek early legal assistance.

Almost without exception, clients come to lawyers in order to determine what their rights are and what is, in the maze of laws and regulations, deemed to be legal and correct. The common law recognizes that the client's confidences must be protected from disclosure. Based upon experience, lawyers know that almost all clients follow the advice given, and the law is upheld.

A fundamental principle in the client-lawyer relationship is that the lawyer maintain confidentiality of information relating to the representation. The client is thereby encouraged to communicate fully and frankly with the lawyer even as to embarrassing or legally damaging subject matter.

The principle of confidentiality is given effect in two related bodies of law, the attorney-client privilege (which includes the work product doctrine) in the law of evidence and the rule of confidentiality established in professional ethics. The attorney-client privilege applies in judicial and other proceedings in which a lawyer may be called as a witness or otherwise required to produce evidence concerning a client. The rule of client-lawyer confidentiality applies in situations other than those where evidence is sought from the lawyer through compulsion of law. The confidentiality rule applies not merely to matters communicated in confidence by the client but also to all information relating to the representation, whatever its source. A lawyer may not disclose such information except as authorized or required by the Rules of Professional Conduct or other law. . . .

The requirement of maintaining confidentiality of information relating to representation applies to government lawyers who may disagree with the policy goals that their representation is designed to advance.

. . .

Disclosure Adverse to Client

The confidentiality rule is subject to limited exceptions. In becoming privy to information about a client, a lawyer may foresee that the client intends serious harm to another person. However, to the extent a lawyer is required or permitted to disclose a client's purposes, the client will be inhibited from revealing facts which would enable the lawyer to counsel against a wrongful course of action. The public is better protected if full and open communication by the client is encouraged than if it is inhibited.

Several situations must be distinguished.

First, the lawyer may not counsel or assist a client in conduct that is criminal or fraudulent. See Rule 1.2(d). Similarly, a lawyer has a duty under Rule 3.3(a)(4) not to use false evidence. This duty is essentially a special instance of the duty prescribed in Rule 1.2(d) to avoid assisting a client in criminal or fraudulent conduct.

Second, the lawyer may have been innocently involved in past conduct by the client that was criminal or fraudulent. In such a situation the lawyer has not violated Rule 1.2(d), because to "counsel or assist" criminal or fraudulent conduct requires knowing that the conduct is of that character.

Third, the lawyer may learn that a client intends prospective conduct that is criminal and likely to result in imminent death or substantial bodily harm. As stated in paragraph (b)(1), the lawyer has professional discretion to reveal information in order to prevent such consequences. The lawyer may make a disclosure in order to prevent homicide or serious bodily injury which the lawyer reasonably believes is intended by a client. It is very difficult for a lawyer to "know" when such a heinous purpose will actually be carried out, for the client may have a change of mind.

The lawyer's exercise of discretion requires consideration of such factors as the nature of the lawyer's relationship with the client and with those who might be injured by the client, the lawyer's own involvement in the transaction and factors that may extenuate the conduct in question. Where practical, the lawyer should seek to persuade the client to take suitable action. In any case, a disclosure adverse to the client's interest should be no greater than the lawyer reasonably believes necessary to the purpose. A lawyer's decision not to take preventive action permitted by paragraph (b)(1) does not violate this Rule.

Withdrawal

If the lawyer's services will be used by the client in materially furthering a course of criminal or fraudulent conduct, the lawyer must withdraw, as stated in Rule 1.16(a)(1).

After withdrawal the lawyer is required to refrain from making disclosure of the clients' confidences, except as otherwise provided in Rule 1.6. Neither this rule nor Rule 1.8(b) nor Rule 1.16(d) prevents the lawyer from giving notice of the fact of withdrawal, and the lawyer may also withdraw or disaffirm any opinion, document, affirmation, or the like.

. . .

Dispute Concerning a Lawyer's Conduct

Where a legal claim or disciplinary charge alleges complicity of the lawyer in a client's conduct or other misconduct of the lawyer involving representation of the client, the lawyer may respond to the extent the lawyer reasonably believes necessary to establish a defense. The same is true with respect to a claim involving the conduct or representation of a former client. The lawyer's right to respond arises when an assertion of such complicity has been made. Paragraph (b)(2) does not require the lawyer to await the commencement of an action or proceeding that charges such complicity, so that the defense may be established by responding directly to a third party who has made such an assertion. The right to defend, of course, applies where a proceeding has been commenced. Where practicable and not prejudicial to the lawyer's ability to establish the defense, the lawyer should advise the client of the third party's assertion and request that the client respond appropriately. In any event, disclosure should be no greater than the lawyer reasonably believes is necessary to vindicate innocence, the disclosure should be made in a manner which limits access to the information to the tribunal or other persons having a need to know it, and appropriate protective orders or other arrangements should be sought by the lawyer to the fullest extent practicable.

If the lawyer is charged with wrongdoing in which the client's conduct is implicated, the rule of confidentiality should not prevent the lawyer from defending against the charge. Such a charge can arise in a civil, criminal or professional disciplinary proceeding, and can be based on a wrong allegedly committed by the lawyer against the client, or on a wrong alleged by a third person; for example, a person claiming to have been defrauded by the lawyer and client acting together. A lawyer entitled to a fee is permitted by paragraph (b)(2) to prove the services rendered in an action to collect it. This aspect of the rule expresses the principle that the beneficiary of a fiduciary relationship may not exploit it to the detriment of the fiduciary. As stated above, the lawyer must make every effort practicable to avoid unnecessary disclosure of information relating to a representation, to limit disclosure to those having the need to know it, and to obtain protective orders or make other arrangements minimizing the risk of disclosure.

Disclosures Otherwise Required or Authorized

The attorney-client privilege is differently defined in various jurisdictions. If a lawyer is called as a witness to give testimony concerning a client, absent waiver by the client, paragraph (a) requires the lawyer to invoke the privilege when it is applicable. The lawyer must comply with the final orders of a court or other tribunal of competent jurisdiction requiring the lawyer to give information about the client.

. . .

Former Client

The duty of confidentiality continues after the client-lawyer relationship has terminated.

ABA Model Rules of Professional Conduct, Adopted August 1983

RULE 1.16 DECLINING OR TERMINATING REPRESENTATION

(a) Except as stated in paragraph (c), a lawyer shall not represent a client or, where representation has commenced, shall withdraw from the representation of a client if:

> (1) the representation will result in violation of the rules of professional conduct or other law;

. . .

(b) except as stated in paragraph (c), a lawyer may withdraw from representing a client if withdrawal can be accomplished without material adverse effect on the interests of the client, or if:

> (1) the client persists in a course of action involving the lawyer's services that the lawyer reasonably believes is criminal or fraudulent;
>
> (2) the client has used the lawyer's services to perpetrate a crime or fraud;
>
> (3) a client insists upon pursuing an objective that the lawyer considers repugnant or imprudent;
>
> . . .

(d) Upon termination of representation, a lawyer shall take steps to the extent reasonably practicable to protect a client's interests, such as giving reasonable notice to the client, allowing time for employment of other counsel, surrendering papers and property to which the client is entitled and refunding any advance payment of fee that has not been earned. The lawyer may retain papers relating to the client to the extent permitted by other law.

Comment

. . .

Mandatory Withdrawal

A lawyer ordinarily must decline or withdraw from representation if the client demands that the lawyer engage in conduct that is illegal or violates the Rules of Professional Conduct or other law. The lawyer is not obligated to decline or withdraw simply because the client suggests such a course of conduct; a client may make such a suggestion in the hope that a lawyer will not be constrained by a professional obligation.

. . .

Optional Withdrawal

A lawyer may withdraw from representation in some circumstances. The lawyer has the option to withdraw if it can be accomplished without material adverse effect on the client's interests. Withdrawal is also justified if the client persists in a course of action that the lawyer reasonably believes is criminal or fraudulent, for a lawyer is not required to be associated with such conduct even if the lawyer does not further it. Withdrawal is also permitted if the lawyer's services were misused in the past even if that would materially prejudice the client. The lawyer also may withdraw where the client insists on a repugnant or imprudent objective.

. . .

Assisting the Client upon Withdrawal

Even if the lawyer has been unfairly discharged by the client, a lawyer must take all reasonable steps to mitigate the consequences to the client. The lawyer may retain papers as security for a fee only to the extent permitted by law.

.   .   .

2.   Divided Loyalties

Food for Thought *

Nancy Barrett had not even finished wrestling with caffeine in soft drinks when she was hit with a new assignment: whether added caffeine had to be included on the label of "Cocolait," a powdered chocolate milk mix.

Barrett was a third year associate working on food and drug law at the large Washington, D.C., law firm of Payne & Brewster (P & B) and had become the firm's expert on caffeine.   Barrett joined the firm in September 1978, primarily because of its reputation in the area of food and drug law.   She majored in biology in college and upon graduating from Stanford University *magna cum laude* went to work as a legislative aide to Senator John Mansfield of California, Chairman of the Committee on Health and Environment.   She worked for the Senator for three years, becoming involved in a number of public health issues including toxic chemicals, pesticides, drug regulation, and food labeling. She was given a great deal of responsibility; however, she realized early on that a law degree was an essential credential in government work: "Most of the 'power brokers' were lawyers."

In September 1975, Barrett entered Boalt Hall School of Law at Berkeley.   She did well in her course work and won the second year moot court competition.   She also maintained her interest in public health and wrote a paper on the history of food and drug law.   P & B, one of the largest and oldest law firms in Washington, was happy to add Nancy Barrett to its ranks.   Although the firm was best known for its antitrust, communications, and banking practices, it also had the largest food and drug practice of any private law firm.   Approximately 15 attorneys practiced food and drug law on a full time basis.   The firm hired only the "cream of the crop" from the top law schools, and Barrett had the right credentials plus experience.

Barrett had had several other attractive offers, including one from the U.S. Food and Drug Administration (FDA), but thought that P & B would provide her with excellent training and experience.   She had qualms about going to work for a large law firm.   Many of her friends at Berkeley thought that anyone who took a job with a firm like P & B was a "sell-out," and she had always considered herself a liberal and a

---

* This case is fiction, adapted (and altered) from several experiences reported by Washington lawyers. The information on caffeine is not comprehensive and should not be relied upon to form any conclusions about its health effects. Research continues on the effects of caffeine on animals and humans.

216

supporter of government regulation. Therefore, her plans were to stay at P & B for two to three years and then go back into the government.

Barrett loved the food and drug law area. It was exciting and full of such important policy issues as public health and safety, consumer freedom of choice, and product development. The history of food and drug law in the U.S. exemplified these conflicting policy tensions.

Congress enacted the Pure Food and Drugs Act in 1906. The Act took a straightforward approach to food regulation. It defined "adulterated" and "misbranded" foods and drugs and prohibited their shipment across state lines. Food was adulterated if it "contained any added poisonous or other deleterious ingredient which could render such article injurious to health." The focus was on whether the food itself, as opposed to the added substance, was injurious to health. A product was "misbranded" if it included statements that were false or misleading or failed to provide required information in labeling.

In 1938, Congress altered food and drug regulation substantially by adopting the Food, Drug, and Cosmetic Act (FDCA). In addition to food and drugs, the FDCA regulated cosmetics and therapeutic devices. It required manufacturers to provide scientific proof that new products were safe before putting them on the market, and prohibited companies from adding poisonous substances to foods unless doing so was unavoidable or required in production. To aid enforcement, the FDCA allowed false drug claims to be barred without proof of fraud and permitted federal court injunctions.

The current food and drug law, which includes the FDCA, the 1958 Food Additives Amendment, the 1960 Color Additives Amendment, and the 1962 Drug Amendments, is lengthy and complicated—the product of many forces and of legislative compromises. Its fundamentals, however, are simple and practical and reflect the framework of the 1906 law. The law prohibits distribution in the United States of products that are "adulterated" or "misbranded." The word "adulterated" applies to products or materials that are defective, unsafe, filthy, or produced under unsanitary conditions. "Misbranded" means statements, designs, or pictures in labeling that are false or misleading, as well as failure to provide required information in labeling.

The Food Additives Amendment to the FDCA

The 1958 Food Additives Amendment to the FDCA was particularly relevant to Barrett's work on caffeine. The amendment, enacted in response to public concern over the content of packaged foods, shifted the burden of proof to the food manufacturer to show the safety of prospective additives before marketing any food containing them. The amendment required the manufacturer to petition the FDA to establish a regulation for safe use of the additive. The petition must include health effect data, dose-response levels, and other evidence of safety investigation as established by lengthy and costly animal tests and sometimes human tests.

The amendment also expanded the definition of "adulterated" to include foods that contain either: (1) a food additive that has not been approved as "safe" by FDA, or (2) an approved food additive that is present in a quantity exceeding a tolerance level established by FDA.

One of the major issues in the ten years of congressional debate on the amendment was how additives then in use would be treated under the new law. In the end, Congress excluded a substantial portion of existing food additives from the extensive testing requirements. Specifically excluded were: (a) "prior sanctioned" substances—those that had received official approval in earlier years and had a type of "grandfather status"; (b) "generally recognized as safe" items, or the GRAS list. The GRAS list, established by regulation, included some 700 substances, among them such well known additives as ascorbic acid (vitamin C), caffeine, cinnamon, MSG, BHA, BHT, sugar, pepper, mustard, cyclamates, and saccharin.

GRAS Review

FDA's decisions to place a substance on the original GRAS list were based on the data available at the time the lists were established and on the then current state of knowledge in the field of toxicology. Likewise, the pre–1958 approvals by FDA that qualified substances for prior-sanctioned status reflected the best safety judgments that could be made at the time. In 1970, FDA initiated a "GRAS review" program and established a select committee on GRAS substances (SCOGS) to evaluate the items on the GRAS list. The review resulted in the initiation by FDA of more than 65 rulemaking proceedings in which the agency proposed either to affirm the GRAS status of the substance under review or, where appropriate, to take action to restrict or prohibit use of the substance.

Caffeine

One of the most interesting GRAS substances, and one that has been the subject of much attention, is caffeine. Caffeine is a strong stimulant of the central nervous system. It occurs naturally in tea leaves and in coffee, cocoa, and kola nuts, but can also be made synthetically. It is often added to soft drinks as a flavor enhancer and because it results in something called "mouth feel" (a distinctive sensation on the tongue). Some consumer groups contend that manufacturers add caffeine to soft drinks because of its addictive qualities in order to get kids "hooked." FDA had specifically listed caffeine as GRAS as a multiple purpose ingredient in cola-type beverages, at a level not to exceed 0.02% of the beverage.

Caffeine has been under scientific study since its isolation in the laboratory in 1820. Short term effects of caffeine on the body are generally well known. The substance: (a) allays drowsiness, (b) enables one to work faster and to think more clearly, (c) stimulates the brain, heart muscle, and kidneys, (d) alters the metabolism of fat, (e) dilates the blood vessels, (f) causes insulin to be released, and (g) increases the production of stomach acid. Persons who drink large amounts of coffee (15–20 cups a day) may develop "caffeinism" which can result in insomnia, a slight fever, and irritability. What is not known is whether caffein has long-term effects on human health.

As a result of GRAS review, in mid 1979, SCOGS determined that "while no evidence in the available information on caffeine demonstrates a hazard to the public when it is used at levels that are now current and in the manner now practiced, uncertainties exist requiring that additional studies . . . be conducted."

FDA's Position on Caffeine—The Scientific Literature

In the October 21, 1980, issue of the *Federal Register,* FDA specifically proposed to remove caffeine from the GRAS list and place it on an interim food additive list and to declare that no prior sanction existed for the use of caffeine as an added food ingredient.

Under the FDA proposal, current uses of added caffeine would be permitted under an interim food additive regulation pending the completion of studies necessary to resolve questions about the safety of caffeine added to food. The questions included the potential fetotoxic and teratogenic properties of caffeine, the metabolism and pharmacokinetic handling of caffeine in humans and experimental animals, the potential behavioral effects of caffeine, particularly in children, and the potential reproductive effects and carcinogenicity of caffeine. [See Appendix 1 for glossary of scientific terms.] FDA proposed to require both animal and human epidemiological studies. Performance of the studies would be a condition to continued use of the substance under the interim regulation.

Due to evidence which had recently been developed concerning the capacity of caffeine to cause birth defects in rats, FDA's primary concern about caffeine was its potential teratogenicity. Although the proposed FDA regulation acknowledged the uncertainty concerning the link between caffeine and birth defects in humans, it concluded that available data from animal studies were significant enough to be of serious concern and to justify additional research to clarify the uncertainties about caffeine's potential teratogenicity in humans.

In addition to studies regarding caffeine's teratogenic effects, FDA proposed to require studies addressing the capacity of caffeine to cause adverse reproductive effects and cancer.

With regard to the teratogenic effects of caffeine, FDA reviewed animal data existing prior to 1979. Many of the studies had deficiencies (e.g., lack of proper control animals, small number of animals, insufficient information on procedures), and many of them were conducted a decade or more ago when teratology study techniques were less developed. Despite these deficiencies, the studies demonstrated that at sufficiently high levels of exposure, well above levels to which humans are normally exposed, caffeine could cause birth defects in animals. The studies were not adequate, however, to determine with any confidence a "no effect level" for the teratogenic effects of caffeine for animals, i.e., the level of exposure at which no teratogenic effects are observed.

Due to the uncertainties left by the existing animal data, the FDA in 1979 initiated two teratology studies of caffeine in laboratory animals using up-to-date teratology test methods. The results of one of the studies—the gavage study, in which mice were force-fed measured amounts of caffeine through a stomach tube—raised serious concerns about caffeine because it was the first large, well designed, and controlled teratology study on caffeine to show irreversible terata (e.g., missing digits) at levels of caffeine exposure not significantly greater than those to which humans might be exposed in the food supply. The problem, however, was whether animal teratology studies in general and rat studies on caffeine in particular were reliable indicators of human risk.

It is difficult to interpret teratology studies. No single test species can be said to predict accurately the human response to a given chemical. For example, there are physiological and biological differences between rats and humans that affect the way the body processes a substance. There is some indication that humans and experimental animals metabolize caffeine differently.

FDA also reviewed six human epidemiological studies that dealt with the teratological effects of caffeine, but most of those studies had methodological problems that made it virtually impossible to draw valid inferences from the results.

With regard to the potential carcinogenic effects of caffeine, FDA concluded in its proposed regulations that the available data were inadequate and incomplete. No lifetime feeding studies of caffeine met currently accepted toxicological testing criteria, nor were there acceptable epidemiological data linking human exposure to caffeine with a significant increase in the incidence of cancer.

Public interest groups supported FDA's efforts to regulate the use of caffeine and, in fact, urged FDA to go further in its control of the additive. The Center for Science in the Public Interest (CSPI), in Washington, D.C., submitted a petition to FDA requesting that it issue a regulation requiring all packages of tea and coffee that contain caffeine to carry a plainly visible warning advising that consumption of the product may be harmful to the unborn children of pregnant women and that FDA initiate an education campaign designed to inform pregnant women about the possibility that excessive consumption of caffeine could interfere with reproduction.

Caffeine and Soft Drinks

One of the most interesting projects Barrett had worked on thus far at P & B was for one of the firm's largest clients: The American Soft Drink Council (ASDC). ASDC had come to P & B five months ago, two weeks after FDA issued its proposal to tighten the regulatory grip on caffeine.

The 1,400 members of the American Soft Drink Council were concerned about FDA's proposed rule to remove caffeine from the GRAS list. Approximately 75 percent of the nation's soft drinks contained added caffeine. Although caffeine is a natural ingredient of cola drinks (as kola nuts contain caffeine), much is removed during processing, and an additional quantity is added to many colas for flavor and to give them extra "spark" or "liveliness."

The ASDC was concerned about the proposed regulation for several reasons. First, the manufacturers would be required to conduct extensive and costly tests on animals and humans. Although the industry was already conducting a number of large scale studies on caffeine it did not want to be required to do all of the tests that FDA was proposing. Second, significant adverse publicity was likely to result. Adverse publicity regarding caffeine had already hurt the industry. Third, and most important, the removal of caffeine from the GRAS list would have serious implications for the industry's international markets. Other countries did not understand the complex regulatory categories established by FDA and might conclude that soft drinks containing caffeine were not safe.

The ASDC was critical of FDA's proposed rule. The trade association specifically criticized the rationale for the rule, citing weaknesses in the studies relied on and the equivocal nature of the data.

With respect to teratogenic effects, ASDC observed that FDA was forced to place nearly total reliance for its October 21, 1980, proposal on the gavage study despite the fact that an internal FDA audit had uncovered serious violations of good laboratory practice regulations in that study.

Other shortcomings of the study noted by ASDC included the possibility that the study seriously misinterpreted the teratogenic effect of ectrodactyly (missing digits) in rats at a dose of 80 mg/kg/day by finding ectrodactyly where none existed. ASDC also attempted to put the dosage in perspective:

> An 80 mg/kg/day dose in a rodent would be equivalent to the following number of 6–ounce soft drink servings per day for persons of the indicated body weight: a 30 kg (66 lb.) person— 135; a 50 kg (110 lb.) person—226; and a 70 kg (154 lb.) person—316. By comparison, the daily intake of caffeine from soft drinks for the average consumer in all age groups is less than three-tenths (0.3) of a mg/kg/day and about 0.2 mg/kg/day for pregnant women. For the heaviest users of soft drinks . . . in special populations such as children or pregnant women, consumption from soft drinks, when all sources of caffeine are considered, is on the order of one (1) mg/kg/day.

ASDC maintained that FDA's proposal was not justified under the law or under the present state of scientific knowledge and requested that FDA reaffirm that added caffeine is generally recognized as safe in soft drinks, including cola-type beverages, pepper-type beverages, and other soda water beverages.

The ASDC came to P & B to have them prepare comments on FDA's proposed regulation. Specifically, the manufacturers contended that (1) FDA sanctioned the use of caffeine in soft drinks prior to 1958, and (2) caffeine should remain on the GRAS list.

The Prior Sanction Issue

Barrett was given the task of preparing the comments for ASDC on the prior sanction issue. She immediately sent a Freedom of Information Act letter to FDA to obtain copies of all the FDA's correspondence on caffeine. Within several months, after pouring through hundreds of FDA files, she had collected five two-inch-thick notebooks full of prior correspondence and FDA pronouncements on the substance. She reviewed the entire file, combing through the documents to determine if FDA had expressly or implicitly approved the use of caffeine as a food additive prior to 1958.

Barrett put together three lines of argument for the proposition that caffeine should be subject to a prior sanction based on FDA's course of conduct, correspondence, and other action between the enactment of the Federal Food and Drug Act of 1906 and the Food Additives Amendment of 1958.

First, she argued that when FDA entered into a court-approved settlement in the case of *United States v. Forty Barrels and Twenty Kegs Coca-Cola* in 1917, the agency thereby approved the use of caffeine in cola drinks at a maximum level equal to the reduced quantity which the parties agreed The Coca-Cola Company could use.

Second, Barrett maintained that FDA letters to consumers, manufacturers, and others from 1938 through 1958 evidenced FDA's pre-1958 determination that the use of caffeine in soft drinks was not injurious to public health. Throughout those years, FDA had been conducting periodic analyses of the caffeine content of soft drinks, and had made no effort to act against these products after evaluating the analyses.

Finally, Barrett referred to a letter written by FDA to The Coca-Cola Company just prior to enactment of the Food Additives Amendment of 1958, which she believed was the culmination of a long line of agency pronouncements and conduct evidencing a prior sanction for the use of added caffeine in soft drinks. Writing to an official of The Coca-Cola Company the then Deputy Commissioner of FDA stated:

> The beverage Coca-Cola has been, in our opinion, in such common use for such a long period of time that its safety, as well as the safety of its components, is well established by this history of food experience. . . . We have long sanctioned the distribution of Coca-Cola and the enactment of H.R. 13254, the Food Additives Amendment of 1958, would not affect our sanction in any way. (Letter from John L. Harvey, Deputy Commissioner, FDA, to Edgar J. Forio, August 20, 1958.)

Harvard School of Public Health Study

Although she believed she had put together a strong case for prior sanction, Nancy wondered if the prior sanction route was appropriate in this case. Just one month ago—March 1981—an article had appeared in the *New England Journal of Medicine* describing research by scientists at the Harvard School of Public Health suggesting a statistical link between the drinking of coffee and cancer of the pancreas.

The researchers questioned 369 patients with cancer of the pancreas about their use of tobacco, alcohol, tea, and coffee. A control group of 644 patients, who were hospitalized for a variety of reasons unrelated to cancer of the pancreas, was asked the same set of questions. A surprisingly strong association was found between coffee consumption and pancreatic cancer in both sexes. The scientists speculated that if the association was confirmed and found to be causal, coffee might be found to contribute to more than half of the 20,000 deaths from this disease each year.

The study obtained significant media coverage. Coffee drinkers were shocked to learn that their daily dose of "java" might contribute to a shorter life span.

Barrett knew that the Harvard study was controversial and had some methodological problems, but she was not sure how serious they were. Just two days ago an article had appeared in the *New York Times*, criticizing the study. The story quoted a medical school dean as saying that the investigators who questioned patients on their pre-hospitalization coffee habits knew in advance which ones had cancer, and that this could have introduced unintentional bias in the results.

Clearly, a number of significant business interests had a stake in FDA's proposed regulation. It sounded to Barrett as if there might be some basis for concern about the link between caffeine and cancer, but she did not have the technical background to evaluate the study results. If the study results were correct, perhaps caffeine should be removed from the GRAS list and perhaps the industry should not press its legal argument that caffeine had received a prior sanction from FDA.

Prior sanction status would protect the industry by putting the burden of proof on FDA to show that caffeine is injurious to health—a difficult task given the equivocal nature of the scientific data. But Barrett started to worry that even if the industry could successfully achieve prior sanction status for its use of caffeine, doing so would impose health risks on the public. She thought that perhaps Congress had been wrong in enacting the prior sanction provision—that the provision might fail to recognize changes in technology and in the ability of modern science to detect harmful substances. If new additives could be used only after a company proved that they were safe, should a showing of safety be required as to caffeine, at least once the ingredient's safety had been challenged by reputable scientists?

Barrett knew that if FDA believed caffeine to be harmful, it could begin a regulatory proceeding and ban use of the substance under 21 C.F.R. 181.1(b). If FDA issued such a rule, the industry could persuade a court to invalidate it only by showing the rule to be "arbitrary and capricious," a difficult test to meet. But she thought the political environment—the strength of the industry and the vast public who consume caffeine daily in soft drinks and coffee—would deter the FDA from putting this particular safety issue at the top of its agenda.

Caffeine and Cocolait

While Barrett was still struggling with the soft drink issue, Donald Porter, a senior partner at the firm, asked her to attend a meeting in his office with a new client. Porter had been at P & B for almost 21 years and was one of the leading food and drug lawyers in the nation. His first assignment at P & B was working on the 1962 Drug Amendments to the FDCA in the wake of the tragic thalidomide case. He had taught about food and drug law at law schools, and had published extensively on the topic. Barrett respected him a great deal.

When Barrett arrived at Porter's office, Porter introduced her to Roger Dubarry, president of Dubarry Foods, Inc. Dubarry was a client of Benjamin Freedland, a corporate attorney at P & B. Freedland had recommended that Dubarry speak to Porter after the company received a letter from FDA asserting that the label of one of Dubarry's canned fruit products did not include all the required information. Although FDA turned out to be mistaken, Dubarry was nervous about another labeling matter.

Dubarry Foods produced a wide variety of food products in the U.S. and imported some specialty items from Europe for distribution here. Among the imported items was "Cocolait," a powdered chocolate milk drink mix. The product had been sold in France for ten years under the name "Cocaulait" and in the U.S. for five years. Dubarry Foods had been marketing Cocolait in this country without disclosure on the label that caffeine was added to the product. Although some caffeine is present naturally in cocoa, an additional amount was added to the chocolate milk drink mix to counteract the soporific effects of warm milk. Dubarry was especially nervous given the recent *New England Journal of Medicine* article on caffeine and pancreatic cancer and the FDA proposal to remove caffeine from the GRAS list.

The Assignment

Roger Dubarry was disturbed by the recent media focus on caffeine and wanted to know whether he was absolutely required to include caffeine on the label of his chocolate milk drink mix. He was under the impression that there were exceptions to the labeling requirements for which he might qualify. He also mentioned that some of his competitors added caffeine to their chocolate milk products and did not list caffeine on their labels. He asked Porter if he could have someone study the issue. Porter asked Barrett to research the caffeine labeling requirements and to have a response for Dubarry by the end of the week.

Barrett was convinced that Dubarry was legally required to include caffeine on the label of its chocolate milk drink mix and that it would be in the public interest for him to do so because the product was primarily consumed by children. Nevertheless, she went through the possible legal arguments why Dubarry should not have to include caffeine on the label:

1. *Caffeine is a natural constituent of cocoa beans and therefore need not be declared on the label.* This argument would not hold water. Although inherent constituents of natural ingredients need not be labelled, the regulations made a clear distinction between natural and "added" ingredients. Added ingredients had to be included on the label, and Dubarry admitted that caffeine was added to the product.

2. *Compliance with the labeling requirements would result in "unfair competition."* This argument was also weak. The statute, 21 U.S.C. § 343(i), provided that a food need not include all ingredients on the label if such labeling resulted in deception or unfair competition. One might argue that because most of Dubarry's competitors were also adding caffeine and not disclosing it on the label, if he were to disclose the fact on his label he would be hurt competitively. But the statute further provided that this provision could only be used if the Secretary of Health and Human Services promulgated a regulation exempting the food from the labeling requirements. No such regulation had been promulgated for chocolate milk.

3. *Caffeine is a "flavoring" and, therefore, exempt from a requirement that it be specifically named on the label.* The statute specifies that if a food is fabricated from two or more ingredients, the label must include "the common or usual name of each such ingredient; except that spices, flavorings and colorings, other than those sold as such, may be designated as spices, flavorings, and colorings without naming each." Regulations provided that both "artificial or natural flavors" could be declared as such in the statement of ingredients. The caffeine added to Cocolait was natural caffeine as opposed to synthetic caffeine and therefore would be a natural flavoring. The regulations defined natural flavoring as any substance whose significant function in food is flavoring rather than nutritional and which is derived from plants or animals. The regulations also provided that natural flavors included the "natural essence or extractives" obtained from plants and other substances listed in the regulations. Caffeine did not appear in any of these lists, but one could argue that it fell within the broad definition of flavors in the regulations. Caffeine is used on a limited basis as an added ingredient in several categories of non-beverage foods, including baked goods, frozen dairy desserts, gelatin puddings, and fillings, in part as a flavoring agent. The "flavor" line was Dubarry's strongest argument. If he did not want to include "caffeine" on the label he might get away with

adding the natural flavor wording. But knowing FDA's most recent thinking about caffeine and its desire to have caffeine separately disclosed on the label as expressed in a recently proposed rule, Barrett did not believe this route would be sanctioned by FDA either.

4. Finally, there was another reason Dubarry might decide not to change its labels—an enforcement reason. *In small amounts it would be almost impossible to detect whether the caffeine was added or within the natural variation of cocoa.* However, Barrett did not believe this was a valid reason and did not think it appropriate to mention it to the company.

Overall, she thought the legal arguments for Dubarry were weak, but she had a difficult time thinking of reasons why it was in the interest of Dubarry Foods to comply, especially given the difficulty of distinguishing added from natural caffeine and therefore the difficulty of enforcement. If it did comply, the company might be hurt competitively. The best argument she could make was that if FDA or a consumer group discovered the company's misrepresentation, there could be serious sanctions and significant adverse publicity that would hurt sales.

On Friday, April 24, she presented the results of her research and her conclusion to Donald Porter. He basically agreed with her assessment. The meeting with Dubarry was scheduled for Monday, April 27th. Unfortunately, Porter was going to be out of town on vacation for the next three weeks so he would not be able to attend the meeting. Benjamin Freedland, who had referred Dubarry to Porter and knew quite a bit about Dubarry Foods, would take his place. Freedland had been at the firm ten years. Early in his career he practiced food and drug law but now he practiced general corporate law. Barrett had worked with him a few times and found him to be a brilliant attorney, always thorough and thoughtful.

The Second Meeting

On Monday, Barrett was prepared to present her findings. She went through the list of legal arguments one by one and shot each one down, concluding that Dubarry had no choice but to include caffeine on the label. She was somewhat taken aback, however, when Freedland quickly jumped in after she presented her conclusion: "Wait a minute, Nancy," he said. "It's not so clear to me that Dubarry must include caffeine on its Cocolait labels. I think that the company would be within the law as long as it included the phrase 'and natural flavors' on the package. There appears to be a solid basis in the law for going that route."

Barrett tried to disagree, but Roger Dubarry broke in: "I agree with Ben. It sounds like we have a pretty good legal argument. Besides, what would FDA do to me if the argument does not hold up? And how likely would it be that they would find out in the first place?"

Freedland took over at this point and answered the question as best he could. First, he explained the difficulty FDA would have in finding out whether caffeine was, in fact, added to the product given that caffeine occurs naturally in cocoa. Second, he indicated that if FDA were to find out it would probably be from a competitor and that this was unlikely since Dubarry's competitors also added caffeine to their products.

At this point Barrett interjected: "But, Mr. Freedland, there's always the possibility that one of Mr. Dubarry's competitors will develop a caffeine free chocolate milk drink mix just like many soft drink manufacturers are doing. Once that happens, the competitor is likely to go to FDA and ask them to enforce the labeling requirement."

Dubarry seemed to think this was unlikely. He asked Freedland what FDA would do if it did decide to enforce the rule.

"First of all," Freedland replied, "the agency would conduct an investigation. Field inspectors would want to collect samples of the product from your warehouses. But, as I said before, even if they analyze the powdered mix in the laboratory it will be difficult for them to determine whether caffeine has been added or is a part of the natural constituents in cocoa, especially if the amount is within the natural variation of caffeine in cocoa."

Freedland continued: "Next, FDA may ask for records of the formula for the mix from your supplier. It is much more difficult for FDA to get records for an imported product than a domestic one but it may be able to obtain them. If it did get a copy, the agency would be able to prove that the product contained added caffeine. If it were able to put together some evidence of added caffeine, the agency would send you a 'regulatory letter,' and might take some significant action such as detaining your imported supply at customs. FDA has virtually unlimited regulatory authority over imported products, much greater than it does over domestic goods. An even more drastic step it could take would be to request that you recall the product that is on the market. Arguably the agency has no legal authority to do this, but if it gets to this stage, it is usually best to comply as FDA does have the authority to take much more drastic legal actions including seizure of the product, bringing criminal suit against the president of the company, or issuing adverse publicity."

"But how likely is it that FDA would require me to recall the product?" Dubarry asked.

"Based on my experience with FDA, not very likely," Freedland responded.

At this point, Barrett broke in. She had been biting her tongue for the last 15 minutes. She was surprised at the way Freedland was handling the issue and did not agree with his assessment at all.

"I'm not so sure that's true in this case, Mr. Freedland," she said. "Given FDA's recent concern about caffeine and the susceptibility of children to caffeine in this type of product, they might request a recall. In addition," she continued, "consumer groups might bring suit for fraud or make adverse public statements about the product. Recently, several consumer groups have been analyzing soft drinks for caffeine and publishing the results. They are likely to do the same thing for chocolate milk products. Also, someone who has an allergic reaction to caffeine might bring suit for your failure to include caffeine on the label."

"But, Nancy," Freedland countered, "if the person is really sensitive to caffeine, the company would be likely to win the suit, given the fact that caffeine is a natural ingredient in chocolate products. And, as I said earlier, there is a strong legal argument that caffeine is a natural flavor, and as such need not be included by name on the label."

Before Barrett could respond, Dubarry broke in. "I agree with you, Ben. It sounds to me like we have a good legal basis for not including caffeine on the label, and I'd like a letter from your law firm on that for my files."

"Sure, Roger," he responded, and turned toward Barrett. "Nancy, I'll leave it to you to work something out with Roger. I suggest you put together a draft for him to look at sometime this week."

On that note, the meeting ended. Nancy Barrett went back to her office. She was sure when she went into the meeting that Dubarry should include caffeine on the label. Now she was less sure, especially given Freedland's response. But she still did not feel comfortable about writing the letter. She wondered if she should talk more to Freedland about it, or wait until Donald Porter got back from his vacation, or talk to Dubarry. Perhaps she should seek guidance from an expert at the FDA, she thought.

It was 12:30 p.m. She was going to meet a friend for lunch, someone she knew and trusted. She hoped her friend could help her sort through her dilemma.

Appendix 1.   Glossary

Carcinogen. A substance or agent producing or inciting cancer.

Epidemiology. The study of the prevalence and spread of disease in a community.

FASEB. Federation of American Societies for Experimental Biology.

Fetotoxic. A substance which has a toxic effect on the fetus.

Gestational. During the period of gestation or pregnancy.

GRAS. FDA category: "Generally Recognized As Safe."

Mutagenic. Having the power to cause mutations (changes in the chromosome structure).

Neurophysiological. Relating to the nervous system.

Pharmoco-kinetic. Relating to the disposition of drugs in the body.

SCOGs. Select Committee on GRAS Substances.

Teratogenic. Causing abnormal development in the fetus (birth defects).

Toxicology. The study of the effects of poisons on the human body.

Discussion Questions

1. Before being assigned to work on the Dubarry problem, Nancy Barrett prepared comments to FDA arguing that the addition of caffeine to soft drinks was legal because caffeine was specifically approved (there was prior sanction) before 1958. In one sense, Barrett's task presented no ethical dilemma. She was expressing the position of her client, the American Soft Drink Council, and it is plainly a respectable argument under the law. But what if she believes that many people may be killed, as the Harvard School of Public Health study on cancer and the pancreas seems to suggest? This would be a result of the very action for which she is attempting to win approval. If an attorney knew that there had been a number of deaths during the early use of a drug in Europe but that there was no requirement that these be made known to the FDA, could she morally file the papers necessary for obtaining approval for use of the drug in the United States? Would she technically be guilty of homicide if she aided and assisted in a course of conduct which she had every reason to believe was likely to cause death negligently or recklessly? Even if not, would there not be some moral responsibility for the result? Is the position of a lawyer in obtaining authority for a client to do a dangerous act any different from the position of the people who advertise a dangerous product or assist in some other way in carrying out the act itself?

What could she do if she believed there was great danger in the actions her client proposed? She could certainly refuse to counsel or assist in the transaction. She could only reveal her concerns to the authorities if she had reason to believe that the client intended to commit a crime (or, perhaps, only if it was a crime likely to result in death or substantial bodily harm). More realistically, she could raise the issue directly and firmly with the client or urge her partner to do this. What factors would enter into a decision to take one of these steps? One is the likelihood of serious harm from the client's action. Another is the availability of the pertinent data to the licensing agency, the FDA in this case. Is it relevant that a commitment to deregulation is making the agency less willing to explore the facts or take serious action? Is the political context which explains an exemption in the regulatory law relevant? What if Barrett were convinced that the exemption were simply the result of special interest lobbying; what if, alternatively, she thought there had been a good reason for it?

2. Question 1 raises the issue of what a lawyer should do in a situation where she may be able to get legal approval for her client to act in a way that may cause serious harm to others. An equally difficult question is what advice a lawyer should give to her client when she thinks what the client wants to do would, in all likelihood, be held illegal by a court, but there is room for doubt. Is there any obligation to go beyond informing the client of the attorney's view of the law and the attorney's prediction as to how courts would handle a dispute about the issue? If the client indicates that he intends to proceed despite advice that the proposed action is almost certainly illegal, does the lawyer have an obligation to remind the client of the immorality of ignoring the law in that way or is it sufficient that the client is aware of the likely consequences? What if the lawyer will be expected to prepare documents or otherwise assist in the transaction? Is it at least proper for the lawyer to take these steps if she believes there is a "presentable" argument for the legality of what the client is proposing to do or should she impose a higher standard?

Would you agree that this is the situation that faces Barrett at the end of the case when Freedland asks her to write an opinion letter? How should she think about the issue? Even if any illegality is purely technical—has no significant economic or health consequences—does Barrett have an obligation to try to persuade Freedland that he should, morally, include caffeine on the label of Cocolait? Does the answer change depending on just how certain she is that such labeling would be required by a court if the issue were in fact litigated? Would she be wrong to continue to participate in and assist the transaction (e.g., by such further steps as negotiating for the purchase of Cocolait labels which she knew did not mention caffeine) if she believed she was furthering a plain violation of the law? Surely writing the requested opinion letter raises this issue for Barrett.

3. Should Barrett draft the letter? Here, in contrast to negotiating with the seller of labels, there is the further issue that she is being asked to state as her own opinion legal views that she does not hold. And the very purpose of the opinion letter is to persuade private associates of Freedland and law enforcement officials that he is acting in good faith. There are three types of letters that Barrett could write in this situation:

(1) An "Opinion Letter" stating that in her opinion the law does not require Dubarry to include caffeine on the label. If she drafts such a letter she will be putting her name and the name of the firm behind it. This is the type of letter Dubarry would like to get.

(2) A letter specifying the legal risks of not including caffeine on the label. In this letter a lawyer need not say whether she thinks the action is legal or not.

(3) A letter defending the client's failure to include caffeine on the label. This letter is a bit closer to the Opinion Letter than option number 2; however, as in option number 2, an attorney need not say that she agrees with her client's position.

Which type of letter would you draft if you were in Barrett's position? None of the letters would help Dubarry much in a court proceeding, but an Opinion Letter or a letter such as that listed as number 3 above might help the company in negotiation with the regulatory agency if the company tried to convince the agency not to take the company to court. What are the implications of preparing a draft to be worked out with the client? Is this ever proper?

4. Another troublesome issue raised by this case is what an attorney should do if she thinks what her client wants to do is illegal but also thinks that the client is not likely to get caught. A particularly difficult variation of this issue is how candid an attorney should be when a client asks her the likelihood of his being "caught" or the probability of his receiving various fines or penalties. How would you have responded to Dubarry's question on p. 225: "What would FDA do to me if the argument [that caffeine is a natural flavoring] does not hold up? And how likely would it be that they would find out in the first place [that we add caffeine to Cocolait]?" Do you agree with the way Benjamin Freedland handled the question? What else could he have done? How much does your response turn on the harmful consequences to others of the illegal conduct?

5. Obviously, Barrett does not agree with Freedland's response to Dubarry regarding the labeling issue. As a junior attorney in a large law firm, what are her options? What would you do in such a situation? How would your responses to questions 1, 2 and 4 affect your decision (i.e. your perspective as to how harmful the consequences to consumers might be if caffeine were not added to the label, whether the act was illegal, how likely you think it is that the FDA would bring an enforcement action)?

Is it relevant that Barrett's law firm is known as a specialist in food and drug practice? Does this give her an additional responsibility to avoid signing her name to views about food and drug law that she does not believe to be her best sense of correct law? Does she have a duty to her law firm to act so as to preserve their reputation as "wise" and "sound" lawyers in this field? If so, was she required to tell the client that this concern would influence her?

At what point would you refuse to work any longer on the case? Would your answer be different if you were in a smaller firm, *i.e.* one with less than twenty lawyers? What if you were a junior attorney in a government agency and you disagreed with the way a senior attorney dealt with a matter? For example, suppose you worked for FDA and the general counsel (your boss) advised the administrator to exempt caffeine from further testing without review of the Harvard School of Public Health study?

In what situations would you feel obligated and would it be proper to report the client's proposed actions to the authorities? Does the Code of Professional Responsibility shed any light on this?

DR 4–101(B) provides: "Except when permitted under DR 4–101(C), a lawyer shall not knowingly: (1) Reveal a confidence or secret of his client. . . ."

DR 4–101(C)(3) provides that a lawyer may reveal "[t]he intention of his client to commit a crime and the information necessary to prevent the crime."

The new Model Rules are more specific.

Rule 1.6(b): "A lawyer may reveal such information to the extent the lawyer reasonably believes necessary: (1) to prevent the client from committing a criminal act that the lawyer believes is likely to result in imminent death or substantial bodily harm; . . . ."

Is this at all helpful? Would it influence your decision?

Rules issued by the U.S. Nuclear Regulatory Commission provide that in certain circumstances employees of a utility who know of a nuclear safety risk must inform government regulators. Should there be such a requirement for anyone knowing of a risk to the public from food or drugs? If there were such a rule, should lawyers for food and drug companies be exempted from the obligation? What is the argument for exempting them? How would you answer that argument?

Epilogue

Regulatory Status of Caffeine

As of September 1984, FDA had not promulgated final regulations on the status of caffeine as a food additive. In recent years, much greater control has been placed over the Agency's pronouncements by the administration and all significant FDA proposed regulations are strictly scrutinized by officials at the Department of Health and Human Services (HHS), the umbrella agency for FDA.

After reviewing all comments on its October 21, 1980, proposed regulations, FDA did recommend to HHS that caffeine in soft drinks be given prior sanction status. HHS has twice told FDA to revise part of its proposal and three years later, FDA was still waiting to hear back from HHS based on its third set of revisions.

Since 1980, a number of additional health studies of caffeine have been published. In August 1981, scientists at Yale Medical School published an article in *The Journal of the American Medical Association* (JAMA) criticizing the Harvard School of Public Health study on caffeine and cancer of the pancreas. Since then the Harvard study has effectively been dismissed. Also, in 1982, two new epidemiologic studies were published on the teratogenic effects of caffeine. Both indicated that there was no association between coffee consumption and adverse outcomes of pregnancy.

As a result of these new studies, the ASDC submitted supplemental comments to FDA on its proposed regulation. In their comments, the firm cited Dr. Brian MacMahon's review of the two epidemiology studies. (Dr. MacMahon was the lead epidemiologist on the Harvard School of Public Health's study on caffeine and pancreatic cancer.) According to P & B, Dr. MacMahon reached the following conclusions in his review:

First, the two recent epidemiologic studies, from unrelated research teams, are of "much higher quality than those previously published" and provide by far the best formal, scientific evidence to date on caffeine and pregnancy outcomes in humans.

Second, the two recent studies "greatly strengthen" [the] . . . conclusion that . . . added caffeine at current consumption levels and uses does not (a) create uncertainties requiring that additional studies be conducted; or (b) pose a reasonable possibility of harm to humans.

Third, the two recent studies are of sufficiently high quality that Dr. MacMahon now concludes that there is a "strong probability that maternal ingestion during pregnancy of caffeine added to cola-type beverages is without harm to the fetus at typical current consumption levels." In other words, these studies "provide important new, carefully assembled human evidence that caffeine use at normal levels is safe, within the usual limitation of the impossibility of proving absolute safety.

Fourth, further epidemiologic studies directed at the relationship between caffeine and pregnancy outcome were not warranted before, and this conclusion is now strongly confirmed by the two recent studies on precisely that subject.[1]

Despite these new results, the Center for Science in the Public Interest still maintains its original position that warnings should be placed on all food products containing added caffeine.

---

[1] Supplemental Comments of the National Soft Drink Association Regarding FDA's Proposal to Delete Caffeine in Cola–Type Beverages From the List of Substances Generally Recognized as Safe and to Issue an Interim Food Additive Regulation Governing its Future Use and Proposed Declaration that no Prior Sanction Exists, Docket No. 80N–0418, April 23, 1982, pp. 2–3.

3. Prosecutorial Discretion

ShelterAd Inc. *

Introduction

In the spring of 1986, the United States Attorney's Office was investigating possible official misconduct in the renewal of a contract to build bus stop shelters for the City of Metropolis, including possible wrongdoing by the City's Comptroller, William Caron.** The prosecutors now had to decide whether to seek grand jury indictments against anyone.

Three critical events occurred during the lengthy bus shelter bidding process that raised questions about possible corruption within Comptroller Caron's office leading to actions favoring City Services Corporation (CSC), a company competing for Metropolis's bus shelter franchise. The first event was the release in November 1983 by the Comptroller's Office of an audit that criticized CSC's competitor, the incumbent franchisee, ShelterAd Inc. The next event was a decision in March 1984 by the staff of a citywide board on which the Comptroller sits, the Board of Review, to require potential bidders to post a performance bond of $3,000 per shelter, a requirement that CSC could meet but ShelterAd could not. The third event was the Board of Review staff's decision in May 1984 to delete a particular contract provision that would have benefitted the incumbent franchise-holder, ShelterAd.

At this stage in the Caron investigation, the only plausible case was against Joseph Vincent, a Michigan Law School graduate and state senator. Vincent had promoted the interests of CSC during a period when his law firm represented minority investors in its competitor, ShelterAd. Now the U.S. Attorney had to decide whether to prosecute Joseph Vincent for this conflict of private interests, a step that would be principally intended to advance the investigation into possible criminal wrongdoing by Comptroller Caron or others in his office.

Background

In 1978, Richard Dupuy, a French businessman, got caught in the rain while waiting for a bus on Main Street and decided that Metropolis

---

* This story is adapted loosely from the facts of *United States v. Bronston*, 658 F.2d 920 (2d Cir.1981). A list of characters and their roles appears at pp. 249–50.

** Caron graduated with honors from Princeton and later attended Stanford Law School. His political career began when he was elected a state senator at the age of 31. In 1979, Caron was elected Comptroller of the City of Metropolis, a position to which he was reelected in 1983 and 1987.

needed bus stop shelters like those in Paris. He saw a way to build shelters for bus passengers, make money for Metropolis, and earn a profit for himself. Dupuy proposed building shelters made of fiberglass roofing and three four-foot wide sheets of safety glass. Two panels, one visible from the inside and the other from the outside of the shelter, would be lighted at night and rented to advertisers at a cost of $250 per month.

Dupuy formed a company named ShelterAd Inc. to attract the capital needed to implement this idea. On May 9, 1981, the Metropolis Board of Review voted unanimously to grant ShelterAd a three year experimental franchise.

The Board of Review is composed of the Mayor, the Comptroller, and the City Council President, elected on a city-wide basis. Under the City Charter, the Board of Review must first approve, after a public hearing, any franchise proposal. The Board of Review must also approve an actual contract, after an additional hearing. The Bureau of Franchises is a subordinate agency of the Board of Review with responsibility for administering public franchises and franchise applications.

The contract between ShelterAd and Metropolis provided that the city would receive five percent of the gross advertising receipts but not less than $5,000 in the first year and $10,000 in each of the second and third years. The three-year contract was to run from September 27, 1981, through September 27, 1984, and required ShelterAd to build between 900 and 2400 shelters in Metropolis over a 26 month period ending in November 1983. Although ShelterAd was to build the shelters by November 1983, the city would continue to receive its stated percentage of the gross advertising receipts until the expiration of the contract in September 1984. Between November 1983 and September 1984, the city would evaluate ShelterAd's performance and the revenue potential of the shelter franchise. The contract also required Shelter-Ad to post $50,000 cash or approved security as a bond for its performance, but did not provide ShelterAd with any renewal or extension rights and gave it no remedy or release from performance in the event that government agencies hindered the company's ability to fulfill its obligations.

In September 1981, Dupuy announced that ShelterAd planned to build 600 shelters within a year. City Comptroller Caron, who had voted with the majority, said, "I am delighted to see we are now expanding the project." However, by September 1982, a year after the contract went into effect, ShelterAd had built only 254 shelters, less than half the number the company had planned to put up by that point. ShelterAd officials explained their slow start by citing their inability to obtain necessary permits from a variety of city agencies.

During the spring of 1983, ShelterAd encountered severe financial problems. "We needed capital badly," said Marie Dupuy, ShelterAd's president at that time, "and we were trying desperately all over town to raise money." ShelterAd was then represented by the law firm of Houston, Blake, Bowman & Cassels. Robert Bowman, a senior partner in the firm, approached Peter Williams in an attempt to raise funds for ShelterAd. Williams, a financial consultant, then contacted Seymour Perkins, the president of Perkins Group, Inc. In April 1983, Richard Dupuy met with Williams and Perkins and offered to sell them a twenty percent interest in ShelterAd. Perkins in turn offered to buy out the current ShelterAd owners and take control of the company. As Paul Cassels, another senior partner in Houston Blake, explained, "someone like Perkins was only going to invest if he could run the whole operation." Dupuy rejected Perkins's offer.

Perkins and Williams then decided to form their own company to compete against ShelterAd in the construction of bus shelters. Perkins and Williams wanted Irwin A. Lowenthal, a close associate of Mayor Charles Harrity and a partner in Stern, Stikeman, Palmer & Davis, to represent their company before the Board of Review. Due to his personal friendship with ShelterAd's public relations consultant and attorneys, Lowenthal decided not to do so. Perkins approached Lowenthal with this proposal on May 18, 1983, through Joseph Vincent, one of Lowenthal's partners at Stern Stikeman. When Lowenthal declined to represent the Perkins–Williams shelter company, Perkins and Williams chose not to retain Stern Stikeman as counsel.

Marie and Richard Dupuy were continuing their search for new investors willing to supply capital to ShelterAd. Eventually two venture capital companies, Midwest Venture Co., a Midwest Bank subsidiary, and United Ventures Inc. tentatively agreed to invest in ShelterAd. On June 2, 1983, these potential minority investors contacted Lowenthal and retained Stern Stikeman to negotiate the terms of their participation in ShelterAd.

Vincent continued to hope that his firm would represent Perkins and Williams. On June 3, Vincent had a Stern Stikeman associate incorporate CSC in Delaware as Perkins's vehicle in the bus shelter competition. CSC's incorporation papers listed Vincent as an officer of the corporation. On June 10, Vincent wrote a memo to the firm's "new business" committee suggesting that Stern Stikeman take on CSC as a client. Richard Davis, a senior partner and member of that committee, told Vincent that the potential minority investors in ShelterAd had retained the firm and that a conflict of interest therefore existed between the firm's representation of those investors and of CSC. Davis instructed Vincent to "render no further services to City Services Corp."

Despite Davis's instructions, a little more than a week later, on June 18, Vincent was elected to a one year term as assistant secretary of CSC. On July 6, Vincent proposed that the firm's bookkeeper establish a client billing number for CSC in case the firm could avoid the conflict of interest problem in the future. Davis agreed, but instructed Vincent that no work was to be done for CSC without his prior approval. In August, after Vincent's efforts to get Stern Stikeman to represent CSC had failed, Perkins retained the law firm of Levin Wright & Schwartz. Samuel Wright, a partner in that firm, was then the Democratic minority leader of the state senate and a political ally of Joseph Vincent.

While Vincent was attempting to get his firm to represent CSC, other Stern Stikeman attorneys, led by partner Henry Their, were working on behalf of the potential minority investors in ShelterAd. The parties signed the minority shareholder participation agreement in the Stern Stikeman offices on August 17, 1983. The agreement provided that the minority investors would supply capital in several installments. The first stage called for the investors to purchase $300,000 worth of secured ShelterAd notes, which they could convert into preferred stock if certain conditions were met. The most important condition was that ShelterAd obtain a renewal of the shelter franchise.

After this deal was completed, Perkins contacted Kyle Myers, the representative of United Ventures, one of ShelterAd's minority investors. According to Myers, Perkins offered Myers double the price United had just paid for rights that could eventually be converted into ShelterAd stock. Myers told Perkins to talk to the Dupuys. Perkins again called Myers the next day. "He went further this time," said Myers, "and stated that if ShelterAd did not sell out to him, he would either make sure they lost the franchise or, if they won, he would make it not worth winning. I asked him what he meant by that and he indicated that he would force a competitive bid situation, which would make us wish we had never gotten into the situation."

Without seeking Davis's approval, Vincent continued to do work for CSC and to bill CSC for that work. Vincent met with Perkins and Andrew Levin, the senior partner of Levin Wright, on August 25 to discuss how to present CSC's interest in acquiring the bus shelter franchise. They agreed at that meeting that Levin Wright should send a letter to the Board of Review publicly announcing CSC's interest in presenting a plan for building and operating bus shelters and introducing the law firm as counsel for CSC. Levin Wright lawyers drafted the letter and Andrew Levin signed it, but they hand-delivered a copy of the draft to Perkins for review before mailing it. Perkins and Vincent reviewed the draft on August 27 and Vincent then called Levin to say he liked it. Vincent noted in his time diary to bill CSC for five hours of services on August 27, specifically including his "review of letter with Seymour Perkins." He also noted to bill CSC for a half-hour of services for his telephone conference with "Andrew Levin re letter." Levin Wright mailed this August 27 letter to Mayor Charles Harrity and the other members of the Board of Review, including Comptroller Caron.

On October 20, 1983, CSC submitted its petition for the bus shelter franchise to the Board of Review. Despite CSC's entry into the bus shelter competition, the Dupuys were confident that ShelterAd's franchise would be renewed. They had just completed negotiations with Howard Meltzer, Director of the Bureau of Franchises, and proofs of the proposed contract had been printed and approved by both parties. On October 30, the Board of Review, with Comptroller Caron's approval, voted to put a resolution renewing ShelterAd's franchise on the agenda of the next Board meeting scheduled for December 2.

Under its contract with the City, ShelterAd was supposed to have built a minimum of 900 shelters before the December 2 meeting date. With the construction stage of the contract completed, the City would then evaluate ShelterAd's performance and the franchise's revenue-generating capacity. Because the October 30 resolution did not contain a requirement that the bus shelter franchise be competitively bid, the Dupuys expected approval of the franchise renewal contract at the December 2 meeting.

Incident One: Release of the Meron–Hofmann Report

Under chapter 5 of the Metropolis City Charter, the City Comptroller has the power and obligation to review the functions and financial operations of city agencies and to review city contracts. Comptroller Caron had two reasons to review ShelterAd's contract. First, he had a duty to determine whether ShelterAd was fulfilling its three-year contract. Second, he had a responsibility to decide whether ShelterAd was the best company to build additional bus shelters. Comptroller Caron had stated that, whenever possible, the City should use competitive bidding to award contracts involving private firms' use of City property as profit-making concessions. In September 1983, Caron wrote to all city commissioners and to Franchise Director Howard Meltzer advocating an increased use of competitive bidding in city concessions.

Caron's office first began analyzing the bus shelter franchise issue during the summer of 1983. In a June 22 memo, Assistant Comptroller John Meron informed First Deputy Comptroller Stanley Klein that he was examining the ShelterAd contract to determine whether the company had complied with its obligations. Meron then assigned Alice

Hofmann to analyze ShelterAd's contractual performance. Hofmann prepared a typed draft of the performance analysis between October 2 and October 21.

On October 29, 1983, Vincent wrote a two-page letter about ShelterAd's franchise to Philip Adams, Caron's executive assistant and the son of Jack Adams, a prominent Caron fundraiser. Vincent wrote his letter to Adams on his State Senate stationery and did not disclose his personal or professional interest in CSC, ShelterAd's competitor. On the cover page, Vincent urged that the city not renew ShelterAd's franchise. "I enclose some figures in connection with the existing franchise which I am sure you have," Vincent wrote, "but which I would like to reiterate. Obviously, a renewal of the existing franchise would not appear to be in the public interest since it might be taken as a reward for non-performance."

The second page of Vincent's letter made three separate points. In the first paragraph Vincent stated that ShelterAd's three year franchise required the company to construct 900 shelters by November 1983, but that it had "constructed less than 400 shelters, and is therefore in default under the terms of its agreement with the City." The second paragraph stated that ShelterAd "should be paying to the City approximately $80,000 to $100,000 per annum, pursuant to the terms of the interim franchise." The last paragraph said:

> Based on the anticipated [CSC] program of building approximately 4,000 shelters (including purchase from the City of the approximately 400 shelters built to date by ShelterAd, Inc.) and assuming payment to the City of between 14–16 percent of gross advertising revenues, the City would receive in excess of $2 million per annum at the conclusion of such construction program.

Vincent derived these three points directly from an October 28, 1983, memorandum from Peter Williams, President of CSC, to Andrew Holms, CSC's public relations consultant, that was designed to promote CSC's own franchise proposal. Vincent copied this CSC internal memo, but changed it in minor respects to eliminate any reference to CSC. The CSC memo, which summarized the advantages of the CSC franchise proposal, somewhat misrepresented ShelterAd's contractual obligations and the amount of revenue that ShelterAd could generate for the City. Although Vincent later said that he had written the letter to Adams "as a senator" because he had "a public interest," on October 29 Vincent noted that he should bill CSC for a "letter to Philip Adams." Vincent wrote this letter and noted his intention to bill CSC without obtaining the approval of Richard Davis.

There is some confusion about whether the Vincent letter was circulated in the Comptroller's Office. Philip Adams later said that he might have sent the second page of Vincent's letter to Meron but that, if he had done so, he had never suggested that Vincent's analysis should influence Meron's review. Meron, however, said that he did not receive Vincent's letter. Philip Adams also stated that when he received the letter from Vincent he did not know of Vincent's connection with CSC and assumed that Vincent had been writing in his official capacity as a state senator.

On November 8, Alice Hofmann, as a follow-up to her performance analysis, wrote a memo to Meron recommending that an additional financial review of ShelterAd be done to deal with certain specified issues. Meron then contacted Trevor King, who headed the group of accountants within the Comptroller's Office that had traditionally conducted franchise audits. King in turn assigned Nicholas Lazzaro, one of the accountants in his unit, to obtain the information that Meron and Hofmann had requested. Before beginning his own audit, Lazzaro met with Meron and Hofmann who gave him a copy of an initial draft of Hofmann's performance analysis, which was very critical of Shelter-Ad. According to Lazzaro, at that meeting Hofmann and Meron "made wild accusations about ShelterAd, trying to influence the direction of my audit." "I asked them why they were giving me this at the start," said Lazzaro. "It had all the earmarks of a prearranged hatchet job."

On November 10, the morning after his re-election as City Comptroller, William Caron met at breakfast with Kyle Myers, the representative of one of ShelterAd's minority investors. Myers, who had requested the meeting, told Caron that he had heard that the shelter franchise was going to be opened to competitive bidding and expressed his opposition to that idea. Caron said he did not know anything about the bus shelter franchise. Caron later stated that when he returned to his office and told his assistant Philip Adams about his meeting with Myers, Adams did not inform him about Vincent's letter urging that ShelterAd's franchise not be renewed.

On the same day, Caron sent a letter to Perkins, thanking Perkins for submitting CSC's franchise petition on October 20. Caron wrote Perkins, "You may be certain that I will have your position very much in mind when the matter comes before the Board of Review for a vote." Caron later characterized that communication to Perkins as a form letter.

After examining ShelterAd's records, Lazzaro submitted an eleven page preliminary report strongly supporting ShelterAd's performance. Lazzaro then notified King that his findings were contrary to Meron's and Hofmann's and that their report "should be held up" until the two analyses could be reconciled. King made the same request to Stanley

Klein, Caron's deputy comptroller. These requests were rejected. On November 28, two days before the Board of Review met to vote on the renewal of ShelterAd's franchise, the Comptroller's Office released only the Meron–Hofmann performance analysis critical of ShelterAd. It did not release Lazzaro's favorable audit. The Meron–Hofmann report recommended that the franchise be competitively bid and was accompanied by a press release that blamed ShelterAd for forcing "long-suffering bus riders to stand in rain and snow" because the company had failed to meet the contractual construction timetable.

At the Board of Review's executive session on November 30, in accordance with the Meron–Hofmann report's recommendations, Caron's staff proposed that the City Transportation Department prepare guidelines for competitive bids on the shelter franchise. Reversing his earlier assurances to ShelterAd, Franchise Director Howard Meltzer also proposed that consideration of the twenty year contract he had negotiated with ShelterAd be held over until January, when Lawrence Collins would begin his term as mayor. Instead of awarding ShelterAd the franchise renewal on December 2 as the Dupuys had expected, the Board of Review directed the Transportation Department to prepare competitive bidding procedures.

Lazzaro completed his audit on December 24, 1983, a month after Meron's report was released. The audit was sent to First Deputy Comptroller Klein, who never released it. "In my opinion," Lazzaro later said, "my audit was intentionally suppressed by the Comptroller's Office because it contradicted the Meron–Hofmann analysis." Meron responded that the Lazzaro report was "full of misinformation" and "a collection of mistakes."

Joseph Vincent was still attempting to find a way for Stern Stikeman to represent CSC. On December 8, Vincent wrote a memo to Richard Davis proposing that Stern Stikeman represent CSC outside of Metropolis. Vincent told Davis that no conflict would exist outside of Metropolis. Davis then assigned an associate to research the question whether it would be permissible for the firm to accept CSC on a non-Metropolis basis if ShelterAd were not, in fact, seeking shelter franchises outside Metropolis. On December 10, Vincent wrote to Perkins and detailed his time charges, but stated that he would not request payment until the parties could agree on "a format through which this can be done."

On January 12, 1984, Henry Their, the Stern Stikeman partner who represented ShelterAd's minority investors, told Davis that ShelterAd was in fact seeking franchises outside Metropolis. At a partnership meeting held on January 13, Vincent's partners instructed Vincent that they would permit no further representation of CSC anywhere in the United States. The next day, January 14, Vincent attended a meeting with Perkins, Myers, and Lowenthal at which Vincent and Lowenthal unsuccessfully tried to reconcile Perkins and ShelterAd.

Incident Two: Addition of a Per–Shelter Bond Requirement

ShelterAd's three year franchise contract contained a total bond requirement of $50,000. In March 1984, Deputy Comptroller David Martin and Franchise Director Meltzer, with the consent of the other Board of Review staff members, drafted a performance bond requirement of $3,000 per shelter. This meant that to build 4,000 shelters the contractor would have to post a performance bond totalling $12 million.

City officials supported the change in the bonding requirement for several reasons. According to both Martin and Meltzer, it would enable the city to construct the shelters if the winning company failed to do so. Meltzer, who retained the new bonding requirement when he released the final bidding procedures in June, added that this change was particularly necessary to protect the City because ShelterAd had failed to build as many shelters as its three year contract had required. When Caron was asked about the new bonding requirement, he defended it, saying, "We wished to protect ourselves on the basis of experience. We were faced with the dilemma of how to prevent some guy with no financial capability from making a bid, then welshing on his performance."

Although ShelterAd did not object to the performance bond requirement at the public hearing held on the bidding guidelines, the company's officials later argued that the bonding requirement was designed to benefit CSC, which had a $10 million line of credit from Metro Bank, as well as funds available from Perkins Insurance Companies, Inc., a subsidiary of Perkins Group, Inc., which Seymour Perkins controlled. ShelterAd made its first formal objection to the new bonding requirement on July 29, 1984, four days before bids were to be submitted. ShelterAd's president Steve Hill called the bond requirement "colossal" and charged that it was intended "to eliminate everybody but City Services."

Incident Three: Deletion of the Match–Bid Provision

When the Board of Review decided to open the bus shelter franchise to competitive bidding, it had to make two separate decisions. The first was which company would be awarded the contract to construct new shelters. The second was which company would maintain the existing shelters and control the revenue those shelters generated.

In his initial draft of the competitive bidding guidelines, Transportation Commissioner Sloane included a match-bid provision that would have allowed ShelterAd to retain the contract for the shelters it had already built if it matched the best bid submitted by any other company. When Sloane submitted his final draft to the Board of Review on January 10, it did not include this match-bid provision. On January 20, 1984, Sloane left city government and eight days later accepted an offer from CSC to become a consultant. The city Board of Ethics investigated and cleared Sloane of any conflict of interest.

When the Board of Review staff reviewed Sloane's proposed bidding guidelines, it reinserted the match-bid provision benefitting ShelterAd. It is unclear at whose request this was done. Kevin LeBlanc, the staffer who had been assigned to revise the proposed procedures, later stated that he thought his boss, Deputy Comptroller David Martin, had directed him to include the match-bid provision. LeBlanc stated that a match-bid provision is unusual in a competitive bidding situation and that he lacked the authority to insert such a provision on his own initiative. Martin, Caron's representative on the Board staff, said he had directed LeBlanc to insert the match-bid provision after discussing the idea with Caron. Comptroller Caron, however, said he had no recollection of this conversation.

Financial Relations Between CSC and the Comptroller

On May 13, 1984, one month before the final bidding guidelines were to be released to potential bidders, Seymour Perkins, William Caron, and Jack Adams, one of Caron's fundraisers and the father of Caron's executive assistant, Philip Adams, had lunch at the Charter Room. At that time, William Caron was three weeks away from announcing his candidacy for governor. Near the end of the lunch, Jack Adams asked Perkins if he would contribute $25,000 to Caron's campaign. Perkins responded that, with the help of some friends, he might be able to contribute three or four times that amount. Both Caron and Jack Adams stated that they did not discuss the topic of bus shelters at the luncheon.

It is unclear whether, at the time of the lunch, Caron knew of Perkins's involvement with CSC. Philip Adams, Caron's executive assistant, stated that, by the time of the May 13 lunch, he knew that Perkins was seeking the bus shelter franchise. He further stated that he could not recall whether, when Caron discussed the lunch with him later that afternoon, he informed Caron of Perkins's association with CSC. Caron denied knowing before the luncheon that Perkins was actively seeking the shelter franchise and denied that Adams informed him of that fact during their discussion after the lunch.

Sometime between May 9 and May 16, 1984, Kevin LeBlanc deleted the match-bid provision from the bidding guidelines. LeBlanc could not recall who directed him to delete this provision or any specific conversations concerning this change in the bidding document. Because the deletion occurred between May 9 and May 16, LeBlanc removed the match-bid provision either shortly before or shortly after the May 13 Caron–Perkins luncheon.

When questioned about the deletion of the match-bid provision, Caron stated that he had initially favored the idea, but that other members of the Board of Review drafting committee had rejected it. Deputy Comptroller Martin said that the drafting committee had voted on the match-bid provision about May 10 and that it had defeated the Comptroller's position favoring the match-bid concept. Other members of the drafting committee, however, recalled that Martin had pressed for the match-bid provision to be stricken from the guidelines, but did not recall the date of the deletion.

When the May 13 lunch was reported in the press, William Caron's reactions raised further suspicion. Responding to *Metropolis Sun–Times* questions about the luncheon, Caron stated that he was sure that his own campaign for governor had not come up. When the *Metropolis Free Press* questioned him, Caron said that no one had mentioned either bus shelters or his upcoming statewide race. But in an interview with the *Metropolis Daily News*, Perkins contended that Caron solicited a $25,000 contribution from him. "There was no purpose to the lunch other than fundraising," said Perkins.

After the *Daily News* published Perkins's statement, Caron retracted his earlier remarks and said that Jack Adams had reminded him that a solicitation had indeed been made toward the end of the meal. "Adams said to Perkins," Caron recalled, "'a lot of us believe that William Caron is an outstanding public official and we want to support him in the campaign. Some people who can are giving $25,000.'" Caron said that Perkins replied "'I'd like to help and I will,'" but that he never received a campaign contribution from Perkins.

Caron equivocated about contacts he had with Perkins following the May 13 lunch. When the *Metropolis Free Press* questioned him, Caron denied ever communicating with Perkins following their lunch at the Charter Room. After he was confronted with evidence that he had telephoned Perkins on June 22 and June 27, Caron said he knew he had not reached Perkins on either attempt and stood by his statement that he did not think he had talked to Perkins since the lunch. He further stated that he did not remember why he had attempted to contact Perkins.

On June 28, one day after Caron's second telephone call to Perkins, Philip Adams had lunch with Joseph Vincent to follow up on Perkins's commitment to contribute to Caron's campaign. That same day, Perkins wrote a check for $12,500 payable to Joseph Vincent. The next day, June 29, Vincent deposited Perkins's check in his personal account at the Main Street Bank. On June 30, Vincent wrote a check for $3500 payable to the "Alliance for Good Government," a Caron campaign organization. The organization reported the check on July 13 in records it filed with the Board of Election. In addition to this check, Perkins contributed $7,500 to the Caron campaign through other associates.

For these actions, Vincent billed Perkins Group, Perkins's company. When later questioned about the $12,500 check, Vincent explained that the $12,500 check from Perkins was a loan and "not compensation." Peter Williams, president of CSC, said Perkins had lent Vincent $12,500 "because he [Vincent] was taking a trip to Europe and he was short on cash." At that time, however, Vincent owned liquid assets exceeding $250,000.

The Investigation Begins

On July 7, a "pre-bidding conference" was held at which prospective bidders were invited to comment on the final bid procedures. No firm at this meeting, including ShelterAd, objected to the deletion of the match-bid provision or the size of the required performance bond. The final bidding regulations were sent to potential bidders on July 11.

On July 18, ShelterAd filed a Freedom of Information Act suit against Caron, requesting access to all his files on ShelterAd and its competitors. Caron chose not to litigate this action and handed his files over that same day. Marie Dupuy began reviewing these records on July 19. Sometime between then and July 21, she discovered Vincent's letter to Philip Adams dated October 29, 1983, urging that ShelterAd's franchise not be renewed. ShelterAd then sought to block the bidding scheduled for August 2. This effort failed.

On July 19, the day after Caron handed over his files to ShelterAd, Vincent telephoned Perkins's office from a hotel in Spain. As a result of this conversation, Vincent sent Perkins a check for $12,500, on the bottom of which he wrote "Repayment of Exchange."

On August 2, Franchise Director Howard Meltzer received four bids for the bus shelter franchise. ShelterAd offered to operate 1,513 shelters and to pay Metropolis 15 percent of its gross advertising revenue. CSC offered to build 4,100 shelters and to pay the City 20.5 percent of its gross advertising revenues.

Despite the deletion of the mandatory match-bid provision in the bidding guidelines, Steve Hill, ShelterAd's president, then offered the City 20.5 percent of its gross advertising revenues to keep control of the shelters the company had already built. Hill charged that a company that paid the City that percentage of its receipts for all of its shelters would probably not maintain them properly, and added that there were not even 4,100 suitable bus stops in the city at which to build shelters.

On August 9, Richard Davis convened a meeting at Stern Stikeman's offices to discuss Vincent's letter to Philip Adams. In attendance were Lowenthal and Their of Stern Stikeman and Steven Paul, Kyle Myers, and Norman Owen representing the ShelterAd minority investors. According to Paul, Davis said that, although Vincent's letter "embarrassed" Stern Stikeman, it believed that Vincent had written it as a state senator and not as a member of the firm. Davis then stated that because Stern Stikeman "obviously would not like to have this issue blown out of proportion and into a highly exposed matter," the firm would "offer to undertake whatever it could do, within reason, to conciliate the investors and resolve the matter." Davis did not, however, ask the minority investors to release the firm from any potential liability arising from Stern Stikeman's conflict of interest.

Stern Stikeman agreed to guarantee a $50,000 loan the minority investors had made to ShelterAd. The document Stern Stikeman drafted required that "neither the execution of the guarantee, the guarantee itself, nor the discussions immediately preceding the execution of the guarantee and related thereto, will be introduced into evidence, referred to, or disclosed directly or indirectly" to any third party. The loan guarantee agreement never went into effect because Marie Dupuy refused to sign it, believing that the agreement barred ShelterAd from revealing the existence of Vincent's letter. The minority investors shared this interpretation of the loan guarantee agreement but Davis did not.

In October 1984, Seymour Perkins invited Paul Cassels and Robert Bowman, the Houston Blake partners representing ShelterAd, to dinner at his apartment. They accepted this invitation without consulting their client. "After dinner," said Cassels, "the men went to the library and, over claret and cigars, Mr. Perkins offered us a deal to buy out ShelterAd. He offered to assume all of Richard Dupuy's personal debts, which were then about a million, to buy out the original investors, and to give the Dupuys a forty percent interest in the company. It was a super deal." Cassels informed Steve Hill, ShelterAd's president, about Perkins's offer. Hill, whom the minority investors had made president of ShelterAd, responded "in a highly abusive way [and] told me to stop any negotiations with Perkins," said Cassels. Neither Cassels nor Bowman informed the Dupuys about Perkins's offer, although the Dupuys would have benefitted personally from the proposed purchase agreement. Questioned about this decision two years later, Cassels said, "I guess in retrospect I should have told the Dupuys about the meeting. Yes, they were my clients and I had a responsibility."

It appeared that the franchise process had come to an end in October 1984, when the Board of Review, in accordance with CSC's high bid, instructed Franchise Director Meltzer to draw up a formal contract with CSC. However, on November 13, in an attempt to re-open the process, ShelterAd officials held a press conference, covered by the Metropolis newspapers, where they charged that Richard Sloane, who had designed the initial bidding guidelines, was now working for CSC in a conflict of interest. One week later, the Board of Ethics reopened its inquiry into Sloane's role in the franchise process. At the request of Investigation Commissioner Edward Garner, who was investigating Sloane's role for the Board of Ethics, the Board of Review on November 23 postponed award of the shelter contract until January 12, 1985. On December 19, CSC filed an $80 million suit against ShelterAd alleging that ShelterAd had conspired to delay the award of the bus shelter franchise to CSC.

On January 11, 1985, the Board of Ethics again cleared Sloane of any conflict of interest, but Commissioner Garner stated that the FBI, which had begun an investigation in early fall, and the Investigation Department were still examining aspects of the bus shelter program. The next day, January 12, the Board of Review unanimously approved granting CSC a ten-year contract to build and maintain 4,100 shelters. The city then filed suit against ShelterAd to obtain title to the existing bus shelters so that it could turn them over to CSC. In response, ShelterAd filed an affidavit that disclosed the existence of Vincent's letter to Philip Adams urging that ShelterAd's franchise not be renewed. The *Metropolis Tribune* reported the disclosure of the Vincent letter on February 27, 1985, under the headline "Bus Shelter Concern Accuses Metropolis Officials of Impropriety."

On March 15, the *Tribune* reported that the FBI and the U.S. Attorney's Office were investigating William Caron, Philip Adams, Jack Adams, and Seymour Perkins to determine whether the relationships among the four men had influenced illegally the award of the shelter franchise to CSC. Mayor Collins reacted that same day by announcing that he would refrain from signing a contract with CSC until all charges had been fully investigated. Collins instructed Edward Garner to begin a formal Department of Investigation inquiry into the bus shelter franchise bidding process. William Caron endorsed Collins's decision.

The Problem

The circumstances surrounding the award of the shelter franchise to CSC and the role played by the Comptroller's Office in that process raised enough questions to create an impression of possible official impropriety. The problem for the U.S. Attorney's Office in this case, as in many public corruption cases, was that it lacked direct, convincing evidence of official illegality.

Furthermore, the U.S. Attorney's Office was under pressure to produce a prosecutable public corruption case. On February 5, 1986, in a lead story entitled "Freedom to Steal: Why Politicians Never Go to Jail," *Metropolis* magazine had lambasted the city's prosecutors for failing "to make a single case against a crooked politician within its jurisdiction" for the past ten years. The article cited the bus shelter franchise investigation as one of eight cases in which a "lack of aggressiveness" was alleged to have "characterized Metropolis's United States Attorney's response" to public corruption. Noting the number of successful political corruption cases prosecuted in other federal districts, the *Metropolis* article concluded that "the records of the office's two nearest neighbors make the absence of the United States Attorney's corruption prosecutions remarkable."

The only prosecutable case at this point in the Caron investigation seemed to be against Joseph Vincent, whom the prosecutors regarded as a key figure in understanding the events that led to the award of the bus shelter franchise to CSC. Senator Vincent's conduct in writing the letter to Philip Adams opposing the extension of ShelterAd's franchise appeared to violate the ethical duty he owed to one of his firm's clients, the minority shareholders in ShelterAd. A state bar disciplinary board, rather than federal prosecutors, normally would deal with this type of unethical conduct. But the fact that Vincent had mailed his letter to Adams brought his unethical behavior within the potential scope of the federal mail fraud statute.

While the mail fraud statute had never before been used to prosecute an attorney for violating his or her fiduciary duty to a client, the pressure on Vincent that would result from the threat of punishment under that statute might be the only way to obtain evidence about what had transpired between Seymour Perkins and the Comptroller's Office in the award of the bus shelter franchise. The U.S. Attorney had to decide whether to bring mail fraud charges against Vincent.

RELEVANT STATUTES AND DISCIPLINARY RULES

18 U.S.C. § 1341 (FEDERAL MAIL FRAUD STATUTE)

Whoever, having devised or intending to devise any scheme or artifice to defraud, or obtaining money or property by means of false or fraudulent pretenses, representations, or promises, or to sell, dispose of, loan, exchange, alter, give away, distribute, supply or furnish or procure for unlawful use any counterfeit or spurious coin, obligation, security, or other article, or anything represented to be or intimated to be held out to be such counterfeit or spurious article, for the purpose of executing such scheme or artifice or attempting to do so, places in any post office or authorized depository for mail matter, any matter or thing whatever to be sent or delivered by the Postal Service, or takes or receives therefrom, any such matter or thing, or knowingly causes to be delivered by mail according to the direction thereon, or at the place at which it is directed to be delivered by the person to whom it is addressed, any such matter or thing, shall be fined not more than $1,000 or imprisoned not more than five years or both.

ABA MODEL CODE OF PROFESSIONAL RESPONSIBILITY: DISCIPLINARY RULES

DR 1–102 Misconduct

(A) A lawyer shall not:

    (1) Violate a Disciplinary Rule.

    . . .

    (3) Engage in illegal conduct involving moral turpitude.

    (4) Engage in conduct involving dishonesty, fraud, deceit, or misrepresentation.

    . . .

    (6) Engage in any other conduct that adversely reflects on his fitness to practice law.

DR 4–101 Preservation of Confidences and Secrets of a Client

. . .

(B) Except when permitted under DR 4–101(C), a lawyer shall not knowingly:

   (1) Reveal a confidence or secret of his client.

   (2) Use a confidence or secret of his client to the disadvantage of the client.

   (3) Use a confidence or secret of his client for the advantage of himself or of a third person, unless the client consents after full disclosure.

DR 5–105 Refusing to Accept or Continue Employment if the Interests of Another Client May Impair the Independent Professional Judgment of the Lawyer

(A) A lawyer shall decline proffered employment if the exercise of his independent professional judgment in behalf of a client will be or is likely to be adversely affected by the acceptance of the proffered employment, . . . except to the extent permitted under DR 5–105(C).

(B) A lawyer shall not continue multiple employment if the exercise of his independent professional judgment in behalf of a client will be or is likely to be adversely affected by his representation of another client, . . . except to the extent permitted under DR 5–105(C).

(C) In the situations covered by DR 5–105(A) and (B), a lawyer may represent multiple clients if it is obvious that he can adequately represent the interest of each and if each consents to the representation after full disclosure of the possible effect of such representation on the exercise of his independent professional judgment on behalf of each.

(D) If a lawyer is required to decline employment or to withdraw from employment under DR 5–105, no partner or associate of his or his firm may accept or continue such employment.

DR 7–101 Representing a Client Zealously

(A) A lawyer shall not intentionally:

   . . .

   (3) Prejudice or damage his client during the course of the professional relationship, except as required under DR 7–102(B).

Characters

William Caron—Comptroller

Joseph Vincent—State Senator;
              Partner, Stern Stikeman;
              Officer and Assistant Secretary, CSC

Richard Dupuy—Founder, ShelterAd Inc.

Marie Dupuy—Richard Dupuy's wife and President of ShelterAd Inc.

Peter Williams—Co-founder and President, CSC

Seymour Perkins—Co-founder, CSC

Robert Bowman—Partner, Houston Blake

Paul Cassels—Partner, Houston Blake

Irwin Lowenthal—Partner, Stern Stikeman

Richard Davis—Partner, Stern Stikeman

Henry Their—Partner, Stern Stikeman

Samuel Wright—Partner, Levin Wright;
              Democratic minority leader of state senate

Andrew Levin—Partner, Levin Wright

Kyle Myers—Representative, United Ventures Inc.

Charles Harrity—Mayor

Howard Meltzer—Director, Bureau of Franchises

John Meron—Assistant Comptroller

Alice Hoffman—Staffer, Comptroller's Office

David Martin—Deputy Comptroller

Stanley Klein—First Deputy Comptroller

Philip Adams—Caron's Executive Assistant

Jack Adams—Father of Philip Adams and Fundraiser for Caron

Andrew Holms—Public Relations Consultant, CSC

Trevor King—Head Accountant, Comptroller's Office

Nicholas Lazzaro—Accountant, Comptroller's Office

Lawrence Collins—Mayor elect

Kevin LeBlanc—Staffer, Board of Review

Richard Sloane—Transportation Commissioner

Edward Garner—Investigation Commissioner

Discussion Questions

1. If you were an Assistant U.S. Attorney would you support the filing of criminal charges against Joseph Vincent?

What is most objectionable about Vincent's conduct is the use of his office as state senator to promote the interests of a private client (CSC) without revealing to the City Comptroller's Office his relationship to the private party.

He acted as if he was playing the public-spirited role of state senator when the views he was pressing on the Comptroller—his criticisms of CSC's rival, ShelterAd—were being carried out as the paid attorney and agent of CSC.

Would it be fair to bring a prosecution on this very general ground if Vincent had no more specific warning that what he was doing might be criminal? Most people do not get warning of what is criminal from reading cases or even statutes. They recognize that certain conduct is socially condemned. Getting an advantage by trickery and using a public office for private financial gain generally fall in the category of matters that people recognize as widely disapproved. That is why the concepts of fraud and corruption, broad as they are, turn out to be manageable even when applied to new situations.

So the question may be a little different. How sure would you want to be that, in the particular context of Metropolis, people in the position of the Comptroller's Office would assume that a state legislator was not being paid for a representation unless the legislator affirmatively revealed that he was working for a client? And how sure should you be that this mistaken assumption would be important in their reactions to the representation?

Perhaps you, as the prosecutor, may feel quite sure of each of those conditions. Still, what if you suspect or believe that this is, nonetheless, a very general practice among state legislators? How should a government lawyer act when he or she believes that a person has violated a statute by actions which the individual knows, or may know, are very common among his associates but which are rarely prosecuted? Is it enough of an answer for the prosecutor to say that there always has to be a first person to be charged with an offense?

Would your opinion change if Vincent offered to show that he had consulted with his attorney and received an assurance that the action was proper? What if Vincent pointed out in addition that the State Senate ethics committee had refused in the past to take action against senators who had advanced the interests of clients of their law firms by influencing the political process without disclosing their private representational interests? While neither of these is a legal defense, would it be fair to prosecute Vincent in either of these circumstances?

Perhaps, in the setting of Metropolis, the only argument Vincent's counsel could make to you for not prosecuting would be something less than any of these. There may be real deception; his conduct may not have been common. But, for now, assume he pointed out that all of the parties involved in the bus shelter competition (CSC, ShelterAd, and the ShelterAd minority investors) sought and obtained counsel who were politically well-connected for the very purpose of using their influence with government officials. He might have added that this is a familiar practice, and an important source of lawyers' revenue, in Washington as well as Metropolis, and in dealing with the legislature as well as with executive agencies. Vincent's counsel might, finally, argue that his conduct was no different from the everyday, accepted practices of well-connected lawyers in every city in the country except that Vincent was currently in office as a state senator whereas the others, though well connected politically, had no formal governmental positions. Does it make a difference that Vincent was currently holding an official position? Different enough to prosecute him?

There are at least two possible distinctions. First, no one in a government position who is approached by a private individual (who may be an ex-official) is likely to assume that the approach was made solely "in the public interest." It may be very different when a present official approaches another official. Second, perhaps Vincent was not only deceiving the Comptroller's Office but also the voters in his electoral district who had a right to expect that he would use the office to which he was elected only to serve the interests of the public and his constituents, not to benefit a paying client. In some cases there is a third distinction: the active government official often has greater capacity to benefit or harm these other officials whose help he seeks for a client. However one resolves these ethical questions of prosecutorial discretion, there are also, of course, hard questions of statutory construction to be addressed. See *McNally v. United States,* 107 S.Ct. 2875 (1987).

2. Is it fair to prosecute Vincent for mail fraud if the central purpose of the prosecution is to discover evidence as to the criminal actions of a third party?

Perhaps the discussion of the decision to prosecute in Question One is like discussing *Hamlet* without mentioning the Prince. The most serious crime that *may* have taken place, as the story unfolds, is the possibility that substantial campaign contributions were paid to the Comptroller by Seymour Perkins as Chairman of CSC in order to win a lucrative city franchise away from Shelter-Ad. It is not generally a crime to give campaign contributions to an official who has some responsibility for making decisions that affect you or your organization. But specifically tying campaign contributions to an official act constitutes bribery or extortion, both of which are matters prosecutable under federal statutes as well as under state law. Under the *Principles of Federal Prosecution,* the Department of Justice's prosecutorial guidelines, a government attorney should not commence or recommend prosecution unless he or she believes that "the admissible evidence will probably be sufficient to obtain and sustain a conviction." On the basis of what you know at the end of the case, as an Assistant U.S. Attorney you simply cannot conclude that there is such evidence making probable the conviction of anyone in Comptroller Caron's office. This standard of belief is not met with regard to a bribery or extortion charge. Should a prosecutor ever bring a case in which he or she believes that the government's case cannot meet this standard?

Still, there is basis for suspicion and, if the suspicion were validated by evidence, the matter would surely be serious enough to warrant vigorous prosecution (although some would argue by state, not federal, prosecutors). Vincent might know if bribery was at the root of the several decisions which promised to undo ShelterAd. Assume he is unwilling to cooperate or that he denies there is anything corrupt to reveal. Even ignoring the possible charges discussed in Question One, Vincent is vulnerable to at least a somewhat technical mail fraud charge. By representing a plainly conflicting interest, CSC, Vincent did deceive the minority ShelterAd investors who were already dealing with his firm on the assumption that the firm was wholeheartedly and unambivalently on their side. The *Code of Professional Responsibility* flatly prohibited such conduct, and he had been so advised explicitly by one of his partners. True, this is a matter that would generally be handled without even state prosecution by, at most, referral to a disciplinary committee of the local bar. Still, it was unmistakably wrong and deceptive. It was thus a fraud and it involved the use of the United States mails.

Prosecuting Vincent for what is technically a mail fraud (but one never previously treated as serious enough to warrant federal prosecution under that statute) may produce the evidence, presently lacking, of bribery between CSC and the Comptroller's Office. Faced with federal felony charges that can be reduced or dismissed if he cooperates or with a conviction after which the length of sentence may depend upon his cooperation, Vincent would be far more likely to talk.

One reason a prosecutor might decide to bring a case he or she otherwise would not bring is in order to increase the pressure on the person charged to testify against another party. Do you agree that, at a minimum, a prosecutor must satisfy several conditions if such conduct is justifiable at all? First, the prosecutor must believe he or she can prove that the individual charged has committed a crime. Second, the prosecutor must have adequate reason to suspect that the third party has committed a serious crime which would surely be prosecuted if sufficient evidence were available. Finally, the prosecutor must have adequate reason to believe that the initial target possesses useful evidence about the third party's criminal behavior. Is meeting these three conditions sufficient to justify prosecuting criminal conduct that would otherwise be ignored?

Epilogue

On April 17, 1986, a federal grand jury indicted Joseph Vincent for two counts of mail fraud. The first count was based on the August 27, 1983, letter Vincent helped draft that introduced CSC to the Board of Review. The second count was based on Vincent's letter to Philip Adams, dated October 29, 1983, opposing the renewal of ShelterAd's franchise. The indictment alleged that Vincent had fraudulently violated his fiduciary duty as an attorney by helping to further the efforts of CSC to obtain the shelter franchise at the same time that his firm, Stern Stikeman, was representing a group of investors in ShelterAd, which was then seeking to renew its franchise.

A jury convicted Vincent on both counts of mail fraud on October 24, 1986. Each count carried a maximum prison sentence of five years and/or a $1,000 fine. At the sentencing hearing, the government argued that Judge Arthur Perry should consider Vincent's refusal to cooperate when imposing sentence. On January 3, 1987, Judge Perry sentenced Joseph Vincent to four months in prison on each count, to be served concurrently.

The United States Attorney's Office ended its investigation of the bus shelter franchise program on July 10, 1987, without seeking any additional indictments. On August 4, 1987, Metropolis Investigation Commissioner Edward Garner released a lengthy report on the shelter franchising program. Garner's report criticized Comptroller Caron for his "lack of candor" and for creating "the appearance of impropriety and favoritism," but concluded that there was "insufficient evidence to establish that the Comptroller in any way abused the power of his office in return for a promise of receiving a substantial campaign contribution from CSC or its principals."

"We reach this conclusion," the report stated, "despite certain facts which might, in the eyes of some, support an inference to the contrary," including:

(1) the issuance of an unfair performance analysis of Shelter-Ad accompanied by an inflammatory press release which effectively ended ShelterAd's hopes for a long-term franchise in December 1983;

(2) the assumption of a lead role in the RFP [bidding guidelines] drafting process which eventually resulted in the inclusion of a multimillion dollar performance bond which limited competition, the deletion of a matching provision designed to reward the incumbent and original franchisee for the successful execution of a difficult and novel concept, and the inclusion of other terms and conditions favorable to a large, well-capitalized, albeit inexperienced company such as CSC;

(3) the timing of the deletion of the matching provision which coincided with the Caron–Perkins lunch, followed shortly by Vincent's campaign contribution; and

(4) subsequent contributions from Perkins and Williams.

"Nonetheless," Garner concluded, "these suspicious circumstances do not rise to the level of evidence needed to support a conclusion that any of these actions were taken in return for or in fulfillment of a promise of a campaign contribution."

The Garner report stated that Caron's campaign had unlawfully accepted $11,000 in "disguised" contributions from Seymour Perkins. Garner concluded that Philip Adams knew that these contributions had come through Perkins conduits, but found no evidence that Caron was aware of these indirect contributions from Perkins. However, Garner noted that "this possibility should not be ruled out entirely given Caron's relationship with Philip Adams."

Vincent's conviction was affirmed in a 2–1 decision by the U.S. Court of Appeals on August 20, 1987. "The evidence was sufficient," the court held, "to allow the jury to convict Vincent of mail fraud based on his breach of his duty of loyalty to his firm's clients, his concealment from the clients of his promotion to their detriment of the interests of

Perkins and CSC in obtaining the franchise, his specific intent thereby to defraud his firm's clients of the very economic value his firm had been retained to protect, and his mailing of two letters in furtherance of the fraudulent scheme."

The Board of Review finally awarded the bus shelter franchise by unanimous vote on September 17, 1987, to Kenmore Sign Associates, which contracted to build 2,523 shelters in the city within a two and a half year period. Kenmore also assumed responsibility for maintaining the existing shelters built by ShelterAd. Kenmore agreed to pay 22.2 percent of its advertising receipts to Metropolis and guaranteed a minimum payment of $3 million. "It's a good contract as far as the City is concerned," said Franchise Director Howard Meltzer.

William Caron, who had been defeated in his 1984 race for governor, was re-elected as the city's Comptroller in 1987.

B. Expenses of Advocacy

1. Injured Workers

a. The Plaintiffs' Lawyers

Lawyering for Fun and Profit: Workers' Compensation and Personal Injury Practice *

"I'm a Mickey Mouse lawyer. Mickey's my hero."

—Raul Lovett, Attorney and Counsellor at Law

Today, as high-tech industries bloom in Connecticut and Massachusetts, Rhode Island remains the region's dowdy neighbor, clinging to old, gritty industries and grappling with big economic problems. Its 10.2% annual average unemployment rate last year was the highest in New England, and those with jobs in the aging textile industry make the second-lowest average manufacturing wages in the country. . . . The Conference of State Manufacturers' Associations rates Rhode Island as having the second worst business climate in the nation (Michigan was worse). The main culprits: high taxes, aggressive unions, and costly energy. . . . A consultant to the state government says Rhode Island can expect to lose 40,000 jobs, or 10% of its current work force, in the next five years, mainly because too many of its businesses are old and uncompetitive. . . . [T]he state's public-school system . . . ranks eighth-lowest nationally in scholastic aptitude scores and 10th-lowest in percentage of high school graduates. . . . Unions, which claim 29% of the work force in the state, are strident and politically powerful . . . "You're either rich or poor in Rhode Island," says Mr. [Edward] Beard, the former congressman. . . .

—*The Wall Street Journal*, June 28, 1983

Within days of publication of *The Wall Street Journal*'s front-page article, and in time for the July 4th weekend, T-shirts reading "What the Hell Does Wall Street Know About Rhode Island?" were being sold and worn in downtown Providence.

---

* This case is based on interviews with Raul Lovett, Bruce Sondler, and several of their colleagues. It was completed in 1983.

A ten-minute walk away, at the bottom of College Hill, a few blocks down from the Rhode Island School of Design and a few more from Brown University, is Raul Lovett's law firm. "Lovett, Morgera, Schefrin & Gallogly," the gray brick building reads. In a second-story plate-glass window stands a six-foot sign of Mickey Mouse. He smiles, holds his tail in his right hand, and extends his left. The sign is electric. It shines at night.

In the waiting room, five portrayals of Mickey Mouse are painted directly on the wall over a couch. In one, Mickey wears huge rings with glistening gems. In another, he stands sad and bow-legged before an unsympathetic-looking judge.

A painted rainbow twists and snakes along one wall. One of the waiting room chairs is a huge plastic hand, bent at the wrist, fingers angled to accommodate a sitting person.

In front of the reception counter is a wooden horse from a merry-go-round. Leaning against the side of the counter are two huge dominoes.

Raul Lovett's office is behind the reception counter. Its door— Mickey Mouse on the outside, mirrored on the inside—is open, and hardly ever closes. It seems occupied, even when empty, because of the human-sized figures congregated there: a full-size cloth doll with a scrooned face, seated cross-legged in a chair; a reproduction of a suit of armor (wearing a Mickey Mouse mask); a skeleton (wearing a dust mask); and a four-foot stuffed Mickey Mouse.

Mickey Mouse is rampant, in stuffed, inflated, porcelain, plastic, and metal versions. There are a Mickey Mouse phone, a Mickey Mouse gumball machine, and four Mickey Mouse clocks, including a giant reproduction of a Mickey Mouse watch hanging on the wall.

The office also teems with lions (Lovett is a Leo), executed in every imaginable medium. A ceramic lion crouches, snarling and roaring, next to the desk. A plastic fountain on the wall, if operating, would spout water from a lion's mouth. Lovett considers himself a classic Leo: "paternal, egotistical, generous, theatrical."

There are Humphrey Bogart mementoes ("That's the greatest guy that ever lived," explains Lovett), including a replica of the Maltese Falcon from the movie of that name. (Lovett's private bathroom, marked "Rick's Cafe Americain, Casablanca," is decorated with a profusion of Bogart posters, photos, and plaques. One reads, "I stick my neck out for nobody!")

Items with motifs of Egypt (which Lovett visited recently) abound, including a reproduction of King Tut's funeral mask on one wall. Lovett's desk chair has hieroglyphics on it (and on top, lying on his stomach like a beach bunny, is a smiling Mickey Mouse).

Lovett's walls are so crowded that some hangings are stacked on the floor against the walls. In addition to the Mickey Mouse, lion, Bogart, and Egyptian hangings, there are photos of Lovett's children (he has four with his wife of 25 years), a membership certificate from the American Trial Lawyers Association, a plaque with a papal blessing, a photo of Lovett pressed up against a state trooper in a crowd picketing Brown & Sharpe (a machine tool company in North Kingstown, Rhode Island, that has been struck by the International Association of Machinists since October 1981), and a mirrored bar plaque proclaiming "Sue the Bastards." There's an enlarged facsimile from *The [Providence] Evening Bulletin* of April 4, 1982, reviewing a television program, "Economic Time Bomb: Workers' Compensation," that the insurance industry persuaded all three local stations to broadcast simultaneously as part of its lobbying campaign against the workers' compensation system. ("It was a snow job," Lovett says. "And it boomeranged.") The *Bulletin* account related:

> The program was, more or less, *The Raul Lovett Show.* Lovett, an attorney whose firm represents many people who have gone before the Workers' Compensation Commission, obviously was a better television performer than most of the other participants. He frequently interrupted other speakers. While his points often seemed valid, the overall effect he created was one of chaos. . . .

Lovett's desk is chaotic; there are Mickey Mouse bric-a-brac and legal files stacked everywhere. There is a large white bust of Pope John XXIII ("The only decent Pope that ever lived," says Lovett) and a framed photo of Lovett next to the Popemobile as John Paul II rides through a crowd in St. Peter's Square. (Lovett is Jewish, and denies that the papal displays are attributable to his clientele being predominantly Roman Catholic—two out of every three Rhode Island residents are Catholic.) There are a jar of Rolaids and plastic reproductions of food, including waffles with butter and syrup, onion rings, McDonald's french fries, and beef stew. An article embedded in lucite, about a case in which Lovett won $500,000 for a group of Kaiser Aluminum workers who were eligible for years of back workers' compensation even though they had returned to work, quotes Lovett: "That's the law as it stood. I only enforced it—I didn't make it." The article also quotes Lovett, who reaped a third of the settlement, reacting to legislators' reactions: "They should spend less time counting my money and more time concentrating on doing the job they're elected to do."

Over his desk, three five-foot Crayola crayons hang from the mirrored-panel ceiling. Nearby are a slot machine and a neon sculpture reading "RAUL".

A Reputation for High Quality and Volume

It's July 1, 1983, the Friday before the July 4th weekend. Several minutes past 9 a.m., Raul Lovett, head of Rhode Island's fifth largest law firm and generally considered Rhode Island's ablest and most successful workers' compensation lawyer, arrives at his office. He is wearing cordovan-colored cowboy boots, a cream-colored feathered cowboy hat (with a Mickey Mouse pinned to it), a bright green blazer (with a Mickey Mouse lapel pin), and a matching Ralph Lauren tie (with a Mickey Mouse stick pin). He has a Santa Claus belly and a white Santa Claus beard (which he has dyed green on St. Patrick's Day). He is wearing nine rings on eight fingers (he wears up to 14 at a time), including one Mickey Mouse ring, and a ring with six lion heads. He is wearing two watches (one a Mickey Mouse) and a silver bracelet on his left hand. On his right hand, he is wearing a turquoise bracelet and a thick gold bracelet with four recumbent lions.

Lovett, 48, is soon on the phone to make a few calls, one to a union he represents. He talks with an insurance adjuster: "They underpay you so you don't give big offers," he says. The adjuster reports that he will be leaving for another insurance company. "They have a very paranoid attitude there," Lovett says of the adjuster's old company. "Any time they have a bit of a freethinker, and I say that sincerely, bingo, they get shot down." Lovett's voice is sonorous, his delivery polished.

Lovett hands his Mickey Mouse briefcase to his intern, Jane Lehman, 25, who recently completed her first year at Albany Law School. During the car ride to the courthouse, she holds his Mickey Mouse mug of coffee and his unlit cigar. (He usually smokes Havana cigars, which he says he buys four or five hundred at a time during an annual trip to Cuba.)

Lovett's white Mercedes convertible (Rhode Island plates: "MMOUSE") is one of his 15 vehicles, he says. (Among the others: five motorcycles, three Rolls Royces, two London taxis, and a 1937 firetruck.) He parks in a no-parking zone outside the J. Joseph Garrahy Judicial Complex, a spacious, orderly, and new building comprising Family Court, (State) District Court, and the Workers' Compensation Commission. Hearings before the commission begin at 9:30 a.m.

Lovett greets three attorneys on the street. One, employed by the state, wears a Mickey Mouse tie. He calls it his "voodoo tie" and wears it when he is scheduled to oppose one of Lovett's attorneys.

"How you doing, cutie?" a female guard calls to Lovett as he enters the building. A client stops him to talk.

H. & L. Soc.Resp.Lawyers UCB—10

On the elevator, he compliments a man's green jacket and a woman's ring. He gets off on the Family Court floor. The halls are a swirl of people and smoke.

A lawyer who has asked to join Lovett's firm approaches him to find out when a decision on hiring will be made. (Later, while waiting to speak with Lovett again, the lawyer lists his reasons for wanting to work for him: He can't fit the mold of a blue chip Providence firm; he has a beard—which he wants to keep—and does not have an Ivy League background. He also does not want to wait a few years before being allowed to go to court. Lovett, he says, handles "99.99 percent" of workers' compensation claims in the state, and is recognized as an expert. The firm, a general practice firm in addition to specializing in workers' compensation and personal injury, has a reputation for high quality as well as for high volume.)

Lovett passes through the halls, tapping shoulders, shaking hands, exchanging pleasantries, like a politician working the crowd. People waiting for their court sessions watch him as he goes by. Some smile at his attire. A client lights his cigar.

Lovett cannot find the person he is seeking. He gets back on the elevator, and as he does, a lawyer offers him $35,000 to settle a case. "I'll take it," Lovett says. The elevator doors begin to close. The lawyer is still standing in the hallway. "But I want more money for California," Lovett calls out about another case.

Lovett goes to the small conference room that his firm uses as its courthouse headquarters. "We took it over by adverse possession," Lovett says. "We've had it since the building opened." Says Jack Kaveny, a 25–year–old paralegal, "We're there probably the earliest of anybody and we're there the latest so it just kind of evolved that it's our room."

In addition to Lovett, two of his attorneys are operating out of the conference room that day (there are usually three), as well as two summer clerks and one paralegal (there are usually three). His attorneys hand him papers to look over and sign.

"You're Going to Hear From My Lawyer"

The attorneys are conservatively and impeccably dressed, as are the overwhelming majority of the people who work for Lovett. Among the reasons offered by people at the firm for dressing in contrast to Lovett are not wanting to be seen as imitating him and not being established enough to get away with his flamboyance. Lovett in effect offered another explanation when he told a writer from *The East Side Monthly,* a Providence community newspaper, that he would not hire anyone who dressed as he does. From his first floor corner office,

Lovett can watch people from his firm come and go through the mirrored vertical blinds on his windows.

> When I see people from the office going out to lunch with their jackets over their shoulders, I'm negatively impressed and I let them know about it.

Lovett leaves his cowboy hat in the conference room. His brown hair is graying and thinning. He takes a client, a sad-looking woman, to the hearing room next door. He tries unsuccessfully to balance his cigar on the plaque designating the hearing room by number, and finally takes the cigar in with him.

Lovett briefs the woman for her commutation hearing. (Commutation in Rhode Island is the replacement of weekly workers' compensation benefits with a lump-sum settlement.)

> The questions will be as follows: "You have been receiving workman compensation benefits, as a result of injuries you sustained on or about December 24, 1979; is that correct?" Now the reason that's correct is because we are entering papers today where they have agreed to pay you for that period of time, so the answer would be "yes" to that. "You have decided to settle your case for a lump-sum settlement . . .; is that correct?". . . . "[T]he total amount is [$]25,000 and you will net [$]20,000." "You have decided that it's in your best interest to settle any future sum to which you may be entitled, to a lump sum?" [You'll say,] "Yes, I do." "You appreciate the fact that if this is approved by Commissioner _____, who will be hearing the case, that this is the end of the case for any and all times? You appreciate that in addition to this compensation that you are being paid that any and all outstanding medical bills up through today's date will be paid by the insurance company?" And that is true. . . .

His client will receive a $20,000 settlement after counsel fees.

Lovett brings his client back into the hall. She smiles for the only time that morning. "How 'bout throwing one of those rings into the settlement?" she asks.

Lovett is much wealthier than most of his clientele. But he insists that his clients do not resent it; instead, he says, they take pleasure in seeing his jewelry and his cars and knowing how successful their lawyer is.

> You see, to the lower end of the blue-collar scale, the only status the guy . . . has or the poor guy out in South Providence . . . [has is:] "You'll hear from my lawyer." He's got something; he's got a lawyer. The banker got his lawyer, and

this guy's got his lawyer and [can say,] "You're going to hear from my lawyer. Lovett's my lawyer."

In the hallway, another client, a man wearing a Molson Golden Ale polo shirt, invites Lovett to his home if Lovett will be in the vicinity of Bristol, Rhode Island, during the weekend. (Lovett, however, will be at his vacation house on Cape Cod in Hyannisport, Massachusetts, for the weekend and the following week.) Lovett checks the firm's docket sheet to figure out the man's name. (The firm has 23 workers' compensation cases scheduled before the commission that day. All case files include a Polaroid photograph of the client on the inside cover to facilitate identifying and locating clients in the courthouse bustle.)

He constantly scans the hall as he chats with clients and lawyers, only occasionally making eye contact. He conducts a hallway examination of a client's wrist scar, measuring it with his fingers. He lifts his eyebrows and says semi-facetiously, "A kid, a kid. A *horrible* scar for the rest of her life."

"We Can Hold Off 'til We Get the Right Bargain"

Lovett conducts a commutation hearing, and then stands outside a hearing room, talking with the attorney he will oppose in the next hearing. Lovett tells him about the departing insurance adjuster, and discusses another adjuster:

He didn't give away the company store, but we were on the same wavelength. I'd rather deal with a seasoned adjuster who tells me to go to hell than someone who keeps saying, "I'll get back to you."

The upcoming hearing is for the woman whom Lovett briefed earlier that morning. "Don't ask her too many questions," Lovett says to the opposing attorney. "She's nervous."

Lovett balances his cigar on the plaque with the hearing room's number and enters the room. It has blond wood furnishings and carpeted walls, an elevated bench for a commissioner and counsel tables.

The Workers' Compensation commissioner is in short sleeves. The client looks tired and vacant-eyed. She says, "Yes," or "Yes, I do," to Lovett's leading questions (which are allowed in commutation hearings) without seeming to mean it or understand. She does not answer one of the questions, but Lovett keeps asking them. Even when he is speaking quickly, the words do not sound rushed.

Conducting a compensation hearing often entails asking a standard set of questions. Lovett's attorneys have conducted hearings even when the files could not be located, as occurs occasionally. "It doesn't take that long to get the whole feeling of a case," says Lovett.

It's not winging it. That wouldn't be fair to the client, but there's no reason why with 22 years of experience in . . . compensation matters on a regular basis that I can't take a file and look at it and, bingo, know what's going on.

Lovett says he does not conduct extensive research for individual compensation cases, although he does stay informed of developments in compensation law. To orient a recent law school graduate to compensation law would take nine months to a year, he says. The first three months of the orientation would consist of the new lawyer following Lovett around and observing him, much as his summer intern Lehman does. Eventually Lovett would let the lawyer conduct simple direct examinations, then more complicated ones, and then cross examinations.

The woman's commutation hearing is informal and short, lasting about ten minutes. Commutations must be approved by a Workers' Compensation commissioner; since they usually have been agreed to beforehand by both the employee and the insurer, approval typically amounts to ratification.

A commutation agreement between an employee and an insurer provides for counsel fees which, like the rest of the agreement, must be approved by a commissioner. Counsel fees may not exceed 20 percent of the settlement, which Lovett typically charges.

Lovett estimates that 10 percent of his workers' compensation cases are settled through commutation. Another 20 percent are settled before they reach the compensation commission. In these settlements, recalcitrant insurance companies that have delayed paying Lovett's clients agree to start paying them weekly benefits, sometimes retroactively. The settlements can include Lovett's fees. But he sometimes waives them if it appears that insurers will hold up his clients' benefits while counsel fees are negotiated.

Commissioners set fees for non-commutation hearings, in which employees contest denial of compensation benefits, or insurers contest their granting. (The issues at contested hearings include whether an injury occurred, whether disability resulted, and whether disability is as severe as claimed. Witnesses are usually the employee, the employee's physician(s), the insurer's physician(s), and the employer's personnel manager. Of the 40,000 on-the-job injuries that Dennis Revena, deputy administrator of the commission, estimates occurred in 1982 in Rhode Island, 5,079 were disputed before the compensation commission.) Commissioners, who sit separately, have varying criteria for awarding fees for contested hearings. According to Commissioner

Moses Kando, the rule of thumb is to award the attorney $225 for filing the hearing petition and $50 for each hearing thereafter. (The hearings last from 15 to 90 minutes, according to Lovett.) The rule is flexible; Kando says he awards higher fees for a case that requires, for example, an out-of-state deposition. He will not reward attorneys for stringing out a case over three hearings when one would have sufficed. The prevailing attorney is typically awarded $350 to $450 per case, says Kando.

Most of the compensation hearings Lovett's firm conducts are contested, meaning that it receives about $400 per claim, rather than the 20 percent that it can collect from a commutation settlement. The firm can survive, and even prosper, on $400 awards because it has so many compensation cases: Lovett estimates that his firm opens and closes 2,000 per year.

The volume of cases has another advantage:

[W]e probably get better money than most firms, because we have such a huge volume the [insurance] companies know we can hold off 'til we get the right bargain—that we won't settle cheap.

His firm has no real competition in compensation, he says. He guesses that he and his three compensation attorneys are among only 20 attorneys in the state handling compensation. Of the 48 cases scheduled before the Workers' Compensation Commission on that day, 23 are for clients of Lovett's firm.

"If They Represent Themselves, They Are Going to Hurt Themselves"

The Rhode Island Workers' Compensation Commission is a seven-person body with power to subpoena. Its members, appointed by the governor and confirmed by the State Senate, sit separately and act as judges. Its decisions are appealable to the Rhode Island Supreme Court.

Claimants may appear before the commission *pro se*. "If they represent themselves, they are going to hurt themselves," says Lovett, because lay people do not know what injuries are worth.

Many times a client will say, "Get me $20,000 and I'll be satisfied," and I'll get him 50. I don't leave it up to them to decide what they want to get because most of them don't know what's in their best interest; most of them cut low.

Lovett contends that his reputation, let alone his legal experience and expertise, will net a client more money:

I'm trying not to boast, but if my name is on a compensation case, they [insurance companies] automatically know it's going to cost them more money than it would [otherwise].

The average commutation settlement, when it was last computed in 1982, was $20,000, according to Revens, the commission's deputy administrator. Lovett says his average commutation settlement is double that.

"How About Paying This Guy? Now."

Says Lovett,

A typical case would be, the person is injured at work, and. . . . [h]e's out of work. . . . [T]he insurance company calls him and says, "You'll hear from us next week or in two weeks," or "We'll get back to you," and they don't. . . . [H]is brother, his cousin, his doctor or someone says, "You ought to call Raul." . . . When he calls . . . he's given an appointment within 48 hours. Every new client is seen within 48 hours by hook or by crook. They'll come down and they'll see a paralegal who will do the intake . . . and I'll sit down with the client . . . I will dictate a letter to the company asking if they will pay voluntarily or whether I have to file a petition [for compensation]. [If] I have a chance, I'll call the adjuster right then and there, say, "What's going on? How about paying this guy? Now." Many times they will.

We'll fill out the temporary disability forms so that they can get some other income in the meantime. . . . [W]e'll check into trying to get them on Social Security. . . . [W]e'll find out if they have any loans that should be paid for by private insurance . . . and then send them on their way, advising them that they have to call back in ten days to see what's going on.

The next step . . . [is] that we file a petition for compensation benefits. . . . Within usually ten days, we go to a pre-trial hearing and there the commissioner can either order the [insurance] company to put the man on [compensation] without a determination or say, "I don't have enough information to make a determination." If he doesn't make a determination, the case is then placed on what they call a regular calendar. The case is continued for about two months.

At that time, we go back to the compensation commission . . . and the client will testify, will be [direct] examined by us, and of course [cross] examined by the insurance lawyer. Then the case will be continued for us to bring in our medical [reports]. Then it will be continued for them to bring in their medical [reports]. Then the judge writes a decision. If it's favorable, and they [insurance companies] don't take an appeal, he [the client] gets paid. If it's not favorable, we take an appeal and we start the appellate work. From start to finish, it could take three to six months. . . . [I]t takes nine months to a year if they want to play long and hard.

Fifty-five percent of the firm's work is workers' compensation, Lovett estimates. Approximately 20 percent is personal injury, 15 percent domestic cases, 5 percent criminal cases, and the remaining 5 percent spread over real estate, wills, trusts, labor, arbitration, and other areas. "I don't think there's that much profit in domestic," says Lovett. "There's certainly profit in the liability and comp. . . ."

Lovett spends most of his time working on compensation cases. But each year he tries to do a criminal and a civil trial (preferably before a jury) as well as argue before the Rhode Island Supreme Court.

"Every Year Just Got Better"

Lovett conducts another workers' compensation hearing, retrieves his hat from the firm's conference room, and strides out of the Judicial Complex by 12:30.

Lovett was born and bred in Providence, where he still lives. He attended the University of Rhode Island for six months, Emerson College in Boston for three and a half years, and then the University of Miami for six months. After that, he took night courses at Brown University. His B.A. is in Radio and Television; he minored in English and Philosophy. (When Lovett applied to Boston University Law School, it questioned his academic record and accepted only his English and Philosophy courses as college work.)

After college, Lovett worked for a year as a disc jockey and news announcer at a radio station in New Bedford, Massachusetts, from 6–9 a.m. and 10 a.m. to noon, and at a radio station in Pawtucket, Rhode Island, from 2–6 p.m. The cost of driving to New Bedford exceeded his salary at the station there, he recalls.

(Lovett would return to radio or go into theater if he ever gave up law. "When it stops being fun, I'll quit," he says. But it's still fun: "I'm the luckiest guy in the world. I get paid to do what I enjoy.")

Lovett was accepted by Boston University as a special law student upon a strong letter of recommendation from M. Louis Abedon, a Providence lawyer. Lovett made law review and received his J.D. in 1960. He returned to Rhode Island to clerk with Abedon's firm. "It's just the roll of the dice as far as what kind of firm you get a job with." The firm did "compensation, personal injury, divorce, everything . . .

so I started doing it, enjoyed it, liked it, and continued on." In 1966, he launched his own firm.

"I had three kids, a pregnant wife, I'd just bought a house, and was on my own. It was a challenge. I was scared shit."

Lovett's firm began as a labor law firm. It still does legal work for unions representing aluminum, electrical, rubber, health, and transit workers; machinists, state employees, carpenters, and teamsters.

Lovett's work with unions brought in individual compensation and general practice clients, mostly blue-collar. "They liked two things, from what I understand," says Aram Schefrin, an attorney with the firm and a 1966 graduate of Harvard Law School:

> One was that . . . the door was open. This place never closed. Raul was never home. Raul was always out doing work on something, seeing a client. He was here constantly. Even when I got here five years ago, he would never go home. . . . And they liked his attitude, because they felt that since he was flying in the face of convention and everything else, he was also kicking ass to represent their rights, which he was. . . . It was just booting the who-is's on behalf of the who-isn't's.

Says Lovett:

> Every year just got better. The first year out was better than the last year working for somebody else and each year has been better. . . . I started on my own, and I hired another person and hired another person and hired another one and hired another one.

The firm, a corporation whose sole stockholder is Lovett, now employs 66 people, including Louis Abedon's grandson, who is a summer clerk. There are 16 attorneys in addition to Lovett, all associates. "Everybody works for me," he says. Despite the name of the firm, "Lovett, Morgera, Schefrin & Gallogly," Lovett has no partners.

Lovett has three legal secretaries and an appointments secretary. There are night secretaries to transcribe dictation, and two interpreters, for Spanish and Portugese clients. (In addition, one lawyer and two secretaries speak Spanish, and one lawyer, one secretary, and one paralegal speak Portugese.) One woman spends all day answering the firm's 23 telephone lines, and typing the names of callers waiting to speak with Lovett into a video display terminal on his desk. Some clients wait on the phone for two or three hours to speak with him. The number of callers on hold (easy-listening radio is fed to them over the phone) often jams all 23 lines.

Says Bruce Sondler, a 29–year–old litigator at the firm,

> I had to go to a beeper, because people just couldn't get
> through. With the beeper system, people . . . ring my num-
> ber, and it just says, "Bruce, call me at such and such a
> number."

Lovett also has three private phone lines in his office. He provides
his home phone number on his business card (as do some other
attorneys at the firm). He has five lines at home. At night, most
clients call him there, rather than leaving messages with his 24–hour
answering service. Some of the calls to his answering service are from
clients arrested for drunken driving.

As late as 1977, there were 16 people at the firm. But at the end of
the 70s, two things caused business to explode: paid advertising and
free publicity.

A Favorite of the Press

Over lunch at the Aurora Civic Association, a private club, with
Lehman, his intern, and Patricia Betz, 35, his office manager, Lovett
discusses the type faces for a full-page ad in a July 4 supplement to *The
Providence Journal–Bulletin*. The firm also places ads in weeklies and
monthlies (including Spanish and Portugese ones) throughout the state
to announce new associates and to offer Christmas greetings to the
public. It purchases space in programs for civic associations, a cinema,
and artistic performances.

"I'm against advertising," says Lovett,

> but if they are going to allow it, then I'm going to do more than
> anybody else. But I think it is terrible to have. You start
> with advertising and then what do you get? You get competi-
> tion. If someone comes in to see me, I think I am the best, so I
> advertise, but I see some sleazes, people I think who are sleazy,
> who advertise, and people go to them too.

The firm purchases full-page three-color ads on the inside rear
cover of the Yellow Pages in Providence, Bristol, Narragansett, New-
port, and Woonsocket. The firm is also listed under "Lawyers" in
every Yellow Pages in the state. The ads and listings (those outside
Providence provide the firm's toll-free intrastate phone number) cost
between $40,000 and $50,000 a year, says Betz.

The ads were the subject of a federal district court decision in 1979,
holding that the Rhode Island Supreme Court could not restrict lawyers' ads in telephone directories to the Yellow Pages' listings for
lawyers, but could limit implied assertions of legal specialization, even
if accompanied by disclaimers. The Rhode Island Supreme Court later

voided its own restriction on implied assertions of specialization. (In 1977 the U.S. Supreme Court ruled in *Bates v. State Bar of Arizona*, 433 U.S. 350 (1977), that truthful newspaper advertising of the availability and terms of routine legal services is protected by the First Amendment.)

"We picked up a lot of people from it," says Lovett about the Yellow Pages ad. The firm also obtains clients through referrals from physicians, judges, unions, and other clients. In addition, Lovett gets free media attention.

> The television thing, when I was on for two hours on every channel ["Economic Timebomb: Workers' Compensation," April 8, 1982], that brought in a lot of people. Martha Smith of *The [Providence] Journal* did an article on me [Sunday, April 15, 1979; full-page], that brought in a lot of people. Being on television and radio brings in more people, being active on the picket line at Brown & Sharpe brought in a lot of people.

(Lovett picketed every morning before work for over a year, he says. One of the firm's attorneys says that Lovett has an "uncanny ability to get press" because he is charming, witty, colorful, and quotable.)

"I have always been a favorite of the press here," Lovett says.

> This week alone I was on television two different nights, and I was on radio one night, and they did a newspaper story on me last week. So the name is usually bandied about. . . . It's a small town so it's easy to be a big fish. . . . Wednesday I was coming out of the courthouse and a TV reporter came up to me and said, "Did you see *The Wall Street Journal* with the article about Rhode Island?" I said, "Yes," and she said, "Would you mind being interviewed?"

The previous day, a client called Lovett about the greyhound-raising business she is starting. Lovett gave her quick advice about dog licensing and business partnerships, and then asked that a greyhound be named after him. A similar request to the owner of 3 Steeple Street (a restaurant a block from the firm), whom Lovett opposed in a divorce case, led to a menu item called the Raul Burger. "You'll Lovett!" proclaims the menu.

"The Hi–Bye"

"It's a legal factory," says one employee about the firm. And the factory seems fueled by the publicity that Lovett generates. "It hasn't hurt me, being with him," says Sondler, "because he's got the reputation, and possibly part of that reputation that he's developed is because he's so outrageous."

"It's a gimmick and it works," says Kaveny about Mickey Mouse being in effect the firm's mascot. "He laughs all the way to the bank," says Sondler. Still, not everyone is pleased. Another attorney gestures toward the six-foot electric Mickey Mouse sign in the window and says, "It's hard to maintain an air of professionalism with that out there." Attorneys' offices at the firm are generally furnished conservatively.

The clients apparently do not mind the Mickey Mouse trappings. "He likes to have it around," says one woman waiting for her appointment with Lovett. "It helps him to think better. I guess everyone has their own thing." A male client says, "The man is very smart. He remembers your name. He remembers your case. He's a super guy, I guess. . . . Whatever he does, it works."

Lovett was not always unconventional.

[Y]oung lawyers, and I was one of them, come out and see themselves as the most important people in the world, paragons of virtue, and pontificating all the time. . . . I had a briefcase, *The Wall Street Journal,* the whole thing.

He adopted Mickey Mouse, he says, to remind himself not to take himself too seriously.

"When someone goes to see a lawyer, they're very uptight; they've got a problem," says Lovett. His office and his waiting room are furnished in an effort to get people to relax, he says, and to occupy them while they wait to speak with him. Even making it into his office does not entail getting his undistracted attention.

The waiting room is crowded when Lovett breezes through it on the way to his office at about 3:30. His appointment schedule began at 3:00. (Lovett says his lunch break, which sometimes includes running professional errands, usually takes an hour and a half.)

The people waiting for Lovett have already been seen by someone at the firm who conducted an intake interview. Paralegals conduct intake for compensation cases, and record such basic information as clients' employers and treating physicians, average weekly wages, and whether injuries come under the old or revised workers' compensation statute. Intake for non-compensation cases is usually conducted by attorneys in whose area of specialty the case falls.

After intake, clients are usually taken to Lovett for "the hi-bye."

I like to see every single client. So I know who my clients are. Sometimes someone will come down and see another lawyer, but I haven't met them. So even if I'm tied up seeing a client there will be enough time for "hi-bye," meaning, "How are you. I'll look into the case." At least I see their face. They see me and they know I exist and I know that they exist.

The hi-bye entails giving the client the impression that Lovett will be handling the case or at least involved in it, says one attorney.

(On the previous day, clients in the waiting room talked with each other about how Lovett is handling their cases personally with the assistance of associates. One woman was irritated that two associates showed up at her hearings when she thought she had retained Lovett.)

Some clients, upon being sent to one of Lovett's attorneys, insist on being represented by Lovett himself. Says Schefrin,

> If they're really adamant, you send them down to Raul. Otherwise, you just tell them, "Look, he doesn't try those kinds of cases anymore . . ." or sometimes we tell them that we're just working the case up for him. Some of them we have to ease into the idea that he personally is not going to be able to do the case.

During appointments that do not amount to hi-bye (i.e., those with clients whose cases he works on), Lovett asks clients for updated information, calls physicians' offices and insurance companies, and dictates memos to the file. Lovett says the work is routine, but,

> No one will ever do it as well as I would have done it myself. . . . [I]f I have my choice to . . . have nobody working for me and handling every single case myself, that's what I would do, because that way I know what's being done.

Additionally, Lovett has established personal relationships with many of the people he contacts.

> [T]he development of the rapport in the insurance company, where I can just call someone, he knows my voice and I know his voice and have a rapport going back and forth where I can call him a silly son-of-a-bitch and . . . he can call me a crazy bastard and we'll still settle a case, that comes from winning cases in the past. That comes from beating them. That comes from respect.

Holding Court

Lovett estimates that he sees 10 to 12 clients (including five or six new ones) in a typical afternoon. A hi-bye can consist of several exchanges totaling three minutes spread over a half hour. One reason is that Lovett speaks on the phone with what he estimates to be 50 to 60 people a day, and many calls don't have to do with the client who might be in his office at the time.

Lovett sometimes takes two calls at once, one on a regular phone, one on a speaker phone, which has no receiver and which amplifies the other party's voice. While one client waits in his office, Lovett listens to another client on the speaker phone accuse a physician of examining her breasts unnecessarily, and then dictates a memo.

He smokes cigars, dictates memos, calls to the receptionist to bring him another client, and signs checks while on the phone. He takes people off hold, assures them he will get to them, and puts them back on hold. Employees climb around him, avoiding the phone cord, looking for files on, underneath, behind, and beside his desk.

Clients sit patiently—some look bored, some amused—during the interruptions. A friend steps into the office—the door stays open during almost all appointments—to introduce Lovett to his daughter, who is home for the summer. They banter for a while.

Attorneys, secretaries, summer clerks, and paralegals, often five people, sometimes more, stand in Lovett's office waiting to ask a question between or during appointments. An attorney flips through a copy of *Gentlemen's Quarterly* on Lovett's desk. Other employees chat quietly. One turns to another and jokes, "Are you next in line to speak with His Highness?" It is almost as if Lovett, sitting in his throne-like desk chair, is holding court, or that his office is a family room. At the end of the day, employees stop in to call their good-nights to Lovett or to discuss July 4th plans with him. (On the previous day, an employee stopped in to show Lovett the little lawn chair she had bought her nephew. Bruce Sondler, an associate, went to Lovett to collect his birthday greetings, and wound up with a kiss on the cheek as well.)

The paper boy comes in and leaves *The Providence Journal* on Lovett's desk; Lovett tips him. Lovett turns from his phone conversation with a client to comment on an employee's haircut. He calls to the receptionist for a file.

In Lovett's office, flashes of light can be seen coming from the waiting room; photos of new clients are being taken for their files. The front door bell chimes constantly, and the receptionist buzzes people through the locked door (there have been thefts from the office.) The sound of clients talking in the waiting room (the receptionist asks them pre-intake questions—the nature and cause of their injuries) mixes with the sound of traffic and sirens; Lovett's first-floor corner office is at the intersection of two busy streets. People walk by on the sidewalk and look through the blinds, pointing to the decor.

A Full–Service Firm

It is 5:30 on a Friday afternoon before a long weekend, and clients are still waiting for Lovett in his waiting room and office.

Lovett remains calm. He has the demeanor of a country doctor. "Stop worrying," he tells clients. He is at ease with them and tries to put them at ease.

"My manner is to treat my clients as friends, and they are. And I'm 'Raul,' not 'Mr. Lovett' to them." (He is "Raul" to his attorneys, but "Mr. Lovett" to the rest of his employees.) His firm sent between 8,000 and 10,000 Christmas cards last year, he says.

Lovett's personal and professional concern for his clients merges. "Are you interested in getting more of an education, or retraining of some type?" he asks a client whose back is injured.

> While you are out and collecting compensation, it might be the proper time to do it for you, and what you might think in terms of is having some vocational rehabilitation, to retrain you. Use your brains instead of your back.

He advises one client to "get rid of the goddamn cigarettes" and another client with a jammed shoulder to avoid further cortisone injections.

Lovett sees his firm as a full-service blue-collar law firm. He pays clients' parking-lot fees while they visit his office. When the Workers' Compensation Commission moved, Lovett provided a van, complete with Mickey Mouse signs and license plates reading "WKCOMP," to shuttle clients from the old to the new location.

> I always found it easier to keep people out of trouble than to get them out of trouble. I try to educate everyone. I'll tell people, don't sign anything but birthday cards until they see me first. Once they've made contact, I try to give them a total service. . . . [I]f somebody has an automobile accident, I want to be sure that, number one, their needs are being taken care of: the car is being repaired, and it's being taken care of by a proper body shop, not a hack shop. Number two, that if they have medical problems that they are being seen by the best doctor, that if they have an orthopedic problem, that they are being seen by an orthopedic man. . . . I ask them . . ., "What kind of insurance do you carry? What are your limits of liability? What are you paying? Do you have Medicaid? Do you have an uninsured motorist? Bring over the policy. Let me take a look at it." I'll ask them, as soon as somebody comes in, and he's been injured on the job or injured in an accident . . ., "Do you have any loans of any type? . . . Do you have insurance on that loan?" and check to see whether they are entitled to have the premium paid while they are disabled. So you go the full route, not just . . . talk about the accident and nothing else.

"They'll call me about anything," he says about clients. "They'll call me for advice on who to see as a doctor." (When Lovett refers clients to physicians, he weighs two factors: the physician's competence—he sends clients to physicians he and his family use—and the physician's willingness and availability to testify at trials and hearings.) "They'll call me for advice as to whether to make an investment or not make an investment, call me on advice on what kind of car to buy." (An attorney says, "[H]is clients will call him up 15, 16 times a day.") Lovett is seen as an all-purpose advisor. "No charges made for first conference on any matter," says the firm's Yellow Pages ad.

To a client worried about paying legal fees, he says,

> If there is litigation and we're successful in defending you, in representing you, then the insurance company pays my bill. If . . . you do go back to work and get your job back and everything, fine and dandy. That's the end of that and I don't get paid. But I have established goodwill for the next time.

For non-compensation cases on a contingent basis, the firm charges 33 percent of a pre-trial settlement and 40 percent of a post-trial award.

About his non-contingency fees, Lovett says,

> If I'm handling a case personally, again depending on who and what it is, if it's Joe Zilch from the union, or it's a blue-collar worker or something, I charge them the base of [$]50 an hour or even less, knock something off if he can't afford it, or charge nothing. On the other hand, if it's a doctor or someone who can afford the time and knows what's going into it, then they pay $100 an hour. Which is cheap.

"Dogs"

Although no case is too small, Lovett estimates that he declines two or three cases a week on behalf of his firm. He says he will not accept a case without merit, but still takes most cases that come his way.

"That's how he built his practice. He does not look kindly on turning away a client," says an employee.

> His attitude is: Handle a case, good or bad. Bring it to a result, win, lose, or draw. His approach is: Service the client. We do anything, we do everything, with exceptions. If they want something done in the future, they come to us, even if we haven't been successful in the past. So we end up taking a lot of "dogs." But the trend is away from that.

"Dogs" is the firm's term for weak cases. There are also "pain-in-the-ass" cases.

As examples of "pain-in-the-ass" cases, Lovett cites disputes among neighbors over backyard fences and street parking:

Someone's a long-time client, he's a union member, he's sent business down to us, you can't say, "Well, I'm not going to handle the case." So it's that sort of case we'll take.

Lovett estimates that his firm accepts 50 such cases each year—"too many," he says.

An intake of a person with a weak or "pain-in-the-ass" case who is not a prior client is less likely to be accepted, says an attorney; the firm will ask for a retainer of between $750 to $1000 to discourage potential clients from pressing cases, such as injunctions, that do not result in monetary settlements from which costs and counsel fees can be collected.

The firm appeals all but the most frivolous cases that are decided adversely. Lovett says,

I want the [insurance] companies to know and the clients to know that in each case we go to the end. And if we don't win, that we lie on our back and kick our feet, but at least we tried.

Accepting and appealing most cases has created an active caseload that Lovett estimates to be 5,000. (Computerization, which is in progress, will make a more accurate count possible.) Lovett maintains that 90 percent of the cases are his.

One attorney says he has 150 to 200 active cases. Schefrin estimates he has 300 cases. Sondler, a personal injury attorney, estimates that he has 1,000 cases, 700 of the firm's and 300 of his own. "[Y]ou become familiar with them," he says. "For some reason, they stick in your head. A lot of them do anyway." He gets five or six new cases a week, and completes five or six trials a week. An average case requires ten hours of research, he says.

Says Schefrin,

Sometimes I feel like we don't, we're not able to delve into all the cases in a lot of detail because of the volume. But it seems to be that the ones that really need the kind of comprehensive work-up, we will research, setting up the discovery so that you pick it all up and we manage to do it. I don't usually feel that we're going to court missing something.

"None of them slide," says Lovett of the 5,000 cases. "They're all pushed."

Schefrin says,

We try not to let any of them slide. First of all, we can't really do that. Obviously you know which ones are worth more money. But those aren't necessarily the ones that need most of the work. It's not that hard to retain what has to be done or the essence of 300 [cases].

"Do we just let them sit on the back burner?" asks an attorney, who replies:

> Yes. There are cases that are best off not being pressed. An insurance company will contact you at some later date regarding settlement. You might be handling a claim that you don't have the most faith in, but for one reason or another, you've taken the case. You're handling a case where there are no witnesses that exist. Many different ways, just because you settle a case quickly doesn't mean you've done a good job for your client. . . .

An attorney points out that under Rhode Island's comparative negligence system, a plaintiff with a weak case and a counterclaim against him can end up paying more damages than he collects. "Why make him pay the money today if he's going to pay the same money four years from now?" the attorney asks.

File Chasers

Cases whose clients are considered annoying are moved faster, according to an attorney. One paralegal says that disabled clients who are not receiving any form of government assistance often receive priority attention.

Attorneys at the firm receive 50 percent of the fees generated by cases they personally bring in, no matter who at the firm works on them. (Lovett estimates that 10 percent of the cases handled at the firm are under this arrangement.) One attorney reports that attorneys work harder on these cases, because they have brought them in or they are prodded by colleagues who did.

Cases are managed on a crisis basis, says an attorney. He notes that many interrogatories are answered and requested documents produced, not within the 40 days provided for in state civil procedure, but in response to motions for dismissal for failure to comply with orders compelling answers and production. He adds, however, that such delays are standard in the state.

"I don't think there's any firm that could say that they didn't blow a statute of limitations somewhere along the line," says an attorney.

(The only disciplinary case involving Lovett that is public information concerned his Yellow Pages advertising, on which he ultimately prevailed. There is one complaint against him pending before the Disciplinary Counsel, he says, which sounds, as he describes it, like the result of a misunderstanding. "Nothing will come of it," he says.)

Case files at the firm are occasionally misplaced. "They stay lost for a period of time, and then they'll show up again," says an employee.

Finding a client's file can take 45 minutes, says a file clerk, also known as a file chaser; computerization has not made it easier to find the physical files. Neither has the establishment of a central file grouping, according to a paralegal. If compensation files are being worked on,

> they could be on my desk, they could be with [another parale-gal], who doesn't even have a desk. So it just depends on where he's sitting for the week. Could be in any of the attorneys' offices that handle comp . . . could be with some-body handling a Social Security case. . . . It could be any-where sometimes.

Clients as Friends, Employees as Family

Confusion at the support staff level is compounded by high turn-over and nonexistent orientation of new employees, according to a former employee. In addition:

> Most people feel underpaid and overworked. Everyone com-plains about that. There's a lot of resentment. Everyone feels they aren't getting paid enough and Raul Lovett is driving around in a Rolls Royce.

"I treat my staff like I treat my kids," says Lovett. "I kiss them and I kick them in the ass, whichever is necessary. . . ." A plaque on his desk declares: "Whether I'm Right or Wrong, I'M STILL THE BOSS."

Lovett says he will not ever take partners. He wants to run the firm his way and take vacations when he wants without anyone's permission.

Lovett views the firm as his family. He claims to hire attorneys for life, attorneys who do not plan to leave after two years. But the attorneys see it differently.

One attorney, expressing no illusion about making partner, says he came to the firm to get experience and will leave when he's gained enough. Another jokes that making it to the top of the firm's letter-head can be achieved by default—by waiting for everyone else to move on.

Sink or Swim

Lovett's attorneys attended various law schools: the University of Connecticut, Villanova, Boston University, Harvard, and John Mar-shall, among others. Their work weeks range from approximately 50 to 65 hours. Their pay scales and vacation benefits are not standard-ized. They are not paid commissions per case. They usually receive

Christmas bonuses, but have not received them in the past two years.
Lovett says an attorney's salary

> depends upon the year's gross receipts. It depends upon
> whether they've contributed toward the receipts. It depends
> upon time, effort, energy they've expended. Whether they're
> here 9 to 5 or are they here on weekends and nights working
> on cases. . . . Whether they're socializing, whether they're
> building up a clientele. There are just so many variables.

The variables, an attorney contends, include how much salary an
attorney requested upon being hired, whether Lovett likes the attorney,
and how persistent the attorney is. Lovett, he says, "is a master of the
put-off. A master."

One attorney says that a recent law school graduate hired by the
firm can end up receiving $200 a week. Another attorney says of
Lovett,

> He's very generous to someone he perceives is in need. He
> once paid for the funeral of a poor client. When it comes to
> employees, you have to scatch and claw. . . . It's hard to get
> anything out of him.

An associate characterizes Lovett's attitude as: I am giving you experience, not money.

Says Sondler, "I applied here because you get thrown right into it.
You go into court three days after you're here." Sondler, who received
his degree from John Marshall Law School in Chicago, wonders

> why so many students from Harvard, the University of Chica-
> go, and other schools insist on joining large Wall Street firms,
> Chicago firms, Massachusetts firms, where you're going to be
> put into a room, you're going to be doing the research, some-
> body else is going to be examining it, somebody else is going to
> be ripping it apart, somebody else is going to be signing their
> name to it, somebody else is going to be litigating it, and you're
> in the back? And maybe ten years from now, somebody's
> going to come along and discover you, John Doe, in the back
> room. . . . For so many years. Why do they do it?

"You don't hang around here watching people do things for very
long," says Schefrin. "New lawyers . . . sink or swim." But an
attorney charges that opportunities for experience at the firm come at
the expense of supervision and training. One new lawyer was reportedly assigned a case at 12:30 p.m. on which jury impanelment was
scheduled for 1:00 p.m.

"Amazingly," says one attorney of Lovett, "he has a knack for
hiring people who think they deserve only what they get." But he

reports that one of his colleagues was so dissatisfied with salary levels and caseloads that he investigated the possibility of organizing a lawyers' union in a firm that originally specialized in labor law. He learned that attorneys at the firm have too much managerial control to be considered employees under the National Labor Relations Act.

Creating Order

Annexed to the gray brick building that contains Lovett's office is a wooden house that has been converted to offices; it is hard to tell from inside that it was formerly residential. Most of the firm's litigators—who handle non-compensation cases—have their offices there. It is so isolated that one litigator doubts Lovett is aware that the litigator has developed a speciality since he was hired.

Lovett does not have the time to supervise litigation, says an attorney; Lovett runs the firm as if it were a four-person operation even though it is too large for that. He says that the litigators consciously decided to organize their work, make it more professional, and exert more control over it.

The attorneys at the firm who handle neither workers' compensation nor domestic cases (which are, in effect, separate departments) hold a weekly intake meeting. With Lovett rarely in attendance, they discuss and assign new cases. The meetings also produce decisions not to litigate 20 percent of the intake, according to one of the litigators. He says one reason is that the firm is already litigating too many "dogs" that were accepted three or four years ago.

In addition to the weekly intake meetings, there is a weekly meeting of all the firm's attorneys to make sure that upcoming court cases are covered and to discuss problematic cases and general office policy. These meetings start at 6 p.m. and can last three hours. Lovett usually attends.

Lovett says he also receives weekly memos, not too detailed, from attorneys reporting on their work. One attorney, however, says he is unaware of such memos, and another attorney says that he consults with Lovett only irregularly and informally.

Flying Cars

Bruce Sondler has been with Lovett's firm for four years. A litigator, he specializes in personal injury, property damage, auto accidents, and breach of contract. One issue he faces as a litigator arises when an insurance company offers $8,000 to settle a case he is convinced is worth $20,000.

If the client insists that he doesn't want to go into the court-room and believes that it is in his best interest, I'll take the $8,000. . . .   My duty to that client is to do the best job I can within the bounds of the law.   My duty to myself and my future client is to protect them the best I can.   If I start settling every case for a minimal amount of money, I'm not going to be able to command what is necessary for other clients.   So what do you do?

Sondler believes that "a client is never more honest than on the first day, because a client is never more uncomfortable with you than on the first day."

I'll let them tell me the story of what happened.   And I'll tell my client the weak points of the case in the beginning, and I'll make notes to myself of what I told the client in the beginning, because I'm not going to let that client come back to me a year or two years down the line, and have them say, "You told me this, that, or the other."

Sondler does not want his client's story breaking down on the witness stand:

I must handle 200 T-intersection accidents a year.   Somebody's taking a left-handed turn and gets hit, or taking a right-hand turn and gets hit by on-coming traffic.   Now, more times than not you ask the client, "How far away was that car when you first saw it?". . . .   The client will tell you, "That car was 100 to 200 feet away when I saw it."
"And where were you?"
"I was stopped with my blinker on."
"And what did you do while it was 100 feet away?"
"I started to take a left-hand turn."
You hear so many of these cases.   You, as a lawyer, going home at night, on many occasions, stop, wait until oncoming traffic is . . . 25 feet away and start to take your turn as slow as you want.   And time after time, you don't get hit.   You don't even come close. . . .   It makes it more difficult to take the client's story at face value, because I can see that this flying car story just doesn't follow. . . .   I don't care if they have headlights on, if it's broad daylight, midnight; they don't fly, but people believe the stories.   They've built it into their own head.   Half the time, it's a kid who tells that story to their parents, because he doesn't want to go home and say, "Dad, I made a mistake.   I didn't see him; I didn't look."   Or it's a wife who doesn't want to tell her husband, or a husband who doesn't want to tell his wife. . . .   It starts . . . within the family.   People don't want to admit they were wrong.   "He hit

me; therefore, he must be at fault". . . . When a client comes in the first time, don't let him come in with any other member of the family who wasn't involved.

Sondler discusses evaluating personal injuries:

If a bone doesn't set properly, if a leg is going to be shorter than another leg, . . . if it [a break]'s over by a joint, is there going to be arthritis? . . . What's a broken leg worth? No two broken bones are worth the same thing. Depending on where the break was, depending on the type of breaks, depending on the individual. . . . [L]et's say you trip in a restaurant, fall up against the jukebox and you fracture three ribs, and [in a similar accident, a] 67–year–old man also fractures three ribs. Are his ribs going to heal as completely as yours? Is he going to heal as quick as you are? Is his case worth more or less because he's elderly and he isn't as mobile as you are? Maybe he doesn't have the earning capacity, etc. These are all things to be considered.

Sondler says he sees four or five clients and works on up to 30 cases (not including phones calls from clients) each day. He usually takes calls as they come in.

Sondler says it is not always feasible to engage in complete discovery. "It's one of the things that you explain to a client in the beginning." The constraint comes from monetary cost, not time pressure.

The backlog in the state's superior courts, which have sole jurisdiction of matters worth over $10,000 and concurrent jurisdiction with the state's district courts over matters worth between $5,000 and $10,000, is three years. The backlog in district courts, which have sole jurisdiction of matters valued under $5,000, is about six months. "So you can pretty much do the discovery you want to do," says Sondler. "I wouldn't say that time constraint is a problem."

It's a hell of a lot easier now, granted, becoming involved with the computers and the word processors. I can get discovery out of here in no time at all because I can look at a thousand interrogatories and pick the 30 most relevant to the case, as 30 is the maximum that the court allows me to ask. . . .

When he goes to trial Sondler settles 75 percent of his cases. One thing he fears is to have his $8,000 case heard by a jury with members who have just heard a $150,000 case. He senses the jury members wondering:

Why are they bothering the court system with this case? Why are they taking up this judge and this courtroom and this jury and these days for $8,000?

Lovett says his firm could not survive on $10,000 personal injury cases; it has had a few multi-million dollar ones. Personal injury settlements and awards average $50,000 for his firm, he says.

Eating Peas

By 6 p.m., Lovett's office and waiting room are empty of clients. Twelve employees have drifted into Lovett's office. Most of them are male attorneys (the firm has two female attorneys), winding down after work. Someone mentions an insurance company; an attorney suggests "We'd rather lose than pay" is its attitude. "Make me," another suggests. One litigator notices that he is bleeding through the pants leg of his summer suit. "Is this work-related?" he muses. Lovett is still on the phone.

It takes half an hour, but the badinage turns into business again; the work day is not over. The door is closed, and discussion begins over whether to hire the lawyer who has applied to join the firm. The firm plans to take on two new associates, one for criminal, one for civil work.

Lehman, Betz, and five male attorneys are left in Lovett's office. One attorney runs down the applicant's qualifications and background; the applicant's law school is not mentioned until midway through. The attorneys relate what they know of the applicant. One says his impression is that the applicant delves into cases too much, which is not desirable for fast case turnover.

The attorneys question whether the applicant hustles, whether he is experienced or abrasive. There is a slight controversy over whether abrasiveness is an attribute. Lovett decides the issue; he does not want to hire anyone abrasive. (An associate says later that the firm values in attorneys the ability to think quickly on their feet and, if necessary, to make convincing representations they do not know are true.)

Lovett decides to hire the applicant on a one-week trial basis. (Later he decides that the new lawyer will be paid $200 a week.) At 6:55 p.m., Lovett sees one last client.

During the winter, Lovett frequently works 14 hours a day on weekdays and six hours a day on weekends. He works so late that he carries a .25 magnum, for which he is licensed, for protection. His summer hours are not as long, and he has recently begun taking every sixth week off. "I work like hell and play like hell," he says. His upcoming week's vacation starts as soon as he leaves the office.

Lovett sees personal injury and workers' compensation practice as one of the most important legal practices.

Take a compensation case. That person, if he loses his case,
he's done forever. If he's a working man with five children
and he loses that pay, everyone loses. He doesn't get paid his
weekly compensation, his kids have no money, [he can't] support them with secondary education. That just multiplies
down; that can go from generation to generation. So the
person who is injured, although he's not making a million
dollars, but at least gets something to get by on while he is
incapacitated. He doesn't lose his house. He doesn't lose his
car. He's able to make things go along for a certain period of
time until he's able to get back on his feet. So in winning his
case, I would feel that I'm really doing something positive.

"I feel everybody should do something to add to the betterment of
mankind. That should be a goal. That's my goal," says Lovett. "I feel
I can best do it by what I'm doing, in helping the working man, the
little guy, work his way through the bureaucracy."

Lovett says he received "zero" inquiries from students at prestigious law schools about working at his firm for the summer. He knows
that most of the students at those schools do not consider practicing
compensation law.

It's all right to shy away from it once you know [what] you are
shying away from. . . . [I]f you don't like peas, fine, eat
them once. If you don't like them, spit them out and don't eat
them again, but at least eat them once. The same thing with
law.

Lovett enjoys his work, and is well compensated for it. But there is
another reward.

It's a good feeling, a feeling that you have accomplished something in a small way, granted, . . . [by] winning a case and
taking on a corporation, a large corporation, or a bank, or the
state, or an insurance company, and helping somebody in some
small way. [It's] very rewarding, very.

Workers' Compensation

History

Workers' compensation, America's first social insurance program,
pays benefits on a no-fault basis to employees who are injured or
become ill as a result of their employment. The states administer the
workers' compensation system and today every state has one.

Workers' compensation laws were enacted in response to the failure of the tort system to respond adequately to the high rate of

industrial accidents in the late nineteenth and early twentieth centuries. Prior to the enactment of workers' compensation laws an employee who was injured at work could only recover compensation from his employer by bringing a tort action. To prevail the worker had to prove that his injury was caused by the employer's negligence. It was difficult for a worker to prove negligence, but even if he could his employer often escaped liability through three powerful common law defenses: assumption of risk, the fellow-servant rule, and contributory negligence.

Dissatisfaction with tort law prompted most states to enact employers' liability laws to modify the assumption of risk doctrine and the fellow-servant rule. But even with these modifications, recovery under the tort system continued to be unsatisfactory and the states soon recognized that further reforms were needed.

Progressive employer groups played a major role in the reform movement by arguing that business should pay the social cost of injuries that are part of the production process, that business should have a financial incentive to make the workplace safe, and that predictable and insurable workers' compensation payments were preferable to the uncertain risks of large tort judgments. What employers obtained from workers' compensation was freedom from tort liability (and its attendant risk of jury-set punitive damages or pain and suffering awards). As one commentator has noted:

> The unique "bargain" struck by workers' compensation laws remains an unusually clear example of compromise between the traditional rights of individuals and the practical necessities of industrial economies. Under these laws, the injured employee surrenders his (or her) right to full compensation for nonmedical costs in [re]turn for his employer's prompt payment of medical and subsistence expenses. This plan is meant to avoid a costly and time-consuming legal process to determine whether and to what degree the employer's or the employee's negligence contributed to the injury. The employer, on the other hand, gives up the immunity which he would gain by disproving negligence in return for the certainty that his liability will be limited to a schedule of finite benefits set by a public body according to injury classes.[1]

Following the lead of other western industrialized nations, states began to enact workers' compensation laws in 1911. By 1948 every state had established a program.

---

[1] Shubert, *Foreword* to L. Darling–Hammond & T. Kniesner, The Law and Economics of Workers' Compensation at v (Rand Institute for Civil Justice, 1980).

Structure

Workers' compensation programs require employers to provide cash benefits, medical care, and rehabilitative services for workers who suffer injuries or illnesses arising out of and in the course of their employment. All laws provide benefits for workers with occupational diseases, but they do not all cover every form of occupational disease.

Cash benefits compensate injured workers for lost income and earning capacity. These benefits are classified as temporary total, temporary partial, permanent total, permanent partial, and death benefits. Temporary total benefits are paid for injuries that prevent an employee from working until he is fully recovered. Temporary partial benefits are paid during a period of reduced earnings and cease when the worker returns to full wages or is found eligible for permanent total or permanent partial benefits. Permanent total benefits are paid to workers who are completely disabled for an indefinite time. Permanent partial benefits are paid to employees who suffer an impairment that causes a permanent but partial loss of wages or wage-earning capacity. If the worker is fatally injured, the employer is required to provide burial expenses and to pay benefits to specified dependent survivors. For each category of benefits, all states prescribe a maximum weekly payment. Some states place limits on duration or total amount or both for certain classes of benefits.

Workers' compensation programs provide medical benefits, usually without dollar or time limits. Most states also pay for medical and vocational rehabilitation for workers who suffer severe disabilities.

Employers meet their statutory obligation to compensate injured workers through various forms of insurance. Private insurance carriers pay approximately two-thirds of all workers' compensation benefits. State-run insurance funds pay about 23 percent of all claims. The remainder are covered by employers through self-insurance.

In cases in which an injured worker's right to recovery is undisputed, benefit payments may be initiated by either agreement or direct payment. The agreement system operates in a majority of states. Under that system, the employer does not begin payments until it and the injured worker have reached an agreement in writing regarding the benefits to be paid. Because of the delays and potential bargaining disadvantages occasioned by the agreement system, many workers retain lawyers even though their claims are uncontested. If an agreement cannot be reached, the claim is referred to the workers' compensation commission. In direct payment states, the employer must begin paying benefits to the injured worker within a prescribed number of days, or else file a notice with the state administrative agency of its intent to contest the claim.

After an employer's liability has been established, the extent or duration of that liability may be limited through compromise and release settlements. Under these settlements, the employer pays benefits to the injured worker in a lump sum in exchange for a release from further liability. This system has both advantages and disadvantages for the injured worker and for society:

> [Compromise and release agreements] may deprive the employee of his rights to medical care should the need recur, . . . they may seriously underestimate the extent or duration of the impairment, and . . . they may later shift the costs of the disability to other social insurance programs if the employee has expended the amount of the award before he can return to work. On the other hand, such agreements may reduce the administrative load of the state agency; they may allow compensation to a worker when there are legitimate doubts concerning employer liability and prevent costly litigation which would otherwise ensue; and they may contribute to the employee's vocational rehabilitation by allowing him to pursue training opportunities or to invest in a small business.[2]

Current Data on Workers' Compensation Coverage and Costs

In 1984, more than 90 percent of the American workforce (82.6 million workers) were covered by workers' compensation programs. Employers paid a total of $25.1 billion in insurance premiums. Of the $19.5 billion the insurers paid out in compensation, $13.1 billion was for cash benefits and $6.4 billion was for medical care and rehabilitation costs. Private insurance carriers paid $10.6 billion of the total benefits, state and federal funds paid $5.3 billion, and self-insurers paid $3.6 billion.[3]

The Workers' Compensation System and Litigation

One goal of the workers' compensation system was to reduce substantially the need for litigation. This ideal has never been realized in practice. Some commentators place the continued need for litigation in a broad perspective:

> The dream of a self-administering system has not been realized because (a) determinations of compensability and extent of

---

[2] L. Darling–Hammond & T. Kniesner, *supra* note 1, at 37.

[3] Price, *Workers' Compensation: Coverage, Benefits, and Costs, 1984,* 49 Social Security Bulletin, No. 12, at 20, 23 (1986).

disability are controversial; (b) state agencies have not sufficiently participated in clarifying statutes and settling disputes;
and (c) societal values have, over time, expanded the purview
of the system and obscured the differences between its goals
and those of other social insurance mechanisms. Litigation is
often a technique for rearguing the social policy underlying the
system. . . . The adversarial atmosphere surrounding the
workers' compensation system may explain why many workers
choose not to submit injury and occupational disease claims to
the system but to a variety of other social insurance programs
instead. . . .

[T]he changing view of the compensation system's boundaries, reflected in expanded coverage and broader definitions of
employer liability, has created an atmosphere of uncertainty
and of increased litigation that is troubling to workers, employers, and insurers alike. The process of renegotiating those
boundaries has engendered debate over issues of causation and
employer fault, third party liability, compensation adequacy
and overlap, and the efficacy of current administrative practices. Much of this debate is based on the underlying tension
in the concept of workers' compensation between the principles
and goals of liability-based compensation and those of social
insurance for health and income maintenance.[4]

There are also specific structural explanations for why injured
workers continue to litigate. First, workers whose claims are disputed
must establish their right to compensation. Second, several gaps in the
system afford workers an opportunity to sue their employers in tort.
Third, workers can seek damages from third parties whose actions
contributed to their injuries.

1. Disputed Claims

When an injured worker files a claim for benefits, the employer's
insurer can contest it on one of two grounds. First, the insurer can
argue that the injury is not compensable. Second, the insurer can
admit liability but challenge the extent of disability caused by the
injury.

Compensable Injuries. The most frequently litigated question in
the workers' compensation system is whether or not a particular injury
is compensable. The requirement that an injury "arise out of and in
the course of employment" can present difficult questions of causation.
For example, how can a worker prove that an increased risk of heart
attack or chronic nervousness arose out of employment? Similarly, is a

---

[4] L. Darling–Hammond & T. Kniesner, *supra* note 1, at xiv, 6–7.

worker acting in the course of employment who becomes injured during an altercation in the firm lunch room? Occupational diseases, which originally were not covered by workers' compensation, pose special problems. Not only is it difficult to establish a causal link between a worker's job and a disease, but the employer's insurer may use the long latency period to question whether the injury occurred while the worker was employed.

Extent of Disability. Even if the worker can prove that an injury is compensable, the insurer can still dispute the extent of disability. Controversies frequently arise over the injured worker's medical record. This record may be incomplete, inconclusive, or incorrect. Where the record is sufficient, the insurer may challenge the worker's interpretation of it. Some injuries, such as back pain, cannot be objectively determined and the medical record is of little help. Beyond the uncertainty inherent in the medical record, a determination of how debilitating the injury is or how long the worker will be impaired is affected by a host of personal factors, including the worker's age, weight, and lifestyle.

The following table summarizes the distribution of these two sources of disputes:

Table 1 *

PERCENTAGE OF WORKERS' COMPENSATION CLAIMS CONTESTED BY CASE TYPE AND REASONS FOR CONTESTING

	Occupational Disease	Heart	Accident
% of Claims Contested	62.7	55.2	9.8
Primary Reason for Contesting Claims			
Work relatedness (%)	72.5	76.0	20.6
Extent of disability (%)	12.0	11.6	55.8
Other issues (%)	15.5	12.4	23.6
Subsample	1,052	434	8,146

Claim disputes create additional costs for the workers' compensation system. According to a federal government study:

about 60 percent of the [Workers' Compensation] premium dollar [goes] for workers' compensation benefits, from which, however, must be deducted the amounts injured workers must pay their own lawyers. The latter amounts have been estimated at about eight percent of the benefits so that it appears that about 52 percent of the premium dollar goes to the claimant as

* Reproduced from L. Darling–Hammond & T. Kniesner, *supra* note 1, at 33.

benefits. The most recent data indicate an insurance loss adjustment expense factor of about 9 percent of premiums. Thus the total for adjudication of claims amounts to about 17 percent of benefits [insurance adjustment expense plus claimant payments to their lawyers].[5]

2. Tort Actions Against Employers

The workers' compensation system was designed to eliminate job-related tort actions against employers by guaranteeing benefits to workers through an administrative process. Although the number of lawsuits brought by employees has been reduced significantly, workers continue to sue their employers in tort. The principal reason for this is that, while the workers' compensation system guarantees the worker a minimum amount of support during recuperation, the tort system offers a chance for full compensation for all losses.

An injured employee may bring a tort action against an employer if:

(1) The injury occurred outside the course of employment and was the result of the employer's negligence;

(2) The injury is not considered to have arisen out of and in the course of employment (for example, certain occupational diseases are caused by the employer's negligence but are not covered by the workers' compensation act);

(3) The employer harmed the worker with a "deliberate intent to injure";

(4) The injury is covered by the Federal Employer's Liability Act (for railroad workers) or the Jones Act (for maritime workers); or

(5) The employer is dealing with the worker in a "dual capacity" (for example, the employer manufactured the equipment the worker is using or provides medical care to the worker) and the injury is caused by the employer's exercise of the second function.

3. Third Party Lawsuits

A worker barred from suing an employer may still recover additional compensation from a third party. For example, an injured worker may sue the manufacturer of the defective machine or product that caused the injury. Third party actions arise frequently and result in substantial awards. According to one estimate reported in a study by the Rand Corporation's Institute for Civil Justice, 31,500 of the 1.5

---

[5] Interdepartmental Workers' Compensation Task Force, Workers' Compensation: Is There a Better Way? 9 (1977).

million compensation claims filed in 1974 resulted in lawsuits against third parties. The damage awards in these cases totaled $1.5 billion.

Discussion Questions

1. What do the best lawyers do for their clients? They help them understand complicated official systems; they give wise and detached guidance; and they share their "connections" and experience in the ways of the world. On the surface Raul Lovett looks very different. For example, what do you think of his Mickey Mouse routine? Presumably he does it to give clients an impression different from the austere tradition just described. Mickey Mouse says that he is against the system, not part of it. And it advertises effectively as do his ads in the yellow pages, his regular appearances on television, and his highly publicized appearance on a picket line. Do these seem unprofessional to you? Is Lovett merely a modern example of someone furnishing the traditional services but to a new clientele? If he is something new and different, what are his innovative contributions?

2. Is what Lovett offers the traditional services—expert knowledge, wise counsel, connections and experience—supplemented by an atmosphere that makes the client feel like something other than a piece on a legal chessboard? Even if any number of lawyers were equally good at obtaining maximum awards for a particular injury, perhaps many clients would want Lovett's service because it treats them with informality and good humor, while conveying a sense of independence from the system and of power brought to their cause.

Which of the following do you think Lovett is doing and selling? Does he sell expert knowledge of the system and its rules? In this view the client has a problem. Lovett knows the rules and procedures and can get the maximum outcome. It is more than worthwhile paying his fee because the amount by which he can be expected to increase your award is well in excess of what he charges. Does he instead sell assertiveness and confidence to people who would be intimidated in even the relatively informal setting of a workers' compensation proceeding, especially when faced by the representative of a large insurance company? In this view he is an intermediary between injured working people and a complicated bureaucratic apparatus that they could not successfully approach on their own. He is empowering clients, and making sure they receive their due less by reason of his expert knowledge than by reason of his confidence and assertiveness in a situation that is otherwise intimidating. Is he a person whose contacts and experience the client is purchasing? In this view it is not his expert knowledge of the procedures and the rules but his collegial relations with insurance company adjustors and his knowledge of their ways and the ways of the administrative judges which are worth 20 percent of the client's award.

Perhaps what brings clients to Lovett is less the hope of receiving an additional award than the supportive relationship he provides at a time when people are in great need of such support. In this view, Lovett sells a service. He has studied the market and has realized that clients want exactly what he supplies—including the hugs, the "hi-byes," the waiting time in the office (and on "hold" on the telephone), and the business cards. No client is forced to come to Lovett, yet he has a large market share of the total workers' compensation business in Rhode Island. In this view, Lovett is a successful businessman in a competitive environment.

Which interpretation is most true? If all are true, is the total picture compatible with your sense of a lawyer? Of the legal profession? Of your own role as a legal professional?

Would you be good at Lovett's work? Would you like to work for him? Is it not clear that he and his associates provide important services to persons who would otherwise not be so adequately represented? If you agree with that statement, are you willing to do Lovett's work yourself? If not, why not?

3. What is wrong with the U.S. Workers' Compensation system? Does it use lawyers too much? Too little? The original goal of workers' compensation was to do without lawyers and operate at low expense. The study cited at p. 290 above concluded that injured workers received as benefits only 52 percent of each Workers' Compensation premium dollar. One reason lawyers play a large and expensive role (as they do in all states—not only in Rhode Island) is that a simple system has become complicated as rules have been adapted to meet a vast range of fact situations. Another reason is that it is a *system*, more open to an expert who knows the officials and the routines. But should we and can we replace the current program with one that is cheaper to administer and uses fewer lawyers? There are two ways in which this system could be changed so as to make lawyers less necessary to claimants:

(a) The system could be made simpler. Is it inevitable that rules and distinctions proliferate? How would you make workers' compensation less complicated? Even if you could, lawyers might still be needed. Keep in mind that workers' compensation is part of a multi-dimensional system of income transfers (unemployment insurance, retirement, other disability programs, food stamps, health benefits), that income tax consequences intersect with worker income calculations, and that a worker is affected by regulatory arrangements (occupational safety and health, anti-discrimination, union authority and responsibility, and so on). Many workers' compensation claimants must consider rights in tort against the employer or a third party. The injured or sick worker can benefit from a great deal of sophisticated advice, and also from expert help in making his or her way through the various procedural stages required to obtain what may well be the worker's entitlements.

(b) The worker could be provided competent representation by someone other than a lawyer. This could be:

(i) A union. About 17 percent of private sector workers belong to a union. That percentage has been declining steadily.

(ii) Government. In Europe, workers (and other claimants under income-transfer programs) expect a government office to assist them in obtaining what they deserve. Individuals have greater respect for the accuracy of the information they will receive and the fairness with which they will be treated. Americans are more likely to distrust government and to expect that adversarial challenges to government decisions will be effective. Is that a good or a bad thing about our system of government? If it is bad, how could we begin the process of changing it?

b. The Defendants' Lawyers

Asbestos Litigation *

Lively Wilson

Lively Wilson remembers the lawyers in Bowling Green, the small Kentucky town where he grew up, as upstanding citizens who contributed significantly to the community. When he graduated from Western Kentucky State College in 1948, Wilson toyed with the idea of entering the ministry. But feeling admiration and respect for the Bowling Green lawyers, he enrolled instead at Harvard Law School.

Upon graduating from Harvard in the spring of 1951, Wilson took a job as Secretary to the Kentucky Public Service Commission. After two years, he left the government for private practice, and joined a nine-lawyer firm in Louisville.

The law firm had a general practice. As Wilson recalls:

> We were a collection of eight or nine generalists. We did a little bit of everything that had to be done. We did wills and estates. We administered trusts. We did a little labor law. We did a little tort work. We did whatever the client had to offer.

The firm's largest clients were utility and insurance companies, and much of the law work involved defending these clients against tort suits. In the early years, Wilson spent his time writing opinion letters for the Illinois Central Railroad and handling automobile accident claims arising from rear-end collisions.

Over time, the firm grew to more than forty lawyers. As it expanded, its members quit doing "a little bit of everything" and began to specialize in particular fields of law. Wilson concentrated on trying liability lawsuits and eventually became a nationally recognized defense attorney. Wilson's reputation as a defense lawyer prompted Johns–Manville, then the country's largest asbestos manufacturer, to retain him in 1976 to represent it in a suit brought on behalf of the estate of William Sampson, a worker who had died as a result of his exposure to asbestos.

Background: Asbestos Litigation Generally

Asbestos is a tensile, fibrous mineral with a high resistance to heat, fire, and corrosion. Together, these qualities make asbestos well-suited

---

* This case is based on an interview with Lively Wilson and on published sources.

for a wide variety of uses. Since 1900, the United States has consumed more than 30 million tons of asbestos in some 3,000 products, including electrical insulation, brakedrums, wallboard, pot holders, and pipes.

Despite its utility, asbestos can be very dangerous. When inhaled, asbestos can cause several diseases, some of which may remain dormant for as long as 40 years after exposure. The three most serious asbestos-related illnesses are asbestosis (a clogging and scarring of the lungs that severely reduces breathing capacity), mesothelioma (a rapid and fatal form of cancer that attacks the lining of the chest and abdomen), and bronchogenic carcinoma (a type of lung cancer).

Asbestos disease is dose-related; the heavier the exposure, the greater the likelihood of contracting the disease. Since the 1960s, industry has reduced workplace exposures, and the incidence of serious asbestosis has dropped markedly. However, cigarette smoking has a synergistic effect, and the risk of lung cancer to a cigarette smoker exposed to substantial quantities of asbestos can be as high as 50 times the risk to the general population.

These diseases are not confined to individuals directly involved in the mining and manufacture of asbestos. They also affect persons who install and remove asbestos-containing materials, who reside near asbestos plants, and who live in the same houses as workers exposed to asbestos. In all, as many as 27 million Americans may have been exposed to dangerous levels of asbestos in one form or another.

By far the heaviest exposure to asbestos has been in the workplace. Between 8 and 11 million people have come into contact with asbestos because of their work. Four million of these were exposed to asbestos while employed by the United States government in naval shipyards during the Second World War.

Since the early 1970s, more than 30,000 people have filed claims against asbestos manufacturers in courts around the country seeking compensation for injuries due to asbestos exposure. In the coming decades, tens of thousands of new claims will probably be filed.

The onslaught of asbestos product liability claims can be traced to the ruling by the United States Court of Appeals for the Fifth Circuit in *Borel v. Fibreboard Paper Products Corporation*, 493 F.2d 1076 (5th Cir. 1973). The *Borel* court held a manufacturer liable under Section 402A of the Restatement of Torts for failure to warn a worker who died of asbestosis about the dangers of asbestos exposure.

Section 402A states: "One who sells any product in a defective condition unreasonably dangerous to the user or consumer . . . is subject to liability for physical harm thereby caused to the ultimate user or consumer." Generally a product is "unreasonably dangerous" if the danger associated with its use is "reasonably foreseeable" and "on balance, the utility of the product does not outweigh the magnitude of the danger." *Borel,* 493 F.2d at 1087. Where a product's danger is not greater than its utility, it is said to be "unavoidably unsafe" because it possesses "both unparalleled utility and unquestioned danger." 493 F.2d at 1088. A manufacturer can market an "unavoidably unsafe" product, but it must warn the consumer or user of the dangers involved. Otherwise the sale is "unreasonably dangerous."

Prior to *Borel,* courts had never applied Section 402A to asbestos products. In that case, however, the court recognized for the first time that:

> The utility of an insulation product containing asbestos may outweigh the known or foreseeable risk to the insulation workers and thus justify its marketing. The product could still be unreasonably dangerous, however, if unaccompanied by adequate warnings. 493 F.2d at 1089.

According to the court's application of Section 402A, the case turned on whether the dangers associated with the asbestos product in question were "reasonably foreseeable" by the defendant. Asserting that an asbestos manufacturer is an "expert," the court held that it must "keep abreast of scientific knowledge, discoveries, and advances and is presumed to know what is imparted thereby," *id.,* and that it has a duty to test and inspect its products in a manner "commensurate with the dangers involved." *Id.* at 1090. The court then concluded that, because there was sufficient evidence of the dangers of asbestos in the medical literature at the time the defendant manufactured the asbestos products to which the plaintiff was exposed, the manufacturer had a duty to warn workers handling its products. Because the defendant had breached this duty, the court deemed the product "unreasonably dangerous" and held the defendant liable under Section 402A.

After *Borel,* asbestos manufacturers sought to escape liability by proving that the dangers associated with their products first became "reasonably foreseeable" in 1964 when Dr. Irving J. Selikoff of the Mount Sinai School of Medicine published the results of his two-year study of asbestos-insulation workers.

Lively Wilson's Involvement in the Asbestos Litigation

Lively Wilson first became involved in asbestos litigation in 1976 when he defended Johns–Manville in the suit brought by William Sampson's administrator. After working with asbestos products manufactured by Johns–Manville, Mr. Sampson developed mesothelioma and died in 1972. Although Mr. Sampson was exposed to asbestos prior to 1964, and Wilson argued that Johns–Manville did not know before that date that exposure to asbestos in Mr. Sampson's circumstances was unsafe, the jury awarded the estate $90,000.

After the Sampson case, Johns–Manville retained Lively Wilson to represent it in a number of other asbestos suits. In these cases Wilson continued to argue that under tort law Johns–Manville should not be liable to victims who were exposed to asbestos products prior to 1964.

As the volume of asbestos litigation grew, plaintiffs' lawyers searched for evidence about when manufacturers learned asbestos was dangerous. They unearthed two key findings. First, in 1975, a plaintiff's lawyer deposed Dr. Kenneth Smith, a former medical director with Johns–Manville, who testified that the company had considered placing warning labels on its asbestos insulation products in the early 1950s. Second, in 1976, another plaintiff's lawyer discovered minutes of meetings the Asbestos Textile Institute held in 1944. These indicated that the institute's members, including Johns–Manville, Raybestos–Manhattan, and others, knew then that working with asbestos could pose hazards.

Confronted with the plaintiffs' evidence, Lively Wilson adopted a three-part strategy to establish that Johns–Manville did not know of the dangers associated with asbestos before Dr. Selikoff's findings were published in 1964. First, he emphasized the results of a 1946 study conducted by Walter Fleischer and Philip Drinker of the Harvard School of Public Health. They studied military shipyard workers who installed asbestos insulation and concluded that these workers were not involved in a hazardous occupation. Thus, even though asbestos manufacturers may have known their employees were at risk, they did not believe workers who used their products during part of their work also were at risk. Second, Wilson introduced this information through two highly regarded medical experts who testified that the medical community had no knowledge of the dangers of asbestos until 1964. These witnesses were especially persuasive because they were older and more experienced than the plaintiffs' experts who, as Wilson told the jury, had not even started medical school when Selikoff was conducting his studies. Third, Wilson argued that workers using Johns–Manville's products were not exposed to asbestos beyond the levels permitted at that time by the United States Government.

Taken together, these arguments provided support for the claim by Johns–Manville and other asbestos manufacturers that they did not know of the risks attending asbestos until at least 1964. Although plaintiffs had achieved a number of victories early on, by 1978 plaintiffs and defendants had each won eight of the sixteen asbestos suits that had gone to trial.

The Plaintiffs' Breakthrough

Lawyers for plaintiffs continued to search for evidence to counter the asbestos manufacturers' defense. Their most important discovery came in 1977 when Carl Asch, an attorney for plaintiffs, found the papers of Sumner Simpson, a former chief executive officer with Raybestos–Manhattan. In 1930, a British trade journal had published the results of a study indicating that exposure to asbestos in English factories caused asbestosis among workers. In an exchange of letters in 1935, Simpson and Vandiver Brown, Johns–Manville's corporate counsel, discussed the possibility of publishing these findings in an American asbestos industry magazine. They decided that, because the amount of exposure in American factories was less than in British factories, it would be best if they did not publicize these findings in the United States. Plaintiffs portrayed this as a calculated cover-up.

By 1978, plaintiffs' lawyers were using the Simpson–Brown correspondence to persuade juries that manufacturers knew their products' dangers well before 1964. Subsequent disclosures buttressed this argument. In late 1978 and early 1979, attorneys for plaintiffs discovered three additional pieces of evidence: (1) the minutes of a 1933 Johns–Manville board of directors meeting at which the directors authorized the company's president to settle eleven pending lawsuits by Manville manufacturing employees who had contracted asbestosis; (2) the notes of several health review committee meetings held in 1957 and 1958 indicating that Johns–Manville had developed a corporate policy of concealing from sick employees the true nature of their illnesses; and (3) dozens of workers' compensation claims that insulators had filed in the 1950s while working for contract units Johns–Manville and other asbestos manufacturers owned.

Mass Tort Litigation

The claims against Johns–Manville and other manufacturers, distributors, and suppliers of asbestos-containing materials constitute mass tort litigation on an unprecedented scale. By July 1985, asbestos victims had filed more than 33,000 lawsuits. As many as 200,000 more may be brought in the next thirty years. On average, four to five years pass between the filing of a claim and settlement or trial.

A major study by the Rand Corporation's Institute for Civil Justice found that between 1970 and 1982, the asbestos litigation cost defendant companies almost $1 billion. For every dollar spent, the victim or his family received 39 cents, with trial costs and legal fees accounting for the remaining 61 cents. The Rand study also estimated that future outlays by companies defending against asbestos lawsuits will range from $4 billion to $87 billion.

Alternatives to the Tort System

Congressional Response

Faced with mounting asbestos lawsuits and damage awards, industry representatives turned to Congress for statutory relief. The first bill to deal with their concerns was the Asbestos Health Hazards Compensation Act introduced in the House in August 1977. The bill's sponsor was Millicent Fenwick, a Republican representative from New Jersey whose congressional district included the town of Manville. Fenwick's proposal, drafted with the assistance of Johns–Manville's attorneys, provided for the United States government to compensate all asbestos victims who filed claims before January 1, 1980, and for all subsequent claims to be paid out of a fund made up of contributions by the asbestos and tobacco industries and the federal government. The bill was never voted out of committee.

In December 1981, Representative Fenwick reintroduced the legislation in a substantially altered form. The second version provided for asbestos victims to be compensated from a fund administered by the federal treasury but created only with contributions from the asbestos and tobacco industries. This bill also died in committee.

In the meantime, asbestos manufacturers were attempting to have the Senate enact legislation as well. John McKinney, Johns–Manville's chairman and chief executive officer, spoke with Gary Hart, a Senator from Colorado, the state in which the company's headquarters were located, and Johns–Manville's Washington lobbyists conferred with Senator Hart's aides. In 1980, Senator Hart introduced a comprehensive program that called for existing state workers' compensation boards to administer asbestos claims based on standards for recovery set by a commission composed of government, health, labor, and industry representatives. It also provided for various "responsible parties," including employers, mining companies, manufacturers, importers, and federal and state governments, to compensate successful claimants. This bill was never voted out of committee. Senator Hart reintroduced the legislation the following year, but again it died in committee.

Uniform Product Liability Law

Bob Kasten, a Republican senator from Wisconsin, has proposed a federal Uniform Product Liability Law. This law would preempt all state causes of action, whether in tort or contract, that serve as a basis for recovering losses caused by a product sold in interstate commerce. Several of its provisions would be favorable to manufacturers defending against asbestos claims. First, the law would eliminate liability for injuries resulting solely from failure to warn by requiring a claimant to prove that a manufacturer was negligent because it knew, or should have known, that its product was "defective." Second, the law would exculpate a manufacturer who had failed to warn the immediate users of the dangers associated with its product if the manufacturer had advised retailers or employers of the potential hazards. Third, the bill would prohibit an asbestos victim from suing a manufacturer more than two years after he discovered, or should have discovered, his injury and its cause. Fourth, it would limit the circumstances under which a court could award punitive damages by requiring a claimant to prove with clear and convincing evidence (not a preponderance of the evidence) that the defendant had been reckless (not negligent). Although the jury could decide whether or not to award punitive damages, the judge would set the amount.

Senator Kasten first introduced the Uniform Product Liability Law in 1983. The Commerce Committee voted it out the following March, but that autumn opponents prevented it from coming to the Senate floor. Although Senator Kasten reintroduced the bill in January of 1985, a tie vote in May of that year stopped it from being reported out of the Commerce Committee. As of 1987, the Senate had not enacted the bill.

The Asbestos Claims Facility

Harry Wellington, the former Dean of Yale Law School, devised a plan for an administrative structure called the Asbestos Claims Facility (ACF) as an alternative to traditional tort litigation. Asbestos producers and their insurers organize and operate the ACF by subscribing to a formal "Agreement Concerning Asbestos Related Claims." The ACF is a non-profit corporation with a board of directors composed of representatives from the member producers and insurers, a chief executive officer hired by the board of directors, and a staff of trained professionals.

Instead of filing suit in court, an injured party has the option of bringing a claim to the ACF. An ACF attorney handles this claim for the manufacturers. The attorney's first priority is to negotiate a satisfactory settlement as early in the process as possible. If this does not work, the ACF attempts to arbitrate the claim. Only when all administrative efforts fail does the case go to court, where the ACF serves as defense counsel.

The ACF pays awards which are limited to compensatory damages. Each member producer and insurer pays the ACF a percentage of liability payments and allocated expenses based on the claims the ACF handles on its behalf.

Although twenty-eight asbestos producers, seventeen insurers, and five unidentified companies have subscribed to the ACF, the program has not received a large volume of cases. The principal stumbling block is the reluctance of plaintiffs' lawyers to participate in a dispute resolution system that does not include all producers and insurers and that prohibits punitive damage awards.

Changes in Laws to Limit Awards in Liability Suits

The tendency of juries to award large amounts in tort cases has affected the cost and availability of liability insurance. Liability insurance premiums have skyrocketed, increasing by as much as 100 percent in 1985 alone, and insurance companies have become more selective about who they will insure. Some members of high risk groups, such as doctors, cities, and some businesses, cannot purchase liability coverage at any price.

To deal with this situation, many states have changed, or are considering changing, their civil liability systems. These changes include capping awards for noneconomic losses (pain and suffering is often the largest part of a damage award), limiting punitive damages, curtailing joint and several liability, and allowing defendants to pay large damage awards over time rather than in a lump sum.

In April 1986 President Reagan endorsed federal legislation addressing this problem. His proposals included limits on pain and suffering and punitive damages, arrangements to permit damages to be paid in installments, and a sliding scale for attorneys' fees to reduce fee percentages as awards increased. In late September, majority leader Robert Dole removed this bill from the Senate legislative agenda, arguing that the Senate did not have time for a long debate on the bill before it adjourned in early October. The bill was not reintroduced in the new Congress.

Approaches in Other Countries

Other countries have adopted different approaches for dealing with torts. One approach has been to discourage litigation in various ways. For example, England and Australia prohibit contingency fee arrangements. They pay lawyers at an hourly rate and subsidize legal fees for qualified low-income plaintiffs. England, Australia, and Canada require the losing party to pay the other side's legal costs, including attorneys' fees, which often provides an incentive to settle before trial.

Another approach involves limiting damages. For example, Canada caps pain and suffering damages at $125,000. Judges instruct juries that they cannot award more than this amount and that they should only make maximum awards in the most severe cases.

A third approach lets judges, rather than juries, determine the amount of damage awards. England has adopted this system and has found that awards generally are lower and more predictable.

New Zealand's system for compensating accident victims is perhaps the most different from the United States' approach. In 1974, New Zealand abolished personal injury lawsuits and created a national no-fault compensation system. This system compensates injured parties for lost earnings up to an inflation-adjusted ceiling that was $350 a week in 1986. Victims also may receive a maximum lump sum of $8,500 for loss of a limb, unrelated to medical expenses, which the country's national health care system covers.

Johns–Manville's Bankruptcy Filing

On August 25, 1982, Lively Wilson traveled to Frankfort, Kentucky, to attend a hearing in one of the asbestos cases he was overseeing. In the early afternoon, he received a telephone call from a paralegal in his Louisville office who told him "something is amiss" and urged him to contact Johns–Manville's general counsel. Wilson immediately telephoned the company's head office in Denver. In that conversation, Wilson learned that his client was planning to file for bankruptcy.

The following day, August 26, Johns–Manville filed a Chapter 11 petition in the United States Bankruptcy Court for the Southern District of New York. The filing shocked the business community. At the time, Johns–Manville was the world's largest asbestos company. It employed 25,000 people, operated more than fifty factories and mines, and had an estimated net worth of $1.1 billion. By all accounts, Johns–Manville was in sound financial condition.

Despite this appearance, the company claimed that the asbestos litigation threatened its very existence. At the time of the bankruptcy filing, Johns–Manville had been named as a defendant in 16,500 lawsuits. The company commissioned a study by Epidemiology Resources, Inc., which concluded that it eventually could face as many as 52,000 claims, amounting to more than $2 billion in liability. Under standard accounting principles, this meant the company had to establish a reserve fund in that amount to guarantee that it could pay these claims. With a net worth of only $1.1 billion, the company was unable to set up this reserve.

In the press release announcing its Chapter 11 petition, Johns–Manville claimed that it was filing for bankruptcy as a last resort. Its insurers were disputing the company's liability coverage and had refused to renew its policies. Although half of all the plaintiffs who were suing Johns–Manville had been exposed to asbestos in the Navy shipyards during the 1940s, Manville's attempts to have the federal government accept responsibility had failed. And Congress had declined to enact a statutory system for compensating asbestos victims.

Johns–Manville's bankruptcy had an immediate effect on the many asbestos cases in which the company was a defendant. The filing froze all court proceedings, stopped all settlement payments, and prevented asbestos victims from filing new claims after six months. As Lively Wilson described it: "Manville went into bankruptcy on August 26 and all of a sudden there were no more cases to try."

Epilogue

On the morning of July 28, 1985, shortly before the third anniversary of the bankruptcy filing, three of Johns–Manville's top executives boarded a plane in Denver bound for New York. Once in New York, they joined the company's attorneys and traveled to the offices of Fried, Frank, Harris, Shriver & Jacobson overlooking New York harbor. There they met with Leon Silverman, a Fried, Frank partner the bankruptcy judge had appointed to represent the interests of the future claimants, and several of Mr. Silverman's associates. For the next eight hours, they hammered out the details of a comprehensive reorganization plan and, by the end of the day, had reached an agreement in principle.

The agreement was modified in negotiations and took effect December 31, 1986. The plan immunized the company's operating business unit from future lawsuits by setting up two separate funds that will receive more than $2.6 billion to settle all pending and future asbestos claims.

The first fund, a $2.5 billion trust based on immediate contributions from Johns–Manville and its insurers and annual payments out of the company's earnings over the next twenty-five years, will compensate victims for personal injuries and losses. Of this, only $5 million will be earmarked for punitive damages. Johns–Manville will set up a facility, not unlike the Asbestos Claims Facility Professor Wellington recommended, to administer the fund.

The second fund will pay property damage claims based on the costs of removing asbestos from buildings. Johns–Manville created it with an initial contribution of $125 million, and it may be supplemented in the future with several hundred million dollars from insurance payments, company earnings, and unclaimed proceeds from the personal injury fund.

Affected parties did not endorse the reorganization plan unanimously. Johns–Manville's trade creditors and equity holders argued that the plan unfairly favors health claimants. Some representatives of asbestos victims maintained that the fund is too small because it underestimates the total number of potential claimants. In responding to these concerns, G. Earl Parker, Johns–Manville's senior vice-president for corporate and public affairs and the reorganization plan's chief architect, stated the company's position as follows: "Enough or not, the $2.5 billion is all Manville has."

Discussion Questions

1. The *Asbestos Litigation* case raises questions as to both the responsibility of the defense attorney and the fairness of the system for compensating individuals injured by a dangerous product. Consider first the defense attorney's obligations in tort litigation to his client and, perhaps, to the plaintiff. Johns–Manville first retained Lively Wilson to defend an "ordinary" tort case. What was his job as the defendant's lawyer? How deeply should he have dug into the company's prior knowledge about the danger of asbestos? Imagine (not this case) that a defense lawyer learns that the company's files include evidence of forty year old studies of asbestos dangers, but that plaintiffs' lawyers do not yet know of those studies and have not asked in discovery the questions that will unearth them. What should the defense lawyer do? What if the question asked in discovery is plainly intended to unearth any such information but was so poorly worded that the defense lawyer can answer in a way that conceals the existence of the damaging evidence?

2. Assume you are the defense lawyer in a case in which the plaintiff has poor or indifferent representation and you know that in other cases effective representation has greatly strengthened the plaintiff's hand. Is it right to propose a small settlement for this plaintiff, if you know that someone with the same medical condition and the same background facts will be offered a settlement ten times larger because she has a tough and effective lawyer? Is it Lively Wilson's job, or the job of anyone working for Johns–Manville, to be concerned about equity among tort plaintiffs? Is the situation any different in the most extreme case, for example if Wilson was aware that one plaintiff had discovered a crucial document that was wholly unknown to the attorney for another plaintiff with whom he was arranging a settlement?

3. The answer to these questions in a litigation context may be that each party can be trusted to represent its own interests. But what about attempts to change the structure of liability through legislation? Here the organized asbestos industry or, more broadly, the cooperative efforts of all those industries facing product liability claims may be far more effective with Congress than the disorganized opposition of many relatively poor asbestos victims. Do the attorneys for Johns–Manville or the asbestos industry have a special obligation of fairness when they turn to Congress for its help in resolving the conflict between the industry and those suffering from the effects of asbestos? Do plaintiffs' attorneys have a sufficient interest in products liability litigation to be counted on to provide adequate legislative representation? In this regard it is worth considering the case titled *No-fault, No Fee: The Legal Profession and Federal No–Fault Automobile Insurance Legislation* at p. 309.

4. When litigation involves hundreds of suits by separate plaintiffs against a single defendant, it may be in the defendant's interest to settle, at almost any reasonable price, potentially damaging cases. The damage may come from unusually effective discovery, from the development of novel arguments at trial, or from the favorable resolution of a crucial issue on appeal. In these situations, others may use the work of the particularly effective plaintiff or the result in a particularly sympathetic case to the defendant's detriment. Is there anything wrong with the defense seeking to eliminate, by favorable settlement, the more effective plaintiffs and the more compelling cases? What if the terms of settlement involve a particular plaintiff keeping secret that he has discovered an unusually damaging document, perhaps indicating that Johns–Manville was aware of the dangers of asbestos-related diseases at a very early date?

5. The most effective long range strategy for a company such as Johns–Manville faced with many claims by needy plaintiffs may be to contest each claim vigorously so that the costs of litigation and the burdens of delay will discourage some new claimants and reduce the amount at which others will be willing to settle. Is this proper? What if Johns–Manville finds that it has lost nine of its ten last cases because the plaintiffs' bar discovered crucial and very damaging documents? Is it still proper to continue to litigate at length every successive similar claim?

6. What would you tell a corporation today if you were its lawyer and learned that a product it once made was unsafe? Would you tell the company to offer compensation to victims even if you thought it might be possible to defend cases for five to ten years more before plaintiffs got the information they needed to start winning cases? Is this fair advice to give, considering that today's shareholders will pay money because of business decisions made long before these shareholders bought stock? Is any other course fair to the victims who might not receive compensation for years to come? What would you tell the company if it is making something that you suspect will cause disease decades from now? In connection with this consider the *Food For Thought* case at p. 213.

7. Consider the social utility of the work Lively Wilson does for Johns–Manville. He helps the company defeat some claims that are not well founded. He helps them make their best arguments, which will sometimes hold down the amount plaintiffs win. He gives them good advice about when to offer settlements, and for how much. He is a master at persuading juries. Is this work more or less socially useful than the work of plaintiffs' lawyers, who assemble the same facts, evaluate the strength of cases, argue (sometimes brilliantly) before juries, and recommend which settlement offers to accept? Is there some reason to prefer one role to the other? Would you rather work in asbestos-type cases for the injured plaintiff or for the defendant company? Why?

8. As the asbestos story shows, the current U.S. tort system has high transaction costs: a large part of the total amount tort defendants pay goes to lawyers and others involved in the process of determining who recovers how much. The transaction costs are attributable largely to the difficulties of resolving the issue of fault, of damages flowing from pain and suffering, and of punitive damages. The difficulty is compounded by the use of a jury, a far more cumbersome device than a judge. The costs are also greater because of our American practice of contingency fees for plaintiffs' attorneys, a system that provides substantial encouragement to bringing cases and that results in large attorneys' fees in successful cases. But there are serious costs to any of the steps that might be taken to reduce the percentage of the total amount paid by tort defendants that goes to lawyers for the two sides. In thinking about possible ways to restructure the current system, consider:

(a) One problem with the tort system is that, although their injuries may be similar, some individuals get a large judgment and others very little. "Pain and suffering" is a vague concept. Many people in society experience pain and suffering with no opportunity to collect money damages for it. Would you limit tort recovery to identifiable and provable money loss (as for lost wages and medical expenses)? Would you give additional compensation for—say—loss of a limb, beyond the impact of the loss on wages or medical expenses? If so, would you assign a standardized value to that limb, whether lost by a person who is rich or poor, young or old, appealing or unappealing as a plaintiff before a jury? (The Workers' Compensation system assigns a dollar value to each part of the body. Lawyers call these statutory provisions a "meat chart." See the *Lawyering for Fun and Profit: Workers' Compensation and Personal Injury Practice* case at p. 258.)

(b) Similarly, would you continue to allow punitive damages against companies that have behaved badly, even if you doubted whether juries have objective standards for assigning such damages or setting the amount? Without occasional large recoveries, defendants might have too little incentive to find safe production methods. But is this a kind of quasi-criminal determination that should require a higher standard of proof than a civil determination can supply? And in a case like that of asbestos, are companies deterred today by the fear that tort plaintiffs may, in forty years, recover against them for the decisions they make now? The tort system surely influences conduct where damages will be paid fairly soon. But how much effect can it have in asbestos-type cases? If fear of tort recoveries will not adequately encourage safety, presumably the only alternative is government regulation, as by the U.S. Occupational Safety and Health Administration, notwithstanding the risk that regulatory interventions will be clumsy and enforcement imperfect.

(c) Would you do away with the civil jury entirely, as most countries have (England uses civil juries only in defamation cases)? Why not let these determinations be made by trained judges, who can bring at least a degree of standardization to the general run of cases?

(d) Some plaintiffs' lawyers make vast sums (through contingency fees) for the work they do. Has the injured victim who signs a contingency fee agreement to pay one-third (or more) of any recovery (even if obtained quickly via a settlement, with the lawyer having invested very little time) made a voluntary and knowing agreement? Should we enforce contingency fee agreements, or instead should we limit lawyer fees (as nearly every European country does), and in particular require judicial review of whether the fee is fair, considering the case, the circumstances, and the extent of the lawyer's effort? Without the possibility of a large contingency fee, would any lawyer have hunted long enough to find Sumner Simpson's letters? Is it good that occasional large fees encourage lawyers to put great effort into tort cases, many of which lead to no recovery for plaintiff or lawyer, but all of which impose costs on defendant companies and insurance companies?

2. Lawyer Lobbyists

No–Fault, No Fee: The Legal Profession and Federal No–Fault Automobile Insurance Legislation *

On July 12, 1977, 20–year–old Rosemary Pryor wheeled herself before the Senate Commerce Committee and read the following statement:

> On August 16, 1974, in Clare, Michigan, I was riding home with some friends when the driver lost control and hit a tree— no other cars were involved. The result was seven injured girls with four of them seriously hurt. My injuries were four broken ribs, two severe head lacerations, and a severed spinal cord. The severed spinal cord has left me paralyzed from the waist down. Of course, I was in need of immediate medical care. But even after that, I was in need of rehabilitation.
>
> All of this meant lots of money would be needed to put me back in society as a productive human being. Because Michigan has no-fault insurance, my father's insurance picked up the expenses. They were very good to my family and me. The insurance company said not to worry about a thing because they would pay for whatever was needed. So far that has meant that they have paid $52,128.49 for medical, rehabilitation, and three years of lost wages. The expenses broke down this way: medical—$8,870.16; wage loss—$6,969.60; rehabilitation—$36,288.73.
>
> I truly believe no-fault has helped me through the changes I have had to make. I did not have to worry about my parents going into debt and losing out on things they have worked years to gain. They did not have to worry about the money. That left them the time and energy to help me face what I was going through. That left me with the energy to accept what my life was now to be.
>
> Today I still get all my medical bills paid for that are relevant to my injuries from that accident. My insurance company makes sure that I go to the clinic at least once a year to make sure that things are going okay. They make sure that I get the tests, medication, and equipment that is needed to keep me healthy—both physically and mentally. It allows me to get

---

* This account is derived from published sources.

the medical attention I may need immediately instead of neglecting problems until they get worse because of lack of funds.

Because Ms. Pryor's injuries were sufficiently severe to satisfy the Michigan no-fault law's tort threshold, she also sought recovery through the tort liability system. Ms. Pryor's parents knew only one attorney, a divorce lawyer in a nearby town. He took the case, filed suit, and settled out-of-court for $90,000, from which he exacted his $30,000 fee. Ms. Pryor, in response to questions from Senator Riegle, expressed dissatisfaction with the role her lawyer played:

> [B]ecause we settled out of court, he did not do that much work. I was trying to figure out how many hours he did put in, say 20–30 hours at the most. That is $1000 per hour.

> He has a very well-paid job. I just did not approve. Here I am trying to compensate for some of the hardships that I go through—not that money can ever repay the loss of my legs, but mentally it can help out at times.

> It's just really hard to watch somebody walk away with that money, especially when you feel, you know, sometimes I feel I should have received more.

Ms. Pryor's testimony came a month after a U.S. Government study of the sixteen state no-fault laws that restricted access to the tort system concluded that "[n]o-fault automobile insurance works." The study revealed that no-fault compensated a higher percentage of automobile crash victims, particularly those injured in one-car crashes who had no chance of recovery under the tort liability system.

In addition, the study concluded that no-fault plans represented an improvement over the tort liability system in terms of the timeliness and coordination of benefits, the efficiency of administering the automobile accident reparations system, the reduction of motor vehicle tort litigation, the rehabilitation of crash victims, and the stability of insurance premiums. The study attributed the problems it encountered largely to the fact that the no-fault plans enacted "reflect *not* the no-fault advocate's conception of a sound and effective accident reparation plan but rather imperfect compromises wrought through the political process. . . ." The study hailed the Michigan law, which provides for unlimited medical benefits and stringent tort thresholds, as the best accident reparations plan.

Deficiencies in the Tort Liability System

In the last few decades, a steadily increasing number of automobile accidents has resulted in an unprecedented number of personal injuries. Under the tort liability system, the party whose fault or negligence caused the accident bears the cost of these injuries. To recover for her injuries, the victim normally must hire a lawyer, file a lawsuit, prove the defendant was negligent, establish that the defendant's negligence caused the plaintiff's injuries, demonstrate that the plaintiff herself was not contributorily negligent, and settle or succeed at trial.

In the 1960's, criticism of the tort liability system's performance as an automobile accident compensation mechanism focused on four issues. First, automobile accident cases were overtaxing the judicial system, which faced potential lawsuits arising from some 15 million motor vehicle accidents each year in the United States. Although not all of these resulted in law suits, accident victims filed enough suits that, by the late 1960s, automobile cases clogged the courts. In Massachusetts Superior Court, for example, 23,024 of the 33,784 civil cases filed in 1969 were motor vehicle tort cases. One effect of court overcrowding was substantial delays in compensating automobile accident victims. For those who did not have the financial means to meet their accident-related expenses while their suits were pending, these delays often meant they had to settle for less than they otherwise might have received.

Second, the tort liability system created huge gaps in compensation. A Department of Transportation (DOT) study showed that only one-third to one-half of traffic accident victims received any compensation at all for the injuries they sustained. In fact, of the $13.1 billion in compensable loss automobile accidents caused in 1970, victims recovered only $4.5 billion. Several factors explain why accident victims are often either precluded from recovery under the tort liability system or receive compensation bearing little relationship to the cost of the injuries they sustain. To begin with, the driver may not have been negligent or the accident victim may have been contributorily negligent. Even if the driver was negligent, he may be unidentifiable, insolvent, or uninsured. Moreover, because of the fear of incurring litigation costs that exceed claims, insurance companies tend to settle small claims for more than they are worth and to challenge large claims, resulting on average in recovery of one-third of total economic loss.

Third, the tort liability system's constituent legal doctrines presented problems of their own. Proving negligence in an automobile accident that occurred years before was a "surreal" process, and the resulting fault determination was a "crap shoot." General damages (pain and suffering) commonly awarded to successful plaintiffs in personal injury cases were a legal fiction at best, a "charade" or fraud at worst. These imperfections in the legal doctrines encouraged dishonesty. To maximize general damages, accident victims remembered selectively the facts surrounding their injuries and exaggerated the harm they suffered. Increasingly, general damage awards became a device to ensure that accident victims could pay their legal fees (which normally amounted to more than 35 percent of any judgment or settlement) and still be fully compensated for their economic losses.

Finally, the tort liability system was an extremely expensive compensation mechanism. In addition to the costs taxpayers paid to maintain the courts, insurance companies incurred significant costs in administering liability insurance (the primary source of compensation to accident victims). And the legal fees and ancillary litigation costs borne by the parties to the accident litigation consumed as much as 23 percent of insurance premiums. In all, the DOT study found that the tort liability insurance system cost approximately $1.07 in administrative expenses for every $1.00 it delivered in net benefits.

History of Reform Proposals

The tort liability system's inability to handle automobile accident claims has been apparent for some time. The initial response was to remove some of the doctrinal barriers to recovery by automobile accident victims. Most notable was the movement the plaintiff's bar led to replace contributory negligence with some form of comparative negligence.

Some scholars felt, however, that more fundamental changes were necessary. In 1932, Columbia University's Council for Research in the Social Sciences studied the automobile accident reparations system and proposed compulsory liability insurance, no-fault liability for persons whose vehicles caused injuries, and "no-fault" access to the owner's insurer as the victim's exclusive remedy. Due in part to a barrage of criticism from the insurance industry and bar associations, only four states considered the Columbia Plan and none adopted its recommendations.

In 1965, Professors Robert Keeton of Harvard Law School and Jeffrey O'Connell of the University of Illinois College of Law published *Basic Protection for the Traffic Victim: A Blueprint for Reforming Automobile Insurance,* a book that galvanized the tort liability system's critics. Their proposal, dubbed the Keeton–O'Connell Plan, contained four elements: (1) compulsory "Basic Protection" insurance that compensated accident victims without regard to fault for losses up to $10,000 per injured person or $100,000 per accident; (2) coverage for losses attributable to medical expenses and lost wages of up to $750 per month, but *not* "pain and suffering"; (3) tort "thresholds" that precluded an accident victim from suing in tort unless her losses covered by the Basic Protection exceeded $10,000 or her pain and suffering losses were greater than $5,000; and (4) deductions from Basic Protection compensation for all benefits received from collateral sources (and vice-versa) in cases exceeding the Basic Protection limit.

The Keeton–O'Connell Plan spawned a host of different no-fault plans. Companies, organizations, and professional associations with vested interests in automobile accident reparations published proposals suggesting various changes. Some of these proposals represented genuine attempts either to improve on the substantive provisions of the Keeton–O'Connell formulation or to make the Keeton–O'Connell Plan more politically palatable. Other proposals which claimed to be versions of "no-fault" effectively gutted the major features of the Keeton–O'Connell Plan.

The ambiguity inherent in the term "no-fault" itself contributed to the widespread confusion that surrounded all the no-fault plans. The various proposals, all called no-fault, can be evaluated by whether and to what extent they contained two basic features: mandatory first-party coverage and a tort threshold.

Under first-party coverage, the driver/owner of the automobile involved in a one-car accident takes financial responsibility for some or all losses sustained by herself, injured pedestrians, and occupants of her vehicle. If two cars are involved, vehicle owners recover from their insurers and vehicle occupants recover from their own insurers, if they have first-party insurance. If they do not have insurance, they recover from the insurer of the driver/owner of the vehicle they were in, regardless of whether the driver/owner would have been liable in tort. Because the driver/owner's insurer pays regardless of fault, the tort remedy becomes superfluous (assuming that the insurer compensates 100 percent of the losses the victim sustained). Thus, under a "pure" no-fault system, the driver/owner is exempted from tort liability.

To keep premiums down, all no-fault proposals placed some ceiling on losses recoverable on a no-fault basis. Most no-fault plans provided that, beyond the point where the no-fault coverage ends, accident victims had recourse to the courts to seek recovery to the full extent of their injuries. Despite the obvious logical connection between the tort threshold and the insurance benefits ceiling, statutory no-fault proposals often linked the two variables only if it was politically expedient.

A common feature all no-fault laws shared was that they were mandatory: they required all vehicle owners to carry first-party insurance. Because an insurance scheme that permitted some vehicle owners to carry first-party insurance, others to carry third-party ("liability") insurance, and still others to carry no accident insurance at all would be inequitable, particularly for injured pedestrians and vehicle occupants, no-fault opponents usually did not attack the compulsory nature of first-party coverage.

No-fault critics based their opposition on the argument that no-fault's superiority over the tort system was grounded in the fundamental mischaracterization of the fault system as a compensation mechanism. As Richard Posner wrote in his ABA–commissioned no-fault study:

> Negligence liability is rooted in age-old notions of corrective justice, in concepts of moral responsibility, and in the concept of economic efficiency, which is closely related to the intuitive notion of due care. Negligence liability creates rights against that form of wrongful conduct which consists of carelessly injuring another. Its purpose was never to insure people against mishaps.

In short, the fault system is designed to provide remedies for wrongful acts rather than to compensate accident victims.

On a more tangible level, supporters of the tort liability system argued that society benefits from a remedy against wrongful conduct in driving automobiles. Most notably, the prospect of paying for all the harm her behavior causes deters a person from driving carelessly. If that driver has liability insurance, the deterrent takes the form of higher insurance premiums.

Although all insurance schemes that provide for first-party coverage "reward the guilty at the expense of the innocent," some "Oregon-type" no-fault plans, which did not restrict access to the tort liability system, won the grudging support of the most dogmatic no-fault critics. These proposals, however, are completely unacceptable to no-fault supporters, who believe a dual compensation system is largely self-defeating. Such a system would be confusing and burdened by severe administrative costs. More importantly, court congestion is unlikely to be eased. Accident victims with relatively minor injuries, encouraged by the knowledge that they will receive, on average, 4–5 times their actual economic loss in the tort liability system, will file suit instead of or in addition to receiving first party benefits. Because no-fault proponents believe that eliminating the legal fees and court costs incidental to the tort liability system (which consume more than 18 cents out of the premium dollar) will increase compensation, any formulation that does not restrict access to the tort system frustrates this primary objective.

Effects of the Keeton–O'Connell Plan

The Keeton–O'Connell Plan had two important, relatively immediate effects. First, the Massachusetts legislature used it as a model when it enacted the country's first no-fault plan. Second, it prompted the Senate Commerce Committee to fund a two-year, $2 million study of the automobile accident reparation system by the Secretary of Transportation. Both the DOT study and the Massachusetts law, in turn, played a major role in the debate over no-fault that raged through the 1970s.

Massachusetts Personal Injury Protection (PIP)

In August 1969, the Massachusetts House of Representatives approved a no-fault bill sponsored by state representative Michael Dukakis. The bill's passage at first surprised the insurance industry and state bar organizations, but they organized quickly and defeated the bill in the state senate. Dukakis, who described some members of the local bar's opposition as "hysterical," reintroduced the bill in the legislature's 1970 session. Both chambers passed it and Governor Francis Sargent signed it into law.

Some viewed Massachusetts's no-fault law as a radical change in the automobile accident compensation system and as a triumph for no-fault proponents. In fact, the law was not as significant as it might have been. For example, legislative opponents moderated the bill by lowering the first-party no-fault compensation ceiling to $2000 for medical expenses, cost of replacement services, and lost wages. In addition, no-fault advocates believed the tort threshold was far too low. Professors Keeton and O'Connell considered the Massachusetts law "a breakthrough for the no-fault concept" but refused to "recommend it as a model for adoption elsewhere."

Between 1970 and 1976, 23 other states enacted no-fault legislation. However, like Massachusetts, few states adopted true no-fault schemes. Eight states simply enacted "add-on" schemes that placed no restrictions on the right to recover in tort. Thirteen states followed the Massachusetts model and adopted "modified" no-fault laws that used thresholds to eliminate partially the tort remedy. Although no state completely eliminated access to the tort liability system, New York and Michigan enacted "almost pure" no-fault plans by setting their tort thresholds sufficiently high to preclude almost all lawsuits.

No-fault proponents attributed their defeats and limited successes at the state level to the state lawyers associations' political influence. From the inception of the no-fault movement, state trial lawyers associations linked campaign contributions to no-fault opposition and sponsored their own candidates in unsympathetic legislators' districts. State representatives who shared the lawyers' opposition to no-fault often held key legislative positions. (*See* Table 1).

Table 1

REPRESENTATION OF LAWYERS AND INSURANCE AGENTS
ON COMMITTEES WITH JURISDICTION OVER NO–FAULT LEG-
ISLATION IN SELECTED STATE LEGISLATURES (1970)

STATE	HOUSE			SENATE		
	Total Committee	Lawyers	Insurance Agents	Total Committee	Lawyers	Insurance Agents
California	14	7*	1	9	4*	0
Florida	13	2*	1	7	2*	1
Illinois	17	8	4	12	6*	3
Michigan	11	2*	1	5	1*	0
Mississippi	17	8*	6	8	5*	1
New Jersey	7	2*	1	5	5*	0
New York	18	10*	5	18	14*	1
N. Carolina	21	11	3	17	14*	1
Pennsylvania	23	9*	8	14	1	4*
Texas	21	9	7	17	13*	0

* Includes Chairman

As Table 1 indicates, lawyers chaired the insurance committees in *both* chambers in six states, and in at least one chamber in all ten states. This is significant because a committee chairman can often block undesirable legislation through control over scheduling and other legislative devices.

U.S. Department of Transportation

The Department of Transportation began its study in 1969 and published its findings in a 24–volume report over the next two years. The DOT study, which was the most comprehensive, factual, and impartial of all automobile accident reparations system studies, revealed a great deal about the legal profession's stake in the status quo. Although attorneys represented only 46.2 percent of all paid claimants, those claimants suffered 73.2 percent of the total economic loss and received 77.0 percent of all payments. Attorneys fees accounted for 35.5 percent of the average claim and 27.3 percent of total payments to all claimants. Including defendants' legal fees, payments to lawyers amounted to more than one billion dollars in 1968 alone.

More threatening to the legal profession was the light the DOT statistics shed on the impact of various no-fault proposals' tort thresholds on fees. The Keeton–O'Connell Plan, for example, barred a tort suit unless the injured party suffered more than $10,000 in economic losses. According to the DOT study, only 0.8 percent of all automobile accident claimants whom attorneys represented and who received payment had sustained more than $10,000 in economic loss, and those claimants were responsible for a mere 7.7 percent of the attorneys' fee income from automobile accident litigation.

Notwithstanding its factual findings, the DOT study's most important effect was to signal the beginning of congressional involvement in the area. The members of the Senate Commerce Committee who had provided the impetus for commissioning the DOT study were certain to introduce no-fault legislation once the DOT study was concluded. Concerned groups used the years while the study was in progress to formulate and publicize their positions on the no-fault issue. By the time Senators Hart and Magnuson introduced the first federal no-fault bill in 1971, the special interests were ready.

Interest Group Alignment on the Hart–Magnuson Bill

The goals that united the interest groups who lobbied for the Hart–Magnuson bills included increased compensation for automobile accident victims and reduced insurance premiums for all motor vehicle owners. Among the most active advocates for federal no-fault legislation were the Consumer Federation of America, International Brotherhood of Teamsters, United Auto Workers, American Association of Retired Persons, and AFL–CIO. Many of the consumer organizations, unions, and insurance companies that supported national no-fault legislation formed umbrella organizations to coordinate lobbying efforts. The first such organization, the National Committee for Effective No–Fault, was succeeded in 1977 by the Committee for Consumers No–Fault.

Ralph Nader was notably absent from those who endorsed the Hart–Magnuson bill. In testimony before the Commerce Committee, Nader repeatedly declined to take a position on the bill, ostensibly on the grounds that he had not yet studied it. Nader's focus was entirely on preventive measures, such as improving automobile safety. According to one source Nader was "unable to align himself with a coalition that included the big insurance companies against the trial lawyers, his allies in past battles against the automobile industry."

The insurance industry, however, was almost evenly split on the federal no-fault issue. The first insurance industry supporter of the Hart–Magnuson bill was Frederick D. Watkins, President of Aetna, who endorsed S.945 on November 9, 1971. Aetna brought into the no-fault fold the American Insurance Association (AIA), a group of 122 stock companies that wrote about 33 percent of the premium volume and covered 25 percent of the automobiles insured at that time. The AIA even promulgated its own no-fault plan, the "Complete Personal Protection Plan," eliminating recovery for pain and suffering entirely.

Both the National Association of Independent Insurers (NAII) and the American Mutual Insurance Association (AMIA) were opposed to the federal no-fault bills. The NAII and AMIA, which represented 386 independent insurance companies and 110 mutual insurance companies, respectively, both formulated no-fault proposals designed for state enactment that featured relatively low tort thresholds. The AMIA and NAII predicated their divergence from the AIA regarding the merits of federal no-fault on the belief that a national insurance law would disadvantage the smaller mutual and independent insurers vis-a-vis the AIA's large stock companies.

The dispute within the insurance industry over the Hart–Magnuson bills was bitter, but the issues the insurance associations fought about were intra-industry concerns not particularly comprehensible to either the public or Congress. Although lawyers frequently characterized themselves as a profession of "Davids" confronting a monolithic insurance "Goliath" seeking to impose no-fault schemes on an unwilling public, the insurance industry actually was so divided that it effectively neutralized itself before Congress.

Internal Decision–Making of the Legal Profession

The legal profession's stake in the no-fault issue was evident from the beginning. Professors Keeton and O'Connell made clear their intent to make the automobile accident reparations system more efficient by drastically reducing legal expenses. Nevertheless, some scholars hoped that the legal profession as a whole would support the movement because only a relatively small percentage of the profession actually was engaged in automobile accident litigation. However, the primary danger no-fault posed to the legal profession was as a precedent.

No-fault scholars saw automobile insurance as only the second of four fields in which to implement a no-fault scheme. The first had been workers' compensation. The third would be product liability. And the fourth would be professional malpractice. Many lawyers feared that the imposition of no-fault systems in all these areas would effectively destroy the personal injury bar. By the time the first Hart–Magnuson bill was introduced in 1971, the American Bar Association (ABA), the Association of Trial Lawyers of America (ATLA), the American College of Trial Lawyers (ACTL), and many state and local bar associations had studied no-fault automobile insurance and issued proposals to reform the automobile accident compensation system.

The American Bar Association

The ABA is the world's largest voluntary professional organization and the oldest legal professional organization in the United States.

Although less than half of America's lawyers belong to it, the organization speaks for 97 percent of the legal profession because state and local bar associations are represented in the ABA House of Delegates.

During the 1960s, the ABA maintained that it limited its lobbying efforts to those issues to which it could apply "the knowledge and experience of the profession to the promotion of the public good." The no-fault issue threatened the ABA's effort to nurture a public interest reputation. No-fault proponents, such as Daniel Patrick Moynihan, were quick to question the legal profession's motives: "If the bar cannot do anything but proceed with the squalid concerns that have characterized its dealing with this issue for the past 20 years, then the bar is sicker than anyone knows, and we are in deeper trouble than we know." However, the ABA also would have problems if it failed to oppose no-fault legislation because, just as the ABA carefully fosters its public interest reputation, it zealously guards its status as the "primary voice of the legal profession." ATLA, which came out early and aggressively against no-fault, threatened to supplant the ABA, at least for the 30,000 lawyers in the ABA Section of Insurance, Negligence, and Compensation Law.*

The A.B.A. appointed a special committee to examine automobile accident reparations. The committee's nine members all had handled automobile negligence cases. Some no-fault proponents, most notably Professor Keeton and Michael Pertschuk, were appointed to the advisory commission. The Powers Committee presented its findings to the House of Delegates in January 1969. The committee's four general proposals were: continuation of the special committee; retention of the tort liability system with fault to be determined by the adversary method of trial by judge or jury, but with certain modifications; opposition to proposals, such as the Keeton–O'Connell plan, that would alter substantially the tort basis for automobile accident reparations; and designation by the ABA president of persons to oppose legislation inconsistent with these resolutions. There was no significant dissent to any of the Powers Committee's major recommendations either from within the committee or in the House of Delegates. The Powers Committee's recommendations, as approved by the House of Delegates, were the ABA's official position at the time the first Hart–Magnuson bill was introduced in the U.S. Senate.

---

* By the February 1968 meeting of the House of Delegates in Chicago, the ABA's Negligence Section already had the findings of its own special committee (the Powers Committee) outlining the serious danger the no-fault concept posed to the fault liability system. The committee said that the fault system was grounded in "the religious belief that each of us is responsible to his God for his own conduct."

The Association of Trial Lawyers of America

ATLA led the fight against no-fault legislation. The organization's spiritual father, Roscoe Pound, articulated its guiding philosophy when he commended ATLA's members for "not thinking of yourself as a trained, organized body striving for the advancement of the economic conditions of the practitioner, but thinking and working for the improvement of justice in this field." ATLA describes itself as the "lawyers for society's victims."

Since its inception, ATLA has grown to 46,000 members with a $7 million annual budget (1981–2) and an 84–person national staff. To a large extent, ATLA has patterned itself structurally after the ABA. It publishes a monthly journal (*Trial*), holds annual meetings, has substantive law sections, and is led by a Board of Governors and executive triumvirate (president, president-elect, and vice-president). ATLA also has 84 law school chapters and its own code of professional responsibility. ATLA differs from the ABA by having directly subordinate state and local subunits and a much more homogenous membership.

The ATLA membership's homogeneity is a product principally of the association's charter. A prospective ATLA member must subscribe in writing to the organization's stated objectives, which include promoting "fair trials," the adversary system, and a just result for the injured, the accused, and those whose rights are jeopardized (one practical application of this requirement is to exclude attorneys who regularly represent insurance companies). The oath to the adversary system helps explain the absence of internal debate preceding ATLA's public opposition to no-fault legislation.

ATLA established a committee on automobile accident reparations whose function was to coordinate ATLA's opposition to all pure or modified no-fault proposals. To oppose the Hart–Magnuson bill, ATLA published a position paper, raised state and national dues, hired a public relations firm, opened a Washington office, and in September 1971 registered for the first time as a lobbying organization.

No–Fault in Congress

92nd Congress (1971–1972)

ATLA attracted attention to itself and the legal profession during the Senate Commerce Committee hearings on the Hart–Magnuson bill (S.945) in May 1971 when its staff member, Robert Joost, testified as the Committee's lead-off witness on the fifth day of the hearings. Disillusioned by ATLA's position on no-fault automobile insurance and the activities ATLA had engaged in to defeat no-fault legislation, Joost decided after much soul-searching to reveal ATLA's activities to the Commerce Committee.

ATLA had employed Joost intermittently for almost ten years. A magna cum laude graduate of both Yale College and Harvard Law School, where he was an editor on the law review, Joost progressed from assistant editor of the *National Association of Claimants' Counsel of America Law Journal* in 1962 to assistant to the chairman of the ATLA legislative section and consulting editor of *Trial* in 1969. During that period, Joost also worked for Sheff & McGarry, a Boston law firm specializing in automobile negligence work, taught labor and housing law at New England School of Law, and participated in the revision of the Massachusetts mental health code.

From the beginning of his career, Joost had believed that trial lawyers played a crucial role in American society. By bringing damage actions and seeking injunctions on behalf of private citizens injured by those who pollute, discriminate, rent substandard housing, or otherwise exploit consumers, he felt trial lawyers acted as "private attorney generals." Thus, without plaintiffs' lawyers, the environmental, civil rights, and housing laws would not be enforced.

Apparently, however, Joost's two year exposure to automobile negligence litigation at Sheff & McGarry convinced him that that particular form of litigation was inappropriate for the trial bar. Joost began to think of automobile accident lawyers as "rug merchants," making a living "selling broken bones and blood." Soon after he left Sheff & McGarry, Joost reviewed for the Portia Law Journal "Basic Protection for the Traffic Victim," the "trailblazing" book cowritten by his law school torts professor Robert Keeton. In his review, Joost applauded the Keeton–O'Connell plan:

> The proposed statute is a careful attempt at reform. If substantially enacted, it would provide a fairer and more sensible solution to the grave national problem of compensating automobile accident victims.

The position Joost took on the Keeton–O'Connell plan proved difficult to square with his work at ATLA. When ATLA hired Joost on a permanent basis in 1967, it was on the condition that he make no public statements opposing ATLA's position on no-fault legislation. Although Joost honored his pledge for several years, his further study of the issue increased his enthusiasm for no-fault automobile insurance, and he freely confided to friends his support for no-fault and his dismay with ATLA's efforts to sidetrack no-fault legislation.

At the same time, S. Lynn Sutcliffe, the Senate Commerce Committee's majority staff director, was preparing the witness list for the impending opening round of hearings on S.945. The trial lawyers already loomed as the legislation's major opponent. When a committee staff member told Sutcliffe that a highly placed ATLA employee might be willing to testify before the committee in favor of the bill, Sutcliffe jumped at the chance.

Joost was surprised and troubled by the invitation to testify. His immediate reaction was to decline the offer. On a substantive level, Joost could justify his decision because he believed state no-fault legislation was preferable to a federal no-fault act. Nonetheless, during the first few weeks of April 1971 Joost reconsidered his decision not to testify. One of the tasks Joost was performing for ATLA at that time involved organizing and attending regional "key men" meetings devoted to formulating strategies to defeat no-fault insurance in the state legislatures. Joost had followed closely the no-fault battle in his native Massachusetts and was well aware that it had taken a fortuitous alignment of political forces to enact what he felt was a weak no-fault statute. What Joost heard at a "key men" meeting in Chicago on April 24 convinced him that no-fault legislation was doomed politically at the state level. The effective choice, therefore, was between federal no-fault and no no-fault at all.

When Joost returned to Cambridge, he immediately mailed a written statement to the Senate Commerce Committee. Almost simultaneously, ATLA's executive committee met in Chicago to adopt a drastic budget reallocation to finance a new department that would coordinate the battle against no-fault automobile insurance on both the federal and state levels. The reallocation eliminated Joost's job. Because Joost already had decided his testimony would make it impossible for him to continue working at ATLA, he submitted his two-week notice to the editor of *Trial*. As he sat before the Senate Commerce Committee on May 6th, Joost was working his next-to-last day on ATLA's payroll.

In his testimony, Joost argued for federal legislation because ATLA's influence in the state legislatures made meaningful state reform politically impossible.

Joost revealed that ATLA had held a series of regional meetings of "key-men," at which several ATLA members boasted that the trial lawyers had enough control over key chokepoints in their state legislatures to make passage of undesirable no-fault legislation impossible. The state "key-men" also bragged about using campaign contributions to influence state legislative action.

On the national level, Joost revealed that the ATLA executive committee recently had decided to create a Federal–State Relations Department with an annual budget of $322,000. This new department instantly became ATLA's largest, consuming more than 25 percent of

ATLA's total budget. ATLA used a significant chunk of the $322,000 to retain a public relations firm to assist in the fight against no-fault legislation.

Although Joost focused his testimony on ATLA, it implicated the entire legal profession. In his disappointment with ATLA, Joost made little effort to distinguish the other lawyers' associations: "When you come right down to it, the bar associations, at least the American Trial Lawyers Association, is nothing more, nothing less than a trade association." He concluded his statement by declaring that "the trial lawyers of America, who should be out there litigating for America, a better America, are vegetating in the pork barrel of automobile negligence work."

After Joost concluded his testimony, Senator Philip Hart, Democrat of Michigan, commented on what Joost had just done:

> Let me make one last comment. Normally when this comment is made it reflects a feeling that because of some act of individual courage and sensitive conscience somebody has put themselves into the army of the unemployed by coming in here and testifying. With your extraordinary talents, there would never be the danger that your services would not be sought. So I know that when you decided, as you put it here, "finally I concluded I had to accept the call to testify," that you did not face economic deprivation from the decision, but that really is not the most difficult part of stepping up and speaking hard truths. Lots of people who are the beneficiaries of enormous trust income never speak.
>
> The fact that you would come as you have to us as one who has been a trial lawyers' lawyer and told us that no-fault is the answer is an act, I think, of considerable courage.

Joost in fact did find employment for the next few years—on the staff of the Senate Commerce Committee.

Joost's testimony rebutted the remarks ATLA president Richard Markus had made to the committee the previous day. Markus had testified that ATLA did not oppose all no-fault, only bad no-fault. Joost asserted that ATLA would oppose virtually all no-fault, state and federal. Joost's testimony came as a surprise to Markus and the ATLA staff. When he was informed of the nature of Joost's testimony, Markus feared that Joost's allegations would be "generally perceived as an indication of nefarious conduct by ATLA on a hot legislative topic." Markus immediately sent a telegram to the Senate Commerce Committee requesting permission to appear before the committee again to answer Joost's charges. In an extraordinary development, the Senate

Commerce Committee granted this request, and on May 7, a mere 24 hours after Robert Joost, Richard Markus again appeared as a witness.

Markus, in his hurriedly prepared rebuttal, sought to deflect the committee's focus from ATLA to the insurance industry. After downplaying his organization's lobbying strength ("We are probably the world's crummiest lobby"), Markus concluded his brief statement by estimating that the insurance industry had spent upwards of $10 million to promote no-fault legislation.

Senator Hart refused to shift the committee's focus from ATLA:

Senator: Do you dispute any of the facts that Mr. Joost gave us?

Mr. Markus: I believe that some of the statements, if the Senator requests, are, I think overstatements and I would prefer not to quibble with them.

Markus, however, did not at any point in his testimony directly contradict Joost. Instead, he sought to cast Joost's most damaging assertions in a more favorable light. Senator Hart's increasing skepticism turned to open sarcasm when Markus vigorously asserted ATLA's altruism on the no-fault issue:

Mr. Markus: . . . whenever our governing body has met, to the best of my recollection, if anyone dared to suggest that we should take any position because it was in the self-interest of our members or our association, he would promptly be excluded from the room. We have rather strongly felt—

Senator Hart: He would be sent to an insane asylum, wouldn't he?

The Joost–Markus joust was the highlight of the month-long committee hearings.

The Commerce Committee spent the next full year revising the complicated bill. One change it made was to limit the right to sue in tort to victims who suffered "catastrophic harm." According to one staff member, "We didn't win any friends among the lawyers in redrafting our bill."

As revised, S.945 contemplated a "cooperative federalism" scheme, under which states were free to enact their own no-fault laws. However, if the states did not enact no-fault laws, or if the proposals they enacted did not meet the prescribed federal standards, a federal no-fault plan (Title III) was imposed directly. The federal minimum standards were set so high under Title III that only one state no-fault law, Michigan's, qualified. This prompted critics to charge that the revised S.945's purported preservation of the benefits of state experimentation was illusory. They also denounced as unconstitutional the effective subordination of state insurance commissioners to the Secretary of Transportation, arguing that the Constitution limited Congress to choosing between preempting the field entirely with a federal plan that used federal officials to administer it or leaving the field open to state regulation.

However, the constitutional objections no-fault opponents posed did not deter the Senate Commerce Committee. On May 25, 1972, the Committee approved the fifth revision of S.945 by a 15–4 vote.

When S.945 reached the Senate floor in early August, many Senators were concerned about the bill's complexity, the federal-state question, and the keen interest of powerful special interests in the bill. Opponents of S.945, led by Senator Roman Hruska, moved to refer the bill to the Judiciary Committee, ostensibly to study potential constitutional problems. The Senate voted 49–46 to refer S.945 to the Judiciary Committee, where it died a few months later.

93rd Congress (1973–1974)

S.945's sponsors reintroduced a revised bill in early 1973. This bill, S.354, invited the states to enact their own federal no-fault plans in compliance with minimum federal standards (Title II). If a state did not enact such a plan within two years, a federal no-fault plan (Title III) would be imposed upon it. The drafters patterned the high threshold and minimum no-fault coverage provisions of S.354 after the recently-promulgated Uniform Motor Vehicle Automobile Reparations Act (UMVARA).

The use of UMVARA as a model for S.354 put the ABA in a difficult position because UMVARA had emerged as a cooperative effort of ABA and the federal government. The National Conference of Commissioners on Uniform State Laws (NCCUSL) drafted UMVARA at the behest of and with funding from the DOT. The ABA had founded NCCUSL and continued to have close ties with it. In fact, the ABA House of Delegates traditionally voted on model uniform state legislation NCCUSL proposed. In NCCUSL's 76–year history, the House of Delegates had approved all of the more than 70 uniform proposals NCCUSL had submitted to it. The House of Delegates planned to consider UMVARA at the February 1973 midyear Convention in Cleveland. UMVARA posed a difficult problem for ABA President Robert Meserve and his Board of Governors. Although there were certain to be UMVARA supporters within the House of Delegates, there seemed no conceivable way that the House of Delegates would reverse itself on the no-fault issue. The Board sought a way out by supporting state, but not federal, no-fault legislation. In this way the ABA could oppose S. 354 but still support legislation that had the NCCUSL proposal for its prototype.

Meserve and other ABA leaders were concerned about being lumped together with ATLA on the no-fault issue. Besides disliking the ATLA leadership and wanting to prevent ATLA from becoming the "tail wagging the (ABA) dog," they were concerned about the notoriety ATLA was attracting because of its lobbying tactics in the states. On January 25, 1972, Virginia Knauer, President Nixon's Special Assistant for Consumer Affairs, had written to then ABA President Leon Jaworsky requesting that the ABA investigate ATLA's lobbying techniques, which Knauer described as "devious, misleading and blatantly self-serving." The ABA declined. The popular press, which almost uniformly supported pure or modified no-fault legislation, often did not distinguish between the ABA and ATLA in criticizing lawyers' self-serving position on no-fault legislation.

Meserve also had to consider his personal views about no-fault. He had kept his own counsel regarding no-fault while ABA president, but he had been convinced early on that the movement begun by his close friend, Robert Keeton, represented the wave of the future. An eminent Boston trial attorney himself, Meserve had grown increasingly concerned with the burden automobile accident litigation placed on the judicial system.

Meserve had no illusions about the Bar's impartiality on the no-fault issue. He believed the majority of lawyers who handled no personal injury litigation favored some form of no-fault, but he knew that those who did handle such cases were almost uniformly opposed to all no-fault proposals that limited tort recoveries. Although he recognized that a primary function of the ABA was to serve as an advocate for its membership and that a clear majority of the membership opposed no-fault legislation in the states, Meserve had sought unsuccessfully to prevent the House of Delegates from adopting that position.

As ABA president, Meserve's duties included explaining and defending important ABA positions on Capitol Hill. To represent adequately the House of Delegates's position while remaining true to his personal beliefs, Meserve decided to avoid testifying about the merits of no-fault and to concentrate exclusively on the shortcomings of federal involvement in the area.

The Commerce Committee approved S.354 on August 3, by a 15–3 vote. Threatened with another time-consuming debate over a motion to refer, Warren Magnuson reached an agreement with Judiciary Chairman James Eastland by which the Senate would refer S.354 to the Judiciary Committee with the understanding that the Committee report it back by February 15, 1974. The no-fault opponents' success in once again avoiding a Senate vote on no-fault legislation caused one exasperated staff member to complain, "For every one step forward, we take two back."

The Judiciary Committee provided an ideal forum for lawyers who wished to express their constitutional objections to S.354. In ten days of hearings, the Judiciary Committee heard testimony from ten representatives of national and state legal associations, all of whom opposed S.354. ATLA President Leonard Ring, testifying on February 5, 1974, made it clear that his organization opposed S.354 while noting for the record that "we do support and have always supported progressive reform in the automobile insurance system on a state-by-state basis." Two days later, Chesterfield Smith, Meserve's successor as ABA President, called for 4–5 years experimentation with existing no-fault laws. Smith acknowledged that many ABA members disagreed with the organization's position, but he denied that he had dissented, despite his past support for the threshold plan his native state of Florida had enacted. Smith speculated that had 5–9 years of state experimentation preceded UMVARA the House of Delegates would have adopted it.

An unenthusiastic Judiciary Committee reported S.354 back to the Senate on February 18, 1974. Given one more month to prepare its report, the Judiciary Committee voted 8–7 on March 20 to report S.354 favorably without alteration. Thus, the only significant result of committal to the Judiciary Committee had been a delay of more than seven months.

As floor consideration of S.354 approached, ATLA had its members contact personal acquaintances within Congress. Although the ABA had a long history of using this tactic, ATLA systematized it by developing an extensive network of association members.

As the vote approached, no-fault proponents worried about whether the 65 lawyers in the Senate would be influenced by the economic interests of their past, and possibly future, profession. The few indications available were mixed. Immediately prior to offering an amendment substantially reducing the tort restrictions of S.354, Senator Howard Baker candidly admitted on the Senate floor that his immediate reaction to no-fault legislation after practicing law for 17 years was overwhelmingly negative. On the other hand, Senator Adlai Stevenson rebuked a state bar association representative during Commerce Committee hearings by saying:

> I hope that you would not presume to represent the uniform opinion of all lawyers. If anything in my own personal experience has made me a fervent believer in no-fault, it has been my experience as a defense lawyer in the courts, and if anything in my own personal experience has convinced me that the time has come for federal action, it has been my experience as a state legislator.

During the seven-day floor debate over S.354 in April, floor manager Frank Moss bitterly attacked President Nixon for failing to endorse the bill and ATLA for its lobbying techniques. In particular, Moss denounced ATLA's inundation of the president and nine designated senators with anti–S.354 telegrams. The ATLA membership's high response rate was a result of the apocalyptic tone of the ATLA leadership's message:

> URGENT, act instantly, minutes count. Just learned Federal no-fault will be voted on in U.S. Senate Thursday. In its area, this will end tort system, jury system, adversary system. . . .

Senator Moss questioned the ethics of ATLA's activities: "I believe that these new techniques employing electronic technology to disguise a highly organized lobbying effort by an affected interest group which is disguised as a groundswell of public opinion from ordinary citizens is questionable."

The defeat on April 25 by a 53–31 vote of an amendment designed to reduce S.354's tort threshold indicated that ATLA and the ABA would be unsuccessful in stemming the no-fault tide. With Senate approval imminent, Senator Magnuson vented three years of frustration with one final denunciation of his antagonists:

> I am just hopeful that over the weekend each senator can decide to support the bill. I do not know what the purpose of waiting that long is, unless the trial lawyers are doing something over the weekend. Of course, I know what the trial lawyers have been doing. I know what they have been doing to me. I suppose I know what they will be trying to do to me this fall.

On May 1, 1974, the Senate approved S.354 by a vote of 53 to 42.

Although a House Interstate and Foreign Commerce subcommittee had held extensive hearings on a variety of no-fault bills in April 1971, Chairman Harley Staggers had decided to await Senate approval before seriously addressing the no-fault question. As the Senate moved towards passage of S.354 in early 1974, Subcommittee Chairman John E. Moss scheduled hearings for April but Staggers delayed giving Representative Moss permission to begin the hearings until July.

Representative Moss's subcommittee rushed through a long list of witnesses in just two weeks. The subcommittee had under consideration not only S.354, but also no-fault proposals introduced by Moss (H.R. 10) and subcommittee member Bob Eckhardt (H.R.1400). As the last summer of Watergate came to an end, interest in S.354 among subcommittee members waned. The chances were extremely slim that, even if reported out of the subcommittee, a no-fault bill could be approved by the whole committee, secure passage in the House of Representatives in a form identical to S.354, and then avoid presidential veto. Furthermore, subcommittee members were hesitant to antagonize ATLA in an election year. S.354 met a quiet death in the 93rd Congress in September 1974 when Representative Moss was unable to assemble a subcommittee quorum to mark up no-fault legislation.

94th and 95th Congresses (1975–1978)

No-fault proponents on Capitol Hill sought to circumvent the delaying tactics that killed S.945 and S.354 by proceeding simultaneously with no-fault legislation in both chambers of the 94th Congress. The Senate Commerce Committee and the newly-formed House Interstate and Foreign Commerce Subcommittee on Consumer Protection and Finance both held hearings. The Senate committee, after fine-tuning S.354 in response to constitutional misgivings Attorney General Levi expressed, approved the bill by voice vote on June 27, 1975.

The House subcommittee had a more difficult time reporting out H.R.9650, S.354's companion bill. Representative Jack McCollister prolonged the mark-up sessions for weeks by insisting on a line-by-line reading of the bill, during which he offered a steady stream of amendments. On October 29, McCollister unexpectedly relented and the subcommittee reported H.R.9650 favorably to the Interstate and Foreign Commerce Committee by a 5–4 vote.

The subcommittee's vote was a cause for celebration among the legislation's supporters because this was the first time a no-fault bill had gotten beyond a subcommittee in the House of Representatives. The optimism no-fault proponents felt in October 1975, however, was tempered by the Federal Election Commission's announcement that a newly-formed campaign fund, the Attorney's Congressional Campaign Trust, had raised more than $400,000 in its first seven months.

The Trust was not connected formally to either ATLA or the no-fault issue, but virtually all the contributors were ATLA members and its chairman was ATLA past president Leonard Ring. Although Ring denied that the sole criterion for allocating funds from the Trust would be potential recipients' positions on no-fault, the Trust's symbiotic connection with ATLA, "the nation's first single-issue lobby," made it obvious on Capitol Hill that contributions from the Trust would in fact be tied only to no-fault.

ATLA used its political action fund not only as a carrot (by contributing directly to members of Congress) but as a stick (by telling members of Congress who threatened to oppose ATLA that it would use the funds to finance the campaign of an opponent, possibly recruited from the ATLA membership, in the next election). The fact that trial lawyers are a large part of the pool from which congressional candidates are drawn gave added weight to these threats.

Although formation of the trust did not win ATLA much popularity in the Senate, it had the desired effect. Despite the eloquent plea of Senator Pastore, who began by calling the nonthreshold no-fault plans ATLA championed "trial lawyers' relief acts," and ended by saying, "Trial lawyers have their self-interest, but what about the public interest? What about the people?", the Senate killed S.354 by a 49–45 vote to recommit to the Commerce Committee.

In light of ATLA's rapidly expanding strength, the Senate's recommittal vote seemed to signal the end of no-fault legislation in Congress. President Jimmy Carter breathed new life into the no-fault movement in 1977, however, when he strongly endorsed federal no-fault legislation. S. Lynn Sutcliffe, who had left the Senate Commerce Committee staff after working on no-fault legislation for eight years, agreed to serve as president of the reconstituted Committee on Consumers No–Fault.

Sutcliffe's committee attempted to combat the strength of the no-fault opponents by marshalling its constituent organizations' grass-roots forces and by launching a publicity campaign aimed both at highlighting no-fault legislation's merits and exposing the legal profession's self-interest. Sutcliffe unleashed another storm of criticism of the legal profession in the nation's newspapers.

Under increasing pressure from elements within the Association to be more outspoken in opposition to no-fault legislation, the ABA again formed a special committee on automobile insurance litigation to review its position in light of the recent political developments. This ABA special committee shed all pretense of impartiality. To write the committee's report, the ABA hired a legal scholar, Richard Posner, known to be strongly opposed to no-fault.

The ABA need not have abandoned its pretense of impartiality. ATLA had the political situation under control. For the 95th Congress, ATLA supplemented its experienced lobbying staff by retaining professional lobbyists Thomas Hale Boggs and William Timmons. The combination of ATLA's usual delaying tactics, as perfected by Boggs and Timmons, and its huge campaign fund proved too strong for no-fault supporters to overcome. The bill died its last death in the 95th Congress.

Discussion Questions

1. The account of efforts to obtain a federal "no-fault" statute for automobile accidents radiates disillusionment and even cynicism about the Bar. The case study assumes that no-fault is a socially desirable development that has

been systematically prevented from enactment by the spirited opposition of self-interested lawyers and their organizations. No issue of legal reform is that simple. In this, as in every case, there were opponents as well as supporters who believed deeply and disinterestedly in their cause. But the case does encourage consideration of a fundamental ethical issue that faces the lawyer who is asked to represent a cause he does not believe in before a legislative body.

Consider the tax attorney whom the trade association of a particular industry has hired to press for a favorable change in the Internal Revenue Code. Assume that he has become expert in the area by representing firms in that industry who have lost before the courts and that the lawyer's personal belief is that the courts have been correct not only legally but also because there is no adequate basis for a special exemption such as the one on behalf of which he has been hired to testify. Indeed, he believes that there are highly persuasive arguments against the special exemption but these are known only to a few experts like himself.

If an attorney is employed to testify before a legislative or administrative body on behalf of his client, he must represent the client's position. However, he must make it clear to the legislative body whom he is representing and that he is not appearing on his own behalf. The Code of Professional Responsibility, EC 8–4, addresses this issue:

> Whenever a lawyer seeks legislative or administrative changes, he should identify the capacity in which he appears, whether on behalf of himself, a client or the public. [Furthermore], a lawyer may advocate such changes on behalf of a client even though he does not agree with them. But, when a lawyer purports to act on behalf of the public, he should espouse only those changes which he conscientiously believes to be in the public interest.

The American Bar Association's Model Rules are similar. Rule 3.9 states that "a lawyer representing a client before a legislative . . . tribunal . . . shall disclose that the appearance is in a representative capacity. . . ."

Are these the only obligations of a lawyer lobbyist? Rule 3.9 of the ABA Model Rules makes all of the obligations of basic honesty applicable to legislative testimony by incorporating the provisions of more general rules. But it specifically omits and thereby fails to mandate compliance with the general requirement of Rule 3.3(d) that "in an *ex parte* proceeding, a lawyer shall inform the tribunal of all material facts known to the lawyer which will enable the tribunal to make an informed decision, whether or not the facts are adverse." Surely the assumption that any facts that one lawyer omits are likely to be brought out by an opposing party, doubtful as it may be in many litigating contexts, cannot be accepted and relied upon in a legislative context. Here it frequently is true that important interests are unrepresented. Why should the obligation of Rule 3.3(d) not apply to legislative testimony?

Even if the lawyer's only obligation is to make clear that he is appearing on behalf of a client in a representational capacity, is this as easy as the rules' wording suggests? If a client hires a lawyer who was once Secretary of State to urge its position on a tariff bill, is not the very purpose to suggest that the lawyer is acting "on behalf of the public," a situation in which the Code of

Professional Responsibility requires that "he should espouse only those changes which he conscientiously believes to be in the public interest"? What if the lawyer was formerly Assistant Attorney General in charge of the Tax Division of the Department of Justice, a history he brings out in the course of introducing himself as the representative of the particular industry? Is there not a clear suggestion that the views are his expert, personal views? How does a lawyer in this position, or anyone recognized by a legislative committee as expert in the area, respond if he is asked by a senator or representative what is his personal opinion?

Many lawyers become expert in the law affecting the business of their clients. That was surely true, for example, of Raul Lovett in the field of workers' compensation (see the *Lawyering for Fun and Profit: Workers' Compensation and Personal Injury Practice* case at p. 256 and of Lively Wilson in the area of asbestos litigation (see the *Asbestos Litigation* case at p. 293). A high proportion of those who know the most about the Internal Revenue Code, the National Labor Relations Act, or the Federal Communications Act are the lawyers for clients who have called upon them to deal with these bodies of law. Are these lawyer-experts free to volunteer their own experience to legislative or administrative bodies in situations where they have not been asked to represent a client but in which they know their client's interest and position is contrary to what the lawyer would urge as best for the country?

What if his opinion and his expertise on the subject are based on information he obtained while working for the client? Even if the information is not confidential, the attorney only acquired it because his client retained him to research and investigate the issue. The potential conflict of interest argues against the lawyer testifying. On the other hand, a lawyer has an obligation to assist in improving the legal system. EC 8–1 provides that:

> By reason of education and experience, lawyers are especially qualified to recognize deficiencies in the legal system and to initiate corrective measures therein. Thus, they should participate in proposing and supporting legislation and programs to improve the system, without regard to the general interests or desires of clients or former clients.

If lawyers, who both have the best chance to know when a law is working badly and the special competence to put it in order, are prevented from testifying on such issues, who else will take the initiative?

A 1958 Report by the Joint Conference on Professional Responsibility of the ABA admonished the members of the organization for failing to propose needed legal reforms. The committee reminded its members that "[t]he lawyer tempted to repose should recall the heavy costs paid by his profession when needed legal reform has to be accomplished through the initiative of public spirited laymen. Where change must be thrust from without upon an unwilling Bar, the public's least flattering picture of the lawyer seems confirmed."

2. Now turn from the obligation of the lawyer as representative of an industry or firm to the obligations of organizations of lawyers when these organizations are taking a position before the legislature. Is there anything wrong with ATLA representing the economic interests of its members in a legislative contest over an issue such as no-fault that greatly affects their economic well-being? Does it have some obligation to take a more principled stand or adopt a wider vision? Does an affirmative answer to these questions depend upon the assumption that a majority of the members of ATLA honestly believe that no-fault would be better for the country? What if most members believe it would make worse-off those injured in automobile accidents but would reduce the costs of automobile insurance to the average driver?

Why would one give an affirmative answer to these questions in any event? Are not the interests of trial lawyers as entitled to representation as those of any other economic group? If ATLA does not represent their interests, who will? Is the problem that ATLA has some fiduciary responsibility because it has a near monopoly of expertise about the present automobile accident liability system? Is this true? Are not insurance companies equally well-informed and equally well-represented?

Perhaps the problem is that ATLA does not purport to be a special interest. In the case study we see its president denying that economic self-interest affected its position. But all organized interests that appear before the Congress describe their special concerns in language about the common good. That is the way lobbyists talk. Indeed any advocate before a governmental body will press for a conception of the common good that is consistent with the interests of the party he represents. Is ATLA doing anything different?

Would it be better for the country if an organization such as ATLA were given special deference because of its claim that it was able to rise above economic interests in arriving at its position; *i.e.,* because it claimed to speak for justice and efficiency rather than for the interests of trial lawyers? Is not an organization such as ATLA inevitably biased by its own economic interests? If it is, is it not better that it represent those interests forthrightly and without any claim to more, at least when the other side is adequately represented? Would it be better if ATLA gave up any pretense of being different from other special interests?

Is the ABA's position any different? It represents a broader constituency of lawyers with more diverse interests. Still, on many issues the interests of most lawyers are consistent and clear. And on many more the intense interest of some groups of lawyers, such as the Criminal Defense Bar, will enjoy deference from many other members who are relatively uninterested in the subject but would like to be supported by their colleagues on future occasions. Still the claim of a particular economic interest to be zealously represented before the Congress or a state legislature is less compelling for the leaders of the ABA.

The ABA has never considered itself a trade association created to advance the self-interest of its membership. The original ABA Constitution (1878) listed as the new organization's objectives: (1) advancing the science of jurisprudence; (2) promoting the administration of justice; (3) promoting uniformity of legislation; (4) upholding the honor of the profession; and (5) encouraging cordial intercourse among members of the Bar. However, the ABA does not purport to be completely altruistic. When matters of interest to the legal profession arise, the ABA staff collects information and disseminates it to the membership. If the membership, through its representative body, the House of Delegates, takes a stance on a particular issue, the ABA articulates and publicizes that position.

The ultimate power of the ABA is vested in the House of Delegates, a democratic body in the sense that its members are representatives of all the constituent elements of the ABA. Twenty percent of the House of Delegates are directly elected from the 52 state bar associations (including the District of Columbia and Puerto Rico). The remaining members are delegates because of their office (e.g., U.S. Attorney–General), status (e.g., past ABA presidents), or as representatives of their sections. The 52 state representatives within the House of Delegates have the responsibility of electing the president of the Board of Governors. The Board, in which is vested the power to authorize ABA action on an interim basis, is the day-to-day ruling body of the ABA. The ABA president, aided to a large but informal degree by the president-elect and the treasurer, wields the executive power of the association.

Does the ABA have an obligation to resist the self-interest of lawyers in stating its position on issues such as no-fault? The answer is "yes" if the ABA claims a special position of respect and leadership in national debates about issues of this sort. Could the Bar Association expect to have its views given unusual weight if it frankly admitted that the economic or other interests of its members would be given great weight in arriving at those views?

Is the question then what role we want the ABA to play in the legislative resolution of matters about which lawyers are likely to be unusually expert or experienced but in which they also are likely to have a substantial economic interest? Would the country be better served by a frank denial of any special responsibility on behalf of the Bar? Can the same question be asked of organizations of doctors, scientists, architects, accountants, and others? Do not legislators often want to defer to the views of such professional associations on major policy issues affecting their fields of special expertise? What responsibilities come with that deference?

If the ABA were to decide to declare frankly that it would represent the interests of its lawyer members at least as much as the interests of the nation as a whole when these interests might conflict, what would be the effect on respect for lawyers, courts, and the law? What would the message be to lawyers about their community responsibilities, whether to furnish *pro bono* services or call to a court's attention a precedent the opponent has overlooked?

Should the ABA have a position on major political issues? The other side of the coin of disinterestedness is the risk that the ABA or a local bar association may, in complete good faith, confuse the economic or social class interest of its clients or the beliefs of those with whom the members associate with the public interest, whatever that may be. No question of legislative policy is so technical that the views of lawyers as experts on an area of law involve nothing more than specialized, professional judgment. Even if the profession has no economic stake in the legislative matter, the organization may set forth, in the guise of expert professional judgment, the beliefs and views of limited social groups. Members of the House of Delegates of the ABA are not even a particularly representative cross-section of the legal profession.

Should the ABA take a position only on matters as to which the component of "expert legal judgment" is very high? That would not include support for legal services for the poor, a matter on which many think the Bar should speak out. In 1965 Justice Louis Powell, then President of the ABA, used all the powers of persuasion at his disposal to bring the Bar to endorse federal funding for legal services for the poor, over the objection of influential segments of the ABA. Should it only take a position when its membership (or, even broader, the population of lawyers in the United States) are likely to share a common view or at least are not badly divided? Not so long ago this would have precluded taking stands on civil rights issues which now seem matters of elemental justice. What, then, are the issues on which a national or local bar association should speak in the name of all lawyers?

3.   Sanctioning Lawyers

When to Give Up a Law Suit: Davidoff vs. Meyerson *

Alan Parker, a partner at Fried & Campbell (F & C), a large and prestigious Boston law firm, looked at the clock on his office wall. It was 9:45 p.m. on a Thursday night (March 28, 1987). He had told his nine year old daughter, Melissa, that he would be home at 9:30 to watch "Cheers," her favorite TV show. He was angry at himself for missing their "date" but he was so preoccupied with his work that he had not only forgotten the time, but his stomach as well—he had not eaten since noon.

He was in the midst of deciding whether to file a complaint in the case he had been investigating for the past three months. The statute of limitations was about to run and his client was pressuring him to file by Monday. Two days ago he had been confident about filing—now, he was not so sure. Gary Abrams, counsel for the defendant, had remarked offhand that such a suit could be challenged as frivolous. Parker was so disturbed by the comment that he asked Joe Campbell, a fifth year associate at F & C and the best devil's advocate he had ever met, to look into the issue and prepare a memo on the merits of the case, given the substantive law on securities as well as the law on frivolous litigation. Joe's memo, which he received yesterday, troubled him.

Parker had also discussed the case briefly with Donald Armstrong, a senior partner in the corporate division. He expected Armstrong to be supportive, as he usually was and as other partners in the litigation department had been, but instead Armstrong cautioned: "We don't want to be known as a firm that engages in frivolous litigation. That's not the kind of reputation we want. . . . I'd hate to see us get involved in something like that. I just read a piece last week in the *National Law Journal* where a firm was required to pay $10,000 of the defendant's legal fees for bringing a frivolous action. You'll be awfully unpopular around here if that happens."

Parker had to decide what to do. He called his daughter and apologized for missing her program and said he would be home very late. He went back to the case, reviewing all the facts he had put together.

---

* This case is modeled after *Nemeroff v. Abelson,* 620 F.2d 339 (2d Cir.1980). However, the names and many of the facts have been changed to make the case a more useful tool for teaching purposes.

The Facts

Parker's involvement in the case began on January 14, 1987. On that day, he was present at a meeting between one of his partners and a longstanding client, Philip Stone. Mr. Stone told them he had information that a forthcoming issue of *Baker's Monthly* (a well known financial journal) would carry an article by Ronald Meyerson (a financial reporter who wrote a column published on the front page of the magazine entitled "Up and Down the Stock Market"). Stone was apprehensive the article would contain comments critical of a company ("Dentrex") in which he had a substantial equity interest. He portrayed the publication of the negative comments as part of a scheme designed to cause a fall in the price of Dentrex stock—an outcome that would redound to the benefit of particular investors who had sold Dentrex short.* Stone stated that this scheme had been successfully employed against another company, Compucare, a manufacturer of medical equipment. The value of Compucare stock had risen for some time after the company went public, and then had declined substantially for no understandable economic reason. Mr. Stone agreed to finance an investigation in an attempt to establish that Mr. Meyerson had leaked information to certain investors. Stone said that he knew other investors who might be willing to bring suit if enough evidence of securities violations could be found.

Mr. Stone had received his information from a broker friend, Harvey Fein, to whom Parker and his partner made a conference call. Fein confirmed Stone's statements, and furnished additional details about trading during the past year in Compucare stock. Donna Galvan, another Wall Street broker, corroborated Fein's statements.

Parker then called Daniel Bortner, *Baker's* managing editor, to tell him of Stone's belief that a forthcoming piece by Meyerson would contain negative comments about Dentrex and ask him either to delete those comments or to inform the magazine's readers that the sources of Meyerson's information were short sellers of Dentrex stock. Bortner

---

* Short sellers agree to sell at a future date shares of stock that they do not currently own. In order for a short sale to be profitable, the market price of the company must decline between the date of the short sale and the subsequent date when the seller must effect a "covering" price. The mechanics of the process are as follows: An order is given to a broker to sell the stock short. The broker executing the sale then "borrows" shares of stock from another broker. The first broker then "loans" the stock to the short seller who sells it at the current market price. The purchaser is unaware whether he is buying from a short seller or from an actual owner of stocks. The market value of the loaned stock is deposited with the lender of the stock. The amount of this deposit varies with changes in the price of the security. If the market price rises, the deposit must be increased; conversely, if the market price drops, the borrower of the stock may request the return of the difference between the amount he has deposited and the then market value of the stock. At the covering date, the investor purchases stock in the market, returns it to the lender, and receives in return the money that has been deposited.

referred Parker to Edward Lewis, an attorney in a New York law firm that did the magazine's legal work.   The interview with Lewis was inconclusive.   Although the next piece in *Baker's* contained no negative comments about Dentrex, a later piece (February 7, 1987) did express some foreboding about Dentrex's future prospects.

Parker also got in touch with Compucare's president, John Graham, who informed him that the company was aware of rumors of manipulation in the trading of his company's stock.   Graham told Parker that he had requested an investigation by both the New York Stock Exchange (NYSE) and the Securities and Exchange Commission (SEC).

On January 18, Parker received a call from Jim O'Hare of the NYSE who inquired into Parker's conversation four days earlier with Daniel Bortner and observed: "the cops at the SEC felt that [Parker's] call had forewarned *Baker's* just before the 'trap was sprung' ".   A Mr. Beecher, from the SEC, called Parker on the same day, asked him about his conversation with Bortner, and requested that he be kept informed. These contacts with the NYSE and the SEC were continued and, on February 8, 1987, Parker met separately with representatives of the NYSE and the SEC.   By the time of these meetings, the focus of Parker's investigations had shifted away from Dentrex and toward the activities of Compucare short sellers and their relationship to Ronald Meyerson.

Parker discovered that allegations of collusive activity among short sellers and Meyerson to depress the price of publicly traded companies were not new.   Parker had received additional information from many persons relating to trading in Compucare: activities of short sellers, alleged family or other personal relationships among *Baker's,* the magazine's personnel, and various hedge funds,* alleged financial interests of magazine personnel in certain stocks, alleged secret investments or bank accounts of certain editors at *Baker's,* suggestions of a company-wide conspiracy at Prescott Brown (a publisher of financial reports) affecting wire service reports relating to certain securities and the content of articles appearing in the *Wall Street Times,* the participation by the NYSE specialists in Compucare in conspiracies to drive down the price of Compucare stock, the participation in such conspiracies of certain analysts and traders, and many other matters.   In each instance, Parker took steps to investigate the allegations, but for most of them he was unable to obtain supporting evidence.

Parker's investigation focused primarily on the relationship between Meyerson and the short sellers.   On January 25, 1987, Parker

---

* Hedge funds are groups of investors, usually in the form of limited partnerships, that employ speculative techniques in the hope of obtaining large capital gains.

received a call from a New York attorney representing Information Networks and Control (INC). The caller told Parker that INC had been a victim of raids by short sellers and of a two year assault by Meyerson's columns. The management of the now faltering company believed that there was a relationship between the Meyerson articles and the short selling in INC stock. At meetings with management and attorneys for INC, Parker learned of the existence of a group known as the "Trade Union." This group was made up of money managers who met regularly over meals to discuss stocks. Parker discovered that a negative analysis of INC that had been distributed to the group later formed the core of one of Meyerson's columns. Before the article appeared, two members of the "Union," Douglas Curtis and Melvin Gibson, had taken short positions on INC. Parker considered this information to be evidence corroborating the existence of a relationship between the *Baker's* staff and a small group of short sellers.

A key development in Parker's investigation was his meeting with George Kelly, a financial reporter then working at the *Washington Globe*. As early as 1985, Kelly became suspicious of Meyerson's relationship with hedge funds involved in short selling and published an article about it in *Business News,* a weekly magazine. When Prescott Brown, publisher of *Baker's,* sued *Business News's* publisher, the parties settled the case and *Business News* printed a retraction.

By early February, Parker had gathered a fair number of statements suggesting collusion between Meyerson and certain short sellers. In a telephone conversation on February 3, 1987, Paul Hale, an NYSE employee, told Parker that the NYSE was particularly concerned with trading by Melvin Gibson, a Compucare specialist working for the Exchange, and that one "could conclude that there existed a correlation between Gibson's trades and Meyerson's columns." However, five days later on February 8, Parker met with NYSE employees, including Hale and two senior officials of the section for market surveillance, who informed him that, contrary to Harvey Fein's assertions, the NYSE was satisfied that none of its Compucare specialists were involved in the manipulation of Compucare stock.

Despite these findings, Parker believed there was something "rotten in Denmark." He could find no rational explanation for the decline in Compucare stock. He had obtained copies of many New York firms' recommendations on Compucare, and the almost universal consensus was that the company was fundamentally solid and had a substantial technological lead on its competitors. On the same day he heard from the NYSE, he conferred with officials at the SEC and they informed him that their investigation was still underway.

On February 15, 1987, Albert Ball, an attorney for Prescott Brown, publisher of *Baker's*, telephoned Parker to discuss his investigation of the Stone charges. Ball expressed the view that these charges were unfounded and asked Parker to call him before taking any action about the charges.

By mid-March, however, Parker was satisfied that he had the kind of case his firm would be willing to bring for manipulation of Compucare stock. His partners (except for Donald Armstrong) supported the view. But he still needed two things before he could bring the suit: a plaintiff * and a substantial basis for the allegation of collusion between Meyerson and the short sellers. As to the second obstacle, events that were unfolding in Chicago removed most of his uncertainty.

Between March 7 and March 15, 1987, the price of the common stock of Mohawk Brewing (whose stock was actively traded) dropped from $61 to $28.50. The dramatic drop was preceded by the publication on March 7 in the Meyerson column of negative comments about the company. Parker was able to predict the publication of the Mohawk Brewing article a week before it appeared in print. He had obtained a list of short stocks held by Melvin Gibson, one of the people he suspected of benefiting from Meyerson's columns, and from it was able to predict, with some but not 100 percent accuracy, what Meyerson was going to write about.

Then, on March 14, Dr. Benjamin Davidoff, a client of Harvey Fein's, contacted Parker and indicated that he wanted to sue Meyerson. Dr. Davidoff was a well established dentist in New York who had investments in Compucare ranging from $180,000 to $300,000 during the period in question. When Fein informed him that short sellers were driving down Compucare stock with the assistance of a newspaper writer and that he could sue, Davidoff contacted Parker.

Now Parker had a plaintiff and some evidence about the relationship between Meyerson and the short sellers. Any doubts Parker may have had about bringing the suit were dispelled by an article that had appeared two days earlier in the *Wall Street Times*. The article, which discussed the dramatic drop in Mohawk Brewing's stock, quoted Melvin Gibson as saying: "In the past, I have urged him [Meyerson] to recommend and to disrecommend stocks, and he's done it." For Parker, this was a very significant statement, almost an admission of collusion between the short sellers and Meyerson.

After he saw the article, Parker called Ball to inform him that he would file a suit in the near future. Ball once again tried to dissuade Parker, but Parker was adamant. He had already drafted a complaint against Ronald Meyerson, Daniel Bortner, Prescott Brown and Compa-

---

* Philip Stone would not be an appropriate plaintiff in the suit because he did not own any stock in Compucare, and Parker had not come up with the same evidence of manipulation of Dentrex stock that he had for Compucare.

ny, and nine investor defendants. Among the investor defendants were Thomas Bortner, the brother of Daniel Bortner, who managed an investment house called Hedgewood Associates, Melvin Gibson, Douglas Curtis, Mark Levine, and Harold Klein.

The first count of the complaint alleged that the publisher and investor defendants had conspired to manipulate the price of the stock of Compucare and other selected publicly traded companies for the benefit of investor defendants. According to the complaint, the conspiracy proceeded as follows: Meyerson told the investors he was going to write a column critical of Compucare. Knowing that this would depress the Compucare stock price, the investors sold Compucare short before publication and made covering purchases at the reduced price after publication.

The complaint's second count alleged that the short seller defendants had artificially depressed the price of Compucare stock by increasing their short selling activities whenever necessary to prevent significant increases in the market price of Compucare shares, effecting short sales on certain dates to assure that the closing price of Compucare stock for such days would be artificially low, and undertaking short sales to discourage institutional and other investors from buying Compucare stock, thereby further depressing its market price.

The only thing that gave Parker pause was the memo by Joe Campbell. He had read it four times in the last 24 hours, but now he turned to it again.

Memorandum

TO: Alan Parker
FROM: Joe Campbell RE: Meyerson Case
DATE: March 27, 1987

Issue Presented

You asked me to review the relevant facts of the Meyerson case, as stipulated by you, and evaluate them in light of (1) the relevant Securities law, (2) possible claims of frivolous litigation, and (3) the likelihood of an award of attorneys' fees if the suit is found to be frivolous. I have outlined the relevant law and presented my opinion below.

Securities Law

Courts have tried to identify the scope of liability under the broadly stated prohibitions of Rule 10b–5. According to the case law on the issue, liability depends upon proof that a person used a manipulative or deceptive device in connection with the purchase or sale of a security. In making or facilitating the transaction, the person must have acted with scienter going beyond mere negligence. The plaintiff must show reliance on a material deception or at least that the deception was causally related to his loss.

Causes of Action

Count One

In its present form Count One of the complaint is vague and confused and should be modified to express a clear theory of liability. Liability under Rule 10b–5 may be based on one of the following:

(1) insider trading,

(2) affirmative misrepresentation, or

(3) failure to disclose a material fact.

The SEC and the courts have used Rule 10b–5 as a sanction against trading on "inside information," i.e., private information intended to be available only for corporate purposes. Liability results from disclosure by "insiders" or those with access to inside information (tippers) of "material" inside information to potential traders (tippees) and from use of the information by the tippees to trade on the stock market. The tipper is liable if he knew or should have known that the information he conveyed was nonpublic and that he was breaching his fiduciary duty to shareholders.

The basis for action under the insider trading theory does not appear relevant to the facts in the Meyerson case because it is not at all clear that Meyerson's information about Compucare was given to him by a corporate insider or that he had access to inside information. Rather, it appears that the information was either (a) based on an analysis by Meyerson of the market, or (b) fabricated by Meyerson or the short sellers. Under either of these two scenarios the insider trading theory would not apply.

A more promising cause of action would be one based on either affirmative misrepresentation or nondisclosure of information material to a decision to buy or sell the stock. Under the affirmative misrepresentation theory, you would have to show that Meyerson put forth false or misleading information in his column. However, based on the facts as you have related them, there is no evidence for such an assertion other than the fact that other companies gave Compucare good reviews. Meyerson's negative review of Compucare may simply have been based on different views about the market rather than on fabrication.*

---

*I have reviewed all of the relevant Meyerson columns and although they do not paint a rosy picture of Compucare sales, they appear credible. The reports stated that

The strongest basis for a cause of action under 10b–5 against the publishing defendants is their failure to disclose a "material" fact. There is case law to support this view in a factual situation similar to that in the Meyerson case. In *Zweig v. Hearst Corp.*, 594 F.2d 1261 (9th Cir.1979), plaintiffs sued a financial columnist, alleging that he violated Section 10(b) by purchasing stock in a company at a discount, publishing a favorable column about the company, waiting for a resulting rise in the market, and then selling the stock at a profit. The Ninth Circuit held for the plaintiff, stating that the federal securities laws:

> require a financial columnist, in recommending a security that he or she owns, to provide the public with all material information he or she has on that security, including his or her ownership, and any intent he or she may have (a) to score a quick profit on the recommendation, or (b) to allow or encourage the recommendation to be published as an advertisement in his or her own periodical.

Although the *Zweig* facts are somewhat different from those in the present case in that Meyerson did not actually own Compucare stock, they appear close enough that *Zweig* would be controlling. The alleged fact that Meyerson was reporting in a way that would benefit a few selected short sellers would appear to be a material fact affecting his objectivity and a stockholder's decision to buy or sell. Despite the fact that this theory appears to be the most appropriate to the facts at hand, there are major gaps in the evidence that would be necessary to succeed in such a claim. For example, there is no evidence that:

(1) Meyerson benefited from his own reports; or

(2) Meyerson leaked the information to the short sellers.

Perhaps this information is available, but you have not provided me with it in your account of the facts or in your complaint.

Count Two

Count Two of the complaint is based on Section 9(a) of the Securities and Exchange Act—the "antimanipulation" provision. The rule prohibits trading to induce others to purchase or sell. In order to prove manipulation, a plaintiff must show:

(1) a "series of transactions" on the part of defendants;

---

the market for CAT scanners was going to level out because of various factors, including their high cost and the increasing concern over the rising costs of medical care, increased competition, and state regulation of hospital expenditures. The columns indicated that Compucare would be particularly vulnerable due in part to its proportionately large reliance on CAT scanner sales.

(2) that defendants created "actual or apparent active trading," or that the trading "raised or depressed the security's price"; and

(3) that defendants engaged in the transactions "for the purpose of inducing the purchase or sale of such security by others."

The latter requirement is the most difficult to prove. Authorities presume the purpose was present when the manipulators had a pecuniary interest in achieving a price change *and took steps to effect such change.* Courts have identified a number of actions as steps to effect a price change. These include engaging in concentrated trading, getting others to buy in a bull operation or sell in a bear manipulation, touting or employing others to tout the security, or paying brokers additional compensation to induce customers to trade.

A showing of a valid nonmanipulation reason for the trades, however, will go a long way toward demonstrating that the proscribed purpose was not present; no Section 9(a)(2) manipulation can be established without the requisite intent. There is no indication from the facts in Meyerson that the investor defendants had the intent to mislead others by their active trading. Some evidence that the short sellers paid Meyerson to report negatively about Compucare stock would be the type of information that would substantially help your case.

Frivolous Litigation

The second issue you have asked me to explore is the present status of the law on so-called "frivolous" litigation, specifically: (1) whether the present case might be considered frivolous and (2) whether attorneys' fees can be awarded for such frivolous litigation.

Federal Rule of Civil Procedure 11

The issue of frivolous litigation has become a hot and controversial topic in legal circles primarily as a result of the 1983 amendment to F.R.C.P. 11. Numerous articles analyzing the amended rule and reporting on cases in which attorneys have been required to pay the opposing sides' attorneys fees have been published in both popular and academic legal journals. In the two years following the rule's amendment, there were more than 200 reported cases involving Rule 11 sanctions. *See* Nelken, "Sanctions under Amended Federal Rule 11— Some 'Chilling' Problems in the Struggle Between Compensation and Punishment," 74 Geo.L.J. 1313 (1986). In some cases courts have imposed severe sanctions on counsel and clients. *See Whittington v. Ohio River Co.,* 115 F.R.D. 201, 205 (E.D.Ky.1987).

The amended rule attempts to discourage dilatory or abusive tactics and to help streamline the litigation process by lessening frivolous claims or defenses. *See* Advisory Committee Notes, 1983 Amendments. Under Rule 11, an attorney must sign every pleading, motion, and other paper he files on behalf of his client. The signature certifies that the attorney has read the paper, that "to the best of his knowledge, information and belief formed after reasonable inquiry [the paper] is well grounded in fact and is warranted by existing law or a good faith argument for the extension, modification, or reversal of existing law, and that it is not interposed for any improper purpose, such as to harass or to cause unnecessary delay or needless increase in the cost of litigation."

Before its amendment, Rule 11 did not require lawyers to look into either the factual or legal grounds of a pleading or motion. The lawyer's signature only meant that he had read the pleading, that he believed there was good ground to support it, and that the pleading was not made for the purpose of delay. The courts generally applied a subjective good faith standard in determining whether a lawyer had violated old Rule 11. But good faith is no longer enough. Under the amended rule, the signing attorney must have formed his belief after "reasonable inquiry." There is an affirmative duty to investigate both the facts and the law. This new objective standard is more stringent than the original subjective one. Thus, a greater range of circumstances trigger its violation.

The authority to assess attorneys' fees under Rule 11 is also new. Before the amendment, courts looked outside the federal rules for authority to deal with irresponsible litigators and litigants. But the 1983 amendment authorizes a court to impose costs, including attorneys' fees incurred as a result of the submission of an improper paper. Rule 11 mandates that the Court, upon its own initiative or a motion, impose sanctions upon the attorney, the client, or both, if a violation of the rule's requirements has been found. While the Court must impose sanctions if a violation is found, the nature and amount of sanctions is discretionary.

The amended rule has provoked sharp debate. Of most concern in our situation is the fact that it leaves a number of questions unanswered, specifically:

(1) How much inquiry is required to meet the "reasonable" threshold before filing suit?

(2) Can a lawyer rely on his client's word or does reasonable inquiry require corroboration from independent sources?

The Rule 11 "reasonable inquiry" standard is hardly self-defining. Like "reasonable care," "unreasonable restraint of trade," and "beyond a reasonable doubt," "reasonable inquiry" needs interpretation. But those other phrases have a history of judicial meaning, and so far "reasonable inquiry" does not. The findings of a survey conducted by the Federal Judicial Center in 1985 indicate substantial differences of interpretation among judges as to what constitutes a violation of Rule 11. *See* S.M. Kassin, "An Empirical Study of Rule 11 Sanctions" 38 (Federal Judicial Center 1985). Judicial opinions reported since the amended Rule 11 became effective reflect this lack of consensus and thus lack definitive criteria to determine when the duty of "reasonable inquiry" has been met. For detailed analyses of this problem, see: Note, "Plausible Pleadings: Developing Standards for Rule 11 Sanctions," 100 Harvard L.Rev. 630 (1987); Cavanagh, "Developing Standards Under Amended Rule 11 of the Federal Rules of Civil Procedure," 14 Hofstra Law Review 499 (1986). There are some cases, however, which can assist in evaluating some of the considerations of the "reasonable inquiry" test as it relates to our case.

Although an attorney need not believe a suit will succeed, he must believe the claim is tenable, arguable, or debatable. This requirement establishes a fine line between those claims that an attorney can ethically represent and those that are frivolous. In one relevant case, *Miller v. Schweickart,* 413 F.Supp. 1059 (S.D.N.Y.1976), several defendants were sued for conspiracy to defraud. The court found, however, that the claim advanced against one of the named defendants, Josephal, bordered on being frivolous. The court justified its finding on the grounds that Josephal was named as a defendant merely on the basis of unconfirmed rumors of a most tenuous nature. The court indicated that the plaintiff should have named as defendants only those against whom there was in fact a sufficient basis for suit, and added others later if discovery revealed information justifying their joinder. This case was brought before Rule 11 was amended, when the standard was more relaxed. Given that the standard has been raised, if brought under the amended Rule 11, the court would likely find a violation for insufficient prefiling inquiry and thus would impose sanctions.

It is clear that under the amended rule, reasonable inquiry cannot be established if the attorney has not made any inquiry at all, or if he has relied only on his client, when further investigation of the facts could have been undertaken to confirm or deny the client's story. *See* Schwarzer, "Sanctions Under the New Federal Rule 11—A Closer Look," 104 F.R.D. 181 (1985). On the other hand, an attorney is not required to disbelieve his own client and accept the defendant's assertions. *Friedgood v. Axelrod,* 593 F.Supp. 395 (S.D.N.Y.1984). To determine whether the attorney may depend solely on his client, he should determine "if his knowledge is direct or hearsay and check closely the plausibility of the client's account." If an attorney must depend on his client, "he should question him thoroughly, not accepting the client's version on faith alone." *Nassau–Suffolk Ice Cream v. Integrated Resources, Inc.,* 114 F.R.D. 684 (S.D.N.Y.1987).

One court has advised that before a defendant has been named or a claim brought, "the attorney's file should contain facts admissible in evidence, or at least facts indicating the probable existence of evidence, implicating that defendant or supporting that claim. The shotgun complaint is out." *Whittington v. Ohio River Co.,* 115 F.R.D. 201 (E.D. Ky.1987). Thus, the hope that discovery will reveal something against the defendant as a basis for joining a defendant or asserting a claim against a defendant is insufficient to establish a reasonable inquiry into the facts. These guidelines are aimed at preventing abuse of the litigation process and to discourage pleading a little bit of everything in the hopes that something will stick. *Rodgers v. Lincoln Towing Service, Inc.,* 596 F.Supp. 13 (N.D.Ill.1984), *aff'd,* 771 F.2d 194 (7th Cir.1985). At the same time, however, Rule 11 "is not intended to chill the attorney's enthusiasm or creativity in pursuing factual or legal theories." Advisory Committee Notes, 1983 Amendments.

In one recent case, reliance on newspaper articles was found to be sufficient to meet the "reasonable inquiry" requirement of Rule 11 as a basis for signing a complaint in a shareholder's action. In *Kamerman v. Steinberg,* 113 F.R.D. 511 (S.D.N.Y.1986), plaintiff shareholders alleged that defendants violated Rule 10b–5 of the Securities and Exchange Act in connection with their purchase of shares of stock. Plaintiffs alleged that defendants made material misrepresentations in a schedule filed with the SEC stating that their intention in purchasing the stock was to take over the company. Plaintiffs asserted that defendants actually purchased the securities with the intent of later reselling them to the same company at a premium above the market price. Plaintiffs specifically pled reliance on news articles which appeared in *The Wall Street* and during their depositions, plaintiffs reiterated that their belief that defendants sought to inflate the price of the stock artificially was based upon their examination of news reports. Plaintiffs alleged that they were damaged by this material misrepresentation. The court found that reliance on the newspaper articles was sufficient to meet the requirements of Rule 11 because the articles were evidence of the material misrepresentations upon which plaintiffs may have relied. The plaintiffs had made a strong showing of substantial profit made by defendants from their resale of the stock. While this case may be of help to us, the allegations and facts can be persuasively distinguished. It also does not touch on other weaknesses of our case that could raise Rule 11 objections.

Although I have raised some of the issues involved when considering the requirements to comply with Rule 11, I have not given you much guidance in deciding whether to bring your suit. The Advisory Committee Notes to the 1983 Amendments indicate that the signer's conduct should be tested by inquiring what was reasonable to believe at the time the pleading was submitted. According to the Advisory Committee, what constitutes reasonable inquiry may depend on such factors as:

(1) how much time for investigation was available to the signer;

(2) whether he had to rely on a client for information as to the facts underlying the pleading;

(3) whether the pleading was based on a plausible view of the law;

(4) whether he depended on forwarding counsel or another member of the bar.

I also came across one article that may be of help in evaluating whether or not a suit is frivolous. ("Rule 11: Stop, Think, and Investigate," 11 Litigation 13, Winter 1985.) The article suggests that an attorney ask herself the following questions:

(1) Can your client's story be readily corroborated by information available from other sources?

(2) Is the cost of seeking out other sources prohibitive—that is, is it disproportionate to such factors as the amount at issue and the possible prejudice to the other side?

(3) Is your case based on an established legal theory or pushing the limits of the existing law?

(4) Does your client have actual knowledge of the facts or is his story based on hearsay or rumor?

(5) How well do you know your client? Is she a client of long-standing, in whose credibility you have developed confidence, or is she someone with whom you have had no previous experience?

(6) Is the client's story plausible or does it require independent verification?

All these guidelines raise some troublesome points for the Meyerson suit—

(1) Only Fein has substantiated Davidoff's claims;

(2) Davidoff as named plaintiff has provided you with little information; in fact, you have not even met him and he only came into the picture one week ago;

(3) Any evidence that Meyerson leaked information to the short sellers is tenuous;

(4) You have no evidence that Meyerson benefited from the reduction in the price of the stock and thus a weak basis for a case under Rule 10b–5.

Although Rule 11 has caused the recent controversy over the issue of frivolous litigation, defendants in the present case might employ other bases for the award of legal fees. These include: (1) the "bad faith" exception to the general common law rule that each side pays its own attorney fees; (2) Section 9(e) of the Securities Exchange Act of 1934, 15 U.S.C. § 78i(e); and (3) 28 U.S.C. § 1927. They also might invoke or threaten disciplinary sanctions under the Model Code of Professional Responsibility or the Model Rules of Professional Conduct.

Common Law

The general American rule governing allocation of the costs of litigation places the burden of counsel fees on each party, regardless of the outcome of the action. *See Alyeska Pipeline Services Co. v. Wilderness Society*, 421 U.S. 240 (1975). However, courts can shift fees to the prevailing party under various exceptions to the general rule. Among these is the power to shift fees where a party has commenced or conducted an action "in bad faith, vexatiously, wantonly or for oppressive reasons." The Second Circuit clarified the requirements for a finding of bad faith in *Browning Debenture Holder's Committee v. DASA Corp.*, 560 F.2d 1078 (2d Cir.1977), when it held that there must be "clear evidence" that the claims are "entirely without color and made for reasons of harassment or delay or for other improper purposes."

Section 9(e) of the Securities and Exchange Act

Defendants could also seek to base an award of attorneys' fees on Section 9(e) of the Securities and Exchange Act. The act provides that in actions brought under § 9(e):

> the court may, in its discretion, require an undertaking for the payment of the costs of such suit, and assess reasonable costs, including reasonable attorneys' fees, against either party litigant.

Although the language of § 9(e) makes an award of fees discretionary, the legislative history of this provision indicates that Congress included it to deter bad faith actions and "strike suits." In interpreting a substantially similar provision of the Civil Rights Act of 1964, the Supreme Court concluded that courts should award fees "upon a finding that the plaintiff's action was frivolous, unreasonable or without foundation, even though not brought in subjective bad faith." The Court pointed out that to require less would defeat Congressional efforts to promote vigorous enforcement of the statute, but to require more would be unnecessary in view of the long-standing equitable power to award fees upon a finding of bad faith.

28 U.S.C. § 1927

It is also possible that an attorney who institutes a frivolous lawsuit may find himself liable for attorneys' fees under the recently amended 28 U.S.C. § 1927. Section 1927 states that "any attorney . . . who so multiplies the proceedings in any case unreasonably and vexatiously may be required by the court to satisfy personally the excess costs, expenses, and attorneys' fees reasonably incurred because of such conduct." There are two limits on liability under that statute, however. First, the sanctions the provision refers to will not be imposed for an "unintended inconvenience to the court no matter how annoying it might be. Personal responsibility . . . flows only from an intentional departure from proper conduct, or, at a minimum, from a reckless disregard of the duty owed by counsel to the court."

Second, at least two cases limit an attorney's personal liability under the statute to situations where the attorney prompts the frivolous lawsuit. The attorney escapes liability if she merely acquiesces to the client's demands.

The language of the statute itself also poses some problems. For example, it refers to the attorney who "multiplies" the proceedings. It is unclear whether the drafters intended to include within this term the initial filing of a frivolous suit as well as the prolonging, delaying, or increasing of costs of an existing suit. It is also noteworthy that the section uses the phrase "unreasonably and vexatiously." A "vexatious suit" has been defined as "litigation for the purpose of harassing, annoying and vexing an opponent . . . being invoked . . . to further or satisfy a malicious motive." This definition indicates that there must be some element of intent to constitute vexatious litigation, an element not necessarily present in all frivolous suits.

The Model Code of Professional Responsibility and The Model Rules of Professional Conduct

The Code, which has the force of law in many states, is designed to be a basis for disciplinary action when conduct falls below the minimum standards stated in the disciplinary rules. Three disciplinary rules bear directly on the filing of frivolous lawsuits. DR2–109(A) prohibits a lawyer from accepting employment when he knows the claim is neither warranted under existing law nor supportable by a good faith argument for the extension, modification, or reversal of such law. DR7–102(A)(7) prohibits an attorney from "advancing" a claim under those same circumstances. Finally, DR7–102(A)(1) and DR7–102(A)(7) prohibit both filing a suit that is intended to harass a defendant and assisting a client in carrying out fraudulent conduct. In addition to these rules, courts have the inherent power to prevent the administration of justice from being brought into disrepute by such tactics, and they can use their implied power to supervise and discipline the conduct of attorneys who are officers of the court.

The American Bar Association's Model Rules of Professional Conduct, now being considered for adoption in many states, also attempt to deal with the problem. The Model Rules note that an attorney has responsibilities both to the legal system and to the general public. They say that "a lawyer's advice should include consideration of the client's legal obligations and the interests of other persons who may be affected." Furthermore, the Rules make it clear that there are limitations on the role of an advocate: "There is a limit beyond which legal inventiveness becomes frivolity, and the propriety of a lawyer's conduct in supporting a cause cannot depend simply on personal good faith."

The Rules continue to prohibit lawyers from filing frivolous lawsuits and define a frivolous claim as one of which "a disinterested legal analyst could say it lacks any basis in existing authority and could not be supported by good faith argument for an extension, modification or reversal of existing authority." With this definition in mind, the Model Rules go on to note that a lawyer should not file a complaint unless "according to the lawyer's belief there is good ground to support it," that "an advocate may not present a claim or defense lacking serious merit," and that an attorney shall bring a proceeding "only when a lawyer acting in good faith would conclude that there is a reasonable basis for doing so."

If you have questions about any of my comments or want to talk further about the suit, please do not hesitate to call me.

Parker was confused. He was nervous about this notion of frivolous litigation but also felt his client should have his day in court. If he brought the suit now, he might well be able to get the information he needed in discovery. Davidoff, Fein, and Stone were pushing him to file as soon as possible because they were worried that Meyerson would be writing another negative article about Compucare or Dentrex soon.

Discussion Questions

1. Parker is a partner in a large law firm. What are his concerns and his incentives as he works on this matter? For a time, he has a client. Is that client paying for Parker's time? If not, or after it appears that the original client has no case, on what economic basis is Parker working? The U.S. class

action nd contingency fee system at least opens the possibility that if a substantial fraud can be proved against institutions with deep pockets, the lawyer can eventually collect a hefty fee. Is it a good thing or a bad thing that our system sometimes encourages lawyers to invest substantial effort in seeking to demonstrate wrongdoing in this way?

2. Another route to lawyer compensation is by a fee negotiated as part of a settlement. The expense of a proceeding (and sometimes negative publicity is an expense) encourages a defendant to settle, even if she thinks she ultimately would prevail in litigation. Is it right for Parker to proceed if he thinks the case is weak but he may be able to obtain a settlement that includes substantial attorneys' fees?

3. In filing a complaint a lawyer must be sure that she has enough of a case to avoid sanctions that the court may impose for bringing a frivolous law suit. But does a lawyer have an independent and more stringent ethical responsibility not to bring a case that will in all probability fail? Why would she knowingly bring such a case?

4. DR7–102(A)(1) of the Model Code of Professional Responsibility provides that a lawyer may not "file a suit, assert a position, conduct a defense, delay a trial, or take other action on behalf of his client when he knows or when it is obvious that such action would serve merely to harass or maliciously injure another." Is there evidence that Parker would be in violation of this standard if he filed the suit against Meyerson?

When would an action serve "merely to harrass or maliciously injure another"? One possible standard is that the expected value of bringing the suit, *i.e.*, the probability of success multiplied by the net benefit of success, is less than the cost to the plaintiff of bringing the suit. In such a case the only gain that is likely to come from the action is the settlement amount gained because the other side wants to avoid attorneys' fees.

But even such an apparently minimal standard can be troublesome in certain situations. Such a standard would prohibit some cases where the plaintiff firmly believes he is entitled to a judgment, *i.e.*, where the probability of success is high, but the plaintiff's attorneys' fees are greater than the award he is likely to get if he wins. Assume, for example, that X has taken $80.00 from Y with no justification. Y is outraged and threatens suit. X says "go ahead, but your attorneys' fees will be much greater than $80.00." Y does not care because he thinks it is unjust that X should get away with taking his money and he is prepared to pay the attorneys' fees. Should such a suit be permitted?

5. DR7–102(A)(2) provides that a lawyer shall not:

Knowingly advance a claim or defense that is unwarranted under existing law, except that he may advance such claim or defense if it can be supported by good faith argument for an extension, modification, or reversal of existing law.

The newer Model Rules (Rule 3.1) employ a similar standard but add the requirement that a suit not be "frivolous":

A lawyer shall not bring or defend a proceeding, or assert or controvert an issue therein, unless there is a basis for doing so that is not frivolous, which includes a good faith argument for an extension, modification or reversal of existing law.

In spite of the new wording, lack of good faith remains central to both provisions. Both Rule 3.1 and DR7–102(A)(2) authorize an attorney to bring a suit on a theory she knows is not supported by present law as long as she does so in good faith belief that a change in law is warranted. The problem with the "good faith" requirement is that it is not defined in either the Code or the Rules. What might "good faith" mean in a situation where a lawyer wants to break new legal ground? Do you agree with either of the following interpretations:

(a) as a matter of policy, the attorney thinks it would be good or wise if the law were modified to reflect the position she is urging;

(b) the attorney believes that the court would not be exceeding its proper role or power if it were to adopt the argument she has put forth.

Are such subjective standards appropriate or would it be better if the standard were an objective one?

Should "lack of good faith" or "frivolous" mean anything more than an inordinately small chance of success? The commentary to the Model Rule makes it clear that a lawyer may bring a suit in good faith even if he "believes that the client's position ultimately will not prevail." Should the costs of the suit to the defendant be a factor in deciding whether a suit is frivolous? What about the potential benefits of the suit? Should it make any difference if the benefits accrue not only to the individual plaintiff but also to a significant segment of society by virtue of a change in the law or in the interpretation of a provision of the Constitution?

6. Assuming that the legal theory under which a plaintiff wants to bring a suit is clear, how much evidence should be required before a plaintiff can file a complaint? One possible standard is that a lawyer should only file when he has enough evidence to make out a prima facie case that will survive a motion for summary judgment or for a directed verdict. Such a standard raises two questions:

(a) Should an attorney ever bring a suit without sufficient evidence to make out a prima facie case? What about in situations where crucial evidence is in the hands of the defendant and the only way the plaintiff can get access to it is through discovery? In such cases, it may make sense to allow a plaintiff to bring a suit. This view is consistent with the commentary to Model Rule 3.1 which says that there is no impropriety "merely because the facts have not first been fully substantiated or because the lawyer expects to develop vital evidence only by discovery." What standard should be applied in those situations? Should an attorney be required to request the information he needs from the opposing party before filing a suit? How would she know whether the opposing party is answering honestly?

An additional issue concerning information necessary to filing a law suit is whether or not an attorney should rely completely on the client's version of the facts or whether he should be required to verify the accuracy of the client's statements. Federal Rule 11 seems to require some investigation into the facts—the question is how much. The drafting committee's notes indicate that one factor to consider is whether a lawyer "had to rely on a client for facts . . ." One commentator says this means a lawyer may never rely on the client's word alone where independent verification is available. *See* Marcus, *Reducing Court Costs and Delay: The Potential Impact of the Proposed Amendments to the Federal Rules of Civil Procedure,* 66 Judicature 363 (1983).

(b) The second problem with a prima facie standard is situations where, although a prima facie case could be made out, the case should not be brought. Such situations arise when a plaintiff knows or should know that the defendant has an overwhelming affirmative defense or has evidence that is more than sufficient to rebut elements of the cause of action against him. Given such a possibility, should there be a general obligation to give the opposing party an opportunity to respond to the substance of a proposed complaint before filing a law suit?

In this category of cases, where a prima facie case can be made but can be easily rebutted, there is a high probability of winning on a motion to dismiss but a very low probability of succeeding on the merits. Should the expected value of the judgment to the plaintiff, *i.e.,* the probability of winning multiplied by the likely judgment, determine whether or not it is frivolous? For example, what if there is only a 1 percent chance of winning the suit but the potential reward to the plaintiff is $20,000,000? Does such a suit become frivolous if the attorneys' fees are greater than the expected value of $200,000? Should that be considered? What if the costs to the defendant of the suit are $300,000? Should that matter?

7. Federal Rule of Civil Procedure 11 requires that a court impose appropriate sanctions against lawyers, clients, or both for bringing or continuing a "frivolous" suit. Sanctions may include reasonable attorneys' fees or other expenses. On the one hand such a sanction makes sense in that a lawyer should be responsible for filing a suit that is "frivolous." However, the sanction provision poses enforcement problems. To defend himself in an action for sanctions, an attorney is authorized by the Code of Professional Responsibility to reveal confidences and secrets of his client. Specifically, DR4–101(C) allows an attorney to reveal confidences or secrets necessary to "defend himself . . . against an accusation of wrongful conduct." This possibility may "chill" the defendant's willingness to confide in his attorney in the first place. Does the risk of this result raise doubts about the wisdom of sanctions for this offense?

8. In many areas of law, including fraud, it is difficult to separate legal theories from facts. In the Meyerson case, Parker did not clearly specify a legal theory in his complaint. He purposely wanted to keep the legal theory vague in order to give himself more flexibility to shape the claim later when he was able to get more access to the facts. Are there additional problems when a party has neither sufficient facts nor a clear legal theory under which to bring a complaint? How should a judge respond to a motion to dismiss in such cases? Do such claims pave the way for costly fishing expeditions?

†